Analysing Casual Conversation

Equinox Textbooks and Surveys in Linguistics
Editor: Robin Fawcett, Cardiff University

This two-pronged series provides textbooks for beginning students as well as offering handbooks and surveys of specific research topics.

Published:

Meaning-Centered Grammar: An Introductory Text
Craig Hancock

Language in Psychiatry: A Handbook of Clinical Practice
Jonathan Fine

Multimodal Transcription and Text Analysis
A Multimodal Toolkit and Coursebook with Associated On-line Course
Anthony Baldry and Paul J. Thibault

The Power of Language: How Discourse Influences Society
Lynne Young and Brigid Fitzgerald

Forthcoming:

Intonation in the Grammar of English
M.A.K. Halliday and William S. Greaves

An Introduction to English Sentence Structure: Clauses, Markers, Missing Elements
Jon Jonz

Text Linguistics: The How and Why of Meaning
Jonathan Webster

Genre Relations: Mapping Culture
J.R. Martin and David Rose

Writing Readable Research: A Guide for Students of Social Science
Beverly Lewin

Teaching Multimodal Literacy in English as a Foreign Language
Len Unsworth and Viviane Heberle

The Western Classical Tradition in Linguistics
Keith Allan

Leaning to Write/Reading to Learn: Scaffolding Democracy in Literacy Classrooms
J.R. Martin and David Rose

Sociocultural Theory and the Teaching of Second Languages
Edited by James P. Lantolf and Matthew E. Poehner

Functional Syntax Handbook: Analysing English at the Level of Form
Robin Fawcett

Multimodal Corpus-Based Approaches to Website Analysis
Anthony Baldry and Kay O'Halloran

ANALYSING
Casual Conversation

Suzanne Eggins and Diana Slade

LONDON   OAKVILLE

PE
1074.8
. E38
1997

Published by

Equinox Publishing Ltd.

UK: Unit 6, The Village, 101 Amies St., London SW11 2JW

US: 28 Main Street, Oakville, CT 06779

www.equinoxpub.com

First published by Cassell in 1997.

This paperback edition published by Equinox Publishing Ltd. in 2006 by arrange-
ment with Continuum International Publishing Group Ltd.

© Suzanne Eggins and Diana Slade 1997

All rights reserved. No part of this publication may be reproduced or transmitted
in any form or by any means, electronic or mechanical, including photocopying,
recording or any information storage or retrieval system, without permission in
writing from the publishers.

British Library Cataloguing-in-Publication Data
A catalogue record for this book is available from the British Library.

ISBN-10 1 84553 046 2   Paperback
ISBN-13 978 1 84553 046 4   Paperback

Typeset by Textype Typesetters, Cambridge
Printed and bound by Lightning Source UK Ltd., Milton Keynes
and Lightning Source Inc., La Vergne, TN

IPFW
WITHDRAWN
FEB 19 2009
HELMKE LIBRARY

Contents

List of Figures

List of Tables

List of Texts

Preface

This book arises out of our research into English casual conversation, and is the culmination of the many hundreds of hours we have spent together talking about conversation.

Although every section of the book was discussed in detail with each other, and some chapters were jointly written, other chapters were primarily the responsibility of one author. Chapters 3 and 5 extend and develop Suzanne Eggins' PhD research on the description of the micro-interaction of casual conversation; Chapters 6 and 7 derive from work in Diana Slade's PhD thesis. The work on humour was developed by Suzanne Eggins for two conference plenary talks; the work on attitudinal meanings in text has been developed by Diana Slade in her PhD-related research and by Suzanne Eggins in her work on interpersonal semantics.

As we both have many people that we would like to thank we have decided to write separate subsections to this foreword.

The work of Michael Halliday, particularly as it has been extended into areas of discourse analysis by Jim Martin and colleagues, provides a theoretical framework within which it has been possible to ask interesting questions about casual conversation. Michael Halliday's recognition of the fundamental importance of casual talk as social semiotic encouraged me to listen more carefully to chat, and Jim Martin's willingness to discuss ideas and analyse transcripts has been instrumental in my attempts to come up with some answers. His encouragement to keep working on casual talk over the years, and his general support for my work, have made writing this book not quite the overwhelming task it could have seemed.

My thanks to Rick Iedema for feedback on ideas and drafts, and to Gillian Fuller, Helen Joyce and Lorraine Murphy for editorial rescue missions.

I also express my thanks to the many groups of students at UNSW and Sydney University, and to the participants at various in-services, summer schools and workshops I have contributed to over the past few years, for feedback and encouragement. It has been their interest in casual conversation, and the tricky questions they always seem to ask, that have kept me motivated to see this book through to the end.

It was with great sorrow that I learned in early 1996 of the death of Blair Munro, a student in the School of English at the University of New South Wales. Blair's intelligence, interest and enthusiasm for linguistics provided a rare reminder of just how rewarding teaching about language can be, and how meaningful are the everyday interactions we so casually take for granted.

Finally, I would like to thank George Kozakos for getting me to the finish line in both the Sydney Marathon and in the marathon of writing this book.

Suzanne Eggins

My interest in conversation began over ten years ago as an applied concern about how best to teach conversation to adult ESL learners. It was, however, only when I started teaching in the linguistics department at Sydney University that ways into the analysis and description of casual conversation became evident. There are three colleagues from this early period who inspired me to work in this area. First, Michael Halliday, who from the beginning encouraged me to pursue research on casual conversation and not to feel too daunted by its complexity. I feel extremely privileged to have been able to work with him before he retired. He has been a major source of inspiration for my work as he was with many others before me. Second, to Jim Martin for the many discussions over the years on the analysis of casual conversation. And third, to Christian Matthiessen, for his unfailing support and generosity, and for the detailed and insightful discussions on the analysis of casual conversation in English.

I would also like to thank four other colleagues from this period for their support and the many discussions on aspects of discourse analysis: Chris Nesbitt, Beth Murison, Tim McNamara and Solange Vereza.

During the life of the book, a number of other people have provided me with the encouragement and support necessary to sustain writing over a long period – Alice Caffarel, Sonja Chalmers, Jennifer Hammond, Sue Hood, Graham Lock, Mary Macken, Hermine Scheeres, Bennett Slade, Christina Slade, Nicky Solomon, Sophie Watson and Rosie Wickert.

Many thanks also to Rod Gardner and Erich Steiner for reading and commenting on draft chapters. Also thanks to Rick Iedema and Susan Feez for their discussions on interpersonal analysis. Thanks also to Helen Joyce for her detailed editing advice on the complete manuscript and to Lorraine Murphy for giving us the benefit of her desktop publishing skills.

I would also like to thank Jennifer, Andrew, Chris, Nick and Claire who provided me with quiet havens to work.

I wish also to thank Gwen and John Slade for their extraordinary support over the years and opportunities to pursue the interests and research that were important to me.

The greatest debt I owe to Philip Clark who selflessly supported and encouraged me throughout the period of writing this book. He never begrudged the lost weekends and often sole parenting of our children. I wish to thank him for his patience and consideration, and his interest in my work.

Diana Slade

Introduction: Collecting and transcribing casual conversation

> Perhaps the greatest single event in the history of linguistics was the invention of the tape recorder, which for the first time has captured natural conversation and made it accessible to systematic study. (Halliday 1994: xxiii)

SOURCE OF DATA USED IN THE BOOK

All the casual conversations used in this book were recorded between 1983 and 1995 in naturally occurring situations. That is, the conversations are authentic and spontaneous, occurring in real contexts in the everyday lives of the participants. The data involve casual conversations in the following contexts:

(i)   close friends at a dinner party;
(ii)   immediate family members: parents and adult child;
(iii) extended family members: grandparents and adult grandchild;
(iv)   three groups of workplace acquaintances at coffee breaks:
       (a) all men at a factory
       (b) all women at a hospital
       (c) mixed gender clerical staff.

The data involve variation in age, generation, gender, socioeconomic background, ethnicity, and nationality. Specific details concerning each of the excerpts used in the book will be given at the point at which excerpts are first presented. Except where indicated to the contrary, all the data used were collected by the authors.

The data are presented without any abridgements or deletions as we agree with Atkinson and Heritage (1984:4) that:

> nothing that occurs in interaction can be ruled out, a priori, as random, insignificant or irrelevant.

However, we wish to stress that we do not necessarily share the values and attitudes expressed in any of the conversations presented.

TRANSCRIPTION

In representing the talk in written form, we have chosen to transcribe the conversations in a way that is faithful to the spontaneity and informality of the talk, but is also easily accessible to readers not familiar with conversational literature or phonological/prosodic symbols. Below is the complete transcription key. (See also Table 1.1.)

KEY

Punctuation

Where possible, we have used punctuation to capture information obtained through rhythm and intonation analysis using Halliday's system (see Halliday 1994: chap. 8). Our use of punctuation, as well as the delineation of moves (see Chapter 5), are based on a detailed analysis of rhythm and intonation. However, we have not documented the rhythm and intonation analyses in this book because of constraints of space (see Eggins 1990 and Slade 1997 for details on these analyses).

a) **Full-stops** . These mark termination (whether grammatically complete or not), or certainty, which is usually realized by falling intonation. By implication, the absence of any turn-final punctuation indicates speaker incompletion, either through interruption or trailing off.

b) **Commas** , These signal speaker parcellings of non-final talk. Thus, commas are used to make long utterances readable, and usually correspond to silent beats in the rhythm (but not breaks or pauses, which are marked with ...).

c) **Question marks** ? These are used to indicate questions or to mark uncertainty (typically corresponding to rising intonation or WH-questions).

d) **Exclamation marks** ! These mark the expression of counter-expectation (e.g. surprise, shock, amazement, etc.). Typically corresponding to tone 5 in Halliday's (1994) system of intonation analysis.

e) **Words in capital letters** WOW These are used conservatively to show emphatic syllables.

f) **Quotation marks** " " These capture the marked change in voice quality that occurs when speakers directly quote (or repeat) another's speech.

Other transcription conventions used

a) **Non-transcribable segments of talk** These are indicated by empty parentheses ( ).

b) **Uncertain transcription** Words within parentheses indicate the transcriber's guess, for example (happy).

c) **Paralinguistic and non-verbal information** Information about relevant non-verbal behaviour is given within [square brackets]. Such information is only included where it is judged important in making sense of the interaction. Inferred non-verbal behaviour (i.e. "clues" which the transcriber assumes happened in order for the situation to make sense) are shown with the addition of a question mark.

d) False starts A false start occurs when a speaker "rethinks" out loud and rephrases what they were saying before completing the first version. This is shown with a hyphen. For example:

| 12a | S3 | Did you ever get that – I mean in French what was it? |

This indicates that S3 restarted her clause without any hesitation between *that* and *I mean*.

e) Repetitions All attempts are shown in full.

f) Fillers Following established usage, the most commonly used fillers are represented orthographically as follows:

i)   umm: doubt
ii) ah: staller
iii) mmm, mhm: agreement
iv) eh: query
v)   oh: reaction – what Schiffrin (1987) describes as an "information management" marker.
vi) ohh: an exclamative particle, suggesting surprise, shock, disappointment, etc.
vii) other quasi-linguistic particles are represented phonemically: e.g. aah! (exclamation of pain).

g) Intervals within and between utterances (i.e. hesitations) Hesitations are defined as brief pauses within turns, as opposed to those between turns. They are transcribed by three dots …

h) Intervals between turns (i.e. pauses) Significant pauses or lulls in the conversation are marked between square brackets [ ]. For pauses exceeding three seconds in length, the length of pause is specified in seconds.

i) Overlap phenomena The symbol of a double equals sign == is used in the transcript to represent four types of overlap as follows:

i) Simultaneous/concurrent utterances: when two entire turns occur simultaneously, the symbol == is placed before each of the simultaneous turns/utterances. For example:

4	S2	Really?
5	S3	Umm
6	S2	== Oh I've never heard that before.
7	S4	== I've never heard of that

Here we are indicating that both S2 and S4 produced their turns at the same time (began speaking together). Exact moments at which the overlap ended are not shown.

ii) Overlapping utterances: the point at which the second speaker begins talking is shown by == preceding the point in the first speaker's turn. For example:

2	Jo	She hasn't even come up for ten years' service so it can't even be == classed as long service leave
3	Jenny	==Oh, I don't know.

Here we are indicating that Jenny began saying *Oh, I don't know* just as Jo was saying *classed*. Exact moments at which overlap ended are not indicated.

iii) Contiguous utterances: when there is no interval between adjacent utterances produced by different speakers, this run-on is captured by placing the == symbol at the end of one speaker's line and at the beginning of the subsequent speaker's turn, as in:

66	Bill	Yeah Yeah ==
67	Mavis	== don't ... shrink ==

Here we are indicating that Mavis said "don't" more or less exactly when Bill said "yeah" – i.e. there was no perceptible hesitation.

iv) Concurrent conversations: as distinct from concurrent turns or utterances, concurrent conversations refer to extended passages of dialogue between two or more participants that occurred SIMULTAN-EOUSLY with other passages of dialogue going on between other participants. The boundaries of such concurrent conversations will be clearly indicated by comments on the relevant transcripts.

ANALYTICAL SYMBOLS USED IN TRANSCRIPTIONS

- Turn numbers are shown in arabic numerals: 1, 2, 3.
- Clause numbers are shown in lower case roman numerals: i, ii, iii.
- Move numbers are shown in lower case letters: a, b, c.
- NV indicates non-verbal moves.
- * indicates hypothetical examples.

Table 1.1 Summarized transcription key

Symbol	Meaning
.	certainty, completion (typically falling tone)
no end of turn punctuation	implies non-termination (no final intonation)
,	parcelling of talk; breathing time (silent beats in Halliday's 1985a/94 system)
?	uncertainty (rising tone, or wh-interrogative)
!	"surprised" intonation (rising–falling tone 5 in Halliday's 1994 system)
WORDS IN CAPITALS	emphatic stress and/or increased volume
" "	change in voice quality in reported speech
( )	untranscribable talk
(words within parentheses)	transcriber's guess
[words in square brackets]	non-verbal information
==	overlap (contiguity, simultaneity)
...	short hesitation within a turn (less than three seconds)
[pause – 4 secs]	indication of inter-turn pause length
dash – then talk	false start/restart

1 Making meanings in everyday talk

1.1 INTRODUCTION

As socialized individuals, we spend much of our lives talking, or interacting, with other people. Interacting is not just a mechanical process of taking turns at producing sounds and words. Interacting is a *semantic* activity, a process of making meanings. As we take turns in any interaction we negotiate meanings about what we think is going on in the world, how we feel about it, and how we feel about the people we interact with. This process of exchanging meanings is functionally motivated: we interact with each other in order to accomplish a wide range of tasks. Very often we talk to other people to accomplish quite specific, pragmatic tasks: we talk to buy and to sell, to find out information, to pass on knowledge, to make appointments, to get jobs, and to jointly participate in practical activities.

At other times we talk simply for the sake of talking itself. An example of this is when we get together with friends or workmates over coffee or dinner and just "have a chat". It is to these informal interactions that the label **casual conversation** is usually applied.

As we work through various examples of casual conversation in this book, we will be arguing that, despite its sometimes aimless appearance and apparently trivial content, casual conversation is, in fact, a highly structured, functionally motivated, semantic activity. Motivated by interpersonal needs continually to establish who we are, how we relate to others, and what we think of how the world is, casual conversation is a critical linguistic site for the negotiation of such important dimensions of our social identity as gender, generational location, sexuality, social class membership, ethnicity, and subcultural and group affiliations. In fact, we will be arguing in this book that casual conversation is concerned with the joint construction of social reality.

The original claimants to the title *conversation analysts* were sociologists for whom conversation offered privileged data for studying how people make sense of everyday social life. With early intellectual leadership provided by Harvey Sacks (e.g. 1972a,b, 1974, 1984, 1992a,b), in collaboration with Emmanuel Schegloff, and Gail Jefferson (Sacks *et al.* 1974, Schegloff and Sacks 1974, Jefferson *et al.* 1987) these *ethnomethodological* analysts were the first to engage in the close-up analysis of everyday talk, believing that, as Sacks (1984:18) claimed:

> the detailed study of small phenomena may give an enormous understanding of the way humans do things.

The recognition that conversation is first and foremost a turn-taking activity encouraged a focus on the micro-interactional features of conversation and the interactive nature of topic management. In this book we borrow insights about conversation from this well-developed and still thriving sociological tradition of conversation analysis. All of these insights derive from the initial identification of the functional nature of conversation as a dynamically negotiated 'interactional achievement' (Schegloff 1981).

As linguists, however, our approach differs significantly from that of the sociological conversation analysts in a number of ways. Sociologists ask "How do we do conversation?", and recognize that conversation tells us something about social life. Linguists, on the other hand, ask "How is language structured to *enable* us to do conversation?", and recognize that conversation tells us something about the nature of language as a *resource* for doing social life.

In this book, we draw on a range of functional and semiotic approaches to language to provide a theoretical framework and analytical techniques to describe and explain how language enables us to initiate and sustain casual talk. We treat conversation as an exchange of meanings, as **text**, and recognize its privileged role in the construction of social identities and interpersonal relations. Our position is best stated by the functional linguist, Michael Halliday, when he points out that:

> It is natural to conceive of text first and foremost as conversation: as the spontaneous interchange of meaning in ordinary, everyday interaction. It is in such contexts that reality is constructed, in the microsemiotic encounters of daily life. (1978: 40)

Despite its centrality in our daily lives, casual conversation has not received as much attention from linguists as written texts or formal spoken interactions. In addition, much of the work that has been done has been limited in two respects:

1. Analysis has frequently been fragmentary, dealing only with selected features of casual talk, such as turn-taking or the occurrence of particular discourse units. The limitation is that such partial analysis cannot describe the ways in which patterns from different levels of language (such as word, clause, and turn) interact to produce the meanings of casual talk.
2. Analysis has not sought to explore the connections between the 'social work' achieved through the micro-interactions of everyday life and the macro-social world within which conversations take place. It has not explored the critical contribution that casual conversation makes to our formation as social agents.

Partial descriptions have limited applications, and some of the areas where an understanding of casual conversation would seem extremely useful remain unprovided for. For example, there is still a paucity of adequate materials for teaching casual conversation to learners of English as a second or foreign language. There are also few thorough accounts of casual conversation for students of critical linguistics or social semiotics. In this book we aim to address these current limitations in two ways:

1. We will be offering a comprehensive set of techniques for analysing patterns in casual conversation at a variety of linguistic levels. We will start with the micro-patterns of the grammar of casual conversation, and then move on to examine semantics (e.g. word choice), discourse structure (e.g. turn-taking), and finally the text-types or genres that occur within casual conversations.
2. We will approach conversation analysis with both descriptive and critical goals. By drawing on critical and semiotic accounts which propose that "conversations, like all texts, are motivated by difference" (Kress 1985a: 21), we will explore how the micro patterns of difference realized in everyday chat enable meanings of relevance to the culture at large to be negotiated and contested.

This book will therefore be useful to those readers who are concerned with acquiring skills in analysing casual conversations, and exploring the effects of casual conversation within social life. We are writing, then, for such readers as linguists, social semioticians, tertiary students of English as a discipline, applied linguists and teachers of English as a second or foreign language. By the end of this book, we hope readers will be in a position to analyse and explain the linguistic characteristics and social effects of samples of casual conversation from whatever social contexts are of relevance to them.

In the remainder of this chapter we will deal with essential preliminaries to analysing casual conversation: first we will sketch out the main achievements of casual conversation; then we will suggest an intriguing paradox that casual conversation raises. Finally, we will offer some provisional criteria for differentiating casual conversations from pragmatic conversations.

1.2 THE ACHIEVEMENTS OF CASUAL CONVERSATION

We suggested above that casual conversation is the kind of talk we engage in when we are talking just for the sake of talking. Text 1.1 is a very brief example of such talk. This excerpt of casual conversation involves four speakers at a dinner party. Each participant is identified simply by a speaker number. The transcription conventions used are summarized in the Preface. As you read through this text, you might consider who you think the interactants are – and how you identify them.

Text 1.1. Dead Space

Turn	Speaker	
1	S1	This eh has been a long conversation. Dead space in the conversation.
2	S2	In France they say "An angel is passing"
3	S3	In English too.
4	S2	Really?
5	S3	Umm
6	S2	== Oh I've never heard that before.
7	S4	== I've never heard of that
8	S3	Well I think so. I think I've heard it first in English but maybe they were just translating. I don't know.
9	S2	I thought in English it was "Someone's walked over
10	S3	Oh "over your grave".
==		

[The group now divides into two conversational pairs: S3 and S2's talk occurs simultaneously with that of S4 and S1]

11a	S3	You're probably absolutely right. Maybe I have heard it only in French.

[pause 3 secs]

12a	S3	Did you ever get that – I mean in French what was it? Some of the idioms or sayings are so cute, like that. And one I really like was "manger à belles dents". It's just – you know, it doesn't come out in English, but you know what it means. But it just sounds like sort of Little Red Ridinghood's wolf to me. You know?
13a	S2	Mmm
14a	S3	(it's really nice)
==		

[The following talk between S4 and S1 occurs at the same time as the talk between S3 and S2 in Turns 11a–14a]

11b	S4	[to S3] That's nothing to do with it. [turns to S1] Where's the cigarettes, [name]?
12b	S1	Sorry, [name]. I've cut you off. You said you'd had the last one. You promised me the last one was the last one.
13b	S4	Well I want to have one more.
14b	S1	Cost you a buck.
15b	S4	Oh give me a break, [name]!

(Eggins's data)[1]

Although text 1.1 is very brief, it provides powerful evidence for the central claim of this book: that in casual conversation we see language being used as a resource to negotiate social identity and interpersonal relations.

Although explicit indications of speaker identity have been removed from text 1.1, it is quite likely that you were able to make a great many valid deductions about the speakers. Groups of students to whom we have shown this excerpt have been able to deduce that this group of speakers includes both women and men. You may also be able to suggest which speakers are female and which are male. You may be able to infer the relationships between speakers, and the socioeconomic class, ethnicity, sexuality and preferred conversational strategies of each of the speakers.

Any inferences you make will be based on the way these speakers are using language. Readers of text 1.1 usually point out that all four speakers manage to say something and suggest that this indicates that these four interactants must be fairly close friends, not people meeting for the first time. The fact that S2 and S3 make reference to expressions in French is generally seen as an indication of their educated middle-class status, and female gender. French, our students argue, is a more female topic, than, say, rugby. The categorical dismissal of S3's points and the direct language used to demand a cigarette are seen as indicating that S4 is a male, and this contrasts with S2's more conciliatory tone, as in the offer of an alternative in turn 9. S3's use of concessive back-down in turn 8 is interpreted as female, as is the continuation of the topic and the use of the lexical item "cute" (turn 12a). Students point to the challenging, sparring banter that goes on between S4 and S1 in turns 11b–15b as exemplifying a common mode of interaction for heterosexual white middle-class male friends. S1's and S4's ignoring of S3's topic is also read as male, in contrast to S2's minimally supportive feedback, which is heard as female. Even from this short excerpt students can suggest the general age of the group as being late twenties to early thirties, based on the topics and the relaxed tone. They can also describe the preferred interactional strategies of each interactant: i.e. S1 is an initiator of talk, S2 is a supportive reactor, S3 is a contributor, and S4 is a challenger.[2]

The extraordinary accuracy with which people outside the immediate context of text 1.1 but familiar with the overall cultural context can describe the participants indicates that in the course of this apparently innocuous snippet of conversation, the conversational behaviours of the participants express dimensions of their social identities. As they take turns at talk, the conversationalists are enacting who they are.

The powerful 'social work' that is achieved in casual conversation can be further illustrated by a second excerpt from a casual conversation. This excerpt is from a tea break chat among a group of three women employees in a hospital kitchen. The very different strategies and characteristics of this excerpt indicate some of the variations that any description of casual conversation needs to account for.

Text 1.2 Tamara
Participants: Donna, Jenny and Jo.

Context: the tearoom at the hospital where the three participants work as clerical assistants.

Turn	Speaker	
1	Donna	But this reminds me of Tamara. She comes back from two months away organises an extra month the following year and how she accumulates so many holidays is beyond me.

2	Jo	She hasn't even come up for ten years' service so it can't even be == classed as long service leave
3	Jenny	== Oh, I don't know.
4	Donna	I'm coming up for that, love
5	Jo	Did she see the photos in her coz?[3]
6	Jenny	She walks in … She stopped me she stopped me and she said, umm "Oh, by the way, have you have you seen any photos of == me?" I thought, you know, you're a bit sort of, you know …
7	Jo	== No one told her there were photos.
8	Jenny	She said, "Have you seen any photos of me at the fancy dress?" And I said, I said, "Well, as a matter of fact, I've seen one or two, um, of you Tamara, but you know, nothing …" And, um, she said "Do you know of anyone else who's taken == any photos of me at the fancy dress?"
9	Donna	== I wouldn't be taking any photos. == I mean, I would have asked.
10	Jenny	== I mean, if anyone had taken any photos of me at the fancy dress I'd want them to == burn them.
11	Jo	== Why does she always want to get her picture ( )
12	Jenny	She said, "I just wanted to see how well the costume turned out."
13	Jo	She's pretty insecure, that girl.
14	Donna	I told her… You know what she said? ==I can't believe it.
15	Jenny	== You know what she wore? She wore this suit with a no top, a pair of Lurex tights without feet in them, you know and then, and… she had this old green olive green jumper that her mother must of had …
16	Donna	Yeah, its her mother's. She told me that
17	Jenny	And then she had her face painted green … had her hair in a tight plait or something ==down her back
18	Jo	== Yeah, yeah.
19	Jenny	And she had her face painted green with turquoise upside her long nose and around and up and down, and it had all glitter around here.
20	Jo	Yes. she's a tart.
21	Jenny	And then she had… I can't think what else, I know, … eye shadow and the whole bit and then she had this old stick with a star on it. Um, and she had this stick thing… this stick thing that had a star on it, and then she had a cape around her shoulders or something, and went [poof] or something to people and then started laughing.
22	Donna	== Yeah, here's something. You'd just go and break off a tree and stick a star on it.
23	Jo	Reminds me of my Mum with a Christmas tree every year. We've got pine trees along the back fence, Mum gets up the barbie or whatever she can stand on she's just yanks off a branch and there's the tree.
NV1	ALL	[laughter]
24	Donna	Your Mum lives in Newcastle doesn't she?
(Slade's data)		

As you read this excerpt, you no doubt recognized it as an example of **gossip**, something which we often do in casual talk. In Chapter 7 we explore this common conversational genre in detail. However, we can already note here that it involves participants in exchanging negative opinions and pejorative evaluations about the behaviour of a person who is absent. The achievements of gossip are thus interpersonal, to do with the positioning of participants in relation to each other and to critical issues in their social worlds. By evaluating Tamara's interest in her own appearance as both "tarty" and, implicitly, excessive, Jenny, Donna and Jo use talk both to confirm their affiliation with each other (they are "insiders" and Tamara is definitely an "outsider"), and to reaffirm traditional notions of feminine modesty.

While texts 1.1 and 1.2 both appear to be interpersonally motivated, they illustrate important differences in conversational strategies. Although the talk in text 1.1 is between close friends, it involves a high degree of disagreement. For example, first S3's claim about English is challenged, and then S1 refuses S4's request for a cigarette, which is then challenged in turn. We will see in later chapters that this orientation to confrontation and disagreement is characteristic of the casual conversations we have with those with whom we have the strongest bonds. We will be suggesting that casual conversations between close friends involve as much probing of differences between friends as confirming the similarities which brought them together as friends in the first place.

Text 1.2, on the other hand, is oriented towards the maintenance of solidarity and consensus among the interactants. Jenny, Donna and Jo display substantial agreement in their negative judgements of Tamara. In fact we will see in Chapter 7 that if any of them had disagreed with the negative opinions, the gossip talk would have been aborted. Data that we present in later chapters suggest that this orientation to solidarity and consensus is characteristic of casual conversations which occur in situations (such as the workplace) where we are strongly motivated to get along with people. However, while such talk is explicitly oriented to consensus, our analyses will show that, like all casual conversations, such talk also depends on the exploration of differences. For example, text 1.2 only occurs because Tamara can be positioned as different from Jenny, Donna and Jo. We will see that the construction of group cohesion frequently involves using conversational strategies such as humorous banter, teasing and joking. These strategies allow differences between group members to be presented as not serious challenges to the consensus and similarity of the group.

Texts 1.1 and 1.2 indicate that as we argue or gossip we are enacting our social identity and constructing interpersonal relationships with the other interactants. The distinction between solidarity motivated and difference motivated casual conversations which emerges from a comparison of text 1.1 and 1.2 is one significant generalization we will be exploring in this book. A second important difference between types of casual conversations can be highlighted by considering text 1.3, which involves participants from two very different generations: a granddaughter with her grandmother and great uncle.

Text 1.3 Dr Flannel[4]

Participants: Bill (aged 75, a retired electrician), Mavis (aged 80, Bill's sister-in-law), and Alex, (aged 21, a student, and Mavis's granddaughter).

Context: Alex has dropped in to visit her grandmother. In the chat leading up to this excerpt, the participants had been talking about the best places to go shopping in town, and Mavis had recounted a recent purchase of goods "on special" somewhere...

Turn	Speaker	
1	Bill	I had to laugh. I walked into David Jones's[5] and they're always nice ... people in there, you know
2	Mavis	Mmm ==
3	Alex	== Yeah
4	Bill	And there was two girls behind a counter and I didn't know which ... where to go, to go to ahh ... And she said, I said ah "Good Morning ladies" and one of the girls ==said "Thank you. You're a thorough gentleman."
NV1	Mavis and Alex	== [laugh]
5	Bill	And I said [laughing slightly] "Could you direct me in the direction where the men's singlets are? I'm after ... a Dr Flannel. She said "DR FLANNEL!" She said "What's that?" I said "WAIT A MINUTE!" [Makes motion of tearing shirt open].
NV2	Mavis and Alex	[laughter]
6	Alex	And showed her [laughs]
7	Bill	I said "THAT!" [pointing at singlet]
NV3	Mavis and Alex	[laughter]
8	Alex	And she screamed and == called security. [laughs]
9	Bill	== And I said "Do ya wanta have a look at the hairs on me chest?" I said "Have a look!"
NV4	ALL	[laughter]
10	Mavis	You haven't got any have you?
11	Bill	NO! Haa! [loud laughter] And they started laughin' And another woman came over and said "What's goin' on here?"
NV5	Mavis and Alex	[laughter]
12	Bill	She said "Oh this gentleman here wants to know where the ... the Dr Flannel are. He's just showed us his chest ... == and the hairs on his chest." [laughs]
NV6	Mavis and Alex	== [laughter]
13	Bill	and they said "HE HASN'T GOT ANY!"

NV7	ALL	[laughter]
14	Mavis	What store do you have to go to? Is there a men's store and a women's store?
15	Bill	Yeah. The men's store.
16	Mavis	Yeah. The men's store. Yeah, I was gonna say ...
17	Bill	Ha ha [laughing] And
18	Mavis	They usually
19	Bill	she ha ha she said. "You've got a decent old scar there". ... I said "Oh yeah. [laughing slightly] I said "I'm not gonna == show you where it ends!"
20	Mavis	== Mmm
NV8	ALL	[laughter]
21	Bill	[still laughing] And she said "Why?" I said "It goes a fair way down!" [laughs]
22	Mavis	Did you tell her what you've had?
23	Bill	Yeah ha [laughing] . She said "What you've had an operation?" I said "Yeah, I had a bypass operation". She said "That's what they do?" I said "Yeah". I said "They
24	Mavis	Cut you right open
25	Bill	"Get a saw" I said. And she said "They DON'T!" I said "They DO!"
26	Mavis	They DO! Yeah! They'd have to.
27	Bill	I said "They get like a ah ... fret saw and it's got little, a revolving blade on it. And I said "They go zoom, straight down your chest".
28	Mavis	They cut open your breastbone to ... == pull it back
29	Bill	== Yeah
30	Mavis	Don't they? To be able to do it ... == Open ... Yeah.
31	Bill	== Yeah pull it open like that.
32	Bill	And I said "I've got wire in there". I said "There's three lots of wire down there, figure-eighted". She said "No!"
NV9	Mavis and Alex	[begin laughing]
33	Bill	... I said "Well", I said "You're not == gonna feel it, I can". [laughing]
NV10	ALL	[laughter]
34	Bill	She said. You know the two of them, they said "You've made our day
NV11	Mavis and Alex	[begin laughing]
35	Bill	... It's always SOO dull" [laughs]
NV12	Alex	[laughs]
36	Mavis	Yeah it probably would be ( ) As I say ...
37	Bill	Yeah. [still laughing slightly] She said "We'll remember you for a while."
NV13	Mavis	[laughs]
38	Bill	And when I was goin' out ... They never had any ... They directed me where to go.
39	Mavis	Mmm
40	Bill	[laughing] And when I was goin' out they're laughin'

		their heads off and wavin' to me [laughs]
NV14	Alex	[laughter]
NV15	Bill	[still laughing – the last to stop]
41	Mavis	Yea that, that's what they call them don't they? They call them flannels, don't they?
42	Bill	Yeah. Dr Flannel.
43	Mavis	Yeah. Dr Flannels like um I thought they had a certain name for them.
44	Bill	Never heard of him [laughs]. Dr Flannel. [laughs]
45	Mavis	Well see ... ah ... most of men years ago ... wore
46	Bill	Nothing ==else bar them
47	Mavis	== especially as they got older ... In the winter time ==
48	Bill	== Yeah.
49	Bill	Oh well ah. Oh ah the men. I remember Dad and all the miners wore them.
50	Mavis	I can't remember whether Dad wore them but I think == he did
51	Bill	== All the – Because ah, in the mines see they went ah intake air – the air coming through is colder ... ss
52	Mavis	Oh it would be, yeah
53	Bill	And they're sweatin' like pigs ya know. Workin' like == trojans
54	Mavis	== Mmm Yes
55	Bill	And they're sweatin'
56	Mavis	But I know that um ... Dad must have worn them because I'm almost sure Mum used to always wash them in the same temperature water like ... I think if you wash them in cold water. If you wash them in warm water you're supposed to rinse them in warm water, or something or other so's they
57	Bill	Yeah Yeah ==
58	Mavis	== don't ... shrink ==
59	Bill	== Shrink ==
60	Mavis	And I mean even in those days you didn't have washing machines and everything. You
61	Bill	No No Well
62	Mavis	generally
63	Bill	I wash mine by hand
64	Mavis	Yeah. Well she used to wash Dad's by hand too.
65	Bill	Yeah
66	Mavis	I'm sure it was Dad had them.
67	Bill	I was over there, when was it?

Text 1.3 differs from the previous examples of casual conversation presented in this chapter. One participant, Bill, gets far more talk time than the others. This more monologic pattern in casual talk occurs because Bill is telling a story, a linguistic task which generally requires the production of a chunk of information.

In Chapter 6 we examine in detail the different types of stories which are told in conversation, ranging from highly dramatic narratives to rather mundane recounts. We will be arguing in that chapter that, while storytelling in conversation does perform an entertainment function, just like arguing and gossiping it also enacts social identities and interpersonal relationships. While Bill's story in text 1.3 certainly provides entertainment for Mavis and Alex, it is also a means of confirming Bill's status as an elderly male who considers his experiences worth sharing. He both expects and accepts that his listeners will support him as he tells his story.

However, it is not only Bill whose identity is being negotiated in text 1.3. Although he gets sustained floor time, the conversation is still interactive in that Mavis and Alex provide both verbal and paralinguistic encouragement to Bill to keep talking. Verbally, Mavis enacts compliance with Bill's domination by using strategies which resemble those labelled by Pamela Fishman (1980) as "conversational shitwork". For example, Mavis either asks prompting questions (e.g. turns 10, 14, 22) or she provides supporting information (e.g. turns 24, 26, 30). Alex's verbal contributions (e.g. turns 6, 8) are more assertive than those of Mavis (she volunteers completion of Bill's sentences), but they are nonetheless both supportive and minimal.

The women's most significant demonstration of support for Bill is their laughter, with which they respond to many of his turns. In Chapter 4 we explore some of the functions of humour in casual conversation, arguing that humour is an important resource for achieving serious interpersonal work while not appearing to do anything except have fun. For example in text 1.3 the humour in part signals that the interactants agree that it is in fact funny for an elderly man to undo his shirt and discuss major heart surgery in a slightly naughty and light-hearted way with unfamiliar women. Hence the humour works to enact cultural assumptions about age and gender relations and ideas about serious disease. But the humour in text 1.3 is also contributing to the participants' negotiation of social roles and relationships. Through his own laughter Bill signals to Mavis and Alex just how they should evaluate his story, and by their laughter Mavis and Alex confirm Bill's assumed role of entertainer. Thus in text 1.3 we see conversational behaviours enacting both gender and generational identities.

1.3 THE PARADOX OF CASUAL CONVERSATION

The three excerpts presented so far have suggested that the apparent triviality of casual conversation disguises the significant interpersonal work it achieves as interactants enact and confirm social identities and relations. This is what we regard as the central paradox of casual conversation. The paradox lies in the fact that casual conversation is the type of talk in which we feel most relaxed, most spontaneous and most ourselves, and yet casual conversation is a critical site for the social construction of reality. The relaxed nature of casual conversation leads to a very common perception by those who participate in such talk that it is trivial and that 'nothing happens'.[6] However the evidence of analysis suggests that conversation is anything but trivial. It suggests that casual conversation, in fact, constructs social reality, as Berger and Luckmann so astutely stated some decades ago:

> The most important vehicle of reality-maintenance is conversation. One may view the individual's everyday life in terms of the working away of a conversational apparatus that ongoingly maintains, modifies and reconstructs his [sic] subjective reality. . . . It is important to stress, however, that the greater part of reality-maintenance in conversation is implicit, not explicit. Most conversation does not in so many words define the nature of the world. Rather, it takes place against the background of a world that is silently taken for granted. (Berger and Luckmann 1966: 172–3)

If all this reality construction is going on in casual conversation, then we need to ask why it is not experienced for what it is or, as Fairclough asks:

> How can it be that people are standardly unaware of how their ways of speaking are socially determined, and of what social effects they may cumulatively lead to? (Fairclough 1995a: 36)

For while the "work" casual conversation is doing to construct and maintain culture looks massive when analysed critically, for those involved it obviously does not feel like that. For example, the participants in text 1.1 Dead Space felt that they were just "chatting away about nothing". They certainly did not experience their talk as an enactment of middle-class Anglo-Australian and Western patriarchal sociocultural values and behaviours. Nor did Jenny, Donna and Jo set out to clarify their ideological positionings on definitions of acceptable femininity, any more than Bill was consciously practising Western valorized skills of male aggrandisement, and Mavis those of female supportiveness.

This is the intriguing paradox of casual conversation then. We experience casual conversation as probably the only context in which we are talking in a relaxed, spontaneous and unselfconscious way. We feel it is the only place where we are really free to be ourselves and yet, at the same time, we are hardly free at all. We are in fact very busy reflecting and constituting our social world.

Analysts of casual conversation must try to understand how this enormous feat of invisibility is achieved. Berger and Luckmann suggest that it is the essential "casualness" of chat that does it:

> the great part, if not all, of everyday conversation maintains subjective reality. Indeed, its massivity is achieved by the accumulation and consistency of casual conversation – conversation that can *afford to be* casual precisely because it refers to the routine of a taken-for-granted world. (1966: 172–3) (emphasis in original)

This raises the question of just what we mean by "casualness". Berger and Luckmann point out that to see the taken-for-granted background of everyday life, we need to problematize it in some way. How, then, can we problematize, or denaturalize, the casualness of casual conversation to discover what is going on? In this book we problematize casual conversation in two important ways:

(i)   We problematize the casualness simply by focusing on it. Casual talk is exactly the kind of talk which we do not expect to have taped and transcribed and frozen in written form. When we engage in casual conversation, we assume that anything we say will not be held against us. We usually see casual conversation as the type of talk where we are free from surveillance and accountability. In tape recording, transcribing and presenting excerpts such as texts 1.1, 1.2 and 1.3 above, we have already dismissed these usual assumptions and rejected the usual meanings of the word 'casual' such as 'fleeting', 'transitory', 'one off' and 'forgettable'. In this book we will be arguing that it is this tacit agreement not to take casual talk seriously that, paradoxically, is what allows it to function as a serious resource for constructing social reality.

(ii) We also problematize the casualness of casual conversation by critically analysing it, or, as Fairclough (1995a: 38) suggests, by 'denaturalizing' it. Critical analysis involves describing casual talk in an explicit, systematic and, necessarily, technical way. It involves analysing how language is used in different ways to construct casual conversation and how patterns of interaction reveal the social relations among the interactants.

The main aim of this book is to present a range of techniques for analysing the interactional patterns through which interactants jointly construct social relations. These include:

- grammatical patterns at the clause level which indicate power and subordination within interactions (see Chapter 3);
- semantic patterns which indicate frequency of contact and familiarity among interactants (see Chapter 4);
- conversational structure patterns which indicate affective involvement and shifting alignments within conversation (see Chapter 5);
- the use of text types which give some indication of shared world views about normality and predictability (see Chapter 6).

As we examine these patterns, we will be showing the ways in which the serious work of casual conversation in establishing, confirming or challenging dominant ways of relating in the culture, can remain largely invisible to interactants involved in conversation.

1.4 DEFINING CASUAL CONVERSATION: PRAGMATIC VS. CASUAL CONVERSATIONS

Although the three excerpts presented above are very different, in calling them all "casual conversation" we are implying that they have some features in common. Before we outline our approach to analysing casual conversation, we need to clarify what kind of spoken language we are focusing on in this book. This specification is necessary because in the literature on conversation and discourse analysis terms such as "casual talk", "casual conversation", "informal discourse", and "everyday chat" are used to describe interactions which include telephone calls to emergency services and intimate chat between family members.

We will define casual conversation functionally and, initially at least, negatively, as talk which is NOT motivated by any clear pragmatic purpose. Contrasting texts 1.1, 1.2 and 1.3 above with text 1.4 below illustrates the importance of this definition. Text 1.4 is data collected by Ventola (1987: 239–40):

Text 1.4: Post Office
Participants: Sales assistant; Customer.

Context: over the counter in a post office.

Turn	Speaker	
1	S	yes please
	[C steps forward]	
2	C	can I have these two like that
	[hands over two letters]	
3	S	yes
	[3 secs – S weighs one letter]	
4	S	one's forty-five
	[3 secs – S weighs the other letter]	
5	S	one's twenty-five
6	C	and have you got ... the ... first day covers of .
7	S	yes
8	C	(Anzac)
	[2 secs]	
9	S	how many would you like
10	C	four please
11	S	two of each?
12	C	what have you got
13	S	uh there's two different designs on the-
	[5 secs – S shows C the covers]	
14	C	I'll take two of each
15	S	uhum
	[6 secs – S gets the stamps for the letters and the covers]	
16	S	right ... that's a dollar seventy thank you
	[10 secs – S puts the covers into a bag; C gets out the money]	
17	S	here we are

		[2 secs – S hands over the stamps and the covers; C hands the money to S]
18	C	thank you
19	S	thank you
		[5 secs – S gets the change]
20	S	dollar seventy that's two four and one's five
21	C	thank you very much
22	S	thank you
		[2 secs – C reaches for the letters]
23	S	they'll be right I'll fix those up in a moment
24	C	okay
		[C leaves]

One very obvious difference between text 1.4 and the three texts presented above is the number of participants involved. Texts 1.1, 1.2 and 1.3, like very many of the casual conversations analysed in this book, involve several participants. Text 1.4, like many examples of interactive data you will find in linguistics literature and language teaching materials, involves only two interactants. This difference between **multilogue** and **dialogue** has important consequences for conversations. For example, when there are many interactants, alignments can be formed among interactants, which is something we explore in subsequent chapters. However, the number of participants is not necessarily the most significant difference between texts 1.1, 1.2, 1.3 and 1.4.

Both the participants in text 1.4 achieved a pragmatic goal. One obtained a service, and the other participant provided the service. Together, the participants negotiated a buying-and-selling transaction. Thus, this text differs from texts 1.1, 1.2 and 1.3 in having a clear pragmatic purpose which involves complementarity (one interactant demands and the other gives).

Linguistically, pragmatic interactions such as text 1.4 differ from casual conversations in a number of key respects. First, pragmatically motivated texts tend to be very short. Text 1.4 is a complete interaction, while texts 1.1, 1.2 and 1.3 are merely excerpts from very lengthy conversations. It is difficult to loiter linguistically once your task has been achieved.

A second difference between pragmatically oriented and casual interactions is the level of formality. While text 1.4 exhibits informal characteristics such as colloquial expressions of agreement (e.g. *Yeah, Yep*), texts 1.1, 1.2 and 1.3 are all far more informal and colloquial. In texts 1.1, 1.2 and 1.3 we find colloquialisms (e.g. *give me a break, cost you a buck, she's a tart*), and humour (e.g. Dr Flannel). On the other hand, text 1.4 is conducted in a serious tone and is accompanied by various expressions of politeness (e.g. *Would that be ...? Thanks very much, Just a moment*).

To emphasize the important differences between these different kinds of interactions we will use the term 'pragmatic conversation' to refer to pragmatically oriented interactions of the type exemplified in text 1.4. We reserve the term 'casual conversation' to refer to interactions which are not motivated by a clear pragmatic purpose, and which display informality and humour, as exemplified by texts 1.1, 1.2 and 1.3

1.5   VARIATION IN CASUAL CONVERSATION

We have now indicated grounds for classifying texts 1.1, 1.2 and 1.3 as examples of casual conversation. However, these three texts also illustrate that there is no single variety of casual conversation and that there are a number of important contextual dimensions which impact on the type of casual conversation we are likely to engage in.

Data presented in later chapters will support the patterns which were noted in the three examples of casual conversation presented above and which are summarized below:

- Text 1.1 suggested that talk involving interactants who are close and familiar frequently has a confrontational orientation and results in talk that is quite highly elliptical. In such contexts speakers generally take brief turns at talk, negotiating their challenges and disagreements through rapid speaker change.
- Text 1.2 and 1.3 suggested that in casual conversations involving less intimate participants there is an orientation towards consensus. However, as these two texts show, consensus and solidarity can be explored in different ways. The female participants in text 1.2 actively and jointly negotiate consensus as they each contribute their supporting comments. The apparent lack of negotiation in text 1.3 indicates an assumed rather than a negotiated consensus and a passive rather than an actively constructed solidarity. This suggests that conversation is less interactive in contexts where the participants' social identities represent differences, such as gender, ethnicity and age, which have particular significance in the culture.

1.6   OUTLINE OF THE BOOK

In this chapter we have clarified what we mean by the label "casual conversation". We have also described how the invisibility of the functions of casual conversation challenges the critical conversation analyst. In Chapter 2 we will review a number of approaches to analysing casual conversation which are relevant in developing a comprehensive and critical account of casual talk. From Chapter 3 we begin to explore the ways in which language is used to achieve casual conversation. Each chapter introduces techniques for the analysis of casual conversation at a different linguistic level. We will begin with grammatical patterns in casual conversation in Chapter 3, and then move on to semantic patterns in Chapter 4. Discourse structure will be examined in Chapter 5, followed by generically structured text types in Chapter 6.

In Chapter 7 we explore one of the most intriguing features of casual conversation: that it contains both "chat" and "chunks". This is illustrated through the analysis of a text type very common in casual talk: gossip. Examining gossip in detail allows us to bring together practical analysis and theoretical explanation, as we explore the ways in which gossiping allows interactants to negotiate social identity and interpersonal relations, and to establish solidarity on the basis of difference. In Chapter 8 we offer a summary, and some suggestions as to the relevance of the analysis of casual conversation.

Throughout the book we will draw attention to the tension which characterizes successful casual conversations: a tension between, on the one hand, establishing solidarity through the confirmation of similarities, and, on the other, asserting autonomy through the exploration of differences. In describing how casual conversation involves a constant movement between establishing solidarity and exploring difference, we will be offering an explanation of how casual conversation functions to achieve "social work" at both the micro (interactional) and macro (cultural) levels.

NOTES

1. We wish to note that we do not necessarily share the values and attitudes expressed in any of the conversational excerpts presented throughout the book.
2. The participants, who also feature in a longer excerpt presented in Chapter 5, are David (S1), Liz (S2), Fay (S3) and Nick (S4). All are white, middle-class Australians aged between 25 and 40.
3. "Coz" is common Australian slang for costume.
4. Our thanks to KT and family for permission to use this excerpt, collected by KT.
5. A large, upmarket department store in central Sydney.
6. When asking participants for permission to reproduce and analyse their casual conversations, we were frequently met with a response of amazement. "Why would you want to listen to that", they would exclaim. "Nothing happens – we just chat".

2 Relevant approaches to analysing casual conversation

2.1 INTRODUCTION

Although, as we pointed out in Chapter 1, casual conversation has generally received limited analytical attention, conversation (as a general label for spoken interactive discourse) has been more fortunate. In fact, conversation has been analysed from a variety of perspectives, with sociological, philosophical, linguistic and critical semiotic approaches all making important contributions towards understanding the nature of spoken discourse. In this chapter we briefly review key ideas from the approaches we consider most relevant to the analysis of casual conversation, suggesting that an eclectic approach to analysing casual conversation is not only richer but also essential in dealing with the complexities of casual talk.

2.2 A TYPOLOGY OF RELEVANT APPROACHES TO ANALYSING CASUAL CONVERSATION

The pervasiveness of spoken interaction in daily life has made it an interesting domain of study for researchers with backgrounds in ethnomethodology, sociolinguistics, philosophy, structural-functional linguistics and social semiotics. At various times and in various ways, analysts from all these perspectives have sought to describe aspects of how talk works. Within ethnomethodology, new ways of thinking about conversation emerged in the 1970s from Conversation Analysis, notably the work of Sacks, Schegloff, Jefferson and their followers. Sociolinguistic approaches arise from the interdisciplinary connections between sociology/ anthropology and linguistics. From sociolinguistics we have contributions emerging from the work of Hymes in the Ethnography of Speaking, and Gumperz in Interactional Sociolinguistics, including the work of Labov and associates in Variation Theory. From a more logical–philosophical perspective, both Speech Act Theory and Pragmatics have added important insights to our understanding of how people interpret conversation.[1] And within linguistics, the study of conversation has been pursued most actively by approaches interested in both the structure and the function of authentic discourse, notably the Birmingham School and Systemic Functional Linguistics. More recent perspectives have emerged from social semiotic orientations which arise from interdisciplinary connections between linguistics and critical and cultural theory, including Critical Linguistics and Critical Discourse Analysis (CDA).

Figure 2.1 provides a brief typology of the approaches we consider most relevant to analysing casual conversation. However, although these perspectives have all contributed to ideas about spoken interaction, relatively few of them have specifically addressed the challenge of analysing casual conversation. We have therefore found it most useful to adopt a rather eclectic theoretical base, drawing on insights from all these different approaches, but with particular reference to Conversation Analysis (1), Systemic Functional Linguistics (4b), and Critical Discourse Analysis (5b). From some approaches we take perspectives on the micro-structuring of casual conversation, including the analysis of the localistic organization of turn-taking from Conversation Analysis, itemization of linguistic features relevant to variation in conversational style from Interactional Socio-linguistics, the production and interpretation of speech acts from Speech Act theory and Pragmatics, and the grammatical, semantic and discourse characteristics of casual talk from Systemic Functional Linguistics.

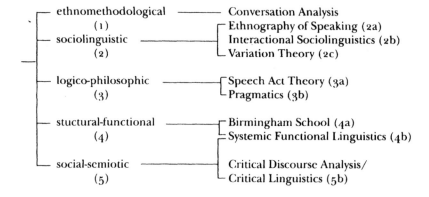

Figure 2.1 Relevant approaches to analysing casual conversation

From other approaches we take perspectives on the more macro patterns of text types or genres. The concept of genre stems from work in traditional literary studies, but for our purposes we are concerned with definitions of genre which have relevance to casual conversation. The term genre is used mainly in Ethnography of Speaking, Systemic Functional Linguistics and Critical Discourse Analysis. In Ethnography of Speaking, genre refers to one component in the complex communicative context of interactions. In Systemic Functional Linguistics, the term has been used to describe how people use language to achieve culturally recognized goals. In Critical Discourse Analysis genre is defined as 'a socially ratified way of using lan-guage in connection with a particular type of social activity (e.g. interview, narrative exposition)' (Fairclough 1995a: 14). In Variation Theory, although the term genre is not used, the notion of 'overall' text structure, corresponding to the notion of generic structure, has been central to much of Labov's (1972a) work on discourse.[2] In the following sections we review the contributions we take from each approach listed in the typology.

2.3 SOCIOLOGICAL PERSPECTIVES ON CASUAL CONVERSATION: ETHNOMETHODOLOGY AND CONVERSATION ANALYSIS (CA)[3] (1)

It is one of the sharper ironies of modern linguistics that the founding work in conversation analysis was done outside the field of linguistics by a group of American sociologists working during the 1960s and 1970s. Their approach to conversation was strongly influenced by the sociologist Harold Garfinkel's concern to understand how social members themselves make sense of everyday life. The "ethnomethodology" he developed centred on: 'paying to the most commonplace activities of daily life the attention usually accorded extraordinary events' (1967: 1). The early conversation analysts, sociologists such as Sacks, Schegloff, Jefferson and their successors, combined a concern with following a rigorously empirical methodology with the ethnomethodological aim of finding methods for making the commonsense world visible.[1] In the study of talk, this meant: 'an insistence on the use of materials collected from naturally occurring occasions of everyday interaction' (Atkinson and Heritage 1984: 2).

Conversation Analysis (CA), as a branch of ethnomethodology, focuses on conversation because it offers a particularly appropriate and accessible resource for ethnomethodological enquiry:

> Seeing the sense of ordinary activities means being able to see what people are doing and saying, and therefore one place in which one might begin to see how making sense is done in terms of the understanding of everyday talk. (Sharrock and Anderson 1987: 299)

In trying to explain how it is that conversation can happen at all, Sacks *et al.* (1974: 700) found it necessary to account for two "grossly apparent facts" that they observed about spoken interactive data. These facts are that:

a) only one person speaks at a time.
b) speaker change recurs.

These two "facts" lie behind our commonsense observation of conversation, that it is, fundamentally, a turn-taking activity. In trying to explain how it is that speakers keep taking turns, the Conversation Analysts modelled conversation as a generative mechanism, designed to fulfil two distinct functions. First, speakers have to be able to work out when it is appropriate to transfer the role of speaker. Second, there has to be a way of determining who the next speaker is to be. For example, in text 1.1, analysis has to account for how a change of speaker occurs once S1 (David) has said *Dead space in the conversation*, and how it is that there is a largely orderly transfer of the speaker role, in this case to S2 (Liz).

Sacks *et al.* (1974) suggested that speakers recognize points of potential speaker change because speakers talk in units which they called **Turn Constructional Units (TCUs)**. They defined a TCU as a grammatically complete unit of language, such as a sentence, clause or phrase, the end of which represents to the interactants a point at which it is possible for speaker transfer to occur. Thus, in text 1.1, when David has completed his sentence, Liz knows it is appropriate to take the turn, as a range of co-occurring factors such as falling intonation, grammatical structure of a completed sentence, posture and gaze, suggest that in this instance the sentence is a TCU. Had Liz begun speaking just as David had said *This has been*, then her talk would have been interpreted as an interruption, rather than orderly turn-taking, as she would have been beginning her talk where there was no TCU boundary.

The second problem of who should be the next speaker also depends on TCUs. Sacks *et al.* (1974) note that at the end of a TCU there are two possibilities for determining the allocation of turns. The first possibility is that the current speaker selects the person who is to be the next speaker. Typical ways by which the current speaker can select the next speaker include the use of names or vocatives, gaze, posture, and the targeting of moves such as directing questions to particular interactants. Thus, for example, in text 1.1, when Nick asks *Where's the cigarettes, David?* he has selected David as the next speaker both by the use of the vocative and by formulating a question. While it would be possible for anyone else present to take the role of speaker at this point, their contributions would be considered to interrupt the orderly transition of speaker role to David. The second possibility is that the next speaker may self-select. Thus, for example, when Liz comes in with *In France they say an angel is passing*, she does so without having been nominated or invited to speak by David. This system of turn allocation is summarized in Figure 2.2.

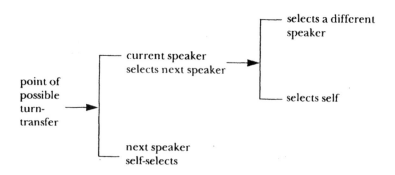

Figure 2.2 The turn-taking system
Source: derived from Sacks *et al.* 1974

Sacks *et al.* (1974) point out that this system operates at the end of every turn or what they call "locally", rather than on an overall or "global" basis. In other words, turn allocation cannot be agreed in advance at the beginning of the conversation, but must be continually renegotiated at each TCU boundary. The system has one aim: to ensure that when the current speaker finishes her turn at talk, some other speaker will start talking. The Conversation Analysts thus modelled conversation as an infinitely generative turn-taking machine, whose design suggests that the major concern of interactants is to avoid **lapse**: the possibility that no one is speaking.

Given that conversation is driven by a turn-taking machinery expressly designed to keep going, it becomes quite problematic to determine how a conversation could ever stop. It was in exploring an answer to this issue of conversational closure that CAs made what many see as their most significant contribution to the analysis of interaction: the identification of the **adjacency pair**. Consider the following pair of turns from text 1.1 in Chapter 1:

| 11b | Nick | [turns to David] Where's the cigarettes, David? |
| 12b | David | Sorry, Nick. I've cut you off. |

Sacks *et al.* (1974) noticed that the occurrence of the second turn can be explained by the first: a question in some ways implies that the next turn will be an answer. Conversational sequences where there was some kind of "special relatedness" operating between adjacent utterances as in this example are called **adjacency pairs**. They were identified as typically having three characteristics:

a) two utterance length
b) adjacent positioning of component utterances
c) different speakers producing each utterance. (Schegloff and Sacks 1974: 238)

The classic adjacency pair is the question/answer sequence, although other adjacency pairs include complaint/denial; compliment/rejection; challenge/ rejection; request/grant; offer/accept; offer/reject and instruct/receipt (Sacks *et al.* 1974: 717).

Adjacency pairs were identified as functioning as a turn-transfer technique, i.e. they function both to allocate the next turn, and to exit from the current turn. It is important to understand that the system is not one of determination, but of expectation. Given that a **first pair part** (the first utterance of the adjacency pair) has been produced, there is a very strong likelihood that the addressed participant will be the next speaker, and will produce a relevant **second pair part**.

The Conversation Analysts recognized that in fact there are two types of second pair parts. There is first a **preferred second pair part**. For example, in text 1.1, had David responded to Nick with *Here, help yourself*, he would have been providing the preferred second pair part: the compliance predicted by Nick's initiating demand. However, as David's actual response indicates, it is always possible for the addressee to produce some kind of discretionary alternative – what in CA terms is referred to as a **dispreferred second pair part**. Preferred responses tend to be briefer, linguistically simpler, supportive or compliant and oriented towards closure. Dispreferred responses tend to be longer as respondents may seek to apologize, explain or otherwise justify their dispreferred response. For example, in text 1.1 David produces four utterances in his refusal of Nick's request, providing an apology and several explanations. Dispreferred responses are therefore linguistically more complex, and involve non-compliance or conflictual action.

The identification of the adjacency pair was the basis for two further developments in CA. The first was the recognition of sequences longer than two units, and the second was the formulation of the theoretical concept of **sequential implicativeness**. Consider the following sequence of turns from text 1.4 in Chapter 1:

6	C	and have you got ... the ... first day covers of ...
7	S	yes
8	C	(Anzac)
	[2 secs]	
9	S	how many would you like
10	C	four please
11	S	two of each?
12	C	what have you got
13	S	uh there's two different designs on the-
	[5 secs – S shows C the covers]	
14	C	I'll take two of each
15	S	uhum

Here we see that turns 6–7 constitute a question/answer adjacency pair. However, this pair is followed by a sequence of seven turns which in some sense seem to "go together" or have a particular relatedness to each other. It takes these seven utterances for the salesperson's question (*How many would you like?*) to be resolved so that the customer's initial request can be complied with. Instances such as these prompted CA to recognize the existence of **sequences**, of which the adjacency pair was merely the minimal version. In their description of sequences, CA has frequently concentrated on those which are particularly "visible" in that they interrupt, suspend, or prepare for the ongoing interaction. The types of sequences referred to most frequently in the CA literature are: insertion sequences (Schegloff 1972), pre-sequences (Schegloff 1980), side sequences (Jefferson 1972), closing sequences (Schegloff and Sacks 1974), and repair or clarification sequences (Schegloff *et al.* 1977).

From the analysis of adjacency pairs and turn sequences came a recognition of the more general principle underlying conversational organization: that of the **sequential relevance** or **sequential implicativeness** of talk (Schegloff and Sacks 1974: 296). This is the notion that conversational turns make sense because they are interpreted in sequence. As Atkinson and Heritage point out: 'no empirically occurring utterance ever occurs outside, or external to, some specific sequence. Whatever is said will be said in some sequential context' (Atkinson and Heritage 1984: 6).

CA suggests that the most significant placement consideration in conversation is that of *adjacency*. Thus, wherever possible the speaker's current turn will be interpreted as implicating some action by the responder in the immediate next turn. Similarly, the respondent's subsequent talk will, where possible, be interpreted as related to the immediately prior turn. Thus, adjacency pairs can be seen as merely the prototypical variety of the general conversational principle of sequential relevance. This principle explains why we will work extremely hard to interpret any two adjacent turns as related, despite the absence of any other indications of cohesion. Consider, for example, the two turns at talk below:

Turn	Speaker	
1	A	What's that floating in the wine?
2	B	There aren't any other solutions.[5]

You will try very hard to find a way of interpreting B's turn as somehow an answer to A's question, even though there is no obvious link between them, apart from their appearance in sequence. Perhaps you will have decided that B took a common solution to a resistant winecork and poked it through into the bottle, and it was floating in the wine. Whatever explanation you came up with, it is unlikely that you looked at the example and simply said "it doesn't make sense", so strong is the implication that adjacent turns relate to each other. Similarly, sequential implicativeness explains why, if a speaker does *not* wish an utterance to be interpreted as related to immediately preceding talk, s/he needs to state that explicitly, using expressions such as *To change the subject ...*, or *By the way ... .*

This orientational perspective of talk is what gives conversation its essential nature as a dynamic process of **recipient design**, another important concept developed by CA and well summarized by Taylor and Cameron:

> My behaviour is designed in light of what I expect your reaction to it will be: i.e. you will react to it as conforming to the relevant rule or as in violation of it, thereby leading you to draw certain conclusions as to why I violated the rule ... Thus, by the inexorable fact that interactions progress, any component action inevitably is temporally situated in a sequential context, a context to which it is an addition and within which it will be interpreted, held accountable and responded to in turn. (1987:103).

At the same time as it focuses close up on the turn-taking organization of talk or who gets to be speaker, CA has always recognized that topic management (what people talk about when they do get to be speaker) is a distinct, though interrelated, aspect of conversational organization. In asking how people manage to get their topics made "mentionable" in a conversation, Schegloff and Sacks (1974), and later others (e.g. Maynard 1980) have developed an account of topic placement and topic fitting which shows the interaction of local and overall conversational structure with topic. Through notions such as step-wise topic progression, topic shift, and topic change, CA has tried to categorize the apparently "natural" or smooth procedures speakers use to progress from one topic to another (Sacks *et al.* 1974, Schegloff and Sacks 1974, Maynard 1980, Jefferson 1984).

Although the focus in CA has not been on contrasting different types of spoken interactions, there are references in Sacks *et al.* (1974) to the relationship between casual conversation and other types of turn-taking interactions. Casual conversation can be positioned at one end of a continuum which reflects the degree to which turns are pre-allocated in an interaction (Sacks *et al.* 1974: 729). The post office interaction of text 1.4 would presumably occur towards the other end of this pole, since turn allocation is largely predetermined by the nature of the social task.

In general, CA work has focused very much on micro structural issues, rather than on the larger, macro-structure of conversation. Thus although Sacks (1992b: 17–32) discusses some of the characteristics of extended talk, i.e. talk that "goes on over more than a single turn" (ibid: 18), his account deals with the micro-features of the talk, rather than with the overall structure of such segments. Jefferson and Lee (1992), in their article on the analysis of "conversations in which 'troubles' are expressed", argue in relation to their conversational corpus that:

> Although many of the conversations were long and multifaceted, they were not amorphous. There seemed to be a shape to them; a shape which recurred across the range of conversations; a shape which could be sensed to be rather well formed in some of the conversations and distorted or incomplete in others. (521–3)

Although they do not use the term 'genre', they discuss a similar phenomenon when they describe the global text structure of talk about troubles:

> we had a strong, if vague, sense of troubles talk as a sequentially formed phenomenon, a seed collection of elements which might constitute the components out of which a troubles-telling "sequence" could be constructed, and a set of categories which might distribute the components across appropriate speakers. In short, we had the basis for a troubles-telling sequence. (Jefferson and Lee 1992: 522)

They argue, however, that although this underlying abstract structure exists, participants negotiate their way through the structure and regularly disrupt it. Thus there are ideal types or 'templates' (ibid: 524) which can be described, but in reality interactants regularly depart from them.

Influenced by this and the Critical Discourse Analysis perspective (discussed below), our description of the storytelling (Chapter 6) and gossip genres (Chapter 7) is an account of the underlying abstract structure that speakers, in particular cultural contexts, orient to. The generic descriptions we present, however, are not to be interpreted as a fixed or rigid schema. Our data support the findings of Jefferson *et al.* that in casual conversation there are often disruptions to the generic flow, but we will be suggesting that the reason that we can recognize these deviations is precisely because there is an underlying abstract structure to each generic type.

A further major contribution of CA has been to make everyday interaction a worthy subject of academic research. Not only have their "discoveries" about conversation drawn attention to the many insights to be gained from its detailed analysis, but they have also offered a powerful way of thinking about casual talk, by emphasizing that it is a dynamic creation of interacting and co-operating participants:

> The discourse should be treated as an achievement; that involves treating the discourse as something 'produced' over time, incrementally accomplished, rather than born naturally whole out of the speaker's forehead. ... The accomplishment or achievement is an interactional one ... it is an ongoing accomplishment, rather than a pact signed at the beginning. (Schegloff 1981: 73)

The strength of the CA observations of conversation comes in part from the fact they are always based on actual recorded data of naturally occurring interactions, transcribed in meticulous detail. Believing that intuition is an extremely unreliable guide for work in conversation, CA has always rejected experimental methods of collecting conversational data such as simulating dialogues or setting up artificial interactive contexts, and has challenged discourse analysts to access the data offered by everyday social life.

The debts owed to early CA by all subsequent approaches to conversation analysis (and to discourse analysis more generally) cannot be overstated, and CA is still a thriving perspective on interaction as collections such as Roger and Bull (1989), Boden and Zimmerman (1991) and Drew and Heritage (1992) attest. However, despite its many contributions, it has three major drawbacks in the analysis of the casual conversational data which we are concerned with. These drawbacks are its lack of systematic analytical categories, its "fragmentary" focus, and its mechanistic interpretation of conversation.

Lack of systematicity is a problem for all aspects of the CA account of conversation. For example, CA has not provided us with an exhaustive list of all adjacency pairs in English, nor, more seriously, has it made clear exactly how adjacency pairs might be recognized. In addition, while CA identified TCUs as the critical units of conversation, it has not specified exactly how a

TCU boundary can be recognized in any one situation.

One of the major problems with this lack of systematicity is that comprehensive quantitative analysis becomes impossible. Yet quantitative analysis is just what is necessary to give empirical validity to claims that conversations are typically organized in particular ways, and to provide evidence of any statistically significant variations in conversational behaviours. To develop such systematic analyses we believe it is necessary to draw very specifically on *linguistic* expertise, employing linguistic methodologies to relate aspects of conversational organization to aspects of the organization of language as a whole. We will suggest in later chapters that specifying criteria for the identification of adjacency pairs requires the use of linguistic categories, terms and analyses. The systematic relationship between categories of first pair parts and their preferred and dispreferred second pair parts needs to be specified in grammatical terms. Specifying TCU boundaries depends on being able to describe the co-occurrence of linguistic patterns, involving rhythm, intonation, grammatical structure and semantics.

The second drawback is that while the close up focus on small excerpts of talk has been responsible for CA's major discoveries about conversation, CA is limited in its ability to deal comprehensively with complete, sustained interactions. While Sacks used fragments to uncover the social meanings being achieved through talk (e.g. how affiliation is achieved, how category membership is determined), much subsequent work in CA has focused on more mechanistic concerns (e.g. the "precision timing" of turn-taking, etc.). This has meant that the reality of conversations (that many are very long and indefinitely sustainable) has not been addressed. A further explanation for this concerns the data CA often works on. While all the data are recorded in authentic situations, relatively little of it constitutes *casual* conversation as we have defined it in this chapter. Thus, some of the very issues which are central for us do not arise for CA.

The final drawback is that while on the one hand CA offers a powerful interpretation of conversation as dynamic interactive achievement, on the other hand it is unable to say just what kind of achievement it is. Modelling conversation as a machine does not explain adequately just what interactants use the machine for, nor how the machine functions in relation to macro social structures.

To address these issues requires a shift of orientation away from conversation as a form of social interaction that is incidentally verbal, and towards conversation as a linguistic interaction that is fundamentally social. Rather than seeing conversation merely as good data for studying social life, analysis needs to view conversation as good data for studying language as it is used to enact social life. We now review some of the most relevant linguistic approaches to analysing casual conversation.

2.4 SOCIOLINGUISTIC APPROACHES TO CONVERSATION

We group together as "sociolinguistic" approaches to discourse analysis those approaches which may have disparate multi-disciplinary origins, but which share in their practice an orientation to the use of language in the social contexts of everyday life.

2.4.1 Ethnography of Speaking: conversation and cultural context

Ethnographic approaches to conversation have been led by Dell Hymes (1972b, 1974) and are concerned with understanding the social context of linguistic interactions. In seeking to account for "who says what to whom, when, where, why, and how" (Hymes 1972b), Hymes developed a schema for analysing context that has as its prime unit of analysis the **speech event** in which language occurs:

> The speech event is to the analysis of verbal interaction what the sentence is to grammar ... It represents an extension in the size of the basic analytical unit from the single utterance to stretches of utterances, as well as a shift in focus from ... text to ... interaction. (17).

The term "speech event" refers to "activities ...that are directly governed by rules or norms for the use of speech" (Hymes 1972b: 56). Speech events include interactions such as a conversation at a party, ordering a meal, etc. Any speech event comprises several components and these are listed in the grid in Table 2.1. With each letter acting as an abbreviation for a different component of communication, Hymes's grid has become known as the "SPEAKING grid".

Table 2.1 Hymes's Speaking Grid (Hymes 1972b)

S	setting	temporal and physical circumstances
	scene	subjective definition of an occasion
P	participant	speaker/sender/addressor/hearer/ receiver/audience/addressee
E	ends	purposes and goals outcomes
A	act sequence	message form and content
K	key	tone, manner
I	instrumentalities	channel (verbal, non-verbal, physical forms of speech drawn from community repertoire)
N	norms of interaction	specific properties attached to speaking
	and interpretation	interpretation of norms within cultural belief system
G	genre	textual categories

Hymes argues that the values of the factors identified in the SPEAKING grid on any specific occasion determine our use of language and our interpretation of what people say. It is the analysis of these components of a speech event that is central to what became known as the "ethnography of communication" or the "ethnography of speaking", with the ethnographer's aim being to discover rules of appropriateness in speech events.

As the SPEAKING grid shows, Hymes used the term "genre" to refer to just one component of the speech event. Defining genre as including such categories as joke, story, lecture, greeting, and conversation, Hymes argued that:

> Genres often coincide with speech events, but must be treated as analytically independent of them. They may occur in (or as) different events. The sermon as a genre is typically identified with a certain place in a church service, but its properties may be invoked, for serious or humorous effect, in other situations. (Hymes 1974: 61)

The SPEAKING grid provides a necessary reminder of the contextual dimensions operating in any casual conversation. These contextual dimensions are similar to the systemic analysis of register, discussed later in this chapter. Hymes's analysis of genre has not been applied to conversation, perhaps because of the lack of explicitness in his account of the relationship between genre and the other components of the SPEAKING grid, and their expression in language. However, the ethnographic framework he initiated led not only to broader notions of the "communicative competence" language users display, but also to a recognition of the close relationship between speech events and their social/cultural contexts.

2.4.2 Interactional Sociolinguistics: the contextualization of discourse

Interactional Sociolinguistics is the label associated with approaches to discourse which grow out of the work of the anthropologist John Gumperz (1982a, b), strongly influenced by the sociologist Erving Goffman (1959, 1967, 1974, 1981). Like Hymes, Gumperz was centrally concerned with the importance of context in the production and interpretation of discourse. Through detailed analyses of grammatical and prosodic features in interactions involving interracial and interethnic groups (e.g. interactions between British and Indian speakers of English in England, see Gumperz 1982a), Gumperz demonstrated that interactants from different socio-cultural backgrounds may "hear" and understand discourse differently according to their interpretation of **contextualization cues** in discourse. For example, intonation contours may be interpreted by some interactants as indicating rudeness and aggression, while for others such intonation patterns denote deference and consideration. As Gumperz explains, our interactions take place against the background of, and are critically affected by, our socio-cultural context:

What we perceive and retain in our mind is a function of our culturally determined predisposition to perceive and assimilate. (1982a: 4)

In other words, in our participation in discourse events we are always bound by our cultural context. Because we interact with orientations only to those contextualization cues that our cultural conditioning prepares us for, miscommunication can occur when we come into contact with interactants who do not share our cultural context. Gumperz's work is strongly focused on exploring the contextualization cues operating in different socio-cultural "styles", in order to identify and explain sources of what are referred to as "communication difficulties". While Gumperz did not focus on the analysis of casual conversation, the most relevant empirical applications of his work to casual conversation include studies by Deborah Tannen (1984, 1989, 1990) and Deborah Schiffrin (1985a,b, 1987, 1990), each of whose work we consider briefly below.

2.4.2.1 Analysing style in casual conversation

Asking questions about overall characteristics of conversational discourse, rather than about its sequential organization, Tannen's approach to conversation draws not only on Hymes's ethnography, but also on Gumperz's work on cross-cultural perspectives on discourse (cf. Gumperz and Hymes 1964, 1972; Gumperz 1982a, b). Her work results in a description in terms of cultural preferences or conventions. Despite the fact that Tannen uses data which fall clearly within the scope of our definition of casual conversation presented in Chapter 1 (Tannen analysed dinner party talk among friends), her work differs from ours in both its aims and approach. Tannen (1984) describes her underlying investigation as asking:

How do people communicate and interpret meaning in conversation? (7)

Her study involves the identification and characterization of different conversational styles in terms of the kind of "rapport" they convey. She suggests that this description of conversational styles is:

a step toward the goal of understanding conversational interaction: what accounts for the impressions made when speakers use specific linguistic devices? What accounts for the mutual understanding or lack of it in conversation? (7)

Tannen identifies a number of stylistic devices as an indication of alternative strategies in creating rapport, and relates the stylistic variation to Lakoff's "Rules of Rapport":

1. Don't impose (Distance)
2. Give options (Deference)
3. Be friendly (Camaraderie). (Lakoff in Tannen 1984: 11)

The features Tannen identifies include: topic choice, pacing, narrative strategies, and "expressive paralinguistics" such as pitch and voice quality. Tannen's analysis results in statements of preferences and conventions. For example, preferences under the "narrative strategies" category include:

a. Tell more stories
b. Tell stories in rounds.
c. Prefer internal evaluation (i.e. point of a story is dramatized rather than lexicalized).(30–31).

Tannen suggests that the use of these features characterizes a "high involvement style" (1984: 31), and she compares two groups of interactants at her dinner party in terms of whether they used and expected this high involvement style or, instead, a high considerateness style.

Tannen's focus on different interactive styles is extremely useful in highlighting the importance of variation in conversational behaviour. Analysis of conversational style reveals that we are not talking about individual speakers so much as groups of speakers sharing common styles. Interactive styles provide recognition criteria for subcultural groups, and indicate dimensions of difference that are significant for cultural members. These dimensions reflect the powerful stratifying dimensions in that culture – typically gender, race, ethnicity and social class. However, the identification of conversational styles which can be empirically correlated with particular social groups demands careful explanation. If, for example, we identify women as showing a preference for certain conversational strategies, and if those preferences differ from men's conversational strategies, we need to explain just what conversational styles mean.

While we share Tannen's interest in uncovering and understanding conversational variation, we reject her suggestion that style differences in conversational behaviour are no more than indications of equal but different modes of behaving. Tannen develops this thesis most clearly in her popular work on male and female conversational behaviour (Tannen 1990), and it relates to what is referred to as the "dominance/difference" debate in studies in language and gender (Cameron 1992). While "difference" advocates (for example Tannen) suggest that subcultural groups, such as women, have different preferred ways of interacting, they are uncritical of the implications of those differences. "Dominance" theorists, on the other hand, point out that some groups are heavily disadvantaged by their conversational style: i.e. that the conversational styles of some groups have unfavourable material consequences for their members (see, for example, Fishman 1980). Thus, speakers whose style is low in conversationally assertive strategies are less likely to get floor time, less likely to be heard seriously, and less likely to control the topic. It is not just that their style may be different from the more assertive strategies used by their co-interlocutors, but that their style of interacting may serve the interests of their co-interlocutors better than it serves their own interests.

The approach to conversational style that will be taken in this book is informed by social semiotics (see critical linguistics/critical discourse analysis, discussed below). By interpreting style in more critical terms, as socially acquired orientations towards particular semantic choices, we are able to explore the material consequences and political implications of particular stylistic features and generic patterns.

2.4.2.2 Analysing conversational continuity

A more micro-focused application of quantitative interactive sociolinguistic analysis is found in the work of Schiffrin (1985a, b), especially Schiffrin's (1987) study of **discourse markers**.

Unlike Tannen's study, which provides an overall characterization of features of conversational talk, Schiffrin's work is localistic in focus, centred on the turn as a basic unit. Her perspective also involves her in issues of sequential organization, since she states her basic concern to be with "the accomplishment of conversational coherence" (Schiffrin 1985a: 640). Schiffrin asks:

> How can what one speaker says be heard as following sensibly from what another has said?

She then draws on CA insights, to focus on the recipient design of utterances: i.e. on how speakers design their utterances so that they are accessible to their listeners. As an explicit example of this recipient design, she looks at a number of "discourse markers", which she defines as: 'sequentially dependent elements which bracket units of talk' (31). Into this category Schiffrin groups a range of items, including: *oh, well, and, but, or, so, because, now, then, y'know,* and *I mean.* As texts 1.1 to 1.3 in Chapter 1 show, these markers occur extremely frequently in casual conversations.

Using a corpus collected through peer-group interviews (thus, not drawn from a naturally occurring situation), Schiffrin argues for the importance of both qualitative and quantitative/distributional analysis in order to determine the function of the different discourse markers in conversation.

Schiffrin's analysis of the function and distribution of a limited number of linguistic devices in conversation offers useful insights into questions of structure, or which turns at talk are signalled as structurally related to others, and of continuity. For example, her discussion of *oh* finds a common function in its various distributional contexts, as a marker of information management, which "initiates an information state transition" (99). The use of *oh* indicates shifts in speaker orientation to information. These shifts occur as speakers and hearers manage the flow of information produced and received during discourse (100–101).

From Schiffrin's work we take specific insights into the function of particular items to signal special sequential relatedness in talk, information which is very relevant in determining the boundaries of conversational exchanges (see below). We also take seriously her concern to explore conversational patterns quantitatively as well as qualitatively. One criteria we demand of the analyses we develop in Chapters 3 to 6 is that results can be quantified, so that sections of one casual conversation can be compared with sections of others. This comparison gives substance to any claims we make about patterns in casual conversation and its varieties.

2.4.3 Variation Theory: texts-in-talk (2c)

A different sociolinguistic perspective which we find relevant to conversational analysis is Variation Theory. This was initially developed by Labov (see, for example, 1972a). Although the major part of Labov's contribution was in the analysis of phonological variation, he has also been involved in important work on the structure of texts within conversations. Of most relevance to our work is the detailed study of narratives, first presented in Labov and Waletzky (1967).

Labov and Waletzky argue that fundamental narrative structures are evident in spoken narratives of personal experience. Although their analysis is based on narratives collected in interviews (and thus not examples of spontaneous conversation), their findings can be usefully extrapolated to an analysis of narratives occurring in spontaneous conversation. They were concerned with relating the formal linguistic properties of narratives to their function. They argue that the 'overall structure' of a fully formed narrative of personal experience involves six stages (1967: 32-41):

1. Abstract
2. Orientation
3. Complication
4. Evaluation
5. Resolution
6. Coda

In this structure the Abstract and Coda stages are optional; and both the Orientation and Evaluation may be realized either before or as part of the Complication and Resolution respectively. Apart from these variations, the stages must occur in this sequence for a text to be a successful narrative.

These structural labels are demonstrated in one of Labov's texts collected in a sociolinguistic interview (Labov 1972a: 358–9). Speaker A is the interviewer and speaker B responds with the narrative.

Text 2.1 The Fight

A: What was the most important fight that you remember, one that sticks in your mind?

Abstract
B: Well, one I think was with a girl.

Orientation

Like I was a kid, you know, and she was the baddest girl, the baddest girl in the neighbourhood. If you didn't bring her candy to school, she would punch you in the mouth; and you had to kiss her when she'd tell you. This girl was only about 12 years old, man, but she was a killer. She didn't take no junk; she whupped all her brothers.

Complication

And I came to school one day and I didn't have no money. My ma wouldn't give me no money ... So I go to school and this girl says "Where's the candy?" I said "I don't have it." She says, powww!

Evaluation

So I says to myself, "There's gonna be times my mother won't give me money because (we're) a poor family. And I can't take this all, you know, every time she don't give me any money." So I say, "Well, I just gotta fight this girl. She's gonna hafta whup me. I hope she don't whup me."

Resolution

And I hit the girl: powwww! And I put something on it. I win the fight.

Coda

That was one of the most important.

(Data and analysis from Labov 1972a: 358–9).

The description of each of the stages that occur in the storytelling genres of spontaneous casual conversation will be explored in Chapter 6.

Labov and Waletzky's analysis was the first attempt to offer a functional description of narratives of personal experience and the strength of their analysis lies in its clarity and applicability. However, there are two main problems in applying their narrative structure to the stories people tell in spontaneous casual conversation.

The first problem is that the accurate identification of the Resolution is problematic, given that it is defined solely by its position within the text, as coming after the Evaluation stage. It is even more problematic when Labov and Waletzky (1967) argue that Evaluation is not only realized as a discrete stage, but is also spread throughout the text. Thus they suggest that there may be more than one Evaluation and 'not all the evaluation sections have the structural feature of suspending the complicating action' (1967: 37). As the criteria for describing the evaluations are semantic and not grammatical, it makes it difficult to locate where an Evaluation is realized discretely, and this in turn makes it difficult to determine exactly where the Resolution begins.

39

The second problem is that Labov and Waletzky's definition of narratives fails to distinguish between narrative texts which have the pivotal stages of Complication and Resolution, and other narrative-like texts, such as recounts that do not have a crisis of any sort but merely involve the temporal retelling of events.[6] As we will see in Chapter 6, participants in casual conversations produce a range of texts which have many features of a narrative, but which do not display the structural changes of a Complication followed by a Resolution. Because Labov and Waletzky's data were elicited in interviews,[7] they did not encounter these different kinds of storytelling texts, leaving later analysts with the task of extending their description of narrative structure to describe the variety of agnate story genres that occur in casual conversation. This is a task we take up in Chapter 6.

2.5 LOGICO-PHILOSOPHIC APPROACHES TO CONVERSATION

Further complementary insights can be drawn from both Speech Act Theory and Pragmatics, which offer a logico-philosophic perspective on conversational organization by focusing on the *interpretation* rather than the production of utterances in discourse.

2.5.1 Speech Act theory : conversation as a sequence of speech acts

All linguistic descriptions of conversational structure owe much to Austin's (1962) and Searle's (1969, 1976) notion of the **illocutionary force** of speech acts. This means that every utterance can be analysed as the realization of the speaker's intent to achieve a particular purpose. The illocutionary force of many utterances is directly derivable from the linguistic form of the utterance. For example, a statement has the illocutionary force to inform. However, Searle and Austin also alerted researchers to the indirectness of many speech acts. Thus, Nick's utterance *Where's the cigarettes, David?* (text 1.1 in Chapter 1) has the same illocutionary force (to request) as its more direct alternative *Can I have a cigarette, David?*

Neither Austin nor Searle were concerned with the analysis of continuous discourse, casual or otherwise. However, other analysts from a range of backgrounds have drawn on the implication of their work, that the **speech act**, or the **illocutionary act**, is the basic unit of discourse analysis. Identification of this unit allowed researchers (such as Labov and Fanshel 1977) to address one of the principal problems of discourse analysis: the lack of a one-to-one match up between discourse function (illocutionary force) and grammatical form (type of clause). For example, Nick (text 1.1) could have asked for a cigarette in any of the following ways:

- *Can I have a cigarette, David?* (modulated interrogative)
- *Where's the cigarettes, David?* (wh-interrogative)
- *Give me a cigarette, David* (imperative)

- *I want a cigarette* (declarative)
- *What I'd do for a cigarette!* (exclamative).

Given that there is extensive variety in the syntactic forms that can realize a particular illocutionary force, speech act accounts explore how the listener can interpret which illocutionary force is meant on any particular occasion. In one development useful for analysing casual conversation, Labov (1970, 1972b) suggested a distinction in interaction between the world as one interactant sees it (A-events) and the world as another interactant sees it (B-events). This enabled him to come up with rules for interpreting utterances as the intended speech act. For example:

> If A makes a statement about a B-event, it is heard as a request for confirmation.
> (Labov 1970: 80)

For example, in the following sequence of turns from text 1.3 in Chapter 1, we see Alex volunteering a completion to Bill's narration in turn 8, when she says *And showed her*. However, Alex cannot be assumed to know what actually happened next as it is a Bill-event. Her declarative clause is in fact heard as needing some kind of confirmation or correction, which is what Bill provides in his next turn, *I said "THAT"*:

6	Bill	And I said "Could you direct me in the direction where the men's singlets are? I'm after … a Dr Flannel. She said "DR FLANNEL!" She said "What's that?" I said "WAIT A MINUTE!" [Makes motion of tearing shirt open].
7	Mavis and Alex	[laughter]
8	Alex	And showed her [laughs]
9	Bill	I said "THAT!" [pointing at singlet]
10	Mavis and Alex	[laughter]

Labov formulated a more complex set of procedures for explaining how our post office customer could have initiated her encounter in text 1.4 in Chapter 1. She could have said *I'd like to post these letters please* and had her declarative recognized as a directive (demand for service) by the salesperson because the following interpretive procedures apply:

> There is a general rule for interpreting any utterance as a request for action (or command) which reads as follows:
> If A requests B to perform an action X at a time T, A's utterance will be heard as a valid command only if the following pre-conditions hold: B believes that A believes (=it is an AB-event that)
> 1. X would be done for a purpose Y
> 2. B has the ability to do X
> 3. B has the obligation to do X
> 4. A has the right to tell B to do X. (Labov 1970: 82)

From Speech Act Theory we take the insight that the basic unit of conversational analysis must be a functionally motivated, rather than formally defined, one. The speech act, under its systemic name of **speech function**, is central to our account of discourse structure in casual conversation (see Chapter 5). Recognition of the tension between discourse function and grammatical expression is also taken up, though reinterpreted through Halliday's (1994) notion of **grammatical metaphor** (explained in Chapter 5). Labov suggests that interaction involves in part the distribution of knowledge, and consequently that roles in discourse are in part the enactment of differential access to knowledge. This suggestion is relevant to the development of models of conversational exchange structure (see the Birmingham School below).

2.5.2 Pragmatics: formulating "maxims" of conversational behaviour (3b)

Another perspective we acknowledge as relevant is that of Gricean Pragmatics (e.g. Grice 1975, Leech 1983, Levinson 1983), which formulates conversational behaviour in terms of general "principles", rather than rules. At the base of the pragmatic approach to conversation analysis is Grice's **co-operative principle (CP)**. This principle seeks to account for not only how participants decide what to DO next in conversation, but also how interlocutors go about interpreting what the previous speaker has just done:

> We might then formulate a rough general principle which participants will be expected (ceteris paribus) to observe, namely: Make your conversational contributions such as is required, at the stage at which it occurs, by the accepted purpose or direction of the talk exchange in which you are engaged. (Grice 1975: 45)

This basic principle is then broken down into specific maxims and submaxims which are implicated in the CP, including maxims of Quantity ("say only as much as is necessary"), Quality ("try to make your contribution one that is true"), Relation ("be relevant") and Manner ("be brief and avoid ambiguity") (46).

Although the pragmatics approach does not lead to a comprehensive description of conversational interactions, the concepts of maxims and principles provide a useful heuristic technique. For example, the description of casual conversation could lead to statements in the form of maxims such as "in casual conversations in specific contexts interactants try to be provocative" and "in other casual conversations they try to be consensual", etc. Such maxims could then provide a useful means of characterizing different varieties of conversation. However, it is important to stress that we regard maxims as merely a shorthand summary of the results of research. The goal of conversation analysis pursued in this book is to offer explicit and detailed linguistic descriptions which can explain any conversational maxims proposed.

Fairclough (1995a: 46) points to a further, more significant problem with the pragmatics approach: that it implies that conversations occur co-operatively, between equals. That is, that power is equally distributed between the consciously co-operating, autonomous conversational contributors. Such an account fails to recognize two facts about casual conversations. First, many conversations involve levels of disagreement and resistance. In fact, we will be offering support later for Kress's claim that:

> most or many conversations are marked by disagreement, and by absence of support. Conversations, like all texts, are motivated by difference. (1985a:21)

Thus, we will be arguing that disagreement is essential to the motivation and the maintenance of casual talk.

Second, in most conversations power is not equally distributed but is in fact constantly under contestation. Gricean pragmatics implies a non-critical idealizing of conversations as homogeneous, co-operative and equal. This view of conversation is hard to sustain if one works, as we do, with authentic examples of spontaneous interactions involving groups of participants from a range of different social backgrounds, rather than with hypothesized examples of decontextualized dialogic utterances.

2.6 STRUCTURAL-FUNCTIONAL APPROACHES TO CONVERSATION

We use the label structural-functional to refer to two major approaches to discourse analysis which have relevance to the analysis of casual conversation: the Birmingham School and Systemic Functional Linguistics. These two approaches share a common orientation to discourse in that they both seek:

> to describe conversation as a distinctive, highly organized level of language. (Taylor and Cameron 1987: 5).

Structural-functional approaches ask just what *is* conversational structure, and attempt to relate the description of conversational structure to that of other units, levels, and structures of language. In addition, both approaches draw on the semantic theory of British linguist J.R. Firth (1957) and Palmer (1968) and seek to offer functional interpretations of discourse structure as the expression of dimensions of the social and cultural context.

2.6.1 The Birmingham School: specifying the structure of the conversational exchange

Logico-philosophic approaches to conversation offer ways of explaining how casual conversation is interpreted. However, we turn to the work of the Birmingham School, characterized as a structuralist-

43

functionalist approach to conversation (cf. Taylor and Cameron 1987),[8] for insights into the linguistic structure of conversational exchanges: i.e. how interactants can keep taking turns. The Birmingham School was established through the work of Sinclair and Coulthard (1975), whose approach to discourse analysis has been extended beyond classroom discourse to conversation by Burton (1978, 1980, 1981), Coulthard and Brazil (1979) and Berry (1981a,b). It shares a common origin with the systemic functional approach discussed later. Both approaches derive from the socio-semantic linguistic theory of J. R. Firth (see Firth 1957, and Palmer 1968), particularly as developed by Halliday in the early description of scale-and-category grammar (Halliday 1961, Halliday and McIntosh 1966). However, the evolution of the two approaches has differed. The Birmingham School has maintained its focus on discourse structure, while Halliday's development of the systemic perspective has led to the semiotic orientation in his work (e.g. Halliday 1978).

The pioneering contribution of the Birmingham School approach involved recognizing **discourse** as a level of language organization quite distinct from the levels of **grammar** and **phonology**. Distinct discourse units, as opposed to grammatical units, were identified for the analysis of interactive talk. These units were seen to be related in terms of **ranks** or levels, i.e. each discourse unit being made up of one or more of the units immediately "below" it. Thus, in Sinclair and Coulthard's (1975) study of classroom discourse, **acts** combined to make up **moves**, which in turn combined to make up **exchanges**. Exchanges combined to make up **transactions**, which finally made up **lessons**, which were the largest identifiable discourse unit in the pedagogic context. Their analysis sought to describe systematically the relationships between these discourse units and grammatical units such as the clause.

The major contribution of the Birmingham School which has relevance for analysing casual conversation is its work on specifying the structure of the conversational exchange. The exchange is the discourse unit which captures the sequencing of turns at talk in terms of a set of functional "slots". While CA recognized the adjacency pair (a two-turn structure) plus a range of different, more extended sequences, it did not propose a general theory of discourse structure. In contrast, Birmingham School analysts have tried to develop a general description, in functional-structural terms, of the exchange as the basic unit of conversational structure. Defining the exchange simply as "two or more utterances" (Sinclair and Coulthard 1975: 21), they suggested that the pedagogic exchange involved the following three moves, or exchange slots:

Initiation ^ (Response) ^ (Feedback)

An example of this three-move pedagogic exchange is:

Exchange	Speaker	
Initiation	Teacher	What is the capital city of Australia?
Response	Student	Canberra
Feedback	Teacher	Right.

However, attempts to apply this exchange formula to non-pedagogic exchanges revealed its limitations – and the peculiarities of the pedagogic context. Conversational exchanges differ from pedagogic exchanges in two main ways:

(i)   At the exchange level pedagogic exchanges typically consist of three "slots", in a sequence motivated by movement towards completion, while casual conversational contexts reveal far more open-ended exchange types. In conversation it is quite typical to find the prolonged multiple-slot exchange identified as sequences by CA. For example, in text 1.1 in Chapter 1, turns 1 to 11a can be read as constituting a single exchange. This example also illustrates the need for more specific criteria to identify the boundaries of conversational exchanges.

(ii) In casual conversation interactants rarely ask questions to which they already know the answers. Therefore the types of moves which occur in Initiating slots of conversation are very different from those in pedagogic exchanges. They include "real" questions, statements of opinions, commands, offers, etc. The slots which occur after the Responding slot do not generally consist of evaluating moves but are either recycling types of moves (queries, challenges) or additional "afterthoughts" of various kinds.

In an attempt to come up with a formula which could describe conversational exchanges, Coulthard and Brazil offered a more explicit definition of the exchange as "basically concerned with the transmission of information" (1979: 41). They replaced the label "feedback" with the label "follow-up" for the third element, and suggested that the conversational exchange could contain slots which were responses to previous initiations and at the same time initiations which elicited responses. The following sequence was necessary to account for conversational exchanges:

Initiation ^ (Re-Initiation) ^ Response ^ (Feedback)

Conversational exchanges thus consist of minimally two elements, and maximally four. Extending on this, they noted that:

(i)   feedback could itself be reacted to with further feedback;
(ii)   sometimes moves occurred which marked the beginning of an exchange without necessarily constraining the next element;
(iii) sometimes moves occurred which indicated the end of an exchange (but which were not necessarily feedback).

Consequently, additional elements were added to their formula, resulting in the following exchange formula (Coulthard and Brazil 1979: 40):

(Open) ∧ Initiation ∧ (Re-Initiation) ∧ Response ∧ (Feedback) ∧ (Feedback) ∧ (Close)

This formula allows for a minimum of two, and a maximum of seven elements of structure in a single exchange. For example, we can use this formula in one possible analysis of the first 11 turns in text 1.1:

Turn	Speaker	Exchange slot/move	
1	S1	Open	This eh has been a long conversation. Dead space in the conversation.
2	S2	Initiation	In France they say "An angel is passing"
3	S3	Response	In English too.
4	S2	Re-initiation	Really?
5	S3	Response	Umm
6	S2	Re-initiation	== Oh I've never heard that before.
7	S4	Re-initiation	== I've never heard of that
8	S3	Response	Well I think so. I think I've heard it first in English but maybe they were just translating. I don't know.
9	S2	Re-initiation	I thought in English it was "Someone's walked over
10	S3	Response	Oh "over your grave".
11a	S3	Close	You're probably absolutely right. Maybe I have heard it only in French.

However, this model still has a number of problems for those interested in the analysis of conversation:

- The criteria for determining the boundaries of exchanges remain unclear. For example, are there perhaps more exchanges in turns 1 to 11a above than we have identified?
- The criteria for allocating different moves to each slot are also unclear.
- The model remains rigidly sequenced and does not recognize that some conversational moves can appear at any point in an exchange. For example, it is possible to query or challenge at any point, thereby achieving a Re-Initiation.

Major retheorizing of Coulthard and Brazil's exchange structure formula was achieved by Margaret Berry (1981a,b), whose four-slot exchange formula drawing on Labov's (1970) distinction between A-events and B-events has proved useful in describing the structure of pragmatic exchanges (see Ventola 1987). However, as it has limited applications to conversational exchanges, we will not review it in detail (see Martin 1992: ch. 2 for a discussion).

One Birmingham analyst who did specifically work on casual conversation, though some of it fictional, was Burton. Building on Coulthard and Brazil, Burton (1978) suggested that exchanges in casual conversation were in fact far more open-ended than the earlier formulae recognized. The typical structure, she argued was that following an Initiation and an obligatory Response, there could be a Re-Initiation (moves which extend on the previous Initiation ^ Response pair). This could then be followed by any number of Responses.

More important than the details of Burton's exchange formula was her observation that the "polite consensus-collaborative model" (1978: 140) which underlies the exchange structure of both Sinclair and Coulthard, and Coulthard and Brazil (and subsequently Berry) did not fit *casual* conversational data well at all. While interactants in pragmatic encounters negotiate in order to achieve exchange closure, casual conversationalists are frequently motivated to do just the opposite: to keep exchanges going as long as possible. One of the ways in which this is achieved, as Burton noted, is for casual conversationalists to choose challenging rather than supporting moves, since challenges, such as moves which withhold the preferred response to an initiation, demand their own responses and thus compel further talk.

In Chapter 5 we will take up these issues in developing an analysis of exchanges in casual conversation and we will integrate Birmingham insights about the structure of the discourse stratum with systemic interpretations of the links between discourse, grammar and semantics in casual talk.

2.6.2 Systemic functional linguistics: a functional-semantic interpretation of conversation (4b)

An important influence on our approach to analysing casual conversation is that of systemic functional linguistics, based on the model of "language as social semiotic" outlined in the work of Halliday (e.g. 1973, 1975, 1978, 1994, Halliday and Hasan 1985). Eggins (1994) provides an introduction to the basic principles of the systemic approach, Eggins and Martin (1995) outline the general approach to discourse/text analysis, and Ventola (1987, 1995) illustrates some applications of the systemic approach to the analysis of pragmatic interactions. The systemic approach offers two major benefits for conversational analysis:

1. It offers an integrated, comprehensive and systematic model of language which enables conversational patterns to be described and quantified at different levels and in different degrees of detail.
2. It theorizes the links between language and social life so that conversation can be approached as a way of doing social life. More specifically, casual conversation can be analysed as involving different linguistic patterns which both enact and construct dimensions of social identity and interpersonal relations.

It is these two advantages of systemic linguistics which are responsible for its applications in a range of domains: e.g. in critical discourse analysis (discussed below), educational fields (Christie 1991a,b, Cope and Kalantzis 1993, Martin 1993), and computational linguistics (e.g. Bateman and Paris 1991, Matthiessen and Bateman 1991). In the following sections we briefly summarize those aspects of the systemic approach which we draw on in our analysis of casual conversation. We are particularly concerned with the realizational relationship between language and context, the analysis of interpersonal meaning in conversation, the levels of analysis for micro-patterns, and the functional interpretation of genre.

2.6.2.1 *Strands of meanings: ideational, textual, interpersonal*

The systemic functional model of language can be glossed as a functional-semantic theory of language. It is a functional theory in that it models conversation as purposeful behaviour. It is semantic in that it interprets conversation as a process of making meanings.

One of the most powerful aspects of the systemic approach is that language is viewed as a resource for making not just one meaning at a time, but several strands of meaning simultaneously. These **simultaneous layers of meaning** can be identified in linguistic units of all sizes: in the word, phrase, clause, sentence, and text. This means that a casual conversation, itself an extended semantic unit or **text**, is modelled as the simultaneous exchange of three types of meaning. These three types of meaning, or **metafunctions**, can be glossed as follows:

(i)   ideational meanings: meanings about the world;
(ii)   interpersonal meanings: meanings about roles and relationships;
(iii) textual meanings: meanings about the message.

The three strands of meaning are summarized and exemplified from text 1.1 in Table 2.2.

As there are different strands of meaning being enacted in talk, so the analyst needs to analyse the talk from different perspectives. Thus different analytical techniques are used to uncover each strand of meaning. For example, to explore the ideational meanings in a text, the analyst focuses on patterns which encode the who, when, where, why, and how of a text. These patterns are seen in the analysis of lexical cohesion (chains of words from similar semantic domains) and the analysis of transitivity (for details see Halliday 1994, Eggins 1994). The systemic model is rich in analytical techniques, allowing the analyst to focus on those patterns which are most relevant to specific data and research interests. This multi-semantic and multi-analytical perspective on language has proved a useful tool for studies of other semiotic systems (cf. Kress and van Leeuwen 1990, 1996, O'Toole 1994). The richness of the model, however, necessitates a careful delimiting of analytical focus.

Table 2.2 Types of meanings in the systemic model

Types of meaning	Gloss/definition	Example: Text 1.1 Dead Space
ideational	meanings about the world, representation of reality (e.g. topics, subject matter)	conversation, expressions; the French language; cigarettes
interpersonal	meanings about roles and relationships (e.g. status, intimacy, contact, sharedness between interactants)	S1 and S4 have a "bantering", conflictual relationship; S2 and S3 have a supportive relationship; S1 takes on role of provoking talk; S4 takes on role of challenging and demanding; S4 is direct and assertive; S3 is less assertive
textual	meanings about the message (e.g. foregrounding/salience; types of cohesion)	rapid turn-taking; cohesion through ellipsis and reference; foregrounding of expressions/idioms

2.6.2.2 Focus on interpersonal meaning in analysing casual conversation

The pluri-semantic model outlined above offers us three main approaches to analysing casual conversation:

(i)   We can focus on the ideational meanings: this involves looking at what topics get talked about, when, by whom, and how topic transition and closure is achieved, etc.
(ii) We can focus on the interpersonal meanings: this involves looking at what kinds of role relations are established through talk, what attitudes interactants express to and about each other, what kinds of things they find funny, and how they negotiate to take turns, etc.
(iii) We can focus on the textual meanings: this involves looking at different types of cohesion used to tie chunks of the talk together, different patterns of salience and foregrounding, etc.

Analysis of casual conversation could explore all of these three dimensions of casual talk. However, for theoretical reasons this book focuses on the analysis of **interpersonal** meanings in casual conversation. We offer the following two reasons for this focus. First, as outlined in Chapter 1, we believe that the primary task of casual conversation is the negotiation of social identity and social relations. Thus casual conversation is "driven" by interpersonal, rather than ideational or textual meanings. To support this claim, we point to:

- the absence of any pragmatic motivations or outcomes to casual talk;
- the observation that anything can be a topic of talk in casual conversation (no topics are a priori barred) which suggests that casual conversation is not focused on ideational meanings;
- the apparent triviality of much of the ideational content of casual talk, which suggests that the important work of casual conversation is not in the exploration of ideational meanings. Rather, any ideational domain (or Field) serves as the environment for the exploration of social similarities and differences.

Second, it is the open-ended, turn-taking organization of conversation that differentiates it from other linguistic activities (Sacks *et al.* 1974). As we will see in later chapters, this turn-by-turn structuring of conversation is realized through interpersonal patterns of mood and conversational structure.

Given the priority of interpersonal meanings in motivating and structuring casual conversation, any comprehensive analysis of casual conversation must be able to offer a framework for describing interpersonal patterns in talk. Our focus, then, is on the interpersonal meanings expressed in casual conversation. In taking the interpersonal as primary, we do not exclude from discussion ideational or textual patterns, but we discuss these as resources mobilized by interpersonal meanings. Ideational dimensions have been explored in detail, both outside systemics and within it, to the comparative neglect of the interpersonal meanings in talk. For example, CA approaches examine topic management (e.g. Schegloff and Sacks 1974, Maynard 1980), and topic development (e.g. Button and Casey 1984) in conversation. Within systemics, although there has been little work on ideational patterns in casual conversation, there is a substantial literature available detailing the kinds of analyses that could be applied (e.g. Halliday and Hasan 1976, 1985, Martin 1992).

Our focus on the interpersonal strand in casual conversation directly implicates the link between interpersonal meanings and the context of casual conversation, which we consider below.

2.6.2.3 *Context: register and genre in the systemic model*

The systemic model is also relevant to conversation analysis because it seeks to explain language as a social resource. The model is based on Halliday's claim that language relates "naturally" to the semiotic environment, that 'language is as it is because of what it has to do' (1973: 34). Halliday claims that the three types of meaning we find represented in language are not there accidentally. They are there because those are the three types of meanings we need to make with each other. This implies that social life requires the negotiation of a shared ideational world. Simultaneously, it requires the continual renegotiation of our places within that world: who we are, how we relate to the other people in it, and how we feel about it all. In the process of negotiating those ideational and interpersonal actualities, we must also negotiate ways of talking about that world: what kinds of texts we can construct to represent ideational and interpersonal meanings.

The tripartite structure of language is therefore an encoding of the tripartite structure of the contexts of situation in which we use language. The systemic interest in the analysis of context through the concept of **register** is the logical extension of Halliday's "natural" language thesis. The three register variables of **field** (activity or topic focus), **mode** (extent and type of feedback possible) and **tenor** (roles and role relationships) are proposed to describe the major dimensions of any situations which have systematically predictable linguistic consequences. Each of the three register variables is realized through patterns in the different metafunctions. The field of a situation is realized through the ideational metafunction, the mode is realized through the textual metafunction, and tenor is realized through the interpersonal metafunction. These links between context of situation and language are summarized in Figure 2.3.

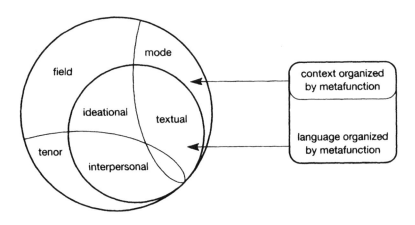

Figure 2.3 Context and language in the systemic function model
Source: Eggins and Martin (in press)

A further level of context important in analysing conversational data is that of **genre** (cf. Eggins and Martin in press), which is discussed in more detail below.

2.6.2.4 *Dimensions of social identity: the register variable of tenor*

By focusing on interpersonal meanings in casual conversation we are choosing to explore the register variable of tenor, of which those interpersonal meanings are the expression. By the term 'tenor' Halliday (1978: 143) is referring to *"the role structure*: the cluster of socially meaningful participant relationships" operating in a situation. Extending on the work of Poynton (1985) and Martin (in press), we will subclassify role relations into four main dimensions: status relations; frequency of contact or level of familiarity; degree of affective involvement; and orientation to affiliation. Each is briefly explained below:

First, **status relations**: the construction of a social self through interaction involves taking on a recognized social role, and attributing to fellow interactants relevant social roles. These may involve an inequality of status, as in functionally differentiated roles such as customer/salesperson, or they may imply the (temporary) assumption of equal status, as in the functionally reciprocal roles friend/friend. As Poynton points out, the legitimation for unequal status relations may come from a number of different sources:

(i)   force;
(ii) authority, where the culture attributes unequal status to particular role relations, eg. parent–child, employer–employee;
(iii) expertise, which will, for example, unequally position the expert in relation to the novice; or
(iv) status symbols, which Poynton defines as 'a matter of relative ranking with respect to some unevenly distributed but socially-desirable object or standing or achievement, e.g. wealth, profession/occupation, level of education, hereditary status, location of residence, overseas travel. (1985: 77)

Second, **affective involvement**: our interpersonal relations also vary according to the degree of affective involvement, the degree to which we "matter" to those with whom we are interacting. Affective involvement can range from nil (distant, unattached) through some (e.g. school friends or particular work colleagues) to high (e.g. lovers, close friends, family). In relationships which are largely low in emotional investment, interpersonal relations are towards the *im*personal end of the continuum. Affective involvement may be positive or negative, and may be a permanent feature of a particular relationship, or may be transient (as in a sudden argument with the bus driver about bus fares, where a typically neutral relationship becomes affectively charged for a short time).

Third, **contact**: interpersonal relations also vary in terms of the level of familiarity constructed to operate between interactants. Familiarity is developed through high frequency of contact. Contact can be characterized as regular (e.g. our relations with our immediate families) or intermittent, with the most intermittent being simply a one-off encounter. At the same time, the contact we have with other people may be voluntary, when we choose to spend our time with them, or involuntary, as in the workplace where we are compelled to spend time with people we might otherwise prefer to avoid. A final dimension relevant to the kind of contact between interactants is the orientation that is operative in their interactions: whether they come into contact largely to achieve pragmatic tasks, or to relate to each other "as people".

Fourth, **orientation to affiliation**: an important part of our social identity derives from our inclination or disinclination to affiliate with various formal and informal social groups, such as family, workmates, fellow students in our tutor group, residents in our area, or other passengers on a bus. Orientation to affiliation refers to the extent to which we seek to identify with the values and beliefs of those we interact with in these different social contexts. We might already be well oriented towards identification with some social groups (e.g. close family), or we may be seeking to be accepted by others as an "insider" (e.g. a new employee in the workplace). On the other hand, we might be happily or unhappily positioned as "other" in a social group (e.g. the marginalized, unaccepted member of the office), or be contesting an affiliation from an earlier time in our social lives (e.g. a rebellious adolescent in the family).

2.6.2.5 *Tenor and patterns of interpersonal meaning in casual conversation*

The systemic model goes beyond simply suggesting a list of tenor dimensions implicated in social identity. It also seeks to offer an account of the ways in which language is used both to reflect and construct these dimensions. As we will demonstrate, there are four main types of linguistic patterns which represent and enact the social identities of participants in casual conversation. These patterns, which operate at different levels or within different linguistic units, are: (i) **grammatical**; (ii) **discourse**; (iii) **semantic**; (iv) **generic patterns**.

i) **Grammatical patterns** – these are patterns which operate *within* turns, and have to do with the mood of the clauses interactants use. For example, whether interactants use declarative, interrogative or imperative clauses. We will be suggesting in Chapter 3 that grammatical patterns of mood choice are a key resource for enacting and constructing status differences. Reciprocal mood choice indicates functional equality of roles, while non-reciprocal mood choice indicates functional differentiation, or the linguistic acting out of status differences.

ii) **Semantic patterns** – this group of patterns is revealed by studying attitudinal and expressive meanings in talk. Semantic patterns often concern the choice of lexical items, and so are revealed by examining the words used by conversationalists. They have to do with the types of evaluative and attitudinal lexis which interactants use, and the directness with which they can speak to or laugh at (or with) each other. We will be suggesting in Chapter 4 that these semantic resources are often used to develop group cohesion and to censure actual or potential deviant group behaviours.

iii) Discourse structure patterns – these patterns operates *across* turns and are thus overtly interactional and sequential. They show us how participants choose to act on each other through their choice of speech functions (i.e. speech acts), such as "demanding", "challenging", "contradicting" or "supporting", and how participants' choices function to sustain or terminate conversational exchanges. We will be suggesting in Chapter 5 that choice of speech function is a key resource for negotiating degrees of familiarity. If interactants wish to explore their interpersonal relations, they must choose speech functions which keep the conversation going, and this frequently means that intimate relations involve interactants reacting to each other in confronting, rather than supporting, moves.

iv) Generic structure patterns – these staging patterns operate to build "chunks" of talk, such as storytelling or gossiping segments within the flow of chat. We will be suggesting in Chapter 6 that the construction of text types or genres within casual talk is one way in which affiliation can be explored and developed. We will now review the work on genre within systemic linguistics.

2.6.2.6   *Genre in systemic-functional linguistics*

Systemic accounts of genre owe much to the Firthian linguist, Mitchell (1957), who developed a detailed account of buying and selling in Cyrenaica. His analysis involved setting up text structures of the following kind for market auction and market transaction contexts. In the formulae below, ^ stands for the typical sequence of realization, although Mitchell notes that some variability and overlap is found.

Market Auction:
Auctioneer's Opening ^ Investigation of Object of Sale ^ Bidding ^ Conclusion

Market Transaction:
Salutation ^ Enquiry as to Object of Sale ^ Investigation ^ Bargaining ^ Conclusion

In the 1970s, Hasan, working in the tradition begun by Mitchell, laid the foundations for a theoretical conception of genre within systemics with her accounts of generic structure. In her early work looking at the structure of nursery tales and later the structure of service encounters (1984, 1985), Hasan introduces the notion of generic structure potential to generalize the range of staging possibilities associated with a particular genre. Her analysis of staging in service encounters (1985: 64) is outlined below.

[(Greeting) (Sale initiation)] ^ [(Sale Enquiry ") {Sale Request ^ Sale Compliance}" ^ Sale] ^ Purchase ^ Purchase Closure ^ (Finis)

This notation is one means by which linguists express what appear to be the obligatory and optional stages of genres. The caret sign ^ means that the stage to the left precedes the one to the right. The stages within the brackets ( ) are optional features of the genre, the brace { }" indicates that the stages within are recursive, and the square brackets [ ] enclose the elements which are recursive. Each stage in the genre (e.g. Sale Enquiry) is given a functional label which attempts to represent its meaning–what it does in semantic terms, in this case making an enquiry about a sale. Of course, people innovate on the basic sequence of obligatory stages and often play, in imaginative ways, with the optional stages of all genres. However, as Bakhtin suggested "genres must be fully mastered to be used creatively" (1986: 80).

Hasan's analysis of service encounters is exemplified in text 2.2 below (from Halliday and Hasan 1985: 59).

Text 2.2 Service Encounter

Sale Request
Customer   Can I have ten oranges and a kilo of bananas please?

Sale Compliance
Vendor   Yes, anything else?
Customer   No thanks

Sale
Vendor   That'll be dollar forty

Purchase
Customer   Two dollars

Purchase Closure
Vendor   Sixty, eighty, two dollars. Thank you.

(Data and analysis from Halliday and Hasan 1985: 59)

Text 2.2 contains the obligatory elements of the structure of a service encounter, i.e. those elements that are a defining feature of the genre. The text begins with a request for goods: *Can I have ten oranges and a kilo of bananas please?* This is then followed by the Sale Compliance, which in this case is the granting of the Sale Request. A positive Sale Compliance is also likely to include an invitation for more purchases, as in text 2.2 when the vendor says *Yes, anything else?* (see Halliday and Hasan 1985: 60). This stage is followed by the exchange of the goods through the three stages of Sale, Purchase and Purchase Closure.

Hasan argues that it is the obligatory elements of structure that define the genre and that:

> the appearance of all these elements in a specific order corresponds to our perception of whether the text is complete or incomplete. (Halliday and Hasan, 1985: 61)

Other elements which are optional may occur in some instances of the genre and may also occur in other genres. However, these do not occur randomly, and the conditions under which they are likely to occur can be described. For example, the optional element Sales Initiation, expressed by *Who's next?*, is likely to occur in a crowded shop where it is necessary to get a customer's attention. It could also occur in other genres, as it is not a defining feature of a service encounter.

Hasan also claims that it is the internal or generic structure of a text that is defining of a genre, so that texts of the same genre will realize the same obligatory elements of structure. Such a model gives us a way of accounting for both the similarities and differences between text 2.2 above and text 1.4, the post office transaction. Text 1.4 contains all the obligatory elements of a service encounter (Sale Request, Sale Compliance, Purchase, and Purchase Closure), but differs from text 2.2 in having both a Sales Initiation and more than one Sale Request ^ Compliance sequence.

Drawing on this work, Martin (1992) developed an alternative but ultimately complementary theory of genre. He defines genre as a:

> staged, goal oriented, purposeful activity in which speakers engage as members of our culture. (1984a: 25)

The concepts within his definition can be elaborated as follows:

- Staged: a genre is staged as the meanings are made in steps; it usually takes more than one step for participants to achieve their goals.
- Goal oriented: a genre is goal oriented in that texts typically move through stages to a point of closure, and are considered incomplete if the culmination is not reached.
- Social process: genres are negotiated interactively and are a realization of a social purpose.

More recently Eggins and Martin (in press: 9) have defined genre as 'a theory of the unfolding structure texts work through to achieve their social purposes'. Genres are enacted in texts, and as texts have different purposes in the culture, texts of different genres will unfold in different ways, or work through different stages or steps. Martin refers to the overall staging patterning of texts as the **schematic structures**. These patternings are a realization of the overall purpose of the text. The stages, as with Hasan's work, are identified in functional terms.

The fact that we can recognize the stages of a text as having particular functions is because of the patterning of language in each stage. For both Hasan (1985) and Martin (1993), each stage is defined by its distinctive semantic and lexico-grammatical realizations. Each genre is seen as having different semantic and lexico-grammatical characteristics, and each stage of the generic structure is realized through specific discourse-semantic and lexico-grammatical patterns.

Considerable work has been carried out on the analysis of written genres using Martin's model. In the 1980s Martin and Rothery analysed in detail some of the key written genres of schooling including reports, narratives, explanations, procedures and argumentative genres such as exposition and discussion (see Martin and Rothery 1986). This work has had a wide impact in education in Australia, and has formed the theoretical underpinning of what is now referred to as the genre-based approach to the teaching of writing in schools.

The work on spoken genres in this paradigm has included the analysis of service encounters (e.g. Ventola 1987), the analysis of spoken, pedagogic discourse (e.g. Christie 1989, Hammond 1995), and narratives elicited from a sociolinguistic interview (Plum 1988). However, as yet there has been very little work in this paradigm on the analysis of the genres that occur in spontaneous, informal conversation. For early applications of the model to conversation, see Eggins (1990), Horvath and Eggins (1995) and Slade (1995).

In Chapters 6 and 7 we will be exploring the structure and function of some of the more common genres that occur in casual talk, building on the techniques developed to describe the more micro-patterns of conversation which are introduced in Chapters 3, 4 and 5. By drawing on analytical techniques offered by systemic linguistics, and also on its theoretical interpretation of the relationship between language and social context, our analysis of casual conversation is simultaneously an analysis of linguistic patterns at several levels, and an account of the work that different linguistic patterns are doing in the construction of social identity.

In the typology of approaches outlined in Figure 2.1 above we have positioned systemic functional linguistics as related to both structural-functional approaches to conversation and to social semiotic approaches. Its focus on structure and function in language (e.g. in the analysis of genre) is complemented by an interpretation of language as a social semiotic resource: a system for making meanings through which language users both reflect and constitute themselves as social agents. This semiotic approach is expressed by Halliday in his recognition of the relationship between the micro- and the macro-social worlds:

> By their everyday acts of meaning, people act out the social structure, affirming their own statuses and roles, and establishing and transmitting the shared systems of value and of knowledge. (1978: 2)

This enactment relationship between language and social structure has provided a foundation for the systemic model. However, since Halliday's development of the more "semiotic-contextual" perspective, systemic analysts have devoted much of their time to developing detailed tools for analysing language patterns. This has often left too little time for interpreting critically the results of their descriptions, and too little time for explaining in accessible terms the social effects of linguistic choices at both micro and macro levels. It is in this area of critical interpretive text analysis that systemics has recently been influenced by, and has also influenced, the last approach we will consider: that of the critical linguists and critical discourse analysts.

2.7 CRITICAL LINGUISTICS AND CRITICAL DISCOURSE ANALYSIS (CDA) (8)

In this final section we group together two approaches to thinking about language which have a "critical" perspective in common. This critical perspective insists that

> the adoption of critical goals means, first and foremost, investigating verbal interactions with an eye to their determination by, and their effects on, social structures. (Fairclough 1995a: 36)

In other words, the micro-interactions of everyday life are viewed by critical analysts as the realization of macro-social structures, so that:

> the question of how discourse cumulatively contributes to the reproduction of macro structures is at the heart of the explanatory endeavour. (1995a: 43)

By the label Critical Linguistics we are referring to social semioticians such as Gunther Kress and his associates (e.g. Kress 1985a, b, 1987, Hodge and Kress 1988, 1993, Kress and van Leeuwen 1996), while the term Critical Discourse Analysis refers to work principally by Norman Fairclough (e.g. Fairclough 1989, 1992, 1995a, b). Both approaches are concerned to 'develop ways of analysing language which address its involvement in the workings of contemporary capitalist society' (Fairclough 1995a: 1). They share a focus on the relationship between language, ideology and power (see, for example, Kress and Hodge 1979, Fairclough 1989) and the relationship between discourse and sociocultural change (see, for example, Fairclough 1992). In these respects the critical strands are similar in focus to much of the work in contemporary critical theory. Where they differ from this work is in their emphasis on relatively detailed textual and lexico-grammatical analysis.

Although researchers in the "critical" tradition have not focused on casual conversation, they have made various comments as to the interest of casual talk, and have provided guidance as to what a critical conversation analysis might look like. We will briefly review the contributions we take from three main areas of their work: (i) notions of text and difference; (ii) methods and techniques of critical discourse/conversation analysis; and (iii) critical accounts of genre.

i) Notions of text and difference One of the major contributions of the critical perspectives has been quite simply exploring why texts happen. Kress (1985a) is one of the few analysts to ask what we consider to be an obvious but unvoiced question for conversation analysts:

> What is the motivation for speech? (11)

Kress's answer, that it is differences which motivate speech, is equally succinct:

> Most speech genres are ostensibly about difference: argument (differences of an ideological kind), interview (differences around power and knowledge), 'gossip' (differences around informal knowledge), lecture (difference around formal knowledge), conversation. (15)

Kress's argument involves recognizing that individuals who come to interactions share membership of particular social groupings, and learn modes of speaking or **discourses** associated with those institutions. Drawing on Foucault, he defines these discourses as:

> systematically-organised sets of statements which give expression to the meanings and values of an institution. . . . A discourse provides a set of possible statements about a given area, and organises and gives structure to the manner in which a particular topic, object, process is to be talked about. In that it provides descriptions, rules, permissions and prohibitions of social and individual actions. (7)

People come to interactions with their own discursive histories, determined by their social history and social position. Interaction with others who do not necessarily share the same discourses (indeed, they cannot, for no two interactants have identical social/discursive histories) creates difficulties that need resolution. As Kress explains:

> There are likely to be problems at any time, arising out of unresolved differences in the individual's discursive history, the individual's present discursive location and the context of discourses in interactions. That difference is the motor that produces texts. Every text arises out of a particular problematic. Texts are therefore manifestations of discourses and the meanings of discourses, and the sites of attempts to resolve particular problems. (12)

He goes on to suggest that dialogues (whether casual conversation or more pragmatic, formal interactions) provide the clearest examples of this "discursive difference" or textual problematic:

> Successful dialogues come about in the tension between (discursive) difference and the attempt to resolve that difference in some way. (13)

This notion of discursive difference explains why couples in longstanding relationships have little to say to each other. They have simply exhausted their differences. To avoid silence they may try to construct difference, for:

> Where there is no difference, no text comes into being. (12)

Kress suggests that the structure of dialogue, of two (or more) interactants taking up positions in discourse and attributing positions to others, makes difference apparent in a way that written text does not. Texts are about (social/discursive) differences, and so texts are fundamentally about (social/discursive) power, for power is nothing more than "relations of difference" (Kress 1985a: 52). The interests of critical linguists and critical discourse analysts in language is not accidental. It arises from their conviction that language and power stand in a particular relationship:

> Because of the constant unity of language and other social matters, language is entwined in social power in a number of ways: it indexes power, expresses power, and language is involved wherever there is contention over and challenge to power. Power does not derive from language, but language may be used to challenge power, to subvert it, and to alter distributions of power in the short or in the longer term. (52)

To understand the social distribution of power, the analyst should look at language, because:

> Language provides the most finely articulated means for a nuanced registration of differences in power in social hierarchical structures, both as a static system and in process. All linguistic forms which can be used to indicate relations of distance, and those which can indicate 'state' or 'process' serve the expression of power. In fact there are few linguistic forms which are not pressed into the service of the expression of power, by a process of syntactic/textual metaphor. (53)

Our analyses in Chapters 3 through 7 are concerned with identifying discursive differences. We will be arguing that these differences invariably express power relationships which have implications beyond the micro-situation of the specific conversation in which they occur.

ii) Methods and techniques of "critical" conversation analysis As well as suggesting *why* conversation occurs, critical analysts have also suggested *how* it could or should be studied. For Fairclough (1995a), as for all critical analysts, the micro-event and the macro-social structures are inextricably linked:

> 'micro' actions or events, including verbal interaction, can in no sense be regarded as of merely 'local' significance to the situations in which they occur, for any and every action contributes to the reproduction of 'macro' structures. (34)

Given this "reproductive" or "reconstituting" relationship between everyday interaction and more global social structures, Fairclough points out that:

> it makes little sense to study verbal interactions *as if* they were unconnected with social structures. (35) (emphasis in original)

Yet this, he claims, is just what many of the approaches to conversation analysis have tried to do. He launches a strong critique against approaches as diverse as the Conversation Analysts, the Birmingham School, and Gricean Pragmatics for only describing the local organization of speech events, and not the social work such events achieve in maintaining social structures. Part of the problem he identifies with such approaches is that they perpetuate views of conversation as the speech events of conscious, independent, social actors, co-operatively achieving self-evident "goals" through homogeneous interactions. Such a view denies the fact that most interactants participate in micro-encounters quite unaware of their ideological/macro-structural implications (cf. Fairclough 1995a: 46ff). In fact, successful ideologies naturalize themselves, effectively making awareness of the social determinations of our actions virtually impossible. Fairclough also points out that:

> The descriptive approach has virtually elevated cooperative conversation between equals into an archetype of verbal interaction in general. As a result, even where attention has been given to 'unequal encounters'...the asymmetrical distribution of discoursal and pragmatic rights and obligations according to status...has not been the focal concern. (46–7)

Thus, the social effects and consequences of power inequalities have not received critical attention.

In contrast to the purely "descriptive" goals pursued by many of these approaches, Fairclough argues for the pursuit of "critical" goals in discourse analysis. Basic to this critical approach is the question we raised earlier when considering the paradox of casual conversation:

> how can it be that people are standardly unaware of how their ways of speaking are socially determined, and of what social effects they may cumulatively lead to? (36)

While Garfinkel and Berger and Luckman sought explanations in the "taken-for-grantedness" of everyday interaction, Fairclough extends this to

61

consider why participants have the impression of "orderliness" in interactions, and feel that "things are as they should be, i.e. as one would normally expect them to be" (28).

Orderliness, he suggests, arises from participants' conformity with their background knowledge about the norms, rights and obligations appropriate in interactions in particular contexts. For example, a lecture at university is "orderly" to the extent that students and lecturer conform to dominant discourse practices whereby the lecturer talks (without invitation), and the students listen (without complaint). Orderliness will be experienced as having been disrupted if, for instance, a student begins interjecting critical comments during the lecturer's discourse, or the lecturer stands up and says *Well, unfortunately I really don't know anything about this topic, so you guys better do the talking today.*

Fairclough suggests that the "knowledge base" which constitutes participants' background knowledge about how orderly interactions proceed involves four components:

- knowledge of language codes,
- knowledge of principles and norms of language use,
- knowledge of situation,
- knowledge of the world. (33)

Fairclough claims that all four of these types of knowledge involve ideology, by which he means:

> each is a particular representation of some aspect of the world (natural or social; what is, what can be, what ought to be) which might be (and may be) alternatively represented and where any given representation can be associated with some particular 'social base'. (31)

This means knowledge is not neutral, and always implies ways of doing which serve the interests of some social group, generally at the expense of others. For example, knowing about the principles and norms of language used in lectures involves knowing a way of using language in that context which serves the interests of one social group (academics, whose position as an educated authority is maintained) at the expense of another (students, who would certainly learn more through other modes and under other conditions). However, participants generally notice neither the social determinations of their speech (e.g. that I behave as a student in lectures in conformity to norms established by an interested social group, academics), nor the social effects (e.g. surrendering of control over my own acquisition of knowledge). It is in the nature of ideology to "naturalize" itself. And thus critical discourse analysis involves "denaturalizing" everyday discourse, to expose the ideologies expressed and therefore the interests served. To achieve this denaturalization, Fairclough argues that:

> Textual analysis demands diversity of focus not only with respect to functions but

also with respect to levels of analysis. (7)

Fairclough finds the most useful linguistic model for achieving this diversity is systemic functional linguistics, which he recognizes to be:

> a functional theory of language oriented to the question of how language is structured to tackle its primary social functions. ... The view of language as social semiotic (Halliday, 1978) incorporates an orientation to mapping relations between language (texts) and social structures and relations. (10)

Like Fairclough, we find the theory of systemic linguistics the most useful one for denaturalizing the ideological processes of casual conversation.

iii) Critical accounts of genre   The third aspect of CDA which has influenced our work is its perspective on genre, where it has contributed to our thinking about analysing both genres *within* conversation and the genre *of* conversation itself. Views of genre within CDA draw less on functional linguistic accounts of structure and more on current reconceptions of genre by critical literary theorists. Drawing on Bakhtin (1986), these accounts make reference to the sociocultural and historical contexts embodied by types of texts and explore the ways in which genres function as discursive practices. Bakhtin's (1986) identification of speech genres, and his argument that the more complex "secondary" genres of writing are derived from these primary speech genres, has broadened the field of enquiry to include everyday as well as literary genres. Bakhtin was interested in the analysis of actual language use and not in the analysis of decontextualized sentences, and consequently his basic unit of analysis is the utterance rather than the sentence. He defines speech genres as:

> the typical form of the utterance associated with a particular sphere of communication (e.g. the workplace, the sewing circle, the military) which have therefore developed into 'relatively stable types' in terms of thematic content, style and compositional structure.' (1986: 52)

Examples of speech genres include 'short rejoinders of daily dialogue', 'everyday narration'', 'business documents' and 'the diverse world of commentary' (60). Their structure derives from the situations from which they arise such that:

> even in the most free, the most unconstrained conversation, we cast our speech in definite generic forms, sometimes rigid and trite ones, sometimes more flexible, plastic and creative ones. ... We learn to cast our speech in generic forms and when hearing others' speech, we guess its genre from the very first words; we predict a certain length and a certain compositional structure; we foresee the end; that is from the very beginning we have a sense of the speech whole. If speech genres did not exist and we had not mastered them, if we had to originate them during the speech process and construct each utterance at will for the first time, speech communication would be almost impossible. (78)

Bakhtin's perspective on genre is similar to that taken in systemic-functional linguistics. Bakhtin claims that the lexical, grammatical and compositional structures of particular genres are a reflection of the specific context of communication and he has identified genres as 'relatively stable types' of interactive utterances with definite and typical forms of construction. These particular features of Bakhtin's analysis are echoed in Martin's approach to genre analysis reviewed above (see Eggins and Martin 1995).

From a CDA perspective, Fairclough defines genre as 'a socially ratified way of using language in connection with a particular type of social activity' (1995a: 14). Genre is 'the abstract constituent of text types' (13). There are the ideal text types which people orient to but do not necessarily conform to, but there are also:

> texts which closely match ideal types (as well as others which do not), so that people learn them from concrete textual experience. (13)

Genres in CDA are seen as social actions occurring within particular social and historical contexts. As Millar argues (1984), the similarities in form and discursive function are seen as deriving from the similarity in the social action undertaken. Thus texts are looked at not only for the textual regularities they display, and therefore also the generic conventions they flout, but also for the class, gender, and ethnic biases they incorporate. Thus, the ways in which the texts position readers or other participants and the ways in which the texts function as discursive practices are explored.

Hodge and Kress's (1988: 8–10) analysis of a billboard advertisement helps to exemplify this approach. Their analysis focuses not on the advertisement format, text structure and lexico-grammatical features, but rather it explores the way that contingent social structures and practices are realized in the advertisement. It considers how the text is institutionally legitimized, how the readers are positioned (e.g. are they positioned as consumers, and in what ways are they able to respond?). The analysis also considers what particular gender, class and ethnic bias is evident in the advertisement (e.g. do the writers of the text want to appeal to a female audience, and if so what 'feminine' stereotypes is the advertisement appealing to?). What is *not* in the text is also considered (e.g. what ideological messages are carried by the very absence of certain features?).

This new conception of genre in CDA sees genres as both social and textual categories, no longer fixed and immutable but dynamic and changing. While recognizing that there are generic conventions in text, both Fairclough and Kress stress the need to see genres not as fixed and rigid schema but as abstract, ideal categories open to negotiation and change. As Kress argues:

> Genres are dynamic, responding to the dynamics of other parts of social systems. Hence genres change historically; hence new genres emerge over time and hence, too, what appears as 'the same' generic form at one level has recognisable distinct forms in differing social groups. (Kress 1987: 42)

Within this general retheorizing of genre, CDA makes passing references to the nature of conversation itself as a generic form. It recognizes the essential similarity which conversation has with other genres, in that it is motivated by difference. It also recognizes conversation as varying from other genres in significant ways. Kress, for example, suggests that of all genres, conversation is that with the "least or no power difference", since:

> in a conversation the participants all speak 'on their own behalf' and take turns on their own initiative, without being directed by any one member of the group. That is, the distribution of power in the interaction is such that the genre of conversation does not provide for any one participant to assume a differentiated directing role. (Kress 1985: 25)

One result of this power equality is, he suggests, that the "mechanisms of interaction", by which he seems to mean the turn-taking procedures, are less foregrounded, allowing the content to be most salient. In contrast, he points out that in genres in which power is unequally distributed (his example is educational genres), the reverse applies. The unequal power foregrounds the interactive conventions, thereby rendering least salient the content or substance of the interaction (Kress 1985: 25).

We agree with Kress that overt differences of power in hierarchically structured interactions generate or are reflected in more "closed" interactions (Kress 1985: 26). However, we believe that the data we will be presenting in the next six chapters challenge the claim that casual conversation is "the genre ... which is formally least about power" (Kress 1985: 26). In fact, what we will show, through detailed, systematic analysis, is that conversation is *always* a struggle over power – but that the struggle goes "underground", being disguised by the *apparent* equality of the casual context. One of the tasks of our analysis is to denaturalize some of the means (e.g. humour) by which the power differences in conversation are rendered opaque for both interactants and "casual" observers.

One final insight we take from CDA is to recognize our own positions as "readers" of the texts we will be presenting:

> The interpretation of texts is a dialectal process resulting from the interface of the variable interpretative resources people bring to bear on the text, *and* properties of the text itself. (Fairclough 1995a: 9)

We recognize that the interpretations of the conversations that we will be presenting throughout this book implicate our own sociohistorical discursive practices.

2.8 CONCLUSION

In this chapter we have reviewed ideas from a range of approaches to discourse analysis that we consider useful in the analysis of casual conversation. In the following chapter we begin our analytical exploration of casual talk by developing a description of the grammar of casual conversation as a resource for realizing interpersonal meanings. In relating grammatical patterns to relations of status, familiarity, affective involvement and affiliation, we will be making a first connection between the "differences" which we negotiate in the micro-semiotic encounters of everyday talk and the "differences" which permeate the macro-social structures of the cultural context within which casual conversations take place.

NOTES

1. All the approaches mentioned so far are cogently reviewed in Schiffrin (1994).
2. It is important also to mention the applied work on genre by Swales (1990) who is concerned to show how a 'genre centred' approach to second language teaching 'offers a workable way of making sense of the myriad communicative events that occur in the contemporary English-speaking academy' (1990:1). His use of the term "genre" is derived from several different traditions (see 1990: 13) and as such is not dealt with separately in this chapter.
3. Note that the term "conversation" is used in the following section as it was used by the Conversation Analysts themselves: that is, it refers to all linguistic interactions, and not only to casual conversational interactions as we have defined them in Chapter 1.
4. CA work can be surveyed in, for example, Sudnow (1972), Schenkein (1978), Psathas (1979), Button and Lee (1987), Atkinson and Heritage (1984), Drew and Heritage (1992).
5. This is an authentic excerpt from data collected by Eggins.
6. See Rothery (1990) for an expansion of this argument in relation to written narratives in primary school.
7. Plum (1988) argues that Labov did not encounter different storytelling texts because during the interviews if a certain stage, such as Resolution, was not mentioned he would elicit it by asking questions such as "What happened then?". This resulted in the storytelling texts having the structure of Complication ^ Resolution.
8. See also Stubbs (1983), McTear (1985) and Wells *et al.* (1979) for extensions of the Birmingham School approach to other discourse varieties.

3 The grammar of casual conversation: enacting role relations

3.1 INTRODUCTION

In Chapter 1 we suggested that casual conversation is motivated by interpersonal goals: people chat not just to "kill time", but rather to clarify and extend the interpersonal ties that have brought them together. In Chapter 2, we used the systemic concept of tenor to suggest that interpersonal ties are the accumulation of values for four main dimensions: the status relationships enacted by participants, the frequency with which they come into contact, the degree of affective involvement they feel towards each other, and their sense of affiliation with each other. In this chapter we will explore the major grammatical resource which English offers for making these interpersonal meanings: the clause systems of Mood. We will show how the analysis of Mood choices in casual conversation can reveal tensions between equality and difference, as interactants enact and construct relations of power through talk.

3.2 GRAMMATICAL PATTERNS IN CASUAL CONVERSATION

In Chapter 1 we demonstrated how we can often deduce many social or contextual factors about interactants from a brief excerpt of casual conversation. A similar claim can be made for text 3.1 below, which involves three participants, Fran, Brad and Dave, who are sitting in a parked car, filling in time. As you read through the text, you might consider how you think these interactants relate to each other (what social roles they are playing), and how you reach your conclusion.

Text 3.1 Philosophy[1]

1, 2, 3 refer to speaker turns. NV indicates a non-verbal action. (i), (ii), (iii) indicate clauses. The full transcription key appears in Table 1.1.

Turn	Speaker	Text
1	Brad	(i) Look. (ii) See that guy. (iii) He plays the double-bass
2	Fran	(i) Does he?
3	Brad	(i) In the orchestra. (ii) He's a funny bastard (iii) and his wife's German (iv) and she's insane.
NV1	Dave	[coughs]

4	Fran	(i)He's funny (ii)== and she's insane?
5	Brad	(i) == ALL Germans are in== sane.
6	Dave	(i) == You know ...(ii)You know a lot of funny people don't you Brad?
7	Brad	(i)Yeah, (ii)everyone at Uni is. ==
8	Dave	== (i)They're ALL mad==
9	Brad	== (i)They're all FREAKS
10	Dave	(i)Except you.
11	Brad	(i)Yeah.
12	Fran	(i)And they're all coming home now.
13	Brad	(i)Whaddya mean? (ii)Coming, oh
14	Fran	(i)Like, they're coming up the hill are they?
15	Brad	(i)No, this ... (ii)For General Studies we've got this ... tutor (iii)and he's German (iv)and he's insane.
16	Fran	(i)I didn't know (ii)you had to do General Studies.
17	Brad	(i)Yeah I, (ii)I got exemption from ==[noise of passing bus] (iii)Bastards!
18	Fran	== (i)Last year
19	Brad	(i)From half of it.
20	Dave	(i)When are you gonna do ... all your odds 'n sods subjects?
21	Brad	(i)Whaddya mean "odds 'n' sods subjects"?
22	Dave	(i)Well, y'know, you can't just do languages can you?
23	Brad	(i)Whaddya talking about?
24	Dave	(i)If you're doing an Arts degree (ii)you got a lot of other garbage to do.
25	Brad	(i)No [falling-rising tone]. (ii)I, (iii)if I wanted to (iv)I could do French, German and Russian ...
26	Fran	== (i)This year?
27	Brad	== (i)In First Year.
28	Fran	== (i)Oh this year.
29	Brad	== (i)I could do ... (ii)In FIRST year you can do whatever you WANT ==
30	Fran	(i)Mmm
31	Brad	== (i)in an Arts Degree ... (ii)as long as you do ... a few General Studies subjects ==
32	Dave	== (i)That's what I mean. (ii)And when are you gonna do your General Studies?
33	Brad	(i)I'm doin it NOW! ==
34	Fran	(i)Mmm
35	Brad	== (i)That's what I'm talking == about.
36	Dave	== (i)And what are your General Studies?
37	Brad	(i)Oh it's ... RUBBISH ... (ii)One of them is alright, (iii)one of them is actually good.
38	Dave	(i)Yeah but what IS it?
39	Brad	(i)Well I'm thinking (ii)what it is.
NV2	Fran	[laughs]
40	Dave	(i)History of Scotch bagpipe == playing?
41	Brad	== (i)It's [laughing] ... (ii)It's bloody ... (iii)it's ... introductory philosophy ... sort of stuff. (iv)It's it's called

... (v)I dunno (vi)what it's called. (vii)Th' they've got weird names like "The Pursuit of Human Rationality" or "Self and Society" (viii)and I, the one, (ix)I think the one that's that's alright is called Human Rationality (x)and it's just introductory philosophy. (xi)They talk about ... Rationalism an. [belches] aah [laughs]

42	Dave	(i)So you gotta pick all those up this year?
43	Brad	(i)I'm doin' em ... at the moment! ==
44	Dave	(i)Right.
45	Brad	==(i)It's look, (ii)it's just a, (iii)it's only a two hours a week subject.
46	Fran	(i)Mmm
47	Brad	(i)And um
48	Dave	(i)But I thought (ii)you dropped a lot of them last year (iii)which you were s'posed to do?
49	Brad	(i)You only have to do, (ii)I onl'... oh [3 sec pause] (iii)I've told you about what POINTS are haven't I?
50	Dave	==(i)Yeah
51	Fran	==(i)Mmm
52	Brad	(i)Right, (ii)so G'... (iii)First Year German is twelve points. (iv)You only have to do eight points of General Studies in your whole in your whole == career.
53	Fran	== (i)Three years.
54	Brad	==(i)Yea
55	Fran	(i)Or whatever, ==(ii)don't you?
56	Brad	==(i)In Second Year, you do ... four points, (ii)and in Third Year you do four points.
57	Fran	(i)Mmm
58	Brad	(i)If you wanted to (ii)you could do ... (iii)you could do ALL your points in the one year.
59	Fran	(i)Mmm
60	Brad	(i)But anyway you th', (ii)it's it's just, (iii)it's just this rubbish subjects that you have to do ==
61	Fran	(i)Mmm
62	Brad	==(i)It's just a ... technicality. (ii)But this one on Philosophy is alright. (iii)We talk about bloody ... Descartes and all these idiots. (iv)It's riDICulous!
63	Fran	(i)Why are they == idiots?
64	Brad	==(i)He sits, (ii)he sits in a room and, and – and the' (iii)and decides (iv)"I think (v)therefore I am" ... (vi)all this stuff. (vii)An', I mean he hasn't got anything better to DO. ... um
65	Fran	(i)He's an abstract thinker.
66	Brad	(i)Yeah but ... (ii)at least he could think abstractly about something that was worth thinking about, like soil erosion or something
NV3	Fran	[laughs]
67	Brad	(i)That's what I'm == thinking ( )
68	Fran	==(i)How to solve the == problem
69	Brad	== (i)I'm wondering these days. (ii)I'm thinking (iii)what

			the hell ... use is anything that I'm doing at University
70	Fran		(i) But even if it meant that you could understand people and therefore HELP them?
71	Brad		(i) Yeah but I don't LIKE people ... um ... (ii) I don't want to be INVOLVED with people. (iii) I'd rather be involved with == soil erosion
72	Fran		== (i) Everybody has to be though. (ii) But I mean
73	Brad		(i) or desalin == ation
74	Dave		== (i) Well there's a, (ii) there's a go. (iii) Get yourself a a degree (iv) and go and work for the Soil Con'
75	Brad		(i) Yeah but ... (ii) yeah, well, that's what I'd like to do (iii) but I don't ==
76	Dave		== (i) And they'd say (ii) "Whaddya know about soil" (iii) and you'd say (iv) "Well I can, (v) I know how, (vi) I know (vii) what it's called in Russian ==
77	Brad		(i) A degree in a degree in Linguistics isn't much use y'know (ii) if you wanna work for Landcare or something, (iii) so == (iv) But anyway
78	Dave		== (i) Well you should have thought of that thought of that three years ago Brad.
79	Brad		(i) I'll get a job, (ii) and I'll make some money, (iii) and then I'll maybe be able to do something meaningful == (with my life)
80	Fran		== (i) However, I mean what you said is, is maybe all very true David (ii) but, I mean, in the Public Service people are transferring from ... areas
81	Brad		(i) Ah I don't wanna be a bloody Public Servant ==
82	Fran		== (i) No no but I'm just saying like. (ii) Like you're saying you know (iii) you don't know anything about soil ... (iv) But people are transferring from Fisheries to Education ... (v) Now I can see no == no bearing
83	Brad		== (i) Yeah but you can't teach (ii) if you haven't got a Diploma in Education ==
84	Fran		== (i) They're not teaching though. (ii) But they're adMINISTERING == teachers
85	Brad		== (i) Yeah well that's different. (ii) That's different. (iii) That's that's that's just a
86	Fran		(i) But whadda they know about education?
87	Brad		(i) Well they know ==
88	Fran		== (i) What have fish gotta do with education?
89	Brad		(i) Who says (ii) they know anything about FISH (iii) just because they were administrating == Fisheries?
90	Fran		== (i) Well they were high up in Fisheries ==
91	Brad		== (i) Yeah but that doesn't mean they have
92	Fran		== (i) Like SAFCOL
NV4	Dave		== [yawns loudly]
93	Fran		== (i) the South Australian Fisheries
94	Brad		(i) They mightn't have had a degree in Biology or anything. (ii) They might have just
95	Fran		(i) They didn't have that either.

96	Brad	(i) Yeah well exactly.
97	Fran	(i) They were just clerks.
98	Brad	(i) Exactly, (ii) so ... if they can administer fish (iii) they can administer bloody schoolkids.
NV5	Fran	[laughs]
99	Fran	(i) Well I, I think ==that's
100	Brad	== (i) That guy that that Bangladeshi that used to live with us he was a a a Limnologist or whatever it's called. ==
101	Fran	== (i) A WHAT? ==
102	Dave	== (i) Who?
103	Brad	(i) Oh not == Limnologist.
104	Fran	== (i) Ichthyologist.
105	Brad	(i) He studied fish. (ii) He studied ... (iii) he was a ... (iv) he was a ...Dip ... (v) Oh what is it called?... (vi) P-H-D in Science.
106	Fran	(i) Yea
107	Brad	(i) An 'e was learnin, studyin Fisheries. (ii) His, his thesis was on the breeding of mullet [laughs] or something
NV6	Fran	[laughs]

You have probably deduced that this group of speakers is very different from the groups contributing to the excerpts presented in Chapter 1. Text 3.1 is not a trio of university friends chatting together, but in fact a family group: Mum (Fran, aged 54), Dad (Dave, aged 57), and university-aged son (Brad, aged 27). Clues to the different social roles can be found in the linguistic choices interactants make. There is an obvious generational difference between Brad on the one hand, and Fran and Dave on the other. This is suggested by Brad's use of colloquial language and intensifying words (e.g. *a funny bastard, it's just this rubbish subjects*) and Fran and Dave's use of more standard, more restrained spoken forms. The ironic teasing by Dave (e.g. turns 40 and 76) is a clue to his patriarchal position (Brad and Fran do not tease Dave). One indication of gender differences between interactants is the non-verbal behaviours displayed by Brad and Dave (belching and yawning), which are not matched by Fran. You may also have noticed that Fran is more frequently interrupted; that she takes the part of the maligned and tries to be even-handed, only to have her reservations interrupted, ignored or undermined; and that she speaks in the most "careful" or standard way of all three interactants.

However, perhaps the most striking pattern enacted in text 3.1 is that which differentiates the parents on the one hand from the son on the other. A close look at text 3.1 reveals an interesting correlation between the social roles and a striking lack of reciprocity in the interaction: the role of "son" appears to carry certain linguistic privileges, while that of "parents" entails conversational responsibilities. Brad is clearly the centre of attention. Only his attitudes and activities are spoken about. He gets the greatest number of turns, and the longest turns, as Fran and Dave ask him questions and follow up on his words. He does not ask any questions of them, nor do we learn anything about their activities.

The most significant example of the unevenness of the talk is found in the choice of clause types. While the parents produce a large number of interrogative clauses (i.e. asking questions), the son produces an overwhelming number of declarative clauses (i.e. making statements). To explore whether this is in fact a pattern rather than an accidental association, we would need to analyse other examples of casual conversation as well. However, in order to undertake such investigations we need to be able to identify reliably features of spoken discourse such as interrogatives and declaratives, and the various other clause types which are possible in English conversation. We could then quantify the relative proportions of each clause type in a text.

Only on the basis of accurate identification of clause selections can we move on to consider the conversational implications of each clause type: what it means when different speakers choose different clause types. We need to consider such issues as the consequences of different clause types. For example, if you produce an interrogative, you are generally agreeing to give up the speaker role for at least one turn, in order for someone to respond to your interrogative. On the other hand, if you produce a declarative this implication of surrendering a turn is not there. We can also consider the evidence from empirical studies of conversation (e.g. Fishman 1980, Holmes 1984) which have suggested, for example, that women produce more of some clause types in mixed conversations than do men, and we need to consider the different explanations that could be proposed for this.

The purpose of this chapter is to present techniques for analysing associations between clause types and social roles. As we present technical categories of grammatical analysis, we will continually re-examine the linguistic behaviour of the three interactants in text 3.1 in order to explore the ways in which the grammatical resources of the language are used to construct and enact personal identity and interpersonal relationships. To begin we will clarify what we mean by grammatical patterns.

3.3 INTERACTING PATTERNS IN CASUAL TALK

We indicated in Chapter 2 that there are four main types of linguistic patterns which contribute to the achievement of casual conversation: grammatical, semantic, discourse and generic patterns.

Grammatical patterns are the focus of this chapter. These patterns are revealed by studying the types of clause structures chosen by interactants and are displayed within each speaker's turns. For example, as mentioned above, in text 3.1 Fran and Dave frequently use interrogative clauses (usually to ask questions), while Brad uses very few interrogatives, producing mostly declaratives (usually to make statements). Such patterned choices are part of what indicates the different social roles being played by the interactants, and how such roles are constructed in our culture. In the uneven distribution of these clause types in text 3.1, we can see how, in this particular cultural context, the social role of "son" gives access to linguistic privileges (the right to make statements, rather than the need to ask questions).

The other linguistic patterns are examined in the following chapters. In Chapter 4, we explore **semantic** patterns, i.e. how attitudinal and expressive meanings are encoded in conversation. For example, in text 3.1 these meanings are conveyed through Brad's use of words such as *funny, insane, freaks,* and Dave's teasing of Brad. In Chapter 5 we will examine the overtly interactive **discourse** patterns of conversation: how people choose to act on each other through their choice of speech functions. For example, in text 3.1 Fran reacts to Brad's opinions with challenges, but her challenges are dismissed. Finally in Chapter 6 we consider **generic** patterns, the way interactants construct longer chunks of continuous talk in order to explore shared social positions.

Since grammatical patterns are patterns which operate *within clauses,* it may seem that we are dealing with monologic issues in this chapter. However, there are two reasons for beginning our analysis of casual conversation by describing what goes on in individual speaker turns:

(i)   Interactive conversation is constructed through the individual contributions of each speaker. As we will see below, through their grammatical choices interactants take up roles in the conversation, thus positioning themselves and other interactants, such that their individual choices are fundamental in making dialogue possible.

(ii) The *interaction* of grammatical, semantic and discourse patterns creates meanings which can only be fully appreciated when we are able to analyse linguistic choices at all three levels. For example, if one speaker announces that *Descartes was an idiot,* a second speaker may challenge in any of the following ways:

(1)   *Why?*
(2)   *What makes you say that?*
(3)   *You should know!*
(4)   *Don't be so bloody sure!*
(5)   *He was an abstract thinker*
(6)   *Maybe he was just an abstract thinker*
(7)   *Really?*

These alternative challenges differ at three levels:

a) They differ grammatically in that

- some of the structures are of different clause types:
  - challenges 1, 2 and 7 are interrogatives
  - challenges 3, 5 and 6 are declaratives
  - challenge 4 is an imperative

- different items function as Subject:
  - *you* is subject in challenges 2, 3 and 4
  - *he* is subject in challenges 5 and 6
- some challenges employ modalities such as *should* and *maybe*

b) They differ semantically with the use of swear words such as *bloody* and minimizing words such as *just*.

c) They differ discoursally in that each challenge makes a different following move more likely, for example:

- *Really* in challenge 7 calls for a clarifying move
- *You should know* in challenge 3 suggests a confrontation is likely in the next move.

To capture differences between these challenges we need first to be able to describe the grammatical choices. We can then analyse how the semantic and discourse choices interact with the choice of clause type.

We are suggesting that a full account of how casual conversation works needs to be able to describe all three of the following:

(i) the expression of meanings through the clauses a speaker uses within each turn (grammar);
(ii) the cumulative expression of attitudes and evaluations negotiated by interactants (semantics);
(iii) the dynamic negotiation of those meanings through the interactional sequencing of turns (discourse).

We therefore need to spend some time acquiring the technical apparatus necessary for describing and comparing the dimensions of clause structure which are most central to encoding interpersonal meaning.

3.4   MOOD: CONSTITUENTS IN CASUAL CONVERSATION

At the clause level, the major patterns which enact roles and role relations are those of **mood**, with the associated subsystems of **polarity** and **modality**. Mood refers to patterns of clause type, such as interrogative, imperative and declarative. These patterns have to do with the presence and configuration of certain "negotiable" elements of clause structure. Polarity is concerned with whether clause elements are asserted or negated, while modality covers the range of options open to interactants to temper or qualify their contributions. We will present and exemplify the techniques for the analysis of these patterns with reference to text 3.1 above. The mood analysis presented below is an abridged version of that found in Halliday (1994:ch. 4). For further details, readers are referred to Halliday, or to re-presentations of Halliday's analysis as in Eggins (1994), Butt *et al.* (1995), and Gerot and Wignell (1994). Below we present only those aspects of mood analysis which are useful in the critical interpretation of casual talk.

3.4.1 Basic mood classes

Differences between interrogatives and declaratives and other clause types are referred to technically as differences in mood. The basic mood types that occur in casual conversation are exemplified by the following set of clauses:

Mood type	Example
declarative: full	*He plays the double-bass.*
declarative: elliptical	*This year.*
imperative: full	* *Look at that man walking up there.*
imperative: elliptical	*Look.*
wh-interrogative: full	*When are you gonna do ... all your odds 'n sods subjects?*
wh-interrogative: elliptical	*Who?*
polar interrogative: full	*Yeah but what IS it?*
polar interrogative: elliptical	*Does he?*
exclamative: full	* *What rubbish you talk, Brad!*
exclamative: elliptical	* *What rubbish!*
minor	*Right.*

(an * indicates a clause which is not taken from text 3.1 above)

Each mood type involves a different configuration of a set of basic clause constituents. **Full** English clauses, that is clauses which have not had any elements left out or **ellipsed** (see section 3.5.7), generally consist of two pivotal constituents: a Subject and a Finite. In addition to these pivotal constituents, we also generally find a Predicator, and some combination of Complements or Adjuncts. Below we will briefly define and exemplify each of these elements, indicating their typical functions in casual conversation.

3.4.2 Subject

i) **Definition** The Subject is the pivotal participant in the clause, the person or thing that the proposition is concerned with and without whose presence there could be no argument or negotiation. A casual conversation cannot proceed unless a Subject is proposed.

ii) **Identification criteria** The Subject is generally a nominal element: i.e. a noun or pronoun. If there is only one nominal element in a clause, it will be the Subject (provided there has been no ellipsis – see below). For example (Subject underlined):

37	Brad	(i) Oh it's ... RUBBISH ... (ii) <u>One of them</u> is alright, (iii) <u>one of them</u> is actually good.

The Subjects of the clauses above are *it* and *one of them*. Since the elements *rubbish*, *alright* and *good* are all adjectives, they could not be the Subject.

As this example shows, not all nominal groups consist of only a single word. With longer nominal groups (e.g. *one of them*), it is the entire nominal group which is Subject: i.e. the head noun and all the modifying and qualifying words which occur before and after it. One test for the scope of the nominal group involves trying to rephrase the clause using one of the subject pronouns (I, you, he/she/it, we, they). All the elements subsumed by the pronoun are part of the same nominal group. For example, <u>one of them</u> is alright could be changed to <u>it</u> is alright, which indicates that the entire nominal group *one of them* is the Subject of the clause.

While there may be two or more nominal groups in a single clause, there will only ever be *one* Subject per clause. The nominal group that is Subject determines whether the first verbal element (the Finite) will be singular or plural. Hence, the Subject can also be identified by changing the number of the verb (from singular to plural, or vice versa) and looking to see which nominal element has to be changed in response.

A further useful test for Subject is the tag test. The Subject is the nominal element which is picked up in pronoun form when you try to "send the clause back" to the other speaker by adding a tag. For example:

37	Brad	(i) Oh it's ... RUBBISH ... (ii) One of them is alright, (iii) one of them is actually good.

tag: Is it?
(*It* = *one of them*; therefore *one of them* = Subject)

As these examples show, the Subject in casual conversation is overwhelmingly a personal pronoun (very often *I* or *we* as casual talk is highly egocentric). However, the Subject may also be an extended nominal group, as in:

77	Brad	(i) <u>A degree in a degree in Linguistics</u> isn't much use y'know

Here, changing the verb from *isn't* to *aren't*, or sending the clause back with a tag (*isn't it?*) or substituting a pronoun (*It isn't much use*) would all indicate that the Subject is the entire nominal group *a degree in Linguistics*. The following example involves an even longer nominal group:

100	Brad	== (i) <u>That guy that that Bangladeshi that used to live with us he</u> was a a a Limnologist or whatever it's called. ==

In fact, in this utterance the nominal group is becoming so unusually long for casual talk that the speaker summarizes by inserting the subject pronoun *he* at the end.

Finally, it is possible for the Subject to be a clause in itself, as in the following example:

80   Fran   ==(i)However, I mean <u>what you said</u> is, is maybe all very true David

Here, all the tests will show that the Subject is not as you might first suspect the *I* of *I mean*. In fact *I mean* is a conjunction, an item which links this speaker's contribution to the prior talk. Nor is the Subject the *you* of *you said*. A tag applied to the first clause (*Is it?*) shows that the *it* stands for *what you said*, which is itself a clause. This is an example of an **embedded** clause as Subject. This means that where we would expect to find a nominal element (a noun phrase or simply a noun or pronoun), we find instead the grammatically more complex unit, the clause. Embedding is a kind of grammatical recycling, a way of getting more information into clauses.

3.4.3 Finite

i) Definition   The Finite expresses the process part of the clause that makes it possible to argue about the Subject participant.

ii) Identification criteria   The Finite is always a verbal element, i.e. it is always realized through a verbal group. The verbal group in a clause is the sequence of words which indicate the process, action or state that the Subject is engaged in. Verbal groups in clauses may consist of one word only, for example (verbal groups *in italics*, Finite <u>underlined</u>):

1   Brad   (iii)He <u>*plays*</u> the double-bass

They may also consist of more than one word, for example:

94   Brad   (i)They <u>*mightn't have had*</u> a degree in Biology or anything.
                             (ii)They <u>*might*</u> *have* just

Where the verbal group consists of more than one word, the Finite is always and only the first element in this verbal group, and corresponds to what is traditionally called the 'auxiliary verb'. Where the verbal group consists of only one word (as is the case in the simple present or simple past tenses, e.g. *eats, ate*), then the Finite is realized in that single word.

3.4.4 The function of Subject and Finite in casual talk

The Subject and Finite together are the essential constituents of a clause from the point of view of dialogue as illustrated in the first exchange of text 3.1:

1	Brad	(i)Look. (ii)See that guy. (iii)He plays the double-bass
2	Fran	(i)Does he?

In his first turn, Brad sets up the Subject *he* and the Finite *plays*. Fran accepts Brad's "terms" for discussion when she reacts with *Does he?*. Fran could also have responded to Brad's proposition by disagreeing, e.g. *No he doesn't*, but again her disagreement would be clearly anchored in the terms of his proposition. However, if Brad had begun the interaction by just saying *Plays*, then negotiation would have been problematic. Before anyone could have argued about *playing* or *not playing* they would have needed to establish WHO plays, i.e. the Subject. Similar problems would have arisen if Brad had begun by saying just *He*. Until this Subject became anchored in a Finite (just what does he DO?), negotiation could not have proceeded intelligibly.

Hence we can say that together the Subject and Finite constitute the "nub" of the proposition: in order to interact we need both something to argue about, and some way in which to argue. However, as Brad's clause *He plays the double-bass* indicates, we often have more to our propositions than just a Subject and Finite. We will now review the other constituents of the clause, and their roles in casual conversation.

3.4.5 Predicator

i) Definition   The Predicator encodes the action or process involved in the clause. It gives content to the verbal element of the proposition, telling listeners what is or was happening.

ii) Identification criteria   Like the Finite, the Predicator is expressed within the verbal group. This means that part of the verbal group is expressing the Finite, and part is expressing the Predicator. As pointed out above, the verbal group may consist of a single word or several words. When there is more than one element within the verbal group, the Predicator is all the constituents of the verbal group minus the Finite, which is always the first verbal element.

When there is only one constituent in the verbal group, then that constituent is functioning both as Finite and as Predicator. This is the case with the simple present or the simple past tense form of a verb. For example (Predicator underlined, verbal group *in italics*):

64	Brad	==(i)He *<u>sits</u>*, (ii)he *<u>sits</u>* in a room and, and – and the (iii)and *<u>decides</u>*

The Predicator in clauses (i), (ii) and (iii) is a single lexical item, so *sits* and *decides* function as both Finite and as Predicator.

These tests to identify the Predicator do not apply to the verbs <u>to be</u> and <u>to have</u> (possess) as these verbs do not have a Predicator element in the present simple or simple past tense. Their verbal groups can be considered to express only a Finite element. For example:

64   Brad   (iv) "I *think* (v) therefore I *am*" ...

In the first clause *think* encodes both a Finite and a Predicator element, but in the second clause *am* is only a Finite, and the clause has no Predicator.

3.4.6   The function of the Predicator in casual talk

While the Finite element serves to anchor the Subject of the talk by specifying such dimensions as polarity, tense and number, the Predicator gives content or representational meaning to the process the Subject is engaged in. Like all elements of the clause, it can become the focus of negotiation, as in the following exchange from text 3.1:

83   Brad   == (i) Yeah but you can't teach (ii) if you haven't got a
                  Diploma in Education ==
84   Fran   == (i) They're not teaching though. (ii) But they're
                  adMINISTERING == teachers

Here Fran does not react to Brad's turn by negotiating the Subject-Finite (e.g. *Can't you? Haven't they?*). Instead she revises his Predicator *teaching* to *administering*. The reason that her response sounds like a side-step is exactly because she has chosen to negotiate the less pivotal element of Predicator.

3.4.7   Complement

i) Definition   The Complement is a participant which is somehow implicated in the proposition, but is not the pivotal participant.

ii) Identification criteria   Like the Subject, the Complement is expressed by a nominal group, either a single pronoun or noun or by a sequence of words dependent on a head noun. This indicates that there can be two nominal groups in a clause, one which will be the Subject, and the other which will be a Complement. The Subject can be determined using the tests given above, and thus by a process of exclusion, the other nominal group must be a Complement.

A more informed test is based on the fact that the Complement is a nominal group which *could* be made the Subject of the clause but has not. To make the Complement become Subject, an active clause would need to be made into a passive, or a passive clause turned into an active. For example, consider the clause below from text 3.1 (Complement under-lined):

1   Brad   (iii) He plays the double-bass

If we try to make something other than *he* the Subject, we find that the only possibility is a passive transformation:

The double-bass is played by him

This shows that the double-bass is a Complement.

While the passive test works to identify all Complements which involve a head noun, there are two situations in which the second nominal group is still a Complement but where the test does not work. The first case is with the verb *to be*. Consider the clause below in which the nominal groups have been underlined:

3   Brad   (ii) He's <u>a funny bastard</u>

Since there is no passive form of the verb *to be*, it is not possible to make a direct passive of such a clause. So we cannot say:

** *A funny bastard is beed by him.*

Nonetheless, the second nominal group *a funny bastard* is still a Complement, since it has a noun as a head word and could potentially become Subject if a verb other than the verb *to be* were used.

The second case concerns related *be* clauses such as those below in which the nominal groups have been underlined:

4   Fran   (i) He's <u>funny</u> (ii)==and she's <u>insane</u>?

In these clauses, the second nominal group does not consist of a head noun, but instead contains an adjective as the main element. Adjectives cannot be made Subject, but are still considered to be Complements since they are nominal groups. For example, the clauses could easily become *He's a funny bastard* or *she's an insane woman*.

Complements in casual conversation are most frequently realized by fairly brief nominal groups, consisting of articles, a head noun and a limited number of qualifying elements. However, as with Subjects, so we can find whole clauses operating as Complements, as in the clause below:

29   Brad   (ii) In FIRST year you can do <u>whatever you WANT</u> ==

Here the Complement is a clause (*whatever you want*), acting in the place where we usually find a nominal group. This is another example of embedding: the occurrence of a clause within another clause.

A few verbs in English, such as those of giving, can take two nominal groups. For example (nominal groups *in italics*):

* *Brad gave introductory philosophy a bad rap*

Since there can be only one Subject in the clause, and since either of the other two nominal groups (*introductory philosophy, a bad rap*) could be made Subject (*Introductory philosophy was given a bad rap; A bad rap was given to introductory philosophy*), both are Complements.

3.4.8 The function of the Complement in casual talk

The presence of Complements in dialogue enables the expansion of the field of negotiation. For example, consider the following exchanges:

| 20 | Dave | (i) When are you gonna do ... all your odds 'n sods subjects? |
| 21 | Brad | (i) Whaddya mean "odds 'n' sods subjects"? |

In this exchange Dave asks a question and Brad continues the dialogue by querying the Complement element.

| 8 | Dave | == (i) They're ALL mad== |
| 9 | Brad | == (i) They're all FREAKS |

In this exchange, Brad reacts to Dave by amending the Complement he offers.

Thus, although Complements are not as pivotal to dialogue as the Subject (many clauses do not have Complements, while all clauses have Subjects), they represent material which is open to negotiation – and often challenged.

3.4.9 Adjunct

i) Definition Adjuncts are, as the label suggests, elements which are additional, rather than essential, to the proposition. They function to add extra information about the events expressed in the core of the proposition.

ii) Identification criteria Adjuncts are expressed through all the parts of speech that do not express Subjects, Complements, Finites and Predicators. That is, they are expressed by: prepositional phrases, adverbs and adverbial groups, or conjunctions. All Adjuncts have two points in common:

- they are not pivotal to the clause (so, they could be left out and the clause would still make sense, although it would not be as informative);
- they are elements which *cannot* be made Subject (since they are not expressed by nominal groups).

There are three main types of Adjuncts: circumstantial, interpersonal and textual. Each type is explained below.

3.4.9.1 Circumstantial Adjuncts

These are adverbs or prepositional phrases which express meanings about when, where, how, why, or with what the proposition occurred. Because they encode representational dimensions, their function is an ideational one. For example, the Adjuncts in the following clauses add circumstantial details to the clause, telling us about the purpose or time of the actions (circumstantial adjuncts <u>underlined</u>):

15	Brad	(ii)<u>For General Studies</u> we've got this ... tutor
43	Brad	(i)I'm doin' em ... <u>at the moment!</u> ==
56	Brad	== (i)<u>In Second Year</u>, you do ... four points, (ii)and <u>in Third Year</u> you do four points.

3.4.9.2 Interpersonal Adjuncts

These are adverbs or prepositional phrases which express meanings to do with judgements and opinions, including meanings about how likely or how intense something is. As these Adjuncts lexicalize interpersonal meanings, they are considered in more detail in Chapter 4. At this stage we simply note some examples of the main types.

Some interpersonal Adjuncts adjust probability, certainty and usuality values in the clause through words such as *probably, maybe, usually, never*, etc. For example, in the following clause the interpersonal Adjunct has been <u>underlined</u>:

| 79 | Brad | (iii)and then I'll <u>maybe</u> be able to do something meaningful == (with my life) |

Metaphorical expressions of probability, such as *I think, I reckon, I guess* where these are not functioning as autonomous clauses also fall into this category of Adjunct.[2]

Other interpersonal adjuncts include vocatives, i.e. names or terms of address used to target the addressee of a clause. For example, the vocative used as an interpersonal Adjunct is <u>underlined</u> in clause (ii) below:

| 6 | Dave | (i) == You know ...(ii)You know a lot of funny people don't you <u>Brad</u>? |

Adverbs or phrases used to either play up or tone down the intensity of clauses are also interpersonal Adjuncts. Examples of amplifiers are *totally, absolutely*. Common mitigators include *just, only, merely*, as well as "vague" expressions such as *or something, or whatever*. For example, the interpersonal Adjuncts which tone down the intensity of the following clauses have been <u>underlined</u>:

| 62 | Brad | == (i)It's <u>just</u> a ... technicality. |

52	Brad	(iv) You <u>only</u> have to do eight points of General Studies in your whole in your whole == career.

In this category we can also place the metaphorical hedge *you know* (with *you* unstressed and often shortened to *y'know*). It is used within a clause to maintain contact without requiring any response from the listener. For example:

77	Brad	(i) A degree in a degree in Linguistics isn't much use <u>y' know</u> (ii) if you wanna work for Landcare or something,

3.4.9.3 *Textual Adjuncts*

Into this third main category of Adjuncts we class adverbs, prepositional phrases or conjunctions which express meanings about the logical links and continuities between one clause and earlier clauses. The three main subclasses of items here are:

i) Conjunctive Adjuncts These are conjunctions which link a current clause with prior talk by expressing logical relations of time (*then, next*), cause/consequence (*so, because*), condition (*if*), addition (*and*), contrast (*but*), or restatement (*I mean, like*), etc. These typically occur at the beginning of clauses. For example (conjunctive Adjuncts <u>underlined</u>):

36	Dave	== (i) <u>And</u> what are your General Studies?
86	Fran	(i) <u>But</u> whadda they know about education?
80	Fran	== (i) However, <u>I mean</u> what you said is, is maybe all very true David (ii) <u>but, I mean</u>, in the Public Service people are transferring from... areas

ii) Continuity Adjuncts These are items which are common in casual conversation and signal that a speaker's clause is coherent with prior talk, without specifying a particular logical relation. The most frequent continuity markers are *oh, well*, as illustrated in the following clauses where continuity markers are <u>underlined</u>:

90	Fran	== (i) <u>Well</u> they were high up in Fisheries ==
99	Fran	(i) <u>Well</u> I, I think == that's

iii) Holding Adjuncts These are words like *umm* and *ah* which speakers use to retain the floor while they organize their message. They often occur in abandoned clauses such as in the exchange below where the holding adjuncts are <u>underlined</u>:

47	Brad	(i) And <u>um</u>
71	Brad	(i) Yeah but I don't LIKE people ... <u>um</u> ... (ii) I don't want to be INVOLVED with people. (iii) I'd rather be involved with == soil erosion

3.4.10 The function of Adjuncts in casual talk

Although not central to the clause, Adjuncts provide one means for interactants to expand the field of negotiation beyond the Subject-Finite. Probing for Circumstantial Adjuncts is one common way of contributing to the dialogue, as Fran does in the following exchange when she prompts Brad:

26	Fran	== (i) This year?
27	Brad	== (i) In First Year.
28	Fran	== (i) Oh this year.

Adding Circumstantial Adjuncts is also a common way for speakers to get back in to the conversation and expand a prior contribution, as Brad does in the exchange below, when he comes back in turn 3:

1	Brad	(i) Look. (ii) See that guy. (iii) He plays the double-bass
2	Fran	(i) Does he?
3	Brad	(i) In the orchestra.

As Interpersonal Adjuncts encode attitudinal meanings, they function to enable the speaker to express a position or assessment on what is being talked about. This is often an assessment in terms of the certainty or usuality of events through words such as *probably, maybe, perhaps, always*. These meanings can be made more fundamental to the clause through the use of Finite modal verbs such as *may, could, might* (see the discussion of modality in section 3.8 below). The intensifying and mitigating Interpersonal Adjuncts function to express the speaker's emotional involvement with the proposition, and their subtypes and functions will be considered more fully in Chapter 4.

Textual Adjuncts function to construct coherence and continuity in talk, with specific adjuncts implying particular logical relations between adjacent clauses. Conjunctive elements, such as *like, and, so,* and *then,* link clauses through relations of restatement, addition, cause/consequence or time, and indicate a speaker's orientation to the logical continuity of their contribution in relation to prior talk (their own, or that of others). There are some continuity adjuncts particular to spoken interactive contexts, such as *well, oh, mmm,* and these indicate a speaker's orientation to the *interactive* continuity of their contribution. For example *well* implies continuity but non-agreement, *oh* implies continuity and the confirmation or querying of information, and *mmm* implies continuity without intervention. For more detailed discussion of a range of functions of various conversational adjuncts, see Schiffrin (1987).

Now that the basic constituents of the clause have been explained, we can rapidly review the major clause types found in English, briefly considering their uses in casual conversation.

3.5 MOOD TYPES

3.5.1 Declarative

Declarative clauses can be identified as clauses in which the structural element of Subject occurs before the Finite element of the clause. For example, all the following clauses are declaratives. The Subject has been underlined, and the Finite element is shown in *italics:*

1	Brad	(iii) He *plays* the double-bass
37	Brad	(i) Oh it's ... RUBBISH ... (ii) One of them *is* alright, (iii) one of them *is* actually good.
64	Brad	==(i) He *sits*, (ii) he *sits* in a room and, and – and the' (iii) and *decides* (iv) "I *think* (v) therefore I *am*" ...
98	Brad	(i) Exactly, (ii) so ... if they *can* administer fish (iii) they *can* administer bloody schoolkids.

3.5.1.1 The function of declaratives in casual conversation

We will see in Chapter 5 that full declarative clauses are typically used to initiate conversational exchanges by putting forward information for negotiation. Thus they construct the speaker as taking on an active, initiatory role in the talk. Declaratives can present both factual information (*He plays the double-bass*) or attitudinal opinion (*He's a funny bastard*). However, declaratives are also used to query prior talk (e.g. Fran's turn 16 *I didn't know you had to do General Studies*), to challenge (e.g. Fran in turn 65 *He's an abstract thinker*) and to counter-challenge (Fran in turn 84 *They're not teaching though. But they're administering*). The implications in the use of declaratives in text 3.1 will be discussed below.

3.5.2 Polar interrogative

Polar interrogatives, also known as yes-no interrogatives, can be identified as clauses where the Finite element occurs before the Subject. Here are some examples taken from texts 1.2 and 1.3 in Chapter 1:

| 5 (1.2) | Jo | (i) Did she see the photos in her coz? |
| 21 (1.3) | Mavis | (ii) Is there a men's store and a women's store? |

As these examples show, in order to construct a polar interrogative in English, the Finite element is separated from the Predicator.

3.5.2.1 The function of polar interrogatives in casual conversation

Full polar interrogatives are typically used to initiate an exchange by requesting information from others. They thus construct the speaker as dependent on the response of other interactants. Because they directly encode an information imbalance, they are not common in casual conversations among close friends or family members, where much of the information circulating is already shared. For example, no full polar interrogatives occur at all in text 3.1.

3.5.3 Tagged declarative

This clause type falls midway between the declarative and polar interrogative. Structurally, it has the sequence of a declarative, with the Subject occurring before the Finite element. However, unlike the simple declarative, the tagged declarative has what is called a "mood tag" added to it. The following are all examples of tagged declaratives: (Subject underlined; Finite in *italics*; Mood tag in **bold**)

6	Dave	(i) == <u>You</u> *know* … (ii)<u>You</u> *know* a lot of funny people **don't you** Brad?
14	Fran	(i) Like, <u>they</u>'*re* coming up the hill **are they**?
22	Dave	(i) Well, y'know, <u>you</u> *can't* just do languages **can you**?
9	Brad	(iii) <u>I</u>'*ve* told you about what POINTS are **haven't I**?

These examples show that when the Finite is picked up in the tag, it often has its polarity reversed. For example, in turn 22 *can't* in the first part of the clause becomes *can* in the mood tag. The effect of the mood tag is to turn a declarative into a kind of polar interrogative, hence their intermediate status.

We can see from these examples that the mood tag consists of:

- the Finite element: if the Finite was merged with the Predicator in the main clause, then it is separated out (i.e. an auxiliary verb is used) in the mood tag;
- the Subject of the main clause, expressed in pronoun form.

3.5.3.1 The function of tagged declaratives in casual conversation

Ever since Lakoff (1975) claimed, on the basis of largely intuitive evidence, that women use tag questions to avoid asserting their opinions (tags invite someone else to offer confirmation), there has been considerable debate about their function and meaning (e.g. Holmes 1984, Cameron 1992). We can simply note here that the grammatical ambiguity of the tagged declarative appears to encode its ambiguous function in dialogue. It both claims the status role of the giver of information, and at the same time recognizes the role of other interactants to confirm or refute the information. We will consider the implications of tagged declaratives in text 3.1 below.

3.5.4 Wh-interrogative

Wh-interrogatives consist of a wh-question word, e.g. *who, what, which, when, where, why, how, in what way, for what reason,* etc. The purpose of the wh-word is to probe for a missing element of clause structure. For example, *when* probes for a circumstantial Adjunct; *who* probes for the Subject; and *what* probes for either the Subject or the Complement of a clause. Wh-interrogatives set up an expectation that the answering clause will fill out (give content to) the missing element of clause structure. The following examples from text 3.1 are all wh-interrogatives (wh-word in *italics*, Subject underlined):

32	Dave	(ii)And *when* are <u>you</u> gonna do your General Studies?
36	Dave	==(i)And *what* are <u>your General Studies</u>?
63	Fran	(i) *Why* are <u>they</u> ==idiots?
88	Fran	==(i) *What* have <u>fish</u> gotta do with education?
89	Brad	(i) <u>*Who*</u> says (ii)they know anything about FISH (iii)just because they were administrating ==Fisheries?

The order of constituents in a wh-interrogative depends on which element of clause structure is being probed. When the element probed for is the Subject, as in turn 89 above, then the wh-word occurs before the Finite element (*says*, in the above example). The structure is thus just like the declarative clause.

However, when the wh-word probes any other element of clause structure (e.g. Complement as in turn 88 or Adjunct as in turn 32), then a separate Finite element must be used, with the Finite element being placed before the Subject. In these examples we see the following order:

Wh-word	^ Finite	^ Subject	^ Predicator	^ Complement or Adjunct
when	*are*	*you*	*gonna do*	*your General Studies*
what	*have*	*fish*	*gotta do*	*with education*

3.5.4.1 *The function of wh-interrogatives in casual conversation*

Full wh-interrogatives are typically used to elicit additional circumstantial information. This may be in an initiatory role (e.g. *When are you gonna do ... all your odds 'n sods subjects?*), in which case repeated use will make the speaker sound like an interrogator. They may also be used by respondents to challenge prior talk (e.g. Fran in turns 86 and 88). However, wh-interrogatives can also be used to achieve commands, as with Nick's turn 11b in text 1.1 (*Where's the cigarettes?*). In this indirect or incongruent function, they provide a means of disguising the dependency relation created by the need to have a command complied with.

3.5.5 Imperative

Imperatives typically do not contain the elements of Subject or Finite but consist of only a Predicator, plus any of the non-core participants of Complement and Adjunct. The following are examples of imperatives (the Predicator is shown in *italics*):

74   Dave   (iii) *Get* yourself a a degree (iv)and *go and work* for the Soil Con'
                             * *Look* at that man coming up the hill.

The omission of the Subject in an imperative occurs because all imperatives are implicitly addressed to the addressee, i.e. there is an implicit "you" acting as Subject for all imperatives. However, in one type of imperative, known as an inclusive imperative, the Subject is made explicit, since it includes both addressee and speaker. This is done through use of the particle *Let's*, as in:

   *Let's *get* ourselves a degree

Similarly, the Finite (in the form of the *do* auxiliary verb) can be made explicit if additional emphasis is required, as in:

   *Do *get* yourself a degree

3.5.5.1 The function of imperatives in casual conversation

As we will see in Chapter 5, imperatives often function to make commands, i.e. to demand that someone does something, as for example when Brad says *Look* in turn 1 of text 3.1. Imperatives set up expectations of a compliant response which may well be non-verbal (e.g. the person turns her eyes to "look", as instructed). However, in casual talk imperatives are often used to negotiate action indirectly, that is they function to encode advice. For example, in turn 74 from text 3.1 below, Dave's imperatives encode his advice/opinion:

74   Dave   (iii)Get yourself a a degree (iv)and go and work for the Soil Con'

In this use (where immediate compliance is not possible nor intended), imperatives position the speaker as having some power over the addressee: you can only advise someone if you assume a dominant position. In addition, the imperative form is a strong advice form since it contrasts with the less authoritarian *should*-form, e.g. *You should get yourself a degree*. Note that Dave also uses this *should*-form in turn 78 from text 3.1 below:

78   Dave   == (i)Well you should have thought of that thought of that three years ago Brad.

We will consider the implications of the use of imperatives when we further analyse text 3.1 below.

3.5.6 Exclamative

An exclamative clause is not merely a word or clause produced with an emphatic or surprised intonation. Exclamative clauses have a specific structure, exemplified by the following exclamative clauses which are not from text 3.1:

> *What an idiot Descartes was!
> *How stupid Descartes was!
> *How amazingly he plays the double-bass!

As these examples show, exclamative clauses involve a wh-word combining with one of the clause elements of either Complement or Adjunct. The order of the constituents is: first the wh-element, followed by the Subject, and then the Finite, Predicator and other constituents. For example, with *What an idiot Descartes was!*, the wh-word *what* becomes part of the Complement *an idiot*, followed by the Subject element *Descartes* and then the Finite *was*. Because this is the verb <u>to be</u>, there is no Predicator involved.

3.5.6.1 The function of exclamatives in casual conversation

Exclamatives are typically used to encode a judgement or evaluation of events. The speaker must thus take on the role of judge, and in so doing positions other interactants as likely to agree with the judgement. Exclamatives can also be used to challenge as in *How dare you talk to me like that*, in which case they amplify the wrong that could be expressed through either an imperative (*Don't talk to me like that*) or a should-declarative (*You shouldn't talk to me like that*), while maintaining the inequality of roles.

3.5.7 Elliptical clauses

All the examples so far have been what we call "full" clauses: clauses where all the elements of structure have been realized. As we will see in Chapter 5, full clauses are produced when speakers are attempting to initiate a new exchange, i.e. when they wish to establish material to be reacted to. However, when interactants react to prior initiations, they typically do so elliptically, producing clauses which depend for their interpretation on a related full initiating clause. Each of the clause types identified so far would typically be realized elliptically when functioning as a response or reaction to an earlier clause.

3.5.7.1 *Elliptical declaratives*

When a speaker produces a declarative as a responding move, they will frequently omit all but the informationally significant components of the structure. Which elements are informationally significant will depend on the prior verbal context. One common context for elliptical declaratives is when a second speaker responds to a first speaker by co-operatively adding some information to the first speaker's clause. In the following example from text 3.1, Dave's elliptical declarative *except you* consists only of a circumstantial Adjunct:

| 9 | Brad | == (i) They're all FREAKS |
| 10 | Dave | (i) Except you. |

The elliptical status of Dave's clause signals to the interactants that the full clause to which it is an Adjunct can be retrieved from prior context, and in this case we only have to look to the immediately prior turn to retrieve the Subject, Finite and Complement to which it adds information. Of course, interactants in conversation do not in fact look back but forward, so it would be more accurate to say that Brad's full declarative sets up expectations for a range of possible elliptical structures to be produced in subsequent turns, and Dave's clause fits in unproblematically.

A second common context for the production of elliptical declaratives is when a respondent reacts not by adding to a prior clause, but by modifying it in some way and, in the process, ellipsing some elements. For example, consider the following exchange from text 3.1:

| 71 | Brad | (i) Yeah but I don't LIKE people ... um ... (ii) I don't want to be INVOLVED with people. (iii) I'd rather be involved with == soil erosion |
| 72 | Fran | == (i) Everybody has to be though. (ii) But I mean |

Here Brad's initial clause consists of a full declarative, *I'd rather be involved with soil erosion*, which Fran has no intention of just accepting and adding to. Rather, she responds with a mild challenge to Brad, using a declarative which is tied to his clause because she ellipses the Predicator in her response *Everybody has to be though*. We can fill out the ellipsis to give *Everybody has to be involved though*. Here her response represents a modification on Brad's clause in that the Subject has been broadened to include *everybody*, the Finite has been reworked to express obligation *has to*, and the conjunction *though* has been added to indicate reservations with Brad's claim. However the ellipsis of the Predicator ties Fran's response to Brad's comment.

The next move in the Brad-and-Fran sequence indicates yet a third context where ellipsis is very common. This is the context where a first speaker gets back in to the conversation and simply tags on another constituent to a prior clause he or she has produced. We can see this in the following example from text 3.1:

90	Fran	==(i) Well they were high up in Fisheries ==
91	Brad	==(i) Yeah but that doesn't mean they have
92	Fran	==(i) Like SAFCOL

Here Fran gets back in with an Adjunct (*well*, indicating that this turn has links with prior talk), a Subject (*they*), a Finite (*were*), a Complement (*high up*, meaning powerful), and finally a circumstantial Adjunct (*in Fisheries*). Brad then takes a turn to challenge this judgement, before Fran gets back in to complete her initiating declarative with a circumstantial Adjunct (*like SAFCOL*).

3.5.7.2 *Elliptical polar interrogatives*

If a speaker wishes to initiate a sequence of talk by finding out a yes/no answer, then they will need to package into the interrogative all the information necessary for the respondent to formulate a response, e.g. *are you doing your General Studies this year?*. However, if the speaker is reacting to prior talk and simply needs, for example, confirmation of something that has been said, then they can abbreviate the interrogative structure. Only the elements of Finite followed by Subject are needed to realize a polar interrogative, so other non-core elements are frequently ellipsed in the flow of interaction, provided that they can be retrieved from prior verbal context. For example, in text 3.1 Fran asks the following question:

2	Fran	(i) Does he?

The listeners make sense of this elliptical clause by relating it to the immediately prior clause

1	Brad	(iii) He plays the double-bass

They therefore could (if they needed to) fill out the ellipsis to construct the non-elliptical interrogative *Does he play the double-bass?*

3.5.7.3 *Elliptical wh-interrogatives*

Any or all elements except the key wh-question word may be ellipsed from a wh-interrogative, provided the ellipsed elements can be clearly retrieved from the context. For example, consider the following exchange:

100	Brad	== (i) That guy that that Bangladeshi that used to live with us he was a a a Limnologist or whatever it's called. ==
101	Fran	== (i) A WHAT? ==

Fran's question involves ellipsis of all elements except the wh-Complement. This can be demonstrated by analysing the non-elliptical version, *What is that Bangladeshi?*, which can be derived from Brad's prior turn. Elliptical wh-interrogatives provide a way of querying, with varying force, any specific element of structure in an earlier clause. For example, let's consider Brad's claim from text 3.1:

| 1 | Brad | (iii) He plays the double-bass |

Any of the following elliptical reactions would be possible:

(i)   Who?
(ii)   Who does?
(iii) What/which instrument?
(iv)   Where?
(v)   When?
(vi)   Why?
(vii) Who/what for?

Response (i) ellipses all but the wh-Subject element, while response (ii) leaves both wh-Subject and Finite and response (iii) ellipses all but the wh-Complement. Responses (iv) to (vii) probe circumstantial details, ellipsing the Subject, Finite, Predicator and Complement of the initiating clause.

3.5.7.4 *Elliptical imperatives*

All elements in an imperative except the Predicator can be ellipsed, giving a typical elliptical imperative structure of:

| 1 | Brad | (i) Look. |

Ellipsis in imperatives is often due to the fact that the ellipsed constituents can be retrieved from the shared physical context. Thus, Brad does not need to say *Look at that man walking up the hill*, since his addressees can see that what he is pointing to is a man walking up the hill.

3.5.7.5 *Elliptical exclamatives*

Elliptical exclamatives must retain the wh-element which is the key to their exclamative import. Thus, where the wh-element was attached to either the Subject or the Complement, typically both Subject and all verbal elements are ellipsed. Thus, for example *What an idiot Descartes was!* can become *What an idiot!* And *How stupid Descartes was!* can become *How stupid!.*

3.5.7.6 Ellipsis in action

The following fragment illustrates ellipsis working to bind together a highly interactive sequence:

100	Brad	== (i) That guy that that Bangladeshi that used to live with us he was a a a Limnologist or whatever it's called. ==
101	Fran	== (i) A WHAT? ==
102	Dave	== (i) Who?
103	Brad	(i) Oh not == Limnologist.
104	Fran	== (i) Ichthyologist.

Brad's turn in 100 initiates the sequence, with a full declarative (Subject, Finite, Complement). Fran then queries this with an elliptical wh-interrogative, which probes for the Complement of the initiating clause. Meanwhile, Dave probes for the Subject of the initiating clause, ellipsing all other elements. Brad then responds to these queries with an elliptical declarative negating the original Complement. The full clause would have been *Oh he's not a Limnologist.* Finally Fran offers an elliptical declarative, providing an alternative Complement. All these clauses relate back in various structural ways to the initiating full clause. This example shows the important role ellipsis plays in signalling to the interactants whether what is being negotiated is new or old (retrievable) information. The discourse implications of this will be considered in Chapter 5.

3.5.7.7 Ellipsis vs referential cohesion

An important distinction can be made between ellipsis (a structural relationship) and a related cohesive (non-structural) device, that of reference. In reference, some portion of prior talk gets repackaged in a reduced form, usually through a pronoun. For example, in the following sequence Dave's interrogative clause is not interpretable without reference to prior context:

| 37 | Brad | (i) Oh it's ... RUBBISH ... (ii) One of them is alright, (iii) one of them is actually good. |
| 38 | Dave | (i) Yeah but what IS it? |

Specifically, we need to know what the *it* refers to, which presents no problem for interactants sharing the unfolding sequential context. However, although the clause therefore depends on prior talk, this kind of dependency is very different from ellipsis. In this non-structural dependency no clause elements need to be retrieved: Dave's interrogative consists of a Subject, Finite and wh-Complement. It is only the *identity* of the Subject that is at issue, not the Subject element of structure itself.

Conversation is tied together by a range of cohesive ties, including reference, lexical cohesion and conjunction. These discourse ties are different from grammatical ties of ellipsis, since elliptical elements are concerned with the presence or absence of structural elements, while discourse cohesion concerns non-structural relations. For a detailed discussion of cohesive patterns, see Halliday (1994: ch. 9), Eggins (1994: ch. 4), Martin (1992) and Eggins and Martin (1995).

3.5.8 Minor clauses

One very important category of clauses in casual conversation is that of minor clauses. These are clauses which have no mood structure at all. All of the following are minor clauses:

44	Dave	(i) Right.
61	Fran	(i) Mmm
96	Brad	(i) Yeah well exactly.
		'Thanks
		'Don't mention it.
		'Hi
		'See ya.

As these examples indicate, minor clauses tend to be very brief, and are often formulaic. However, their brevity is not due to ellipsis. Minor clauses do not have any mood structure, i.e. they do not consist of elements of Subject, Finite, etc. One test for minor clauses is that apparently "missing" elements of structure cannot be unambiguously retrieved. For example, when Dave says *Right*, this is not an ellipsed version of *You're right*, or *I'm right*, or *That sounds right*. The fact that we cannot determine exactly what the Subject might be indicates that no Subject was in fact selected. *Right* in this clause simply operates as an unanalysable chunk.

A second test for minor clauses is that they cannot be negated: i.e. a minor clause cannot be made to take a negative polarity. Attempts to add the negative polarity morpheme *n't*, will not work, e.g. *Rightn't*, *Thankn't*. (See the discussion of polarity and yes/no below.)

There are three common types of minor clauses in casual conversation, all of which have this absence of underlying mood structure:

i) Lexicalized minor clauses   These are minor clauses which are full lexical items which operate in other structures in the language: e.g. *Right* or *Exactly*. These words are usually adjectives or adverbs, and have evaluative dimensions. Swearing when expressed as an autonomous expression (e.g. *Good grief! Bloody hell!*) fits into this category. However, when the swearing is integrated into a full clause (e.g. *We talk about bloody ... Descartes and all these idiots*), then the clause has mood (in this case a declarative). This category also includes words such as *OK, Fine, Great* when used in non-elliptical contexts. These types of minor clauses typically occur as responding contributions, often by a first speaker getting back in for a second turn.

ii) Formulaic expressions These are typically of greeting and thanks: e.g. *Hi, Thanks, G'day, Ciao.* Such minor clauses tend to occur in reciprocated pairs (e.g. speaker A says *Hi*, so speaker B responds *Hi*).

iii) Non-lexical items These function as conventionalized feedback and backchannel indicators: e.g. *Mmm, Uhhuh.* Such items tend to have no standardized written form, and only rarely occur as full lexical items in other contexts (e.g. *He indicated an uhhuh*). They have no experiential content, but play a very important interpersonal role in interactive discourse, as will be indicated in Chapter 5.

3.5.8.1 The function of minor clauses in casual conversation

Minor clauses generally function either as preludes to negotiation, as in the typically reciprocated use of minor clauses in greetings (*Hi!* - *Hi*), or as closures (*Bye* - *Bye*). Within negotiation, they generally encode following up reactions, that is contributions which do not have full negotiation status, as they are not anchored in a Subject-Finite. Most minor clauses therefore position the speaker as a compliant supporter of prior interaction. The function of minor clauses in text 3.1 will be considered in more detail below.

3.5.9 Non-finite clauses

The final clause category we will mention is that of non-finite clauses. A non-finite clause is, as the label suggests, a clause in which there is no Finite element present. Typically they consist only of a Predicator, plus any Complements or Adjuncts. For example, the three main types of non-finite clauses in English can be contrasted with their related finite structure as follows:

He plays the double-bass	Finite clause (declarative)
Playing the double-bass	Non-finite 'ing' clause
Having played the double-bass	Non-finite 'ed' clause
To play the double-bass	Non-finite infinitive clause

As these examples show, non-finite clauses do not only have no Finite element expressed; they also have no Subject. This means that non-finite clauses are not anchored for person (singular or plural) or tense/modality. For these reasons non-finite clauses cannot occur as independent units: they depend for their structural completion on being associated with a finite clause, and so typically occur in sequences such as the following:

Playing the double-bass,	he felt liberated at last.
Having played the double-bass,	he then tried the cello.
To play the double-bass,	first find a comfortable stool.

In the analysis of written text, the mood type 'non-finite clause' would be a very important one. However, in casual conversation non-finite clauses are relatively rare. This is because the structural dependency they involve demands a degree of textual planning that is at odds with the spontaneity and rapidity of the casual context.

3.6 POLARITY

Every clause that has selected for mood (i.e. all clauses except minor clauses) is one of two polarities: either positive or negative. If the polarity is positive, then there will be no explicit indication of that in the clause. For example, all the following clauses have positive polarity:

12	Fran	(i) And they're all coming home now.
20	Dave	(i) When are you gonna do ... all your odds 'n sods subjects?
35	Brad	== (i) That's what I'm talking == about.

Where the polarity is negative, a negative morpheme (either *n't* or *not*) will be expressed. In the following examples the negative polarity marker is underlined:

64	Brad	(vii) An', I mean he has<u>n't</u> got anything better to DO. ...um
71	Brad	(i) Yeah but I do<u>n't</u> LIKE people ... um... (ii) I do<u>n't</u> want to be INVOLVED with people.
95	Fran	(i) They did<u>n't</u> have that either.

Polarity is always considered part of the Finite constituent, and not as a separate constituent in the clause.

3.7 YES/YEAH AND NO/NOPE IN CASUAL CONVERSATION

Polarity is closely related to the words YES and NO, which we often mistakenly think of as polarity markers in English. Clause polarity is always expressed within the Finite. The lexical items YES and NO can function differently according to the context, as we detail below.

3.7.1 Yes, yeah and derivatives

The full lexical item *yes* rarely occurs in rapid interactive casual talk. However, its derivatives of *yeah*, *yep*, *yeo* and others do occur very frequently, and can be seen to function in two different ways:

i) YEAH as a textual continuity Adjunct The commonest use of YEAH in casual conversation is as a textual Adjunct, specifically a continuity marker. In this use YEAH functions to signal or construct continuity between one speaker's turn and another speaker's prior turn. It is common at the beginning of clauses which challenge or dispute a prior contribution. In this usage, YEAH is not stressed, nor does it occur in its own tone group but will be immediately linked to further clause elements. For example:

36	Dave	==(i)And what are your General Studies?
36	Brad	(i)Oh it's ... RUBBISH ... (ii)One of them is alright, (iii)one of them is actually good.
38	Dave	(i)Yeah but what IS it?

Here Dave's *Yeah* is unstressed, and he immediately rushes on to produce the rest of the clause. The only intonational prominence in the clause falls on *IS*.

70	Fran	(i)But even if it meant that you could understand people and therefore HELP them?
71	Brad	(i)Yeah but I don't LIKE people ... um ... (ii)I don't want to be INVOLVED with people. (iii)I'd rather be involved with ==soil erosion

Similarly in the example above, Brad produces *Yeah* without stress or intonation, and with no pause before the rest of the clause. This continuity YEAH could be replaced by another continuity Adjunct, such as *oh* or *well,*

ii) YEAH as a minor clause   YEAH can also occur as a minor clause in casual talk when its function is to confirm and support prior talk. It occurs in response to or in support of prior declarative clauses. For example:

8	Dave	== (i)They're ALL mad ==
9	Brad	== (i)They're all FREAKS
10	Dave	(i)Except you.
11	Brad	(i)Yeah.

Here Brad's *Yeah* is stressed and realized in a distinct intonational contour (i.e. unlike the continuity YEAH it is not produced in the same rhythmic and tone group as following elements). Minor clause YEAH could also be replaced by another lexicalized minor clause (e.g. *right, exactly*) without any change in meaning.

3.7.2   No and its derivatives

While YEAH occurs very frequently in casual talk, NO and its conversational derivatives of *nope, naw, nup,* etc. are relatively infrequent. This appears to be partly because of the more marked status of negation. Rather than say *No*, interactants might try to delay their refusal or prevaricate, by using *Well ...*, *But ...* With NO, different functions are also possible.

i) As a continuity marker NO can function to signal contrastive continuity, as in the example from text 3.1 below:

80	Fran	== (i)However, I mean what you said is, is maybe all very true David (ii)but, I mean, in the Public Service people are transferring from ... areas
81	Brad	(i)Ah I don't wanna be a bloody Public Servant ==
82	Fran	== (i)No no but I'm just saying like. (ii)Like you're saying you know (iii)you don't know anything about soil ... (iv)But people are transferring from Fisheries to Education ... (v)Now I can see no == no bearing

Here, Fran's *No no* in turn 82 is functioning to signal that she has more to say in order to get around Brad's apparent objection. As with the textual Adjunct YEAH, this NO is typically unstressed and is immediately linked to further clause elements. It could be replaced by another (negative) continuity Adjunct, such as *but* or *well.*

ii) NO as a minor clause NO can function to contradict, or to confirm a negative statement. For example:

24	Dave	(i)If you're doing an Arts degree (ii)you got a lot of other garbage to do.
25	Brad	(i)No [falling-rising tone]. (ii)I, (iii)if I wanted to (iv)I could do French, German and Russian ...

Here, Brad's NO indicates disagreement or contradiction.

The importance of differentiating these different types of YES and NO will become more obvious in Chapter 5, when we consider how interactants construct exchanges.

3.8 MODALITY

One final dimension of Mood which needs to be considered in the analysis of casual conversation is that of **modality**. Modality refers to a range of different ways in which speakers can temper or qualify their messages. There are two types of modality: **modalization** and **modulation**. Modalization is a way of tempering the categorical nature of the information we exchange. Modulation is a way of tempering the directness with which we seek to act upon each other. For example, the following declarative is presented as a statement of certain fact, as an absolute:

1	Brad	(iii)He plays the double-bass

Regardless of whether or not it is in fact true, the information is presented as true. The inclusion of any one of various modalities, however, adds an explicit dimension of speaker judgement, and therefore relativity, to the message. For example, none of the following clauses are as neutral or assertive as the original:

He usually plays the double-bass.
He might play the double-bass
He has to play the double-bass
He is willing to play the double-bass.
He can play the double-bass.

Our negotiation of the world involves exploring how things do not always happen, nor are they always definitely established. The variability and uncertainty of our world view becomes part of what is negotiable, and part of our identity. We may seek to act upon each other categorically, as in the following example from text 3.1:

| 74 | Dave | (iii) Get yourself a a degree (iv) and go and work for the Soil Con' |

However, we may also interpret or construct our relationship as one in which we need to place some distance between us and our addressee, invoking external sources for the obligation we are implying, as in the following possible modifications:

You have to get yourself a degree.
You should get yourself a degree.
You're required to get yourself a degree.

We may consider that our social role does not allow us even this degree of directness, and so we may employ modality to express deference, as in:

I think you would probably have to get yourself a degree.

If deference impacts also on our choice of mood, then we may say:

Mightn't you perhaps have to get yourself a degree?

The two main types of modality, then, allow us to temper our conversational contributions. In **modalization**, the tempering of the message is with reference to degrees of frequency or probability, while with modulation, the qualification of the message is with reference to degrees of obligation, inclination, or capability. Each type of meaning can be realized in the clause in a number of different ways. We will now briefly review the major realizations of each category. For more detailed discussion and exemplification of modality, readers are referred to Halliday (1994: 356–63) and Eggins (1994: 178–82, 187–92).

3.8.1 Modalization

There are two main types of modalization: probability and usuality.

3.8.1.1 Probability

In discussing mood, we previously mentioned the two poles of polarity: positive ("yes") and negative ("no"). Propositions may be expressed with either of these polarities, which will be realized in the Finite element of the clause. Either the Finite will be positive (and if so, unmarked), for example:

He plays the double-bass

Or the Finite will be negative, in which case it will be marked by the addition of a negating morpheme *not*, usually contracted in casual talk to *n't*. For example:

He doesn't play the double-bass.

However, very often we judge our information to fall somewhere between these two extremes. Degrees of probability range from 'high' (almost certain) to 'low' (very uncertain), as illustrated in the following examples:

He plays the double-bass	positive polarity
He must definitely play the double-bass	modalized: high probability
He may perhaps play the double-bass	modalized: median probability
He might possibly play the double-bass	modalized: low probability

As these examples show, modalization may be realized in at least two ways in the clause:

i) through the use of a modal Finite: e.g. the auxiliaries *must, may, might*;
ii) through the use of an interpersonal Adjunct: e.g. the adverbs *definitely, perhaps, possibly*.

These means are not mutually exclusive as the clauses above illustrate. Modalization may be expressed both through a modal Finite and through an interpersonal Adjunct in the same clause. In both cases, the fact that a speaker's judgement is being made (since who else could the modalization be attributed to) is left implicit: it is packaged as simply an integral part of the clause.

There are further incongruent ways of realizing modalization in the clause which make the source of the modalization explicit. These realizations are considered incongruent, because they involve the use of grammatical (clause) choices to make meanings that could otherwise be made through single lexical items. Two of these grammatical realizations of modalization are outlined below:

i) Incongruent modalization with explicit subjective source of modalization, for example:

I'm sure he plays the double-bass	modalized: high probability
I think he plays the double-bass	modalized: median probability
I suspect he plays the double-bass	modalized: low probability

Here the speaker uses a clause, usually of mental activity (thinking, guessing, reckoning etc.) to encode the modalization. Note that this method of realizing modalization can also be combined with the other two methods identified earlier, so that we can have, for example:

I'm sure he must definitely play the double-bass	modalized: high probability
I think he may perhaps play the double-bass	modalized: median probability
I suspect he might possibly play the double-bass	modalized: low probability

These subjective explicit modalizations can also be nominalized, giving a further kind of incongruent expression of opinion. Thus, *I think* can be nominalized to *in my opinion*:

In my opinion he must definitely play the double-bass	modalized: high probability

ii) Incongruent modalization with explicit objective source of modalization where an impersonal clause with *it* as Subject and the verb *to be* + *adjective of modality* is used to encode the modalization, for example:

It is certain that he plays the double-bass	modalized: high probability
It is likely that he plays the double-bass	modalized: median probability
It is probable that he plays the double-bass	modalized: low probability

Again, these clauses may also have modalization spread throughout them, as in the example below:

It is certain that he must definitely play the double-bass	modalized: high probability

The objective explicit realizations make it appear as though the judgement being expressed in the modalization is somehow distant from the speaker. Of course, this is just a game, since behind any *it is likely* there lies simply an *I reckon*.

3.8.1.2 Usuality

The second type of modalization is to do with frequency, which ranges again between the polar extremes of *He plays the double-bass* at one end and *He doesn't play the double-bass* at the other, but draws a contrast in terms of the usuality of the event. Thus we can say:

He always plays the double-bass.	Modalization: high usuality
He usually plays the double-bass.	Modalization: median usuality
He sometimes plays the double-bass.	Modalization: low usuality

Resources for realizing usuality meanings are less varied, but three possibilities of realization are:

i) through a modal Finite indicating usuality: e.g. *will*;
ii) through mood Adjuncts: e.g. adverbs of frequency, such as *usually, always, sometimes*;
iii) through an objective explicit clause, which the following statements exemplify:

It is typical for him to play the double-bass.	Modalization: high usuality
It is usual for him to play the double-bass.	Modalization: median usuality
It is rare for him to play the double-bass.	Modalization: low usuality

The expression of modalization in text 3.1 will be considered below.

3.8.2 Modulation

Modulation is a way of tempering the directness with which we seek to act upon each other. We will consider three main types of modulation: obligation, inclination, and capability.

3.8.2.1 Obligation

Modulations of obligation refer to the different alternatives we have between issuing a positive command (*Get a degree*) and a negative injunction (*Don't get a degree*). Again it is useful to recognize three different degrees of obligation, exemplified by the following utterances which range between the unmodulated positive statement and the unmodulated negative statement:

Get a degree.	unmodulated; positive
You must get a degree.	(i) modulated: high obligation: directive
You are required to get a degree.	
It is required that you get a degree.	
You will get a degree.	(ii) modulated: median obligation : advice

You are supposed to get a degree.
It is expected that you get a degree.
You may get a degree.   (iii) modulated: low obligation : permission
You are allowed to get a degree.
It is permitted that you get a degree.
Don't get a degree.   unmodulated; negative

As these examples show, there are three main ways of encoding obligation in a clause:

i)   through a modal Finite expressing obligation: e.g. *must, will, may, have to.* These verbs can carry the implication either that the obligation originates internally, with the Subject (e.g. *you must* get a degree because you owe it to yourself not to flunk out) or that the obligation is imposed by some external source (e.g. *you have to* get a degree because the university insists).

ii) through a *be + -ed* clause with personal Subject: e.g. *you are allowed to get a degree.* These structures imply that the source of the obligation or permission could be named.

iii) through an impersonal *it + -ed* clause: e.g. *it is permitted that you get a degree.* These structures imply an external but unnamed source of the obligation.

3.8.2.2 *Inclination*

A clause may also be tempered according to the degree of inclination or willingness attributed to its Subject. The following examples trace inclination from positive to negative, through the intermediate stages of conviction (high modulation), attitude (median) and undertaking (low):

I will study philosophy next year.   unmodulated; positive
I'm determined to study   (i) inclination: high modulation:
philosophy next year.   conviction
It's a conviction that I'll study
philosophy next year.
I'm keen to study   (ii) inclination: median modulation:
philosophy next year.   attitude
It's a pleasure for me to study
philosophy next year
I'm willing to study   (iii) inclination: low modulation:
philosophy next year.   undertaking
It's a commitment for me to
study philosophy next year.
I won't study philosophy next year.   unmodulated; negative

These examples illustrate the two main realizations of inclination modulations:

i) through a personal Subject + attitudinal adjective structure: e.g. *I'm willing/I'm keen;*
ii) through an impersonal structure with a dummy *it* as Subject and a nominalized mental process (verb of thinking, believing, desiring) as head: e.g. *It's a commitment.*

We make a distinction between inclination modulations and full mental process clauses encoding meanings of desire, such as the following:

> *I love studying philosophy.*
> *I want to study philosophy next year.*

These clauses are not treated as modulations because the verb of desire cannot be omitted to give an unmodulated positive or negative clause. The attitudinal component of these verbs is dealt with under the semantic analysis of Appraisal (Chapter 4).

3.8.2.3 Capability

The final category of modulation is that of capability, exemplified by the following statements:

He plays the double-bass.	unmodulated; positive
He can play the double-bass.	modulated: capability
He is able to play the double-bass.	
He is capable of playing the double-bass.	
He doesn't play the double-bass.	unmodulated; negative

We recognize degrees of capability in these statements, and note that there are two main structural resources for expressing these meanings:

i) through the modal Finite *can* when used to indicate ability and not probability;
ii) through a personal Subject + adjective of capability structure (*he is capable*).

3.8.3 Modality examples in text 3.1

As the number of clauses involving modality in text 3.1 is limited, we list and classify each in the following sections. The modality is underlined in each example.

3.8.3.1 Modalizations in text 3.1.

There are four examples of probability modalizations in text 3.1. The first is median probability; subjective, explicit:

| 41 | Brad | (ix)<u>I think</u> the one that's that's alright is called Human Rationality |

The second example involves a modality which is low probability; objective, implicit:

| 80 | Fran | == (i)However, I mean what you said is, is <u>maybe</u> all very true David (ii)but, I mean, in the Public Service people are transferring from ... areas |

Turn 94 contains two modalities, both low probability, one negative, one positive, both subjective implicit:

| 94 | Brad | (i)They <u>mightn't</u> have had a degree in Biology or anything. (ii)They <u>might</u> have just |

There are no examples of usuality probabilities in text 3.1. The Finite *used to* in turn 100 does not express a modality:

| 100 | Brad | == (i)That guy that that Bangladeshi that used to live with us he was a a a Limnologist or whatever it's called. == |

This is simply the expression of habitual action in the past tense. The present tense equivalent, *that lives with us*, does not express a modality, nor does this past tense version.

3.8.3.2 *Modulations in text 3.1.*

Most of the modalities in text 3.1 are of obligation. They are classified below according to degree and realization.

i) high obligation: directive, subjective implicit:

16	Fran	(i)I didn't know (ii)you <u>had</u> to do General Studies.
42	Dave	(i)So you <u>gotta</u> pick all those up this year?
49	Brad	(i)You only <u>have</u> to do,
52	Brad	(iv)You only <u>have</u> to do eight points of General Studies in your whole in your whole == career.
60	Brad	(i)But anyway you th', (ii)it's it's just, (iii)it's just this rubbish subjects that you <u>have</u> to do ==
72	Fran	== (i)Everybody <u>has</u> to be though.

ii) median obligation: advice; objective, implicit:

| 48 | Dave | (i)But I thought (ii)you dropped a lot of them last year (iii)which you were <u>s'posed</u> to do? |

iii) low obligation: permission. The first is negative, the second positive; both are subjective, implicit:

| 22 | Dave | (i)Well, y'know, you <u>can't</u> just do languages can you? |
| 29 | Brad | (ii)In FIRST year you <u>can</u> do whatever you WANT == |

There are no examples of inclination modulations in text 3.1. However, there are six expressions of capability:

25	Brad	(iii)if I wanted to (iv)I <u>could</u> do French, German and Russian...
29	Brad	== (i)I <u>could</u> do ...
70	Fran	(i)But even if it meant that you <u>could</u> understand people and therefore HELP them?
82	Fran	(v)Now I <u>can</u> see no == no bearing
98	Brad	(i)Exactly, (ii)so ... if they <u>can</u> administer fish (iii)they <u>can</u> administer bloody schoolkids.
79	Brad	(i)I'll get a job, (ii)and I'll make some money, (iii)and then I'll maybe <u>be able</u> to do something meaningful == (with my life)

The implications of these different modality selections will be considered below, in our discussion of patterns in text 3.1.

3.8.4 Modality: summary

The common verbal and adverbial lexis used to encode the various meanings of modality is summarized in Table 3.1, which is a modification of Halliday (1994: 50).

3.9 ANALYSING FOR MOOD AND MODALITY

We will now work through a suggested procedure for applying this technical apparatus for mood analysis of casual conversation, using text 3.1 as our example.

3.9.1 Clause division

In order to carry out a mood analysis, the transcript must first be divided into clauses. A clause can now be identified as a sequence of some of the constituents identified above: Subject + Finite, plus a Predicator, and combinations of Complements and Adjuncts, with some elements possibly ellipsed but recoverable from prior clauses. However, in the dynamics of casual talk speakers do not always finish clauses that they start, either because they run out of steam, or because they are interrupted. It is useful to keep track of these clauses which we call abandoned clauses. They should also be numbered, but assigned some code to indicate their abandoned

status. Depending on how much of the clause is available, it may or may not be possible to state the mood.

We also need to note those clauses which are grammatically dependent (i.e. subordinated) to a main clause, since it is only the mood of the main clause which determines the mood for the clause complex or sentence. Consider the following statement which Brad makes:

25   Brad   (iii) if I wanted to (iv) I could do French, German and Russian ...

Table 3.1 Expressions of modality
Source: modified from Halliday 1994: 49, 82)

Type	Meaning	Examples
probability	how likely? how obvious?	may/will/must; probably, possibly, certainly, perhaps, maybe, of course, surely, obviously
	incongruently	I'm sure/certain; in my opinion; it is sure/certain/likely/probable
usuality	how often? how typical?	usually, sometimes, always, never, for the most part, seldom, often
obligation	how required?	will/should/must; required to/permitted to
inclination	how willing?	will; gladly, willingly, readily
capability	how able?	can; is able to; capably, ably

Although both clauses have declarative mood structure, only the main clause *I could do French* has selected independently for declarative mood. We can see this when we attempt to vary the mood selection of this clause:

If I wanted to,   could I do French, German and Russian? (polar interrogative)

If I wanted to,   what languages could I do? (wh-interrogative)

If I wanted to,   I could. (elliptical declarative)

If I wanted to,   couldn't I? (elliptical interrogative, negative polarity)

While the main clause can be expressed as any mood type, the mood of the dependent clause does not vary. Dependent clauses may be produced before the main clause to which they are attached (as in the example above), or following it (*I could do French, German and Russian if I wanted to*). Dependent clauses are generally linked to the main clause with a subordinating conjunction such as *if, because, when, while, before, after, unless, although,* etc. Clauses which indirectly report the speech or thoughts of a person are also classed as dependent clauses. For example, consider the following clause sequence:

They said   that you could do French, German and Russian,

The second clause is grammatically dependent upon the main, projecting clause *they said.* We will see that this distinction between dependent and independent mood selection becomes important when analysing the interactive structure of the talk (in Chapter 5).[3]

3.9.2 Analysing on a coding sheet

A coding sheet is then used to note down the main mood features of each clause. Typically the coding sheet records the following:

- the turn number and speaker
- clause number, with * indicating incomplete clauses
- the distinction between independent and dependent clauses with # marking dependent clauses
- the Subject of the clause (in parentheses if elliptical)
- clause mood: declarative, interrogative, imperative, minor; elliptical or full; plus (if elliptical), the number of the turn from which the ellipsis can be recovered and the list of all ellipsed constituents;
- negation, if any
- presence of Adjuncts (circumstantial, interpersonal, textual)

Table 3.2 presents an excerpt from a coding sheet for text 3.1.

3.9.3 Quantitative summary

A coding sheet such as shown in Table 3.2 can be used to explore either qualitative or quantitative dimensions of a conversation. Table 3.3 summarizes mood dimensions for each speaker across text 3.1 as a whole, and so gives us a first quantitative perspective on the linguistic patterns in text 3.1.

Table 3.2 Sample coding sheet for mood analysis of text 3.1: Philosophy

Turn no./ speaker	Clause no.	Subject	Mood	Polarity	Adjuncts
1/Brad	i	(you)	imperative		
	ii	(you)	polar interrogative: elliptical (S^F) PC		
	iii	he	declarative: full		
2/Fran	i	he	polar interrogative: elliptical (PC) F^S		
3/Brad	i	(he)	declarative: elliptical: 1 (SFPC) Adj/circumstantial		circumstantial
	ii	he	declarative: full		
	iii	his wife	declarative: full		textual
	iv	she	declarative: full		textual
NV1/Dave	non-verbal				
4/Fran	i	he	declarative: full		textual
	ii	she	declarative: full		
5/Brad	i	all Germans	declarative: full		
6/Dave	i*	you	declarative: full		
	ii	you	declarative: full: tagged		
7/Brad	i		minor		
	ii	everyone at uni	declarative: ellipt: 7 (C) S^F		
8/Dave	i	they	declarative: full		
9/Brad	i	they	declarative: full		
10/Dave	i	(they)	declarative: ellipt: 10 (SFC) Adj/circ		textual
11/Brad	i		minor		
12/Fran	i	they	declarative: full: tagged		textual
13/Brad	i	you	wh-interrogative/ whC: full		
	ii*				
14/Fran	i	they	declarative: full: tagged		textual; circumstantial
15/Brad	i*	this	*		textual
	ii	we	declarative: full		
	iii	he	declarative: full		textual
	iv	he	declarative: full		textual

Key: (elements in parentheses) ellipsed; clause number for retrieval of ellipsis is shown; non-ellipsed elements are shown without parentheses
S=Subject; F=Finite; P=Predicator; A=Adjunct; C=Complement
Wh: wh-element, shown as fused with S, C, or A

Table 3.3 Summary of mood choices in text 3.1: Philosophy

Mood (clause type)	Brad	Dave	Fran
number of clauses (incomplete clauses)	127 27 (21%)	30 4 (13%)	46 2 (4%)
declarative full elliptical	85 (67%) 9 (7%)	17 (56%) 1 (3%)	19 (41%) 7 (15%)
polar interrogative full elliptical			2 (4%)
tagged declarative full elliptical	1 (7%) –	2 (6.6%) –	2 (4%) –
wh-interrogative full elliptical	5 (4%) 2 (1.5%)	3 (10%) 1 (3.3%)	1 (2%) 2 (4%)
imperative	2 (1.5%)	2 (6.6%)	
minor	7 (5.5%)	2 (6.6%)	8 (17%)
most frequent Subject choice	*I* 27 *we* (=*students*) 2 *you* (=*parents*) 2 *you* (=*Dave*) 2 *you* (*generic*) 14 *various 3rd person sg* 51 *3rd p plural* 14	*you* (=*Brad*) 15 *your sth* 1 *3rd p pl* 3 *3rd p sg* 7 *I* 4	*you* (=*Brad*) 7 *you* (=*Dave*) 2 *what you* (*Dave*) *said* 1 *3rd p sg* 10 *3rd p plural* 12 *I* 3
negation	13 (10%)		4 (8.6%)
Adjuncts circumstantial interpersonal textual	17 16 58	3 2 13	10 4 19
Modalization probability high median low	 1 (subjective; expl) 1 (subjective; impl)		 1 (objective; impl)
Modulation (i) obligation high:directive median:advice low:permission	3 1	1 1 1	2
(ii) capability	5		2
total no. of modalities	11	3	5

3.10 INTERPRETING MOOD CHOICES IN TEXT 3.1

Table 3.3 provides us with analytical evidence for some of the grammatical differences in text 3.1 which we noted informally at the beginning of the chapter. It also allows us to argue more confidently about the linguistic construction of status and identities within the text. The major patterns shown in text 3.1 by the analysis are as follows:

i) **Number of clauses** We see a striking difference in the amount of speech produced by Brad as opposed to his parents. Dave speaks least, only one-quarter as much as Brad, and Fran speaks only marginally more. Here we see Brad's dominance of the interaction, as his parents' linguistic behaviour reinforces the centrality of his contribution, and therefore gives him a clear message about his priority as a person.

ii) **Number of incomplete clauses** This shows that although Fran speaks little, she produces very few incomplete clauses. This reinforces the impression of her speech as careful and planned, although it is also related to the very high proportion of minor clauses she produces (see below). Brad's speech contains many incomplete clauses which suggests that he does not have to compete for the floor (he is allowed to remain speaker even when he stumbles and hesitates), and also that he speaks more casually than his parents.

iii) **Declaratives** All speakers produce a high percentage of declaratives, but Brad's percentage is significantly higher than Dave's, and even more markedly higher than Fran's. This suggests that Brad gets to initiate exchanges by giving information more often than the other speakers. Fran's high use of elliptical declaratives is some evidence of her more responding, supporting role (this aspect of the talk will be brought out more clearly using the speech function analysis in Chapter 5).

iv) **Polar interrogatives** It is striking that neither Brad nor Dave produce any polar interrogatives, while Fran produces only two, which are both elliptical. This suggests that Brad and Dave's interaction is not a negotiation of core modal issues of polarity, but rather of supplementary issues of information. Fran's use of elliptical polar interrogatives indicates her orientation towards responding (in these cases, querying, checking), rather than initiating.

v) **Tagged declaratives** Brad does not use this mood choice at all, while Dave makes some significant use of it. We can suggest here that Dave uses this choice to get Brad talking to him (i.e. to establish their special relationship), while not appearing to be dependent on Brad for content.

vi) **Wh-interrogatives** Dave's high use of full wh-interrogatives is another way in which he engages Brad in talk while retaining some status as an initiator.

vii) Imperatives   Although the number of imperatives is small, it is significant that Fran does not produce any imperatives, while the two men do. Brad's imperatives are addressed to both parents, while Dave's are addressed only to Brad. This is one way Dave enacts some authority.

viii) Minor clauses   Fran uses a strikingly high proportion of minor clauses, indicating her supportive, non-initiating role in the interaction. She is often providing feedback, while Brad and Dave are far less frequently in that position.

ix) Most frequent subject choice   This is indeed revealing. We can see that Brad is very frequently the Subject of his own clauses, and while he occasionally makes both his parents or just Dave the Subject, he never makes Fran the Subject. Instead, he talks to his parents as if they were members of a generic class, or he makes things such as philosophy the Subject of his clauses. This suggests some egocentricity, as well as disinterest in his parents – and, strikingly, his mother – as core participants. What he wants to talk about (and what they support him in talking about) is himself and his interests. Dave does refer occasionally to himself as Subject, but is strikingly oriented towards having Brad as Subject. He never makes Fran the Subject either. Meanwhile Fran recognizes both Brad and Dave as clausal Subjects, strongly downplaying herself as Subject.

x) Modalities   While the number of examples here is too low for us to make strong claims, we can see some suggestive contrasts in interactants' use of modalities. Both Fran and Dave modalize slightly more than Brad, which is perhaps more evidence of Brad's assertive status in the interaction. Significantly, Dave does not use any modalizations: he is not concerned with life's uncertainties, but instead all three of his modalities are modulations of obligation. This orientation towards obligation contrasts with Fran's more equitable spread of modalities. She modalizes, and also modulates for both obligation and capability. These patterns are one piece of evidence of Dave's more limited focus in the involvement, while showing Fran to be involved across a greater semantic range, at least in this segment of the interaction. That Brad prefers to modalize subjectively, while Fran's choice is objective, recalls the different ego-orientations revealed by Subject choice. Whether or not these particular patterns are general for the entire conversation is not particularly relevant. The very fact that there are differences in orientations to modalities in this segment is further reinforcement for the different roles and role relations being expressed simultaneously through mood choices.

Taken together, these patterns explain our informal impressions of the marked lack of reciprocity in the interaction. Brad does indeed dominate, and is made to dominate, by the mood choices of all three interactants. Fran does indeed play a lesser and supporting role, her relationship with Brad having no direct linguistic expression (he never directly makes her

Subject). Her isolation is reinforced by Dave's ignoring of her as well. Thus, although Dave produces fewer clauses than Fran, the mood analysis suggests that Fran is the most marginalized of the three interactants.

We are not suggesting here that these grammatical choices are conscious, i.e. that Dave and Brad set out to ignore Fran, or Fran and Dave set out to idolize Brad. But we do suggest that these linguistic choices are both enacting and confirming cultural patterns which go beyond the behaviour of this family group. Every time the family meets and talks like this, they reinforce the importance of the son, the privileging of the father–son relationship, and the isolation of the mother from both son and husband. In acting out these patterns in the many mundane and apparently trivial interactions of daily family life, these interactants are contributing to an ideology of the family that remains pervasive in many white, middle-class, Anglo-Australian contexts.

At this point, then, we have some "hard" evidence of the role grammatical choices play in constructing social identities. While we are aware of the dangers of generalizing on the basis of only one short excerpt, we suggest that similar grammatical patterns would be found in other casual conversations among parents and sons. While not all family conversations will be like this one, text 3.1 is embedded in its culture and therefore does tell us a great deal about that culture, such as what it means linguistically to occupy the social role of a white middle-class father or a young adult son, or a mother of a certain age.

3.11 MOOD IN TEXT 1.3: DR FLANNEL

Further illustration of the information that Mood analysis can provide comes from applying the analytical procedures presented in this chapter to text 1.3: Dr Flannel, the storytelling text presented in Chapter 1. In discussing Dr Flannel we see the importance of being aware of the dynamics of mood choice (i.e. how mood choices are made in sequence) as well as synoptic characteristics (i.e. the overall quantification of mood choices). A synoptic summary of mood choices (i.e. a tabulation of quantitative selections of the type presented above for text 3.1: Philosophy) would show, somewhat surprisingly, that Bill only talks for twice as many clauses as Mavis. However it would also show that a much higher proportion of Mavis's clauses are incomplete clauses (almost one-fifth). Alex appears to enact deference and difference by her very limited contribution. Analysis of Subject choice is revealing, showing that Bill talks most of the time about himself. Not only is he directly Subject as "I" in 34 clauses, but when we add this to all the clauses in which the people in his story also make him Subject we get a total of 42 of his Subjects being Bill. The women in the story are next most frequent Subjects: 29. Then we have unspecified *they* (as in "doctors") as Subject 6 times. In striking contrast we find that Mavis makes herself Subject only 5 times. Bill is not often her Subject either (only 3 times). She is most concerned with unspecified others: *you* (generic) 9 times, and *they* (generic) 9 times. While Bill is anchored in the specific reality of his own actions, Mavis negotiates a world controlled by vague generic classes.

However, a more dynamic analysis of mood choices provides strong evidence for dividing the text into two phases:

- Phase 1: turns 1-40. In this phase Bill clearly dominates, producing full declarative clauses, in turns consisting of up to eleven clauses (turn 23). In this phase Mavis's contribution is largely minor or abandoned clauses.
- Phase 2: from about turn 43 to end. In this second phase Mavis emerges as a more equal contributor. In a grammatical enactment of solidarity, Bill even comes to co-operate with her, offering completion of her clause as in:

46	Mavis	Well see ... ah ... most of men years ago ... wore
47	Bill	Nothing == else bar them
48	Mavis	== especially as they got older ... In the winter time =₹

Although Bill's contribution is supportive, in that he offers completion of Mavis's clause (rather than an initiation of his own), he does still interrupt her. In this, her more assertive phase, however, she is not put off, but comes back in and builds on Bill's contribution. Also in this phase Mavis gets her own chance to produce lengthy clause complexes, with turn 58 containing nine clauses.

Mood analysis also points to an interesting transitional phase in turn 42:

| 42 | Mavis | Yea that, that's what they call them don't they? They call them flannels, don't they? |

Here Mavis's tagged declaratives usefully support Bill's story, but foreshadow her more substantial clause contributions. Having heard his story out, she is perhaps signalling her intention to get a go herself.

We will see in Chapter 6 how mood analysis supports and is extended by a generic analysis of Bill's story. While mood does not give us the full picture, it does begin to explain the linguistic resources interactants draw on to claim discourse roles of "storyteller" or "supportive audience".

3.12 CONCLUSION

In this chapter we have explained the categories and procedures involved in analysing the grammatical resources interactants can draw on to make interpersonal meanings in casual talk. In discussing the results of mood analyses, we have linked these linguistic resources to the construction and negotiation of roles and role relationships, suggesting the importance of reciprocity and difference in pattern use, rather than assigning prescribed meanings to each linguistic choice. Further discussion of mood analysis will be presented in subsequent chapters as we build the cumulative analyses of excerpts.

These grammatical tools represent, we believe, the essential starting point for a comprehensive analysis of casual conversation. Choices in mood have allowed us to explore, confirm and extend our intuitive impressions of the differential roles being enacted by conversationalists in a range of excerpts. We have tried to show how this kind of detailed grammatical analysis can begin to lay bare the linguistic behaviours which are associated with certain social roles and the strategic choices which enable interactants, consciously and unconsciously, to position themselves and their fellow interactants as sociocultural subjects.

However revealing Mood analysis is, it represents only a first perspective on casual talk. In the following chapter we will build on our analysis of individual speaker clauses to look at how interactants negotiate attitudinal meanings in talk, in the process negotiating degrees of solidarity and difference.

NOTES

1. My thanks to the participants for permission to use this excerpt, collected by BM.

2. The status of these elements can be determined by the "tag test", which will often show that the *I* of these elements is not the Subject of the clause. For example, consider:

   43   Brad   (ix) I think the one that's alright is called Human
                  Rationality

   The tag test shows that the Subject is *the one that's alright*. The *I think* is therefore functioning as an Adjunct, expressing the speaker's lack of certainty about the information. The *I* in these metaphorical Adjuncts is also unstressed and the Adjunct occurs within the intonation contour of the larger clause.

3. For further details of the systemic analysis of the (inter-)dependency of clauses, see Halliday's (1994: ch. 7) discussion of the clause complex in English.

4 The semantics of casual conversation: encoding attitude and humour in casual conversation

4.1 INTRODUCTION

In the previous chapter we saw that conversationalists make grammatical choices between clauses of different mood types. Analysing mood choices in a short excerpt of family interaction showed how linguistic choices contribute to both the realization and the construction of role relations between interactants. The social roles (mother, father, son) appeared to give access to a different range of grammatical behaviours, with implications for the power relations between interactants. In this chapter we focus on the attitudes which interactants express towards each other and towards the world. These attitudinal meanings are expressed at the semantic level largely through lexical selections. In reviewing the resources available to speakers through the two semantic systems of Appraisal and Involvement, we will be suggesting that the expression of attitude in casual talk is an important device for constructing and signalling degrees of solidarity and intimacy in relationships. Over many of the casual conversational examples presented, there is a pervasive use of a range of humorous devices such as teasing, ironic remarks, dirty jokes, etc. The final section of the chapter will explore the more common humorous devices used in casual talk, and will investigate their functions. We will be suggesting that humour is not simply used to make talk "fun", but rather that it allows the serious work of casual conversation in asserting and reaffirming values and attitudes to be rendered less visible and its participants held less accountable.

4.2 CONSTRUCTING SOLIDARITY

In Chapter 3 we looked at an example of casual conversation among family members, where roles and relationships are based on longstanding, habitual patterns of interacting with each other, and where the participants played major roles in the joint construction of each other's social identities. In this chapter we will look at an excerpt of casual conversation between people who have much briefer and perhaps more tenuous interpersonal connections. It is a conversation that took place in a workplace, during a morning tea break. In the workplace we are often obliged to interact on a regular basis with people who know us only in that context.

Text 4.1, an example of workplace chat, is a four-minute excerpt from a lunchroom conversation among five men, all factory supervisors at a car factory in Sydney. One of the men, John, an Italian–Australian, has just returned from his "naturalization" ceremony, where he has taken Australian citizenship. His workmates have been congratulating him and asking him about the ceremony. As you read through this excerpt, you might consider how this talk is different from the casual conversation we encountered in Chapter 3.

Text 4.1 Mates

Participants: A group of five workmates, aged from mid-thirties to mid-fifties. Harry, Keith, Steve (all Anglo-Australians), John (a native speaker of Italian) and Jim (Scottish, with a strong accent)

Context: Lunch break at a car factory. John has just returned from his naturalization ceremony. The others have been congratulating him, and asking him about the ceremony.

Key:
Appraising lexis shown in *italics*.
Involvement lexis (vocatives, slang, antilanguage and taboo words): <u>underlined</u> (these categories are exemplified later in the chapter).

Turn	Speaker	Text (numbered for clauses)
NV1	John	[eating lunch]
1	Harry	(i) You've got a mouthful of *bloody* apple-pie there (ii) I know that. (iii) He can't speak now (iv) *even* if he *wanted* to
[pause 2 secs].		
		(v) You're a *guts*, Casher.
2	John	Oh yeah?
3	Keith	(i) You're getting *fat* too. (ii) You'd better watch that heart.
4	Harry	(i) You know when you're a – (ii) when you become a *bloody* <u>blackfella</u> (iii) you gotta share all these <u>goodies</u> with your *bloody* <u>mates</u>.
5	John	(i) Yeah? = (ii) You *want* some?
6	Harry	= (i) Your <u>Aussie</u> mates. (ii) No no
7	John	(i) Yeah?
8	Harry	[while laughing] (i) I don't *want* any
9	Jim	(i) It's your <u>mates</u>, (ii) he said
10	John	(i) Well, YOU *want* some?
NV2	Harry and Jim	[laughter]
[pause 2 secs]		
11	John	(i) Well I went there (ii) and this eh this *pretty* girl come in. (iii) She's *beautiful*
12	Steve	[eating] What she said?
13	John	(i) She said (ii) "Come in". (iii) Started to talk, you know? (iv) She's Italian. (v) *Only this big* – (vi) she had *beautiful* eyes, <u>mate</u>. (vii) My wife next me, (viii) she's *only* talking to me.
NV3	All	[laughter]

14	John	(i)I said (ii)she can answer the question.
15	Keith	(i)Was she Eyetalian (ii)Eyetalian descent was she?
16	John	(i)Yeah. (ii)Oh she's been here ten years (iii)she said.
17	Steve	(i)She's naturalized too (was she?)
18	John	(i)She said (ii)"I'm I'm *very happy* here in Australia (iii)but *only one thing*".
19	Keith	What'd she *wanted*?
20	John	(i)She said (ii) "We got no relatives here"
21	Harry	(i)You should have told her (ii)to have some <u>bambinos</u> (iii)and she can make them herself.
22	John	(i)Well I think she's married. (ii)She had a wedding ring on (iii)but =she said (iv) "It's *only* Mum and Dad".
23	Steve	=(i)You could help her out. (ii)Probably married an <u>Aussie</u>.
24	Harry	(i)Yeah she's (got) [laughter]
25	John	Oh yeah [pause 3 secs]
26	Harry	(i)Oh she'll get over that, <u>John</u>.
27	Steve	(i)I think she's got no one to pay off the house =as well
28	Harry	=(i)So what else did she have to say <u>John</u>?
29	John	er
30	Harry	(i)You didn't go in (ii)an' *just* say that (iii)and <u>knick off</u> out again?
31	John	(i)She asked a lot of questions (ii)they already asked not a lot of questions. (iii)You have to answer a lot of questions on the paper they give you.
32	Steve	(i)Did they ask you about criminal records and *all that sort of thing*?
33	John	NOpe!
34	Steve	No
35	Keith	(i)That would be *wonderful* (ii)if they *ever* asked me
36	Harry	(i)*Just* look at them. (ii)Look at that *little*
37	John	(i) No no (ii)I get angry (iii)because she seemed to be a British subject – (iv)her name was on her (v)there were some Vietnamese there (vi)and they were having a *fucking* big problem *really*
38	Keith	(i)Mmm (ii)she must meet =a lot
39	Steve	=They find it *really hard* to understand
40	Keith	*Hard even* to understand
41	Harry	(i)Some pick it up *like a piece of cake* (ii)and others, <u>Christ</u>
42	Steve	Hmm
43	Harry	(i)Then you got Wallace Bing down the motor inn. (ii)Been there for fifteen *bloody* years
44	Keith	And he understood
45	Harry	(i)*Look* he doesn't *want* to
46	Steve	It's *laziness* though isn't it ( )
47	Harry	Yeah
48	Keith	(i)Did you see (ii)the other day they they they discharged a jury (iii)because =the jurors the jurors couldn't write English
49	Harry	= ( )

50	John	Yeah?
51	Steve	<u>Noosa?</u>
NV₄	All	[laughter]
52	Keith	(i) Well he he told me the day before (ii) that he was going going on jury service (iii) and when I heard on radio (iv) that the jury had been discharged (v) I thought (vi) it might have been him (vii) he said (viii) it wasn't. (ix) The <u>bloke</u> ( )
53	John	He was a Greek.
54	Keith	Eh?
55	John	He was a Greek
56	Keith	(i) Yeah (ii) The <u>bloke</u> pleaded guilty (iii) so they *all* got discharged
57	John	Right
58	Harry	(i) <u>How the *bloody* hell</u> could they should they could call up a person like that?
59	John	I was called a couple of times
60	Keith	I've been once
61	John	And I never went up
62	Keith	You didn't go *at all?*
63	John	No
64	Keith	(i) Never appeared? (ii) Never got summonsed?
65	John	(i) No. (ii) They they sent a letter back (iii) "*Don't worry* about it".
66	Keith	(i) <u>Jesus</u>, you're *lucky.* (ii) It's a two hundred dollar fine, isn't it?
67	John	No = ( )
68	Harry	=(i) He didn't have <u>to front</u> in the finish, (ii) that's what you're saying isn't it?
69	John	(i) Yeah (ii) I didn't have <u>to front</u>.
70	Harry	(i) <u>Gee</u> I wish (ii) you'd speak *bloody* English, <u>bro</u>, (Casher) (iii) so people could understand you. =(iv) You want to be
71	Steve	That's probably why they discharged him.
NV₅	All	[laughter]
72	Harry	Yeah
73	Steve	Couldn't write his letter *properly*
74	Harry	Another *dumb bloody <u>wog</u>*
75	Steve	Yeah another <u>wog</u>.
76	Jim	I might go to these English classes
77	Harry	(i) That's a *good* idea <u>Jim</u>. (ii) The *best* suggestion I've heard you make *all* this year. (iii) Then maybe we can understand you, <u>Jim</u>. (iv) I don't know (v) how Harry understands you.
89	Jim	Who?
79	Harry	Harry
80	Jim	Who's Harry
81	Harry	Harry Krishna!
NV6	All:	[laughter]
82	Keith	(i) Who's Harry – (ii) Harry Krishna
83	Steve	( )

84	Harry	(i) Didn't you say (ii) you were going there?
85	Jim	(i) I told you (ii) I'm I'm breaking away from them now
86	Keith	== He's changed
87	Jim	== I have changed
88	Harry	== You gotta get away?
89	Steve	== He's shaved his <u>mo'</u> off
90	Harry	(i) Hmm. (ii) He's only getting *too lazy to carry his upper lip around.*
91	Keith	(i) Harry Krishna. (ii) Harry
92	Jim	(i) This tablecloth is *good*, isn't it?
93	Keith	(i) Yeah it's Leah's. (ii) She can leave that behind (iii) when she goes (iv) but someone is going to have to take it home (v) and wash it.
94	Jim	I will at a price.
95	Keith	(i) Yeah (ii) Otherwise it *stinks*.
96	Jim	(i) You all put 10 cents each (ii) and I'll wash it.
97	Harry	(i) Yeah. (ii) Well I'd say she's hanging around a few places. (iii) (Seeing her) (iv) I said to her yesterday (v) "I been to church a few times". (vi) She said (vii) "Oh well I been *all* here and *all* up there. (ix) No flannel around the neighbourhood"
NV7	All	[laughter]
·98	Jim	(i) Did you did you hear that one? (ii) The point oh eight one?'
99	Steve	(i) No (ii) I didn't hear that one
100	Jim	(i) Ope John
101	Harry	(i) That's your story
102	John	(i) Oh you know it. (ii) You know it now.
103	Jim	(i) I keep getting it *mixed up*
104	Harry	(i) A <u>fella</u> coming home from the pub drunk every night (ii) calls his <u>missus</u> "point oh five". (iii) One night she asked him why. (iv) And he said (v) "<u>Honey</u>, you're the first *silly* <u>bag</u> I [starts laughing] I <u>get into</u> (vi) when I'm <u>pissed</u> – (vii) I <u>blow</u> in you"
NV8	All	[laughter]
105	Harry	(i) *Silly* enough to ask the question. ... (ii) Reminded me of my wife. (iii) She was *bloody silly* too.
[pause 5 secs].		
106	Harry	(iv) Anyway I told her the one about the <u>flannel</u>.
107	Jim	(i) <u>YOU DIRTY BASTARD!</u>
NV9	Harry and ?	[laughter]

(Slade's data)

Compared with the family data from Chapter 2, Mates will no doubt strike you as far more explicit, humorous, and mysogynistic. The talk might also seem to be more evenly distributed among all five participants, rather than focused on one single person. Applying the procedures for mood analysis outlined in Chapter 3, we can start our exploration of this type of talk by summarizing the grammatical patterns, in Table 4.1.

Table 4.1 Mood choices in text 4.1: Mates

	Harry	John	Steve	Jim	Keith
no. of turns	31	27	16	12	20
no. of clauses (incomplete clauses)	65 (3)	51 (1)	17	17	45
declarative full elliptical incomplete	54 (79.4%) 35 (53.8%) 16 (24.6%) 3	38 (73%) 31 (60.7%) 7 (13.7%)	9 (52%) 6 (35.2%) 3 (17.6%)	10 (58.5) 9 (52.9%) 1 (5.8%)	30 (66.6%) 25 (55.5%) 5 (11.1%)
polar interrogative full elliptical	2 0	– 2	1 –	1 1	4 –
tagged declarative full elliptical	1 –			1 –	1 1
wh-interrogative full elliptical	2 –		2 1	1 –	2 –
imperative	2	2			
minor	5 (7.7%)	10 (19.6%)	4 (23.5%)	2 (11.7%)	6 (13.3%)
most frequent Subject choice	John: 14; I: 5; the woman: 5; you all: 3; migrants: 2; Jim: 4	the woman:18; I:6; they: 3; Jim:3;various: Harry 1	the woman:4; John:2; impersonal:2	John:6; the woman:4; jury:3; Noosa:3; I:3; various	I:8; Harry:1; no other people
negation	7	2	1		2
adjuncts circumstantial interpersonal textual	51 27 12 12	31 15 8 8	9 1 4 4	5 4 1 -	19 8 5 6
modalization in Finites	4		1	1	2
modulation in verbal group	6	2	1	2	5

Note: Throughout this table, bracketed percentages refer to the raw number expressed as a percentage of total clauses produced (excluding incomplete clauses), unless otherwise indicated

Table 4.1 points to some interesting discourse differences among the speakers. We see, for example, that participants contribute very different amounts to the talk. In terms of volume, Harry and John are the most dominant speakers, but Harry gets more value for his turns than John. Keith is the next most dominant speaker, although some way behind Harry and John. Steve gets least value for his turns, but is still heard slightly more than Jim, the Scottish–Australian. Thus, the linguistic evidence implies differential involvement in the talk or social activity.

Table 4.1 also provides evidence to suggest that both dominance and marginalization accrue. So we find that those who get the most clauses also get to produce the highest proportions of declarative clauses, which means that they are more often giving information than other speakers. At the same time, the least heard speaker is also the one who produces fewest declaratives and the fewest full declaratives which implies limited options to initiate exchanges. The most marginal speaker, Jim, is also notably non-elliptical, implying his lack of integration within the group's exchanges.

However, the picture that emerges is more subtle than that of overt domination or marginalization. Harry's domination, for example, is most obvious in his tendency to seize the responding role, with elliptical declaratives, rather than in his monopolizing the initiating role, where both John and Keith outscore him in full declaratives. He gets more information on the floor through adjuncts, but at the same time he makes choices which put someone else in as next speaker through tagged declaratives and full interrogatives. He also makes the heaviest use of modalization. The ambivalence of his role as dominant speaker is also reflected in his preferred Subject choices, where he seems most interested in negotiating about John, rather than about himself. This suggests either a reluctant or a very strategic domination.

Similarly, John's linguistic performance cannot be read off simply as indicating power and status in the group. The analysis suggests that his discourse options are more limited than they are for the Anglo-Australians. For example, only Harry, Keith and Steve (the only Anglo-Australians present) use full elliptical polar interrogatives (to seek information from others), while John's interrogatives are dependent on the clauses of others. Even more striking, Harry and Keith also use the only full wh-interrogatives produced, while John produces none at all. This suggests his dependence on the other speakers and his inability or unwillingness to elicit information. In addition, the percentages of minor clauses suggest that, although John gets extensive floor time, a significant chunk of it is spent in reacting to the turns of others using prefabricated linguistic expressions and not in providing new material for negotiation. John also provides significantly less circumstantial detail than Harry, his nearest match for speech volume, again limiting the amount of information he contributes. Finally, his use of both types of modality is the lowest in the group, suggesting either linguistic difficulties with these systems or a deliberate choice not to use them, whether it be social insecurity about making overt judgements in his contributions or a sense of inappropriacy.

The two minor contributors, Steve and Jim, also need to be carefully differentiated. Of the two, Steve emerges as more involved with the group than Jim. Steve seems to prefer to ask open questions than to offer information himself. He only makes himself Subject of one of his clauses (turn 99, clause (ii)). He produces the most minor clauses. Steve provides almost no circumstantial detail in his turns, but offers his judgements (through interpersonal adjuncts) and constructs his contributions as continuous with the others' talk (through textual adjuncts).

Jim, on the other hand, avoids elliptical structures and minor clauses: when he speaks, it is to offer or demand information. He eschews interpersonal and textual detail, suggesting a distance and lack of continuity from the others, but at the same time his preferred Subject choice is himself.

From these findings emerges a complex, and perhaps confusing, picture of the roles and social relations being enacted in this talk. While mood analysis keys us in to potentially important patterns, it also appears to leave us unable to explain apparent contradictions and ambiguities in the linguistic behaviour of participants.

We will be suggesting in this chapter that the complex linguistic patterns we find in such talk are the enactment of the complex social task being undertaken. The talk in text 3.1: Philosophy, presented in Chapter 3, achieved the reconfirmation of long-established patterns of interacting, however unsatisfactory participants may have found them. The patterns were based on lifelong familiarity, and were established against a background of shared ethnicity, social class and (at least partially) general values. However, the talk in text 4.1: Mates takes place among people who know each other far less well and who do not share ethnicity or socio-cultural background. Hence there are less established common values. The talk is principally concerned with negotiating solidarity. The talk is not just a means of passing the lunchbreak enjoyably but it also constructs cohesive relationships among a group of people who are obliged to co-operate on a daily basis.

Text 4.1, suggests that solidarity for such a group involves formulating a coherent group alignment on central questions which are contested within the culture at large. The questions explored within text 4.1 are principally:

(i)   ethnicity: what does it mean to be an Australian?
(ii)   misogyny: what do we think of women?
(iii) maleness: what do real men do – and not do?

The principle linguistic resources drawn on to explore these alignments include the use of:

- attitudinal vocabulary to appraise and evaluate other's behaviour;
- in-group words or anti-language (terms such as *blackfella*) to indicate group boundaries;
- slang, swearing, and drawing on shared past history to suggest group cohesion;
- abbreviated and Australianized terms of address to indicate levels of intimacy.

In text 4.1 there is also the pervasive use of a range of humorous devices such as teasing, ironic remarks, dirty jokes, etc. We will be suggesting that these devices allow the serious work of chat which involves establishing group values and attitudes, to be largely invisible.

Leaving humour aside for a moment, one of the main resources for exploring these interpersonal alignments is expressed at the semantic level through lexical selections. The choice of one word rather than another expresses interactants' personal attitudes towards each other e.g. favourable/friendly vs. unfavourable/hostile. It also expresses their judgements of the acceptability, normality or appeal of each other's behaviour and beliefs.

In this chapter we review three main areas of interpersonal semantics:

i) Appraisal Appraisal refers to the attitudinal colouring of talk along a range of dimensions including: certainty, emotional response, social evaluation, and intensity. Appraisal analysis enables us to describe what is different between saying that the woman John met in the office was *beautiful/competent/disappointed,* or saying she was *really really beautiful,* or *seemed a bit disappointed sort of,* or *kind of competent.* Appraisal is mainly realized lexically although it can be realized by whole clauses.

ii) Involvement Involvement refers to how interpersonal worlds are shared by interactants. It includes the use of vocatives, slang, anti-language and taboo words. For example: the use of words such as: *bloody/shitty/fucking,* or targeting another interactant through the use of vocatives such as *Brad/Bradley/Daring/Dorkhead* or *mate/Aussie mate* (as in the case of text 4.1).

iii) Humour Humour is a consistent feature of casual conversation; ties and solidarity in many of the conversations are created through teasing each other. For example: in text 3.1: Philosophy where Brad's father suggested that Brad is studying *history of Scotch bagpipe playing* at university and in text 4.1, when Harry says *You're a guts, Casher.*

The role of these semantic patterns will be highlighted by considering text 4.1: Mates, as well as other texts presented in earlier chapters. We will first outline Appraisal meanings, followed by a discussion of Involvement, and finally the role of Humour will be discussed.

4.3 APPRAISAL[z]

One of the least understood and most under-researched areas in linguistics is the domain concerned with interpersonal assessment. There has been work on the interactional and sequential patterns of talk by many different paradigms (see Chapter 2) but very little work on the description of evaluative meanings.

Some exceptions are the studies on the analysis of semantic fields (see Lyons 1977, Lehrer 1974). These studies have focused on experientially coherent lexical fields in natural language. These studies, however, do not focus on interpersonal lexis, and their analysis is not related either to a more micro analysis of grammatical structure, nor to a theory of discourse structure.

Recently Martin (in press), within the systemic framework, has built on early work by Labov (1972a) and Rothery (1990) and Plum (1988) on the role played by interpersonal meanings in narratives; and work by Poynton (1985, 1990) on affect and vocation. Martin has developed a theoretical framework for the analysis of evaluative meanings in texts.

Martin's approach to evaluative meanings in texts is similar in orientation to that of Labov (1972a) and Biber and Finegan (1989). Biber and Finegan (1989) outline categories for identifying 'styles of stance' in English, defining stance as the lexical and grammatical expression of attitudes, feelings, judgements or commitment concerning the propositional content of a message. They include such categories as 'certainty adverbs' (e.g. *actually, certainly*, etc.), 'doubt adverbs' (e.g. *allegedly, apparently*, etc.), affect expressions (e.g. *enjoy, hope*, etc.). Labov (1972a) similarly discussed evaluative devices in relation to spoken narratives where he defined evaluative devices as follows:

> Evaluative devices say to us: this was terrifying, dangerous, weird, wild, crazy; or amusing, hilarious, wonderful; more generally, that it was strange, uncommon, or unusual–that is, worth reporting. It was not ordinary, plain, humdrum, everyday, or run-of the mill. (71)

The main evaluative devices that Labov describes are intensifiers, in which category he includes (i) repetition, expressive phonology, etc; (ii) comparators (e.g. imperatives, questions, negatives, etc.); (iii) correlatives (e.g. progressive verbal tense, double attributives, etc.); and (iv) explicatives (e.g. qualifications: *while, because, since, though*).

Appraisal analysis examines the attitudinal meanings of words used in conversation. Developing our analyses from Martin (1994) we recognize four main categories of appraisal:

- **Appreciation**: speakers' reactions to and evaluations of reality.
- **Affect**: speakers' expression of emotional states, both positive and negative.
- **Judgement**: speakers' judgements about the ethics, morality, or social values of other people.
- **Amplification**: the way speakers magnify or minimize the intensity and degree of the reality they are negotiating.

We will work through each major category in turn, defining and exemplifying it from text 3.1: Philosophy, presented in Chapter 3, text 1.2: Tamara, presented in Chapter 1 and from text 4.1: Mates. We will then present an analysis of the categories as used in the texts seen so far, particularly in text 4.1.

In approaching semantic analysis we need to adopt a more dynamic perspective than was necessary with the mood analysis presented in Chapter 2. Unlike the system of mood, where categories are clearly differentiated on relatively fixed criteria, the analysis of Appraisal and Involvement depends significantly on the co-text: it is often not possible to state whether a lexical item has attitudinal colouring until it is used in context. For example, the word *child* has a very different meaning when used in each of the following sequences:

- Do you have family?
  Yes, I have just one child
- I can't stand this anymore!
  You're such a child!

In addition, lexical meanings are inherently less fixed than grammatical structures. The lexis is the most open area of the language, with new lexis being continually introduced into the language, and with the meanings of words continually under renegotiation and change. For example, when Brad in text 3.1: Philosophy remarks that the double-bass player is *funny* and his wife *insane*, he could be referring to the man's comic abilities and a professional assessment of the wife's psychiatric state. However, the conversational context makes it more likely that the words are being used in their informal sense, expressing Brad's view that the husband and wife do not conform to his idea of socially "normal" people. That the words are being used in this sense of 'a judgement of deviation from a social norm' is evidenced by the way both Brad and the other interactants go on to group the man into a generic class (*all Germans*), with this generic class then described as mad and *freaks*.

The interpretation of the meaning of lexical items is not only dependent on the co-text but also on the sociocultural background and positionings of the interactants. Appraisal analysis must therefore be sensitive to the potential for different readings or "hearings" of attitudinal meanings.

4.3.1 Appreciation: expressing likes and evaluations of an object or process

One of the major attitudinal resources available to conversationalists is that of appreciation, which refers to how speakers evaluate a text (e.g. a painting, music, a work of literature) or a process (e.g. the weather). Appreciation is realized by lexical choices, as well as by whole clauses. Both words and clauses can encode the expression of likes, dislikes, and our personal evaluations of the people, objects or objectified entities we come in contact with. Appreciation can be probed by the question: "What do/did you think of that?". Grammatically, lexical items of Appreciation tend to fit into cognitive mental process structures such as: *I think/know/understand/ believe that it was*.

Because Appreciation lexis functions to encode descriptive evaluations of things, the congruent realization of these meanings is through adjectives. These generally form contrasting pairs, e.g. lovely/horrible; elegant/daggy. However, Appreciation meanings can also be realized incongruently in the following ways:

- Through nominalization we can turn descriptive epithets into objects or things, e.g. *loveliness/horror, elegance/dagginess*. One effect of expressing Appreciation through nouns, and therefore one motivation for nominalizing, is that it allows further attitudinal meanings to be made within the same nominal group. For example, once we have turned *He is lovely* into *His loveliness*, then we can begin further to evaluate his loveliness: *His indescribable/arresting/stunning loveliness*. Because nominalization increases the lexical density of text, (see Halliday 1985), it is more common in the written rather than the spoken mode, but nominalized Appreciations are still quite common in casual talk.
- As adverbs: attitudinal meanings can be relocated to describe how actions and events were achieved (e.g. *Elegantly, he studied the menu; He argued simplistically for two hours*).
- As verbs: descriptive meanings can also be encoded through the Predicator, i.e. as the lexical part of the verbal group. For example, *His hair harmonized with his clothes*; *She challenged him*. This will often involve a nominalization as Subject e.g. His appearance *pleased* her/His loveliness *attracted* everyone.

We may register our Appreciation in one of three ways: reaction, composition and valuation.

i) Reaction   A reaction to an object, or a person treated as an object, expresses whether we like it or find it appealing, e.g. *pleasing, beautiful, splendid* or *plain, ugly, irritating, repulsive*. Reaction lexis answers the probe: "How good/bad did you find it?". For example, in text 3.1 Brad comments:

| 37 | Brad | (ii)One of them is *alright*, (iii)one of them is actually *good*. |

He uses reaction lexis to indicate his ambivalent evaluations of his university subjects. By contrast, John in text 4.1: Mates, says:

| 13 | John | (v) *Only this big –* (vi)she had *beautiful* eyes, mate. |

His use of the reaction lexis *beautiful* refers to a person, showing that he has objectified the woman, and is treating her as a physical object to be admired or criticized.

ii) Composition   Composition is concerned with the texture of the text or process; with the detail or balance, expressed through such evaluations as *harmonious, well-presented, unfinished, assymetrical*, etc. In text 3.1, when Brad is discussing his philosophy subjects he makes the following claim:

| 41 | Brad | (vii)Th' they've got *weird* names like "The Pursuit of Human Rationality" or "Self and Society" |

Here, *weird* indicates his judgement that the names do not really "go with" the subjects.

iii) Valuation   This category of Appraisal is concerned with evaluations of the content or the message being put across. Examples of Valuation include: *challenging, significant, provocative, inspiring, shallow, irrelevant.* Valuation is used quite extensively in text 3.1: Philosophy, usually to denigrate academic subjects. For example, Dave's questions Brad as follows:

> 20   Dave   (i) When are you gonna do ... all your *odds 'n sods* subjects?

By his use of the expression *odds 'n sods*, Dave indicates his ambivalent evaluation of university study. Likewise, Brad expresses his opinion of the subjects using valuation epithets in the following example:

> 62   Brad   ==(i) It's just a ... technicality. (ii) But this one on Philosophy is *alright*. (iii) We talk about bloody ... Descartes and all these idiots. (iv) It's *riDICulous!*

A nominalized example of valuation is also found in text 3.1:

> 24   Dave   (i) If you're doing an Arts degree (ii) you got a lot of other *garbage* to do.

Through the use of the word *garbage*, Dave is incongruently expressing a negative evaluation, which Brad later echoes incongruently:

> 37   Brad   (i) Oh it's ... *RUBBISH* ...

Brad subsequently reiterates this valuation in a congruent mode, using *rubbish* as an adjective this time:

> 60   Brad   (iii) it's just this *rubbish* subjects that you have to do ==

Table 4.2 below summarizes and gives examples of the categories of Appreciation developed above.

The three categories of Appreciation – reaction, composition and valuation – are concerned to encode different kinds of evaluations of a thing or a happening. The distinction between each of the categories can be looked at metafunctionally, i.e. in terms of the three types of meanings recognized in a systemic approach. Thus, reaction codes responses which are to do with the speaker's interpersonal response (whether it was liked), composition is concerned with the textual response (to the overall texture), and valuation with the ideational (the content).

Table 4.2 Categories of Appreciation

	Appreciation: What do you think of it?		
Category	Probe/test	Positive examples	Negative examples
reaction	what did you think of it?	*arresting, pleasing wonderful,*	*uninviting, repulsive*
	mental process of cognition: I think/know/ understand it was …	*fascinating, stunning*	*horrible, boring, dull*
		lovely, beautiful, splendid, great, exhilarating	*plain, ugly, awful, revolting, irritating, depressing*
composition	how did it go together	*harmonious, simple, elegant, spacious, restrained*	*discordant, complex, extravagant, cramped, overdone*
valuation	how did you judge it?	*deep, meaningful, challenging, daring relevant, profound, touching*	*shallow, meaningless, insignificant, irrelevant, reductive*

Source: after Martin 1994

4.3.2 Affect: expressing feelings and emotions

Conversationalists can also encode attitudes that indicate their evaluations of their emotional states: how something makes them *feel*, rather than how something makes them *think*. Affective appraisals are largely realized lexically and generally occur in polar pairs: one positive, one negative. Affect items answer to the probe: "How did/do you feel about it?". Grammatically, they can occur with mental process verbs of affection, such as *like, fear, enjoy*. Again, the realizations are typically adjectival, but incongruent realizations as nouns, adverbs and verbs are also possible. We differentiate three main subtypes of Affect:

i) **Happiness/unhappiness** – when speakers encode feelings to do with sadness, anger, happiness or love. For example, in text 4.1: Mates, John reports the affective comments of the woman in the immigration office:

18   John   (i) She said (ii) "I'm I'm very *happy* here in Australia (iii) but *only* one thing".

ii) **In/security** – when speakers choose lexis which encodes feelings to do with anxiety or confidence. For example, in text 4.1 John reports the legal authorities advice to him as follows:

65   John   (iii) *"Don't worry* about it".

Other examples of lexis expressing insecurity would include *scared, fearful, worried, interested, absorbed.*

iii) **Satisfaction/Dissatisfaction** – when speakers choose lexis which encodes feelings to do with interest or exasperation. This includes such expression of attitudes as *I was fed up, I was absorbed,* and *I was bored,* all of which have to do with dissatisfaction or engagement. This category also includes expressions realized by mental processes of affection, i.e. verbs of liking and hating. For example, in text 3.1, Brad expresses his feelings about the rest of the world in this way:

71   Brad   (i) Yeah but I don't *LIKE* people ... um...

The categories of Affect are summarized in Table 4.3.

Table 4.3 Categories of Affect: congruent realizations

Affect: How do you feel about it?			
Category	**Meaning**	**Positive examples**	**Negative examples**
un/happiness	how happy did you feel?	*happy, cheerful, joyous, buoyant, jubilant*	*down, sad, miserable, distraught*
in/security	how secure did you feel?	*together, confident, assured, composed*	*uneasy, anxious, freaked out, worried*
dis/satisfaction	how satisfied did you feel?	*interested, absorbed, caught up in, engrossed, like*	*tired, fed up, hate, exasperated*

Source: after Martin 1994

4.3.3 Judgement: expressing judgements about people's behaviour

The Appraisal category of Judgement involves expressing evaluations about the ethics, morality, or social values of people's behaviour. The categories of judgement capture the speaker's evaluation of the verbal, mental or physical behaviour of other people, and thus judgement categories represent a resource for evaluating someone's behaviour as either conforming to or transgressing the speaker's social norms. Judgement is usually realized lexically but it can also be realized grammatically in clauses. Judgemental appraisals answer the probe: "How would you judge that behaviour?". There are two major categories, **social sanction** and **social esteem**, both of which we consider below.

i) Social sanction These are the evaluative judgements concerned with moral regulation, or whether the behaviour of a person or group of people is seen as ethical or truthful. This is the domain of "right and wrong". These judgements can be of two kinds. In the first kind, a person's ethical morality is being evaluated as complying with or deviating from the speaker's view of the social system. As Iedema *et al.* (1994: 201) point out:

> the (ethics) system is concerned with assessing compliance with or defiance of a system of social necessity. To comply is to be judged favourably and to attract terms such as right, good, moral, virtuous, ethical, blessed, pious, law abiding, kind, caring, selfless, generous, forgiving, loyal, obedient, responsible, wholesome, modest. To defy these social necessities is to attract terms such as immoral, wrong, evil, corrupt, sinful, damned, mean, cruel, selfish, insensitive, jealous, envious, greedy, treacherous, rude, negligent, lewd, obscene etc.

The second kind of social sanction judgement is where a person's truthfulness is being judged, through lexical items such as *honest, credible, trustworthy, frank, deceitful, dishonest, unconvincing, inconsistent, hypocritical,* etc. (see Iedema *et al.* 1994).

In the following example of judgement by social sanction from text 4.1, we see Harry accusing John of being greedy:

1   Harry   (v) You're a *guts*, Casher.

Later in the same text Jim jokingly questions Harry's ethical morality:

107   Jim   (i) YOU *DIRTY BASTARD!*

Social sanction judgements are also common in gossip, as in this example from text 1.2 presented in Chapter 1:

20   Jo   Yes, she's a *tart*.

Here the gossipers accuse Tamara of being unethical or immoral. The effect of judgements of this kind is to clarify the social values of the speakers.

ii) Social Esteem These are evaluative judgements concerned with the way in which people's behaviour lives up to or fails to live up to socially desirable standards. Iedema *et al.* argue that positive values of social esteem can be associated with:

> an increase in esteem in the eyes of the public while negative values diminish or destroy it. For example, an "outstanding" achievement, a "skilful" performance or a "plucky" display are all "admirable" while "abnormality", "incompetence" or "laziness" are all contemptible or pitiable. (ch. 3. 8: 202)

Judgements of Social Esteem are common in casual conversation in English, with negative judgements particularly common in gossip, as will be discussed in Chapter 7. There are three types of Social Esteem judgements (see Iedema *et al.* 1994). In the first kind the behaviour of a person or group can be sanctioned or approved of in relation to the moral strength or weakness displayed. Someone can be judged as *self-reliant, energetic, brave* or *cowardly.* An example of this type of social esteem is found in text 1.2, when Jo comments on Tamara who is the object of the gossip:

| 13 | Jo | She's pretty *insecure*, that girl. |

Tamara is being judged as not living up to 'desirable' standards.

The second kind of Social Esteem judgement is when the behaviour of a person, or a group of people, is sanctioned by assessing it in terms of its departure from usuality. These are judgements such as *remarkable, unexpected, odd* or *unfortunate.* This is the type of Appraisal expressed in the early sections of text 3.1, as exemplified by the following utterances:

3	Brad	(i)In the orchestra. (ii)He's a *funny* bastard (iii)and his wife's German (iv)and she's *insane.*
NV1	Dave	[coughs]
4	Fran	(i)He's *funny* (ii)==and she's *insane?*
5	Brad	(i) == ALL Germans are *in==sane.*
6	Dave	(i) == You know ... (ii)You know a lot of *funny* people don't you Brad?
7	Brad	(i)Yeah, (ii)everyone at Uni is. ==
8	Dave	== (i)They're ALL *mad* ==
9	Brad	== (i)They're all *FREAKS*

In these eight short turns from text 3.1 there are eight judgemental Appraisal lexical items all of the usuality/abnormality type. In turn 8 the evaluative lexis is elided but understood to be the same type of judgement. By using these particular judgemental lexical items, Brad builds up a picture of universities as places full of strange and unconventional people. Throughout this text Brad is judging others, and is distancing himself from most of the groups and individuals he appraises.

The third kind of Social Esteem judgements are the evaluations concerned with how ably or competently someone has accomplished something. Typical lexical items include *skilful, incompetent, stupid, clever.* This category also includes aesthetic judgements of people's behaviour, where words such as *beautiful, ugly, elegant* are used to assess the extent to which a person's behaviour meets conventional standards in the manner in which actions are carried out. An example of this kind of judgement occurs in text 3.1, when Fran explicitly queries Brad's pejorative evaluation of Descartes' capacity to philosophize:

| 62 | Brad | ==(i)It's just a … technicality. (ii)But this one on Philosophy is alright. (iii)We talk about bloody … Descartes and all these *idiots*. (iv)It's riDICulous! |
| 63 | Fran | (i)Why are they ==*idiots*? |

In text 4.1, Jim deprecates his own inability to tell a joke:

| 103 | Jim | (i)I keep getting it *mixed up* |

These categories of judgement are summarized in Table 4.4.

Table 4.4 Categories of Judgement

| | | Judgement | |
Category	Meaning	Positive example	Negative example
social sanction	how moral?	*moral, upright, ethical*	*immoral, wrong, cruel*
	how believable?	*credible, believable*	*deceitful, dishonest*
social esteem	how strongly committed?	*brave, strong, self-reliant*	*cowardly, weak*
	how usual/destined?	*lucky, blessed, fortunate, extraordinary, normal, outstanding, remarkable*	*unfortunate, unlucky, cursed, ordinary, peculiar odd*
	how able?	*skilful, competent*	*incompetent*

Source: after Martin 1994

4.3.4 Amplification: general resources for grading

Amplification captures the lexical resources speakers can draw on to grade their attitudes towards people, things or events. Amplifications differ from the evaluating systems of appreciation, affect and judgement in the following ways:

- amplification lexis does not occur in positive/negative pairs;
- there is no congruent class realization: many amplifications are adverbs, but other realizations are through nouns, verbs and the use of repetition of elements of structure.

Amplification is perhaps the most complex area as far as casual conversation is concerned. The major subcategories of amplification are enrichment, augmenting and mitigation.

i) Enrichment Enrichment involves a speaker adding an attitudinal colouring to a meaning when a core, neutral word could be used. For example, instead of saying *he won at cards*, a speaker might say *he killed them at cards*. As we will see below, enrichments are closely related to circumstantial elements of clause structure. There are two main resources for achieving this attitudinal colouration:

- The speaker may choose a lexical item which fuses a process or nominal meaning with a circumstance of manner to amplify the expression of how something is done. For example, the speaker can describe someone as *whinging*, or can criticize someone who talks a lot for *yapping* all the time.
- The speaker can add a comparative element which makes explicit the attitudinal meaning, either because the comparative element involves a rhetorical relationship, e.g. *to run like a bat out of hell*, or because it is itself an evaluative word, e.g. *to play like shit*. For example, in text 4.1 Harry post-modifies the negative capacity implied in *lazy* with a colourful rhetorical comparison:

90   Harry   (i)Hmm. (ii)He's only getting *too lazy to carry his upper lip around.*

ii) Augmenting Augmenting involves amplifying attitudinal meaning. This may occur when other Appraisal items are intensified, e.g. *he's beautiful* vs. *he's really amazingly beautiful.* It can also be achieved by making apparently neutral lexis take on an attitudinal meaning through the very process of intensification. For example, repetition can turn a neutral expression into an attitudinally coloured one, e.g. *he won at cards* vs. *he won and won and won at cards.* In amplifying, then, the speaker uses grammatical resources to grade and adjust attitudinal meaning. A basic distinction can be made between intensifying the evaluation or quantifying the degree of amplification.

Intensifying, playing up the force of the evaluation, can be advanced in the following four ways:

a)   Through prosodic features. This is typically accomplished by adding stress to the lexical item which may or may not already express attitudinal meaning. Consider the following turn from text 1.2:

8   Jenny   She said, "Have you seen any photos of me at the fancy dress?" And I said, I said, "Well, as a matter of fact, I've seen one or two, um, of you *Tamara,* but you know, nothing ..." And, um, she said "Do you know of anyone else who's taken == any photos of me at the fancy dress?"

Jenny's emphatic stress on Tamara's name stresses the negative evaluation she is making of Tamara's behaviour.

b)   Repetition may be used to inject attitudinal meaning into lexical items. This occurs frequently in gossip as we will see in Chapter 7. The following is one example from text 1.2:

6   Jenny   She walks in ... She *stopped me* she *stopped me* and she said, umm "Oh, by the way, have you have you seen any photos of == me?" I thought, you know, you're a bit sort of, you know ...

c)   Grading words such as *very, really, incredibly, too* or *so* can be used to intensify an evaluation. For example, in text 4.1 John reports the immigration officer's judgement of her affective state as follows:

18   John   (i) She said (ii) "I'm I'm *very happy* here in Australia (iii) but *only one thing*".

In this example *very* amplifies the affectual Appraisal *happy*. Swear words are often used in this way, to play up the force of a following Appraisal item. For example, in text 4.1 Harry describes his wife first as simply *silly*, but then intensifies this as *bloody silly*:

105   Harry   (i) *Silly* enough to ask the question. ... (ii) Reminded me of my wife. (iii) She was *bloody silly* too.

Swearing that is incorporated within the nominal group can also function as an amplification resource. For example, Harry's use of *bloody* in the following turn:

1   Harry   (i) You've got a mouthful of *bloody* apple-pie there (ii) I know that. (iii) He can't speak now (iv) even if he *wanted* to [pause 2 secs].

In this example, although *bloody* does not intensify an evaluative lexical item but in fact the noun *apple-pie*, it indicates the negative attitude which Harry soon expresses explicitly by calling John a *guts*. Autonomous expressions of swearing, for example, *Bloody hell!* are considered resources of Involvement (see section 4.4).

d)   Amplification can also be achieved by using lexis which quantifies the degree of amplification being encoded. Quantifying may be achieved by adding terms of amount such as *heaps, much,* and *a lot* to positive polarity clauses. For example, in text 3.1, Dave plays along with Brad's representation of his "weird" university life, when he adds:

6   Dave   (i) ==You know ... (ii) You know *a lot* of funny people don't you Brad?

Other ways of amplifying include the use of pronominal expressions such as *all*, and *everyone*. These are very common in casual conversation. For example in text 3.1 both Dave and Brad employ this kind of hyperbole frequently:

5	Brad	(i) == *ALL* Germans are in==sane.
7	Brad	(i) Yeah, (ii) *everyone* at Uni is. ==
8	Dave	== (i) They're *ALL* mad ==
9	Brad	== (i) They're *all* FREAKS

Adverbs like *totally, completely, entirely, utterly, absolutely* can also be used to quantify the extent of the evaluation.

iii) Mitigation As well as intensifying attitudinal meaning, it is also possible for speakers to mitigate or down-play their personal expression. Adverbs such as *just, only, merely, quite, hardly, scarcely,* and (*not*) *much* all play down the effect of surrounding appraisals. There are many examples of the use of *just* to minimize in text 3.1. For example, all the following turns contain mitigating *just*:

22	Dave	(i) Well, y'know, you can't *just* do languages can you?
45	Brad	==(i) It's look, (ii) it's *just* a, (iii) it's *only* a two hours a week subject.
60	Brad	(i) But anyway you th', (ii) it's it's *just*, (iii) it's *just* this rubbish subjects that you have to do==

Only is also commonly used as a minimizer in casual talk, often in close proximity to *just*, as in turn 45 above. A further example from text 3.1 is:

52	Brad	(i) Right, (ii) so G'... (iii) First Year German is twelve points. (iv) You *only* have to do eight points of General Studies in your whole in your whole ==career.

Not much functions in a similar way, as in the following example from text 3.1:

77	Brad	(i) A degree in a degree in Linguistics is*n't much* use y'know (ii) if you wanna work for Landcare or something, (iii) so ==(iv) But anyway

Actually can also be used to minimize, when a speaker wishes to step back from what may be perceived as an evaluation which is too strong. For example, in text 3.1, Brad moderates his initial evaluation of his studies as *rubbish* as follows:

37	Brad	(i) Oh it's ... *RUBBISH*... (ii) One of them is *alright*, (iii) one of them is *actually good*.

In casual conversation, we also find a range of expressions used to indicate vagueness or incompleteness. Common indicators include: *sort of stuff, and everything,* or *anything.* Text 3.1 offers numerous examples of these elements of "vague language" (see Channell 1994):

41	Brad	==(i)It's [laughing] ... (ii)It's bloody ... (iii)it's ... introductory philosophy... *sort of stuff.*
64	Brad	==(i)He sits, (ii)he sits in a room and, and – and the' (iii)and decides (iv) "I think (v)therefore I am" ... (vi)*all this stuff.*
66	Brad	(i)Yeah but ... (ii)at least he could think abstractly about something that was worth thinking about, like soil erosion *or something*
94	Brad	(i)They mightn't have had a degree in Biology *or anything.*

The categories of **Amplification** which have been reviewed above are summarized in Table 4.5.

Table 4.5 Categories of Amplification: congruent realizations

Amplification: General resources for grading		
Category	**Meaning of categories**	**Examples**
enrichment	fusing an evaluative lexical item with the process	*whinging, yapping all the time*
	adding a comparative element	*to run like a bat out of hell, to play like shit*
augmenting	intensifying the evaluation	*repetition: ran and ran, sweet sweet girl* *grading: very, really, incredibly*
	quantifying the degree of amplification	*adverbial: heaps, much a lot, totally* *pronominal: everyone, all*
mitigation	playing down the force of an evaluation	*"vague talk": sort of stuff, or anything* *just, only, not much, actually*

Source: after Martin 1994

4.3.5 Summary of Appraisal

The Appraisal categories outlined above are summarized in Figure 4.1.

4.3.5.1 Procedures for analysing Appraisal in conversation

Having now reviewed the main categories of appraising lexis, we will outline the procedures for analysing Appraisal, and then discuss the analysis of Appraisal in text 4.1. In Chapter 7, the analysis of these interpersonal semantic meanings in text 1.2: Tamara, is discussed in detail.

There are four steps in analysing Appraisal in any conversational excerpt.

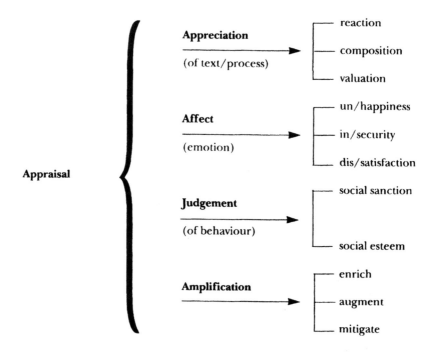

Figure 4.1 A provisional ouline of appraisal resources in English
Source: adapted from Martin 1994

These are:

- identifying Appraisal items;
- classifying Appraisal items;
- summarizing Appraisal choices;
- interpretation of the Appraisal items.

We will now discuss these procedures, illustrating each step with reference to text 4.1: Mates.

i) Identifying Appraisal items The first step is to identify all the Appraising items in a transcript. These will most often be adjectives, but as the discussion above has illustrated, they can also be nominal groups, verbs (particularly of affect and appreciation), adverbs (e.g. mitigations) and phrases (e.g. judgements of capacity). Appraisals in text 4.1 are shown *in italics* in the transcript.

ii) Classifying Appraisal items The second step is to classify each appraising item into one of the four categories outlined above. Categories of semantic analysis cannot be specified in such clear-cut terms as can

Table 4.6 Sample coding sheet for Appraisal in text 4.1: Mates

Turn/speaker	Clause	Lexical item	Appraised	Category	Subcategory
1/H	i	bloody	apple pie	Amplification	augment
	iii	even	if he wanted to	Amplification	augment
	iii	wanted	he (John)	Appreciation	reaction
	v	guts	(John)	Judgement	integrity
3/K	i	fat	(John)	Judgement	normality
4/H	ii	bloody	blackfella	Amplification	augment
	iii	bloody	mates	Amplification	augment
5/J	ii	want	you (Harry)	Appreciation	reaction
8/H	i	want	any (cake)	Appreciation	reaction
10/J	i	want	some (cake)	Appreciation	reaction
11/John	ii	pretty	girl	Appreciation	reaction
	iii	beautiful	girl	Appreciation	reaction
13/J	v	only	girl	Amplification	mitigate
	v	this big	girl	Appreciation	reaction
	vi	beautiful	eyes	Appreciation	reaction
	viii	only	girl	Amplification	mitigate
18/J	ii	very	happy	Amplification	augment
	ii	happy	girl	Affect	unhappiness
	iii	only one thing	(?)	Amplification	mitigate
19/K	i	wanted	what	Appreciation	reaction
22/J	i	only	it	Amplification	mitigate
30/H	ii	just	say	Amplification	mitigate
32/S	i	all that sort of thing	criminal record	Amplification	mitigate
33/J	i	NOpe	-	Amplification	augment
35/K	i	wonderful	that	Judgement	normality
	ii	ever	asked	Amplification	augment
36/H	i	just	look	Amplification	mitigate
37/J	ii	angry	I (=John)	Affect	dissatisfaction
	vi	fucking	big problem	Amplification	augment
	vi	big	problem	Judgement	capacity
	vi	really	big problem	Amplification	augment
39/S	i	really	it	Amplification	augment
	i	hard	it	Appreciation	valuation
40/K	i	hard	it	Appreciation	valuation
	i	even	it	Amplification	mitigate
41/H	i	like a piece of cake	it	Judgement	capacity

grammatical categories (although even grammatical categories often have rather fuzzy boundaries). In determining the category to which a lexical item belongs, it is necessary to consider the context. In particular, analysis must be sensitive to the way in which alternative "readings" of lexical items are negotiated in the flow of talk.

Because of its relative and contextual dimensions, semantic analysis of Appraisal will always be less clear-cut than the grammatical analysis of mood. However, given the categories and examples presented above, it should be possible to arrive at an analysis of the Appraising lexis. This analysis may be displayed directly on the transcript or on a coding sheet.

A sample coding sheet for the Appraisal analysis of text 4.1 is reproduced in Table 4.6. We suggest keeping track of the turn number, speaker and clause in which the appraising lexis occurs. Each appraising lexical item can then be classified as either Appreciation, Affect, Judgement or Amplification, and subcategorized according to the level of delicacy captured in Figure 4.1.

iii) Summarizing Appraisal choices   The third step in the analysis of Appraisal in any conversational excerpt is to summarize the lexical choices. So after identifying and classifying the Appraisal items, it is useful to summarize the kinds of Appraisal items used by different participants. We have done this for text 4.1 in Table 4.7.

iv) Interpretation of the Appraisal items   The last step in the analysis of Appraisal in conversation is the interpretation of the patterns displayed. We will now interpret the coding and summary tables for text 4.1.

4.3.5.2 *Encoding attitude in text 4.1*

The final step in Appraisal analysis is the interpretation of the patterns displayed within the text. From Table 4.7 we can see that in absolute terms Harry produces the greatest number of Appraisal items, followed by John, Keith, Steve, and with Jim producing the least of all. This can be summarized in diagrammatic form as follows:

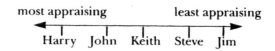

These frequencies reinforce the picture which emerged from the Mood analysis: Harry is the dominant and most expressive speaker and Jim is the participant who is least interpersonally involved in the interaction.

However, expressed as proportions of clauses (i.e. taking into account the different speaker-time each interactant takes), the sequence is slightly different, as is indicated in the following diagram:

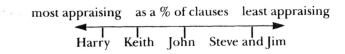

most appraising   as a % of clauses   least appraising

Harry   Keith   John   Steve and Jim

Table 4.7 Summary of Appraisal in text 4.1: Mates

	Harry	**John**	**Jim**	**Keith**	**Steve**
total Appraisal items	29	18	2	9	5
total clauses	65	51	17	17	45
Appreciation					
reaction	5	5	–	2	–
composition	–	–	–	–	–
valuation	–	–	1	1	1
total	5	5	1	3	1
Affect					
un/happiness		1			
in/security		1			
dis/satisf/n		1			
total		3			
Judgement					
social sanction	1	–	–	–	–
social esteem	6	1	1	3	2
total	7	1	1	3	2
Amplification					
enrich	1	–		–	–
augment	14	5		2	1
mitigate	2	4		1	1
total	17	9		3	2

While Harry remains dominant, and Jim, now associated with Steve, still appears to use Appraisal resources lightly, Keith now emerges as using more Appraisal expressions than does John. This suggests that, despite his significant contribution to the conversation, John uses Appraisal resources at a rate below that of the native English speakers.

These observations become more precise when we consider the types of Appraising vocabulary used by each speaker. As Table 4.7 indicates, Harry's appraisals are principally of Amplification and Judgement, with far fewer expressions of Appreciation and no Affect at all. Thus, he is concerned to comment particularly on the social esteem of others and he frequently augments his attitudinal expressions, suggesting the assertiveness with which he puts his opinions forward. His concentration on judgements in terms of capacity implies an orientation to judging others in terms of non-conformity to desirable standards of social behaviour. His judgements are directed at John whom he calls *a guts* and *a dumb bloody wog*, Jim, whom he calls *lazy*, and his wife whom he judges as *silly*.

His amplifications are associated with these judgements, culminating in his *dumb bloody wog* tease of John in turn 74. This explicit judgement of negative capacity is said "humorously", it can be interpreted either as a serious racist insult to John or as a jokey, teasing indication of in-group membership rather than exclusion (see the discussion of humour, including teasing, in this text in section 4.5 below).

Keith's Appraisal choices, although significantly less numerous than Harry's, include Judgements of normality rather than capacity, and most are delivered humorously. In turn 3 he judges John as getting fat, in turn 35 he ironically evaluates as *"wonderful"* the situation of being called for jury service, whereas John is judged *"lucky"* to have avoided it. Thus he appears more oriented towards assessing people's behaviour in terms of their conformity to the "typical". He is less intense in his judgements than Harry, but like Harry he expresses no affect. Also like Harry, the only Appreciation category he employs is that of Reaction, which he uses both to refuse John's mock offers of food and to evaluate the tablecloth – *it stinks*. For Keith as well as for Harry, then, we see that Judgement is an important Appraisal category.

The situation is strikingly different with the next most Appraising participant, John. John expresses only one Judgement, of capacity, in turn 37 when he describes the *fucking big* problem the Vietnamese were experiencing:

37   John   (i) No no (ii) I get angry (iii) because she seemed to be a British subject – (iv) her name was on her (v) there were some Vietnamese there (vi) and they were having a *fucking* big problem *really*

There is some ambiguity as to whether his negative judgement applies to the Vietnamese migrants or to the immigration authorities for not providing adequate services. It could therefore be indicating either solidarity with the migrants, or distance from them.

John is the only participant to express Affect, although two of the three instances involve him reporting the affective comments of the woman at the immigration office (e.g. *happy* in turn 18). He makes use of appreciation lexis to express his objectification of the woman at the immigration office, describing her as *pretty* and *beautiful* (turns 11 and 13). The only other Appraisal resource he draws on is that of Amplification, where he both augments and mitigates his expression of attitude in a more balanced ratio than is the case with Harry.

The two minor participants reflect the patterns of the dominant Anglo speakers, but not to the same extent. Thus, both Steve and Jim offer

Judgements of capacity and normality, and make some use of Appreciation lexis. Steve, although not a highly personal participant in that he does not express much attitude per contribution to the talk, uses both judgement and amplification. However, Jim is the only participant who does not draw on Amplification resources at all. Jim thus makes a very minimal interpersonal contribution to the interaction, Appreciating only once (the tablecloth) and judging once. That judgement (in turn 103) is a self-denigration which enables him to escape the request to be the joke teller. The absence of Amplification in his talk contributes to the construction of what can be read as a reserved manner.

Four general patterns that have emerged so far are:

- When the men discuss their own behaviour judgement is used, establishing shared attitudes and values about how people should behave.
- When they are discussing women, appreciation is used, with women evaluated as 'objects'. The men comment on the women's physical attributes, the only exception being when Harry discusses his wife, who gets assessed as '*silly*'.
- Affect is barely used in this conversation. When it is used it is quoting a woman: she is attributed as having feelings but the men do not express these feelings.
- The different interpersonal contributions from the speakers suggests that the Anglo-Australian members of the group are setting the ethical standards for the group, while the other members judge and grade more sparingly.

Work on the interpersonal semantics of English is still in its very early stages. Grammatical descriptions have so far been biased towards ideational meanings, the interpersonal system not fitting into neat categories nor being as determinate. However, as the primary motivation of casual conversation is interpersonal, this type of analysis is essential to shed light on the nature and function of this kind of talk. The Appraisal systems of interpersonal semantics give us an insight into how in conversations people share their perceptions and feelings about the world, each other and material phenomena.[3]

4.4   INVOLVEMENT: CONSTRUCTING INTIMACY AND AFFILIATION

We have reviewed the ways in which Appraisal lexis reflects and enacts the personal attitudes of interactants towards the world. We have suggested that the use of Appraisal terms is a realization of the construction, maintenance and negotiation of degrees of affective Involvement. In this section of the chapter we consider the second main group of resources used to enact such meanings: the semantics of **involvement**.

Involvement is the name given to a range of semantic systems which offer interactants ways to realize, construct and vary the level of intimacy of an interaction. Involvement resources include lexical systems, such as the use of vocatives, which indicate who is focusing on whom. Other resources include the use of technical or specialized lexis, slang, and swearing. Adapting Martin's (1994) model slightly, we will identify four main subsystems of Involvement:

- 'naming';
- technicality;
- swearing;
- slang or anti-language.

We will consider each of these subsystems in turn, with particular reference to texts 4.1 and 3.1. We will then conclude this chapter with an exploration of humour in casual conversation.

4.4.1   Naming: vocatives and names in casual talk

Naming involves the use of vocatives (an addressee's name or other term of address) to get attention, and to target an utterance. Vocatives thus constitute attempts to control the turn-taking system, by indicating who the current speaker would prefer to see (or hear) as the next speaker. Vocatives are a particularly important resource to examine in multiparty conversations, since they offer speakers a way of attempting to control, manipulate, divide or align the other interactants. The following three aspects of vocative use are of interest in analysing casual conversation:

i) The **user** and the **addressee** of the vocative. This tells us who is seeking to exert control over the turn-taking, and with whom they are seeking to indicate a particular relationship in preference to the other interactants. Of particular interest here is the frequency with which different interactants use vocatives towards other interactants, and whether this usage is reciprocated or not. Repeated use of vocatives between, say, one pair in a multiparty interaction will tend to create a special relationship between them: they come to form a dialogic unit within the larger multiparty context. The effect of this may be to cause friction in the group, as other interactants may come to feel excluded. On the other hand, a dialogic pair may come to be seen as a performing duo, whose dialogue provides entertainment for the other interactants.

ii) The possible **function(s)** of the vocative or why a speaker chooses to use a vocative. The motivations for using a vocative in multiparty talk where there can be no assumptions about who will be next speaker are different from those operating in dialogue because in a two party exchange, it can always be assumed that the next speaker is the other person. In multiparty talk, we will make an important distinction between **targeting** and **redundant** vocative use which are explained below:

a) **Targeting vocative**: a targeting vocative is a vocative used by a current speaker to indicate their choice of preferred next speaker in situations where other contextual clues do not make that person the most likely next speaker. Contextual clues include the fact that the nominated addressee was not the immediately prior speaker; if the turn in which the nomination takes place involves a change of topic, and if that turn does not relate to knowledge/actions known to be attributable to a particular interactant. For example, if you walk in on a family of three who have all been to work, and ask *How was work, John?*, then the vocative is targeting. If John is the only person present who works, however, then the vocative would be redundant. The form of a targeting vocative gives important information about the degree of intimacy between the addresser and addressee – see discussion below.

b) **Redundant vocative**: As the previous example implies, a redundant vocative is one used when there is already sufficient contextual information available for the nominated person to be the assumed next speaker. In other words, strictly speaking no vocative is necessary, as the person concerned will "know" that she/he is being invited to speak next. As in the example above, if one speaker asks a question which everyone present knows only one person can answer, then there will be no need for a vocative. Similarly, if an exchange involving two interactants is ongoing (i.e. has not been resolved or terminated), then the vocative is again redundant, as the other party to the ongoing exchange is the most likely next speaker anyway. The use of redundant vocatives would tend to indicate an attempt by the addresser to establish a closer relationship with the addressee, implying some exclusion of the other participants. The form of the vocative will indicate the affective and status dimensions of the relationship.

iii) The third major dimension of vocative use is that of the **form of the vocative**. Options here include the use of titles and surname, first names only, in full form or modified form, nicknames, terms of endearment or abuse. These major options relevant in casual conversation are captured systematically in Figure 4.2, adapted from Poynton (1984). The type of the vocative tends to indicate the lexical source, while the shape of the vocative indicates any modifications to the form.

In text 3.1 there are only three examples of vocatives. Two are produced by Dave:

| 6 | Dave | (i)== You know ... (ii) You know a lot of funny people don't you Brad? |
| 78 | Dave | ==(i) Well you should have thought of that thought of that three years ago Brad. |

Note that in both these examples Dave uses a truncated form of his son's

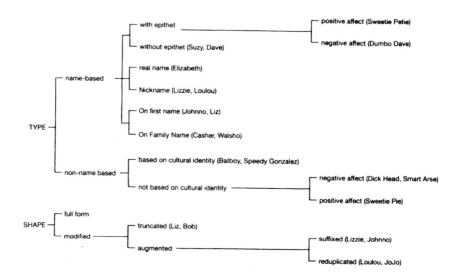

Figure 4.2 Vocatives
Source: adapted from Poynton 1984

name. The vocatives here are redundant: only Brad could be the intended addressee of the two questions. Their use therefore suggests that Dave is marking Fran as an inappropriate next speaker, and that he is indicating a "special bond" between father and son.

The third vocative in 3.1 is from Fran to Dave:

> 80   Fran   == (i)However, I mean what you said is, is maybe all very true David (ii)but, I mean, in the Public Service people are transferring from ... areas

Here we note that Fran produces the full form of her husband's name, suggesting a greater formality in their relationship than that between father and son. In addition, this instance is not a redundant but a targeting vocative which means that Dave has not been the immediately prior speaker, and the comments to which Fran is responding have in fact been spread over a number of his earlier turns. Fran uses the vocative here to avoid potential confusion rather than to silence Brad or to imply a special relationship with Dave. Without the vocative, Brad could think that Fran was saying that what he had said was true.

There are six instances of vocatives in text 4.1. In the first example, Harry uses a redundant vocative, in the form of a modification of John's surname:

> 1   Harry   (i) You've got a mouthful of *bloody* apple-pie there (ii) I know that. (iii) He can't speak now (iv) *even* if he *wanted* to [pause 2 secs]. (v) You're a *guts*, Casher.

The effect is to put John 'on the spot', to set him up as the most likely next speaker, through launching a tease (considered more fully in the discussion of humour below). The form of the nickname suggests some inclusion in the Australian 'mateship' culture, where nicknames derived from physical attributes are common, e.g. Shorty: usually for a very tall man. Modified surnames such as Slanger are also common.

The second vocative use is by John, who uses the general Australian-male vocative "mate" to address Harry:

> 13   John   (i) She said (ii) "Come in". (iii) Started to talk, you know? (iv) She's Italian. (v) *Only this big* – (vi) she had *beautiful* eyes, <u>mate</u>. (vii) My wife next me, (viii) she's *only* talking to me.

This use of the quintessential Australian mateship term contributes to constructing John as "now a *real* Australian". In the next vocative, again produced by Harry to John, we notice that he has switched to using John's first name (or at least the Anglicization of it):

> 26   Harry   (i) Oh she'll get over that, John.
> 27   Steve   (i) I think she's got no one to pay off the house = as well
> 28   Harry   = (i) So what else did she have to say John?

The change to the less intimate term may be in part a reaction to John's "matey" tone, but it also corresponds to Harry's shift from making the direct tease to simply seeking information, to keep John talking. Harry's next vocative to John reverts to his surname, again in a move where he is directing a tease at John:

> 70   Harry   (i) <u>Gee</u> I wish (ii) you'd speak *bloody* English, <u>bro</u>, (Casher) (iii) so people could understand you. = (iv) You want to be

When Jim makes a joke at his own expense (that is, as a Scot, he needs to learn English), we see Harry support Jim by using his first name twice:

> 77   Harry   (i) That's a *good* idea <u>Jim</u>. (ii) The *best* suggestion I've heard you make *all* this year. (iii) Then maybe we can understand you, <u>Jim</u>. (iv) I don't know (v) how Harry understands you.

Harry's use of vocatives indicates that:

- he seeks to exert control over who will be the next speaker;
- he seeks to construct a special relationship between himself and one other, i.e. John;
- he only targets the two potentially marginal members of the group: the now naturalized John, and the non-Australian Jim;
- with John, he switches between forms of vocatives according to whether he is teasing him or not;
- he does not use a matey nickname for Jim, indicating less familiarity.

The only other vocative in text 4.1 is produced by Jim:

| 100 | Jim | (i) Ope John |

Here Jim is trying to get John to 'perform'. There is thus a marked concentration on using vocatives to put or keep John in speaker role, a tactic which simultaneously marks him as "other" but also gives him access to speaking time.

Names are often used in conversation to refer to people who are not present or not involved in the talk. These are usually friends whom the interactants have in common or who are at least known to some of the interactants. Again, the form of the name indicates the relationship being implied between the person using the name and the person referred to. For example in text 4.1 the interactants mention someone called *Noosa* (turn 51). This is apparently the nickname for a fellow workmate. The use of the nickname form, as well as the absence of anyone inquiring *Who's Noosa?*, provides evidence of shared group knowledge. However, naming can also function to exclude or confuse other participants, e.g. when several participants begin talking about someone not known to everyone present. Again the form of the vocative used is significant, with different forms implying differential intimacy with the person being discussed.

4.4.2 Technicality: using technical or commonsense lexis

By **technicality** we are referring to the degree of specialization or commonsenseness with which conversational topics are talked about. For just about any conversational topic we can identify lexical items which are accessible, used and understood by most people without any special background in the particular field. Other lexical items, however, have a more limited circulation and access to them varies according to knowledge of the field. For example, consider this excerpt (text 4.2: Averages) which is from the same dinner party conversation as text 1.1 (this fragment occurs about fifteen minutes later in the talk).

Text 4.2 Averages

Turn	Speaker	Text (technical terms underlined)
1	David	Martins, Johnson and I once did a New South Wales <u>pairs round</u> and as I was handing out the <u>boards</u>... I put them on the wrong tables, right? Out of order, right? And it was <u>across the room scoring</u>. There was about eight thousand <u>pairs</u> playing.
2	Stephen	Maybe eighty, right? You only deduct two noughts this time.
3	David	No, no. There was about there was about two hundred – a hundred and fifty two hundred <u>pairs</u> playing.
4	Stephen	Well, from eight thousand to two hundred!
5	David	Yea well whatever. So, this <u>board</u> that had been – For some reason, I don't know whatever had happened, right. But we had to actually <u>average</u> this <u>board</u> <u>across the field</u>, and we finished at half past five in the morning.
6	Liz	Actually how do they do that? If they say to you, "You haven't got enough time to play this. We'll <u>average</u> it." What does that mean?
7	Stephen	You get an <u>average</u>.
8	David	You'll get an <u>average</u> ( )
9	Stephen	Normally it means if you score
10	Fay	Average the rest of it.
11	Stephen	If you score fifty percent on the night – Do you get <u>percentages</u>? You don't get <u>percentages</u>?
12	Liz	Yea. We get a <u>percentage</u> in the end.
13	Stephen	If you get about sixty percent <u>on the night</u>, you'll just score sixty percent. If you get thirty percent <u>on the night</u> you'll score thirty percent.
14	David	No no no. That's not quite true.
15	Fay	On that <u>board</u> you mean?
16	David	No. That's what – They'll do that in some circumstances, right? But if for some reason they were to give you an exact <u>average</u> on the <u>board</u>, right ... In other words you
17	Liz	It means the average score, what the average
18	Fay	Of the <u>board</u>?
19	David	Yea.
20	Liz	Not what YOU would get on average, but what everybody got.
21	Fay	So if you were really lousy you'd be upped?

Unless you are a bridge player, this excerpt will make little sense to you, as the interaction is peppered with technical vocabulary (technical terms have been underlined). Part of what is going on in this excerpt is that the male interactants are being confirmed as the "experts", while the female interactants are taking the roles of relative, though not complete, "novices". The expert status is confirmed both by David's own use of technical terms in his anecdote, and also by Liz's question in turn 6, which asks for an explanation of a technical term. This move continues to establish David and Stephen as having access to knowledge that Liz does not (yet) share. The males respond to her request, perhaps rather ineptly, by attempting to provide Liz with an answer. While this does expand her access to the field (i.e. next time "averages" are talked about, she will be able to participate in giving, not just querying, information), it also has the effect of reinforcing the superiority and presence of the males. They get to talk about subjects they know about, while the women get to listen and learn.

As this example shows, in looking at who does and does not use technical lexis, we are in fact learning something about the distribution of power in the situation. "Expert" status gives interactants the opportunity to dominate the conversation, while "novices" can be effectively excluded or their participation circumscribed.

In text 3.1, we saw that the interactants have differential access to ideational spheres. Brad, for example, controls the field of university curricula, while his parents need to be initiated into the meaning of terms such as *General Studies* and *points*. Fran appears to have expert knowledge of quangos, seen in her unpacking of the specialist term SAFCOL, implying that the others (Brad?) might not have access to it. There is also some indication of a shared public administration/civil service background in the discussion of *Fisheries*, presumably a subdepartment within the Ministry of Agriculture. Dave does not display expert status, again perhaps reinforcing the narrowness of his involvement in the conversation. But while Brad and Fran talk as experts in different fields, there are important differences in the way their expert knowledge is shared, indicated through the interactions here with mood. Brad's knowledge gets elicited, and is offered somewhat reluctantly, and with exaggerated condescension. On the other hand, Fran volunteers her knowledge to an audience who does not even acknowledge it.

In text 4.1, Harry is the only user of lexis which is non-core, and his use of it achieves recognition of both group solidarity and also internal group differences. For example, Harry says:

21   Harry   (i) You should have told her (ii) to have some <u>bambinos</u>
                   (iii) and she can make them herself.

This use of the Italian word *bambinos*, may be intended as a tokenistic display of a general familiarity with Italian culture. However, it also functions to emphasize the non-Angloness of even naturalized Italo-Australians: they don't have *kids*, they have little foreigners, *bambinos*.

His later pun on Harry/Hare Krishna (turns 79 to 81) works because all members of the group know something of the Hare Krishna movement. His final display of insider knowledge is in the following turn:

106   Harry   (iv) Anyway I told her the one about the <u>flannel</u>.

The reaction from the others implies that they share the understanding of just what *the flannel* refers to (presumably another dirty joke). Thus he uses non-core lexis both to bind and divide the group, in the same way he uses other devices, such as vocatives and, as we will see in the next section, swearing.

4.4.3 Swearing

Casual conversations are punctuated with swear words and expletives. The two relevant dimensions to notice with the use of these are:

i) The degree of integration or autonomy of the expression: i.e. whether the word is inserted within a clause (as an adjective, verb or noun) or is delivered as a separate expletive. Swear words which are inserted within clauses will already have been classified under the Appraisal network (usually as amplification: colour). Under the Involvement system, we note both autonomous and integrated swearing expressions.

ii) the level of explicitness of the item: *Holy smoke* is much milder than *Holy shit* which is still milder than *Fucking hell*. It is difficult to be categorical, but a scale is useful in keeping track of major variations in explicitness.

The frequency of swearing in a conversation gives some indication of the casualness/formality of the talk. However, as with all interpersonal meanings, the most significant variable is not so much quantity as reciprocity. That is, can all interactants swear as much or as little as each other? Differences in frequency of swearing, or in the level of explicitness, construct and reinforce differences in status. For example, there is just this one example of swearing in text 3.1:

17 Brad (i) Yeah I, (ii) I got exemption from == [noise of passing bus] (iii) Bastards!

However, it is significant that it is Brad who produces it (neither parent swears), and that Brad's swear word is very mild, without any sexual explicitness. It thus encodes assertiveness in that he does swear and also deference as he is not as explicit as he perhaps might be in conversations with peers. That he swears at all is signalling his dis-identification with the more restrained behaviour of his parents. And this in turn becomes part of what it means to be a young-adult son: he can swear in front of his parents, but they probably will not swear in front of him.

In text 4.1, on the other hand, there is very frequent swearing, with most examples being integrated. Harry is by far the most frequent swearer, showing a strong attachment to *bloody* as an intensifying swear word. Two of his uses of *bloody* are directed at John. In the first it is an aspect of John's behaviour which is intensified:

| 1 | Harry | (i)You've got a mouthful of *bloody* apple-pie there (ii)I know that. (iii)He can't speak now (iv)*even* if he *wanted* to [pause 2 secs]. |

In the second it is John's new membership status, and the group as a whole, which are intensified:

| 4 | Harry | (i)You know when you're a – (ii)when you become a *bloody* blackfella (iii)you gotta share all these goodies with your *bloody* mates. |

Three uses of *bloody* are directed to the audience at large. The first *bloody* is used to intensify the slang exclamative *How the hell*, which is used to comment on the inadequacies of the legal system:

| 58 | Harry | (i)How the *bloody* hell could they should they could call up a person like that? |

In the second use of bloody, Harry intensifies his mock evaluation of John:

| 74 | Harry | Another *dumb bloody* wog |

In the third example, *bloody* is used to intensify the description of his wife as *silly*:

| 105 | Harry | (i)*Silly* enough to ask the question. ... (ii)Reminded me of my wife. (iii)She was *bloody silly* too. |

John also incorporates an integrated swear word on one occasion. Significantly, he chooses the more explicit word *fucking*, which is perhaps a case of the newcomer demonstrating a willingness to go even further than the insiders:

| 37 | John | (i)No no (ii)I get *angry* (iii)because she seemed to be a British subject – (iv)her name was on her (v)there were some Vietnamese there (vi)and they were having a *fucking* big problem *really* |

Three autonomous swearings occur, all appended as adjuncts to clauses rather than produced as entirely independent moves. All three are derived from Christian vocabulary:

41	Harry	(i)Some pick it up *like a piece of cake* (ii)and others, Christ
66	Keith	(i)Jesus, you're *lucky*. (ii)It's a two hundred dollar fine, isn't it?
70	Harry	(i)Gee I wish (ii)you'd speak *bloody* English, bro, (Casher) (iii)so people could understand you. =(iv)You want to be

There is one example of swearing used as a minor clause, when Jim responds to Harry emphatically with:

107   Jim   (i) YOU DIRTY BASTARD!

These examples suggest that there is some association between swearing and group membership. Harry's use of swearing contributes to his construction of himself as the most macho and aggressive of all the participants. Combined with his domination of the speaker role, and his manipulative use of vocatives, the swearing appears to be one further resource Harry uses to claim the position of group leader: one who articulates the values of the group in the most explicit and consistent form. It is significant that most of his swear words are directed at, or attached to, subordinates or "outsiders" (John, and his wife), the same people who are targets of his racism and misogyny.

Thus it seems that those constructing themselves as dominant in the context of Australian mateship are likely to swear more frequently than others. Those seeking to demonstrate membership may imitate or hypercorrect (overdo) their swearing behaviour. In general, swear words are chosen from the relatively mild end of a continuum, suggesting that although there is a (compulsory) familiarity between these workplace colleagues, they are not close friends.

4.4.4 Slang or 'anti-language': sharing an alternative reality

The category of anti-language draws on Halliday's (1978: 164–82) analysis of those ways of speaking developed by members of "anti-societies", the most studied examples being the anti-languages of criminals and prisoners. Related examples are the so-called mother-in-law languages of some Aboriginal groups in Australia. Such languages generally involve a partial relexicalization of the over-language: i.e. the anti-language involves the creation of an extensive vocabulary which gives new names to things, though not all words of the over-language will have equivalents. In addition, there is typically an *over*-lexicalization (1978: 165) of the significant domains of interest to the anti-society. Halliday cites Mallik's account of the Calcutta underworld language where he found:

> not just one word for 'bomb' but twenty-one; forty-one words for 'police', and so on. (Mallik 1972: 22–3, in Halliday 1978: 165)

Rather than these over-lexicalizations being technical subclassifications (in which case we are dealing with the issue of technicality raised above), the alternative words are essentially synonyms. Halliday (1978) suggests that this proliferation of synonymous lexicalizations relates to a general characteristic of anti-languages, that they:

are typically used for contest and display, with consequent foregrounding of interpersonal elements of all kinds. (180)

While the anti-languages of imprisoned or criminal groups are extreme examples, the use of slang and in-group expressions is a very common and related occurrence in casual conversation. Conversational anti-languages draw on a broad range of contexts for new lexical items, but their functions to indicate or construct a secret, alternative reality are similar.

Although anti-language is closely related to both technical language and swearing, in that all three are resources for realizing degrees of contact and Involvement, it can be clearly differentiated in two respects:

i) slang/anti-language lexical items do not enter into technical taxonomies, that is, their use is not motivated by the need to develop a technical shorthand

ii) slang/anti-language lexis does refer to an ideational content which is unlike swearing, where the ideational content serves to indicate a degree of explicitness rather than any real referent.

Slang is an interpersonal resource because it enables interactants to indicate degrees of identification with each other and an alternative reality, and simultaneously dis-identification with the dominant reality. Unlike technicality, the identification is not in terms of shared knowledge, but in terms of shared rejection of certain values or modes of behaviour. Like technicality, however, what is most relevant about slang use is the extent to which all interactants have access to the code: an anti-language can be used to create and signal solidarity, or to create and signal unequal power and exclusion.

There are two particularly striking examples of anti-language used in text 4.1, both, not surprisingly, are produced by Harry. The first occurs in turn 4 when he says:

4   Harry   (i)You know when you're a – (ii)when you become a
                     bloody <u>blackfella</u> (iii)you gotta share all these <u>goodies</u> with
                     your *bloody* <u>mates</u>.

This example provides fascinating insight into both the process and function of relexicalization. The term *blackfella* is a word that normally carries strong pejorative connotations and is used to refer to the most ostracized and dispossessed group of people, the Australian aborigines. The group of "mates" in 4.1 have relexicalized this term to mean quite the opposite: a full member of Australian society, a legally naturalized citizen. Other conversations recorded among this group revealed that they had developed an anti-language concerned with position inside and outside Anglo-Australian culture. For example, they used the term *alien* to mean a non-naturalized Australian. However, in text 4.1 they use the more widely known term for this:

| 74 | Harry | Another *dumb bloody* <u>wog</u> |
| 75 | Steve | Yeah another <u>wog</u>. |

The humorous tone in which Harry and Steve use the term makes it impossible for John to accuse them of insulting him.

As these examples illustrate, some of the participants in text 4.1 also employ slang terms in general circulation in the Australian context. Thus, in turn 4 cited above, Harry urges John to share his *goodies* (i.e. food) with his *mates*, and the term *mates* is picked up by Jim in turn 9. Keith uses the Australian slang term *bloke* to mean 'man' in turns 52 and 56. Harry uses the slang verbal expressions *to knick off* (turn 30) and *to front* (turn 68), while Steve's one slang contribution is the abbreviation for moustache in turn 89 (*he's shaved his mo' off*). The use of slang by most speakers indicates the general informality of the interaction, while the greater use of Australian slang by Harry and Keith reinforces other linguistic choices which confirm their 'core' status as fully Australian males.

The development and use of slang and anti-language terms by the interactants in text 4.1 simultaneously constructs their solidarity as a group (through their "difference" from other mainstream ways of talking), and their ideological preoccupations (cultural and linguistic assimilation).

In the conversations we will look at throughout this book, anti-language will be only a minor feature, but it is nonetheless an important interpersonal resource available to interactants in casual conversation.

4.5   HUMOUR

The results of the Appraisal and Involvement analyses of text 4.1 presented so far indicate that the interactants are concerned with the evaluation and regulation of the group's behaviour, which is achieved by targeting marginal members and censoring deviance from behavioural norms. However, the apparently serious social work which is being achieved is overlayed by humour and lightheartedness. In this respect text 4.1 is typical of casual conversation, where we have found humour to be a pervasive characteristic, in contrast to its infrequent occurrence in formal, pragmatic interactions (see Mulkay 1988, Adelsward 1989, Eggins 1996). As the very frequent use of humorous devices in casual conversation can be associated with significant strategic effects, we offer here a brief discussion of some of the main types of humour used in several of the excerpts presented so far. We consider humour to be a semantic resource related to Appraisal and Involvement, as humorous devices such as teasing, telling dirty jokes or funny stories, and using hyperbole enable interactants to negotiate attitudes and alignments, and provide a resource for indicating degrees of "otherness" and "in-ness".

4.5.1 Research on humour

Humour is a large research domain, having long attracted research from philosophical, psychological and literary perspectives. Freud (1905), Bergson (1950) and Bateson (1973) are among the major theorists this century who have worked towards explanations of humour, with the most accepted general explanation being that humour arises where there is incongruity of some kind.

However, despite this rich, multi-disciplinary tradition, relatively little of this research has involved empirical analyses of humour in naturally occurring interactions. The research on laughter and jokes carried out individually and collectively by Sacks, Schegloff and Jefferson (e.g. Sacks 1974, 1978, Jefferson 1979, 1985, Jefferson, *et al.* 1987) is an exception, but, while insightful, it displays the same limitations of conversation analysis work outlined in Chapter 2. While very descriptive of the micro-situation, it has limited interest in broader social context, and so pursues what Fairclough (1995a) characterizes as descriptive rather than critical analytical goals.

Within linguistics, interest in humour is relatively recent, generally strongly influenced by conversation analysis, and also by Brown and Levinson's (1978) account of "face". While Brown and Levinson's suggestion that joking is a strategy to minimize the threat to positive face is useful, their account remains too general to describe systematically the range of humorous devices which occur in authentic casual interactions.

It is to anthropology and sociology that we turn to find work on humour from a more critical perspective. For example, the sociologist Michael Mulkay (1988) combines the anthropologist Mary Douglas's (1975) critical social perspective with Koestler's (1964) bisociation theory of humour (itself an incongruity theory). In this explanation, humour is seen as involving at least a duality of meaning, and often a multiplicity of opposing meanings, being made available within the same text. Humour, in other words, involves polysemy, where both a "serious" and a "non-serious" meaning can be recognized. Because simultaneous meanings are made, interactants can claim either that the "serious" meaning was not intended, or that the "non-serious" meaning was not. In either case, humour seems to enable interactants to speak "off the record", to make light of what is perhaps quite serious to them, in other words to say things without strict accountability, either to themselves or to others.

To explain why interactants would want to talk without strict accountability, critical interpretations view humour as the expression of social structure. In these views, humour functions to expose social differences and conflicts. In fact, it depends for its meanings on tensions in the social context. Mary Douglas suggests that joking only arises when the social structure itself involves a 'joke' of some kind (Douglas 1975: 98). In other words, humour enacts contradictions and conflicts in the social relations between interactants. It is these contradictions and ambiguities that interactants simultaneously expose and cover up through their uses of humour.

This position fits very neatly with a critical linguistics approach, reviewed in Chapter 2, which argues that:

Every text arises out of a particular problematic. (Kress 1985a: 12)

There is a suggestive association between Kress's notions of "difference" as the motivation for all texts and Douglas's notion of humour as the expression of difference. We consider that humour does provide a link between differences or tensions in the micro-semiotic interaction and differences or tensions in the macro-social context, as these are realized in text. It is this critical perspective which will be developed in the following discussion of humour in some of the conversational excerpts presented in this book so far.

4.5.2   Identifying humour in casual talk

Analysis of humour raises the question of how we know when interactants are being humorous and not serious. Studies of humour have identified a range of cues or markers which signal entry into what Goffman (developing on ideas from Gregory Bateson's work) has called "play mode" (Goffman 1974), while Hymes talks of a humorous "key" (see the SPEAKING grid, discussed in Chapter 2). Phonological cues include change of pace, volume, intonation or stress, for example, and there are also kinesthetic cues (change of facial expression or physical posture). Our own work also indicates that there are grammatical ways of indicating that remarks are intended as humorous, typically by amplifying the use of negative or positive Appraisal lexis (i.e. by exaggerating – see the discussion of text 3.1: Philosophy below).

However, there is general agreement among humour researchers that the clearest indication that something is humorous is that someone present laughs. For this reason many studies of humour focus on laughter, while recognizing that not all humour is indicated by laughter.

Studies of laughter in naturally occurring spoken interactions have made a number of important observations:

a)   In authentic interactions people often laugh at things that do not seem all that funny (see Mulkay 1988, Norrick 1993). What is funny in one context, for one group of interactants, may well not be in another context for the same or a different group of interactants. This suggests that "funniness" is created contextually, that talk gets to be funny because of its relationship to the social context. If we put this concept together with ideas such as those of Douglas, Mulkay and Kress, we can see that funniness involves relationships between text and both the immediate (micro-) context, and the more abstract cultural or macro-context.

b)   It seems to matter who initiates the laughter, i.e speaker or audience, and whether laughter is reciprocated or not. Gail Jefferson (1979, 1985) pointed to the importance of careful transcription of laughter. Her collaborative work with Schegloff and Sacks (for example, Jefferson *et al.* 1987) demonstrates that laughter initiated by the speaker can offer an invitation to growing intimacy, to which responsive laughter from the listener implies willingness to affiliate, while withheld laughter implies a declining of the invitation. Studies have also shown that laughter often occurs before anything at all funny has been said, and so can signal entry into the humorous "key".

We will now briefly exemplify these points by reviewing the types and effects of humour in texts 4.1: Mates, 1.3: Dr Flannel and 3.1: Philosophy.

4.5.3   Humour in text 4.1: Mates

Text 4.1 illustrates a range of humorous devices common in casual conversation: there is extensive teasing (e.g. turns 1–10, 21–25, 70–75, 77–91), a dirty joke (turn 104), irony (turn 35), and a number of remarks which are met by laughter (e.g. turns 13, 107). In text 4.1, the humorous key is signalled both by frequent laughter and by a general "jokey tone" in that no one takes other participants' comments very seriously, at least not superficially. Our access to other conversations suggests that this is the typical key in which conversations among this group are carried on, and that these workmates interact in what Norrick (1993: 6) describes as a "customary joking relationship".

The excerpt starts with an extended tease sequence, and this is the dominant humorous strategy used throughout. Analysis of the tease sequences reveals a number of points.

First, the tease involves several or all participants teasing one member. For example, the first tease is set up by Harry as an invitation to the other participants to become involved. This is signalled by the change of Subject in clause (iii) of turn 1. Other participants take up Harry's invitation, with Keith and Jim adding to Harry's initial tease. This pattern of a tease-in-the-round is repeated later on in the tease that Harry initiates in turn 21:

21   Harry   (i) You should have told her (ii) to have some bambinos (iii) and she can make them herself.

Again, once Harry has initiated the tease, other participants (in this case Steve) contribute. Similarly, in turns 70 to 75 both Harry and Steve tease John about his English, and then in the Hare Krishna tease from turn 77 to 91, everyone except John becomes involved in teasing Jim.

Second, teasing targets members who are indicated in other ways as being "different" from the group. For example, Mood, Appraisal and Involvement analyses have already suggested a number of respects in which the linguistic behaviour of both John and Jim enacts 'difference'. For example, John is repeatedly invited to be speaker but does not express the same range of mood choices or appraisals as other speakers, while Jim's minimal contributions make him interpersonally disconnected from the group. Neither John nor Jim participate in teasing each other, and the dominant Anglo-males (Harry and Keith) are not teased by other members.

Third, at least some of the teases directed at these participants imply censure of the social attributes or behaviours of the participants rather than merely objections to personal idiosyncrasies. The initiating tease (that John is a "guts") seems personal rather than social and appears to act principally as a strategy to fix John as the centre of attention. However, the later and more amplified tease (that he is a *dumb bloody wog*) explicitly addresses his ethnic otherness from the group. Similarly, Jim is teased for his membership of a non-macho, marginal, spiritual organization, the Hare Krishnas. Beneath the non-serious meaning ("we're just joking") lies the serious meaning: that some members of the group disapprove of these affiliations.

Fourth, participants differ in the strategies they adopt in the face of teasing. In the first tease directed at him, John does not react seriously, as Drew's (1987) analysis of teasing would predict, but instead "plays along", producing the mock offers of food. He appears to react seriously to the tease about the immigration officer (turns 21–25). However, he remains silent after the "dumb wog" tease in turns 74 and 75. Indeed it is difficult to see how he could say anything at that point which would not be interpreted as a challenge to the two teasers, Harry and Steve. Jim, on the other hand, under the pressure of the joint teasing, tries to play along at first (in turns 85 and 87), but then resorts to an abrupt change of topic in turn 92, which effectively deflects attention from him and ends the teasing sequence.

The teasing in text 4.1, then, is targeted at marginal or deviant group members, and appears to function as a way of conveying to them group values and norms. It does not only represent group norms but it also enacts them. The very fact of "being teased" emerges as a test of group solidarity: a marginal member must know how to support a tease, or risk increased marginalization, and group members must be willing to engage in a tease, or look like outsiders themselves.

The teasing in text 4.1 reinforces interpretations of the text based on the analyses of Mood, Appraisal and Involvement presented earlier in the chapter. Patterns of teasing show the tension between integration (solidarity, acceptance) and difference (distance). That the dominant males recurrently tease John enacts his difference from them, his potential "otherness". However, he is able to play his part in the teases by either playing along or shutting up and this enacts his inclusion. In fact, the patterns of teasing suggest that the real Other in text 4.1 is Jim, as he is linguistically less integrated than John (taking few turns, expressing little personal attitude). However, he does also risk more: unlike John, Jim sets himself up for teasing, for example with his suggestion in turn 76 (*I might go to these English classes*) – a move he perhaps comes to regret.

The second major humorous device used in text 1.4 is the dirty joke. Analysis of dirty jokes in conversation (e.g. Sacks 1974, 1978, 1992b: 470–89) suggests that dirty jokes function in part as a test or puzzle for listeners, who may lose face if they are unable to "get" the joke. In this respect, dirty jokes are membership tests. But the specifically sexual meanings of dirty jokes, such as the one Harry tells in turn 104, indicate that they also function to encode ideological positions. In this case Harry's joke reinforces dominant attitudes of mysogyny and the sexual objectification of women. This serious social work achieved by the joke is revealed by the ease with which Harry moves from the joke to talk about his own wife being *bloody silly too* (turn 105). Interestingly, this explicit connection between public attitudes and private life seems to trouble the group, who respond with a long silence. This may be an example of the double standard in action. While it appears to be acceptable to Harry's listeners to denigrate women as a group, they seem to be disconcerted by his explicit denigration of his own wife.

Thus the humour in text 4.1 arises out of tensions in the social context of the interactants. As Mulkay (extending Douglas 1975) suggests:

> Joking takes place because the organized patterns of social life themselves involve contradictions, oppositions and incongruities which find expression through the medium of humorous discourse. (1988: 53)

The all-male workplace in 'multicultural' Australia involves contradictions and tensions, as participants from different ethnic backgrounds, holding different beliefs and values, use talk to define and transmit acceptable alignments with group and sociocultural norms.

4.5.4   Humour in Text 1.3: Dr Flannel

Turning now to consider humour in text 1.3: Dr Flannel, presented in Chapter 1, we find that laughter features strongly in the first phase of this conversational excerpt (turns 1–40). This is also a phase in the text in which one speaker dominates the interaction. As we saw in Chapter 3, mood choice in this first phase is markedly non-reciprocal. Bill's clauses are largely non-elliptical declaratives, while Mavis produces many elliptical inter-rogatives, and both women produce a number of minor clauses expressing feedback. Bill dominates as Subject in both his own and the women's clauses.

This unequal pattern in the first phase of the Dr Flannel excerpt relates to the fact that Bill is telling a story and, as we will see in Chapter 6, storytelling is a linguistic task which generally requires the production of a chunk of monologic talk unfolding in a predictable, staged way. This would therefore seem to necessitate Bill's domination of the talk. However, this is to assume that "telling a story" is just something one interactant or another takes on the task of doing, for the mutual benefit of all concerned. It brushes over the significant strategic achievement that telling a story represents in casual conversation.

In order to tell a story in casual conversation, a prospective narrator must claim the right to tell a story. The narrator must somehow get the fundamental turn-taking mechanism of conversation suspended, at least for a brief time. Going as it does quite against the underlying mechanics of dialogue, and the tacit assumption of equality in the casual context, this suggests that telling a story during a casual conversation is an assertive strategy, even an act of power.

However, in text 1.3: Dr Flannel, the chat does not feel like an act of power, either to the interactants engaged in the talk or to us as "listeners" who are eavesdropping later. Text 1.3 certainly does not seem like talk in which domination is being achieved, power being negotiated. The reason it does not feel like that, either to us or to Mavis, Bill and Alex, is, we would suggest, because the talk is humorous. For in text 1.3 Bill does not just tell a story – he tells a *funny* story. He makes his first move to tell his story in the anaphorically appraising clause in turn 1:

1   Bill   I *had to laugh.*

This move achieves a number of effects. First, it gets the listeners on-side. Bill might be asking them to suspend their turn-taking rights, but he is promising to entertain them in return.

Second, the move sets the affective "key", i.e. it tunes the listeners in to the play frame, suggesting that whatever is said is not really serious.

Third, this move makes the story that follows necessary. The Appraisal points forward, and the move implies that listeners should suspend their right to take a turn (other than to provide supportive feedback) until they find out why Bill had to laugh.

Finally, this move suggests to Bill's listeners how to "read" the sequence of events he is going to narrate. In offering *his* Appraisal of the events, he suggests what their compliant Appraisal should be: that they should laugh – and laugh they do.

Thus Bill's bid for story time, for power in the micro-interactive context, is successful. But in their compliant support for Bill, Mavis and Alex are not just negotiating power relations within their micro-context. The women's acquiescence (not total, but significant) is not the acquiescence of "free and equal individuals". It enacts patterns of female acquiescence to male demands that are institutionalized in public contexts *outside* the privacy of the lounge room.

Empirical studies also suggest that gender makes a difference to the kinds of stories interactants tell (see the discussion of Johnstone's 1993 findings in Chapter 6). Bill's story is, at the end of the day, an extremely positive self-appraisal. Bill tells a story which makes Bill look pretty good. More specifically, it makes Bill look good as a man. In finding funny what Bill finds funny, Mavis and Alex support Bill in a very flattering self-appraisal that plays off institutionalized norms of masculinity.

This claim can be supported by observing that Bill's story could not be told by a woman, or, more accurately, a woman could tell Bill's story, but it would not be funny. The pivotal humour of Bill's story derives from his flirtatious, slightly naughty repartee with the "ladies". Clearly, in a society where heterosexuality is dominant ideology, a woman storyteller would have trouble being heard as flirting with the saleswomen. The loudest, longest laughs in text 1.3 have to do with hairless chests, or rather the incongruity of a man having a hairless chest – and yet clearly being "a bit of a lad". Again, these event sequences would not be "funny" for a woman storyteller because they would not be incongruous.

The humour of Bill's story, therefore, depends on the sexist, patriarchal structures of the culture in which Bill operates. The story derives its humour in part from the simple atypicality of what he did: that his trip to buy a singlet was not at all the dull and boring affair we might usually expect it to be. But the humour relies on his playful, non-serious representation of himself as "naughty" and "a bit of a lad": even as an aging, hairless male, he has managed to flirt with several "ladies" and to display a nonchalant bravado in the face of physical crisis.

Thus the humour in Bill's story arises out of incongruities in both the micro-context and in the social structure. From the micro-contextual perspective, Bill uses the conversation as a platform from which to dominate the talk and restrain the contributions of his audience. From a macro-contextual perspective, an aging, hairless, medically damaged, working-class male is a "joke" in capitalist patriarchy, where youth, virility and vigour are what matter. Yet, in a sense Bill has the last laugh, both literally and figuratively, because he demonstrates that he matters. The shop assistants appraise Bill very positively, saying to Bill (if we believe him) *You've made our day ... We'll remember you for a while*. Bill left them laughing, just as he leaves Mavis and Alex laughing, just as he leaves listeners to whom we have played this excerpt laughing as well.

Bill's flattering representation of himself does not go totally uncontested, however. In turn 8, Alex slips in with an alternative Appraisal that the "ladies" might have given Bill, when she says *and screamed and called security*, suggesting that Bill might have been interpreted more as an object of fear than of enjoyment. But Alex's subversive move is itself told with humour – she laughs at the end of her turn, signalling that her challenge is not really serious, and Bill takes no notice of it whatsoever.

Thus we are suggesting that Bill's funny story is perhaps not just the good laugh it initially seems to be. It is about power, and about connecting the intimate, family interaction to the norms and interests of the public, institutionalized society. The story achieves dominance in the micro-interactive context, as the interactive inequality assumed by Bill suspends the "in principal" equality of status between interactants in casual interactions. In claiming the right to tell his story, Bill brings into Mavis's lounge room patterns of unequal power associated with the macro-institutional contexts of public life. At the same time, Bill's story reinforces dominant representations of masculinity, representations which in turn reinforce his right to assert power in the micro-interactive context. That these implications of the storytelling go unnoticed is due to the use of humour in both the construction and the reception of the story.

4.5.5 Humour in text 3.1: Philosophy

In contrast to both text 4.1: Mates and text 1.3: Dr Flannel, text 3.1: Philosophy presented in Chapter 3 does not initially appear to be a particularly humorous piece of talk, if judged by the frequency and intensity of laughter. There are only three laughs in the excerpt, all produced by Fran, and all occurring immediately after turns by Brad (turns 39, 66 and 107). Nonetheless, it is not possible to understand how the talk makes sense to the interactants involved unless we recognize that it is undertaken in a lighthearted manner. However, its moments of lightheartedness are not accidental: the interactants in text 3.1 make very strategic use of mild humour.

The first indication of humour in the text comes in Brad's first turn. If we interpreted *He's a funny bastard* seriously, we would be likely to challenge in response, demanding perhaps: *Why? What's funny about him? What does he do?*. And then when Brad says of the double-bass player's wife *She's German and she's insane*, we would have to accuse him of racism. Similarly, in saying *All Germans are insane* (turn 5), Brad could mean "seriously" that he is a racist and hates all Germans. However, the more likely reading of his remarks is as humorous, e.g. "these people are a bit different/I find them weird".

As there is little laughter in text 3.1, we need to consider how we know that Brad is being humorous and not serious. Brad's talk shows that the cues to the humorous key may be semantic rather than phonological. His extensive use of amplification, in association with pejorative appraising items, makes many of his remarks hyperbole. And we make sense of his exaggerated claims about *all* Germans being *insane* by reading such comments as humorous. This hyperbolic way of speaking is also, however, associated in Brad's talk with frequent mitigation: Brad makes heavy use of the minimizers *sort of, kind of*. Mitigation creates distance, and when associated with the hyperbole is a further realization of the humorous inflection which Brad keeps running throughout his talk. His speech thus encodes a continuous tension between building up on the one hand, and stepping back on the other, and one way listeners make sense of that apparent contradiction is to interpret his talk as humorous.

Further evidence that Brad does not mean to be taken seriously is the fact that his respondents do not take him seriously, but also enter into the humour. For example, Dave's tag question in turn 6 (*You know a lot of funny people don't you Brad?*), using Brad's appraising lexis but not querying or challenging it, indicates that he "reads" Brad as being funny, not serious.

Brad's humour, then, clearly has effects on his co-interlocutors. In fact the effects of Brad's lighthearted talk both on himself and on others are quite complex, as we can demonstrate by following the talk through dynamically.

In turn 6, we see Dave indicating that he "knows" Brad is being funny. In turn 8 he then joins in the joke, contributing his own exaggeration *They're ALL mad*, which parallels the Appraisal in Brad's turn 5. Brad's humour has thus led to Dave's strengthening of his rapport with Brad, and has also shown Brad what a funny guy Dave thinks he is. Immediately we see that Brad is not the only one to use humour in this chat. Humour is often "catching", and here we see both Dave respond humorously, and then Fran in turn 12 with *Like they're coming up the hill are they?*. Significantly, Fran's joke falls flat and is queried seriously when Brad asks *Whaddya mean?* before being abandoned.

As different interactants become involved in the humour, they use different types of humorous devices. While Brad uses humorous hyperbole, Dave uses teasing. Brad never teases Dave. Beginning in turn 20, Dave initiates a tease sequence, signalled as humorous with the rather antiquated appraising words *odds 'n sods subjects*. This teasing enables Dave to distance himself from the attitude to university study that he is expressing, suggesting that "like you, Brad, I can treat it as nonsense". This strategy may create rapport with Brad, but since at the same time the serious meaning is present, and thus Dave is at least in part saying "what you're doing is a waste of time", his humour is also enacting a conflict between his position and the assumed *serious* position of his son.

Unlike reactions to teasing in text 4.1: Mates, Brad responds seriously to the tease, making a request for clarification in turn 21 (*Whaddya mean?*), distancing himself from the teasing by denying the implied humour. Dave clarifies, still in humorous mode, in turn 24 with the pejorative Appraisal *garbage*:

24   Dave   (i) If you're doing an Arts degree (ii) you got a lot of other garbage to do.

However, Brad continues to respond seriously and Brad's seriousness wins out in this instance, as Dave also comes to question seriously in turn 32 by asking not *When are you going to do that junk?* but *When are you gonna do your General Studies?*. Brad's intensified serious response in turn 33 (*I'm doing it NOW*), encoding irritation, functions to make Dave look a bit slow, and a bit silly. It is perhaps Brad's attempt at a put-down, in return for the tease.

For several turns Dave keeps probing, looking (apparently) for serious details, which Brad cannot or will not provide. When Fran laughs quietly after turn 39, she constructs Brad's lack of knowledge about what he is studying as humorous, which has the effect of Dave's shifting to a "lighter" mode, in turn 40, with the *history of Scotch bagpipe playing* suggestion, at which Brad laughs. Thus, just when the father seemed to be getting heavy, Fran lightens the tone by suggesting a humorous interpretation.

At this point, Brad belches, distancing himself from both what goes on at universities and also from any serious discussion of his university career.

Dave succeeds in getting some serious information out of Brad, but as soon as his explanation is given Brad returns to his humorous evaluation of his subjects as *rubbish* (in turn 60), keeping his distance again. When Fran challenges his flippancy in turn 63, asking why Descartes and his cronies are idiots, Brad responds with more humour. The incongruity of his *soil erosion* comparison in turn 66 makes her laugh. And the effect of Brad's use of humour here is to very effectively cut off Fran's challenge.

We now enter a particularly interesting phase of the conversation, from around turn 69, when Brad says:

69   Brad   == (i)I'm wondering these days. (ii)I'm thinking (iii)what the hell ... use is anything that I'm doing at University

At this point Brad seems to be saying serious things, but because he seems locked into a pattern of reacting flippantly to his mother, he again shifts into humour. This shift makes Dave's humorous advice in turn 74 (to get a degree and work for Soil Con) seem to match. Although Brad responds seriously, Dave has already gone on to make his suggestion into a tease in turn 76:

76   Dave   == (i)And they'd say (ii)"Whaddya know about soil" (iii)and you'd say (iv)"Well I can, (v)I know how, (vi)I know (vii)what it's called in Russian ==

Brad responds seriously to this. To Brad's attempts to explain his problem seriously, Dave responds with an offhand remark in turn 78:

78   Dave   == (i)Well you should have thought of that thought of that three years ago Brad.

In these turns from 69 to 79 Brad seems to be trying to express a serious concern he has, i.e. that his university studies are not useful. But while his father seems likely to agree with him, and his mother seems to want to debate the issue, the humorous dynamics make it impossible for any of them to negotiate "seriously" to what extent Brad might be right, and if so what he might do. Instead, the father has to tease the son and the son has to be flippant to the mother. And so the conversation moves on.

Summarizing the use of humour in text 3.1, then, we find, first, that each interactant uses humour to achieve different strategic purposes:

- Brad uses humour to signal his distance from university and academic culture, and also perhaps to ask indirectly for parental support and even advice
- Dave uses humour to tease Brad, and so to maintain a status difference

and thereby interpersonal distance from his adult son
- Fran uses humour responsively to defuse concentrated exchanges, thereby indicating her approval of Brad (she finds him funny) and enacting her supportive, peace-keeping role.

The consequences of humour for the interpersonal relationships between each interactant also reveal a pattern of differences and contradictions, as follows:

- whenever Dave initiates seriously, Brad responds humorously;
- whenever Brad initiates seriously, Dave responds with humour;
- whenever Brad initiates humorously, Dave responds with humour.

This means that the only connection between Dave and Brad is when Dave can back up Brad's humour! Moreover, there is a perverse outcome to their humorous pattern: Brad seems to be saying, at one level, that university is useless, which seems to be entirely congruent with his father's position. However, they are not able to discover this congruence of attitudes because both of them distance their comments behind humour.

Fran is the least successful at humour. She produces only two "funny lines", with one being queried and the other receiving no laughs. Since what is humorous or not is interactively constructed, we can say that the men's reactions do not construct Fran as funny.

The humour in Philosophy, then, supplements the critical social interpretation we developed of the status inequalities being enacted in this excerpt in Chapter 3. While Brad, Dave and Frans' non-reciprocal mood choices enact differences in social roles, their differential uses of humour enact contradictions and conflicts in the social relations between them not just as individuals but also as socialized agents. The relationship between a financially dependent 27-year-old son yet to complete an undergraduate degree and his father, and the relationships between a mother and both her son and husband are fraught with contradictions in a capitalist patriarchal society. Humour both exposes and covers up these tensions, and renders resistance to such habitual socialized patterns of interacting problematic and unlikely.

4.5.6 Summary of humour

The analyses of humour in text 4.1, 1.3 and 3.1 support four claims we wish to make about humour in casual conversation. These are as follows:

1. Humour is used in casual conversation to make it possible for interactants to do serious work while being able to distance themselves from it. There is a sense in which Harry and his "mates" are racist white Australians and mysogynistic; and there is a sense in which Bill is a conceited old patriarch; and there is a sense in which Brad, too, is racist,

and Dave thinks his son is wasting his time at university. However, none of the interactants could be confronted with such information, and the humorous inflection provides the excuse that they did not really mean it, they were only joking.

2. Humour not only provides distance; it also disguises the serious work that is being achieved through talk. Humour provides interactants in casual conversation with a resource for exercising discursive power, and so slipping out of the non-hierarchic relations of the casual context and into the hierarchic patterns of formal, public contexts. At the same time, however, humour functions to render invisible to interactants that what is being constantly negotiated and contested in casual conversation is power; that they are being positioned and acted upon and socialized as they sit laughing around the table in the kitchen or the lunchroom.

3. Humour, like other linguistic resources we have explored in this book, constructs meanings through difference. Humour arises as interactants make text in contexts which involve conflict, tension, and contradiction. Unlike interactional sociolinguists (e.g. Tannen 1984, 1990), we would not seek to explain the differences as "stylistic misunderstandings". These differences are social, enacting conflicts, tensions and contradictions in the social world.

4. Humour connects the micro-interactive, interpersonal contexts of private life with the macro-social contexts of institutionalized public life. Humour depends on differences whose meanings exceed specific groups or particular interpersonal relationships. Our use of and responses to humour enact our positioning in the culture, not just our personal response to immediately present co-interlocutors.

4.6 CONCLUSION

In this chapter we have presented a range of techniques for analysing the semantic resources interactants draw on to make interpersonal meanings in casual talk. In discussing the results of Appraisal and Involvement analyses, we have linked these linguistic resources to the construction and negotiation of solidarity and difference in attitudes and background. The semantic analyses presented here, combined with the grammatical analyses presented in Chapter 3, provide some initial tools for exploring the ways in which casual conversations achieve serious social effects, while appearing to be no more than ways of "killing time" and "having a few laughs together". In the following chapter we develop a further analytical technique, when we explore the interactive structure of casual talk.

NOTES

1. In New South Wales (Australia), it is illegal to drive a car with blood-alcohol reading of above 0.05. In some countries the limit is 0.08.
2. Although we draw on Martin's analyses of Appraisal and Involvement, we have followed Halliday (1994) in analysing modality as a grammatical system, and thus reviewed modal resources in Chapter 3.
3. An analysis of the evaluative meanings in text 1.2: Tamara, is detailed in Chapter 7, where we combine this analysis with both a generic structure and conversational structure description of gossip, in order to account for the way values and ideological positions are built up through the text.

5 The discourse structure of casual conversation: negotiating support and confrontation

5.1. INTRODUCTION

In the previous chapter we explored ways in which semantic patterns such as humour, involvement and appraisal can be mobilized in the negotiation of solidarity and difference. In this chapter we continue to develop our account of casual conversation as a site for active social work by focusing explicitly on the achievement of interactivity. This will involve, first, a functional interpretation of dialogue as the exchange of speech functions (speech acts), whereby each 'move' in casual talk involves taking on a speech role and positioning other interactants into predicted speech roles. We will then look at the sequencing of moves involved in the joint accomplishment of turn-taking, exploring the unfolding of conversational exchanges. Our analysis will illustrate how the patterns of confrontation and support expressed through conversational structure enable interactants to explore and adjust their alignments and intimacy with each other, and provide evidence of the ongoing negotiation of differences.

5.2. FROM COLLEAGUES TO FRIENDS

The conversational excerpts we have analysed to this point have involved either family groups or workmates. Our analyses have indicated that such contexts are important sites for the exploration of interpersonal relations. Analysis has also shown that, if we can judge from the humour and laughter present, these casual conversations apparently provide at least some enjoyment to their interactants. A common feature of both these contexts is an absence of voluntariness: family members and workplace colleagues are often thrown together by circumstances over which they have little or no control. By contrast, other casual conversations we engage in are optional, for example when we spend time chatting with friends with whom we have chosen to be, in contexts also of our own choosing, away from the home or workplace. Such interactions have the appearance of freedom, of choice. After all, we choose our friends, but have family and workplace colleagues thrust upon us. We choose where we spend our free time with those friends, and what kinds of activities we undertake with them.

One of the social activities enjoyed by white middle-class Anglo-Australians is that of the dinner party, where a group of people voluntarily come together to eat a little and talk a lot. Dinner parties generally involve some participants taking on the role(s) of host. Usually the invited guests do not know each other equally well. Some may be couples, others may be longstanding friends, while some may be meeting for the first time. Where guests are at different levels of familiarity, the dinner party provides an opportunity to explore affective involvement: it offers a context for finding out who is most closely aligned with whom, and what new alignments could potentially be negotiated.

Text 5.1: Allenby below is an excerpt from such a context. In fact, this excerpt is from the same dinner party as text 1.1 (presented in Chapter 1), and occurs immediately following it, about mid-way through a four-hour conversation. As you read text 5.1, you might consider just how this kind of talk is similar to and different from the family and workplace conversations we have already studied. Appraisal and involvement lexis is indicated on the transcript. The analysis presented in the 'conversational structure' column will be explained later in this chapter and can be ignored at this stage.

Text 5.1: Allenby

Participants: David (32), Nick (29), Liz (27), Fay (38), Stephen (28, a New Zealander).

Context: The participants are attending a dinner party hosted by Stephen and his partner (who is in the kitchen throughout the following excerpt). David, Nick and Stephen are longstanding friends who all play bridge semi-professionally. Fay and Liz are novice bridge players who partner each other in local competitions. Fay's partner (not present) is a professional bridge player/teacher, and friend of David, Nick and Stephen. It is through him that Fay and Liz first met David, Nick and Stephen, and began socializing with the bridge community.

Key:
Appraising lexis shown in *italics*
Involvement lexis (vocatives, slang, anti-language and taboo words): <u>underlined</u>.
1, 2, 3 etc: turn numbers
(i), (ii), (iii) etc: clause numbers
O = Opening move
R = Reacting move
D = Developing move
P = Prolonging move
A= Appending move
s = supporting
c = confronting

conversational structure	turn/ move	speaker	text (numbered for clauses)
[pause 7 secs]			
O:I:give opinion	1	David	(i) This conversation needs Allenby.

R:challenge:rebound	2/a	Fay	(i)Oh he's in London (ii)so what can we do?
R:c:contradict	3/a	Nick	(i)We don't want – (ii)we don't need Allenby in the *bloody* conversation.
P:enhance	3/b		(iii)'Cause all you'd get is == him *bloody raving on*
R:D:elaborate	4/a	Fay	[to Liz] == (i)He's a bridge player, a *naughty* bridge player.
P:elaborate	4/b		(ii)He gets banned from everywhere because of his antisocial or drunken behaviour ( )
R:D:extend	5	Nick	(i)And he *just yap yap yaps all the time.*
O:I:question:opinion	6	David	(i)S'pose he gives you a *hard time* Nick?
R:c:contradict	7/a	Nick	(i)Oh I like David a lot.
P:extend	*7/b		(ii))Still but
R:D:elaborate	8	Fay	(i)He has *a very short fuse* with alcohol.
[pause 10 secs. Stephen and Marilyn talking in kitchen]			
O:I:give fact	9/a	Fay	(i)You met his sister that night we were doing the cutting and pasting up.
C:monitor	9/b		(ii)D'you remember?
R:s:acknowledge	10/a	Nick	(i)Oh yea.
P:elaborate	10/b		== (ii)You met Jill.
R:s:acknowledge	11	David	== (i)Oh yea.
R:D:elaborate	12	Fay	(i)That's David's sister.
R:s:acknowledge	13	Liz	(i)Oh right.
A:elaborate	14	Fay	(i)Jill.
O:I:give opinion	15/a	David	(i)Jill's *very bright* actually. (ii)she's *very good.*
R:s:agree	16	Fay	(i)She's *extremely* == *bright*
A:elaborate	17/a	David	== (i)Academ – academically she's probably *brighter* than David …
P:elaborate	17/b		(ii)David's always *precocious* with his …
P:elaborate	17/c		(iii)The *only* sixteen year old *superstar* ( ) arrives in Sydney (iv) to ( ) (v)and straight into the mandies
R:track:check	18	Nick	(i)Straight into the what?
R:track:resolve	19	Fay	(i)Mandies. [laughs]
A:elaborate	20/a	David	(i)He was a *good boy* (ii)but just no tolerance for the alcohol.
P:elaborate	20/b		(iii)I've pulled him out of *so* many fights (iv)it's *ridiculous.*
[pause 5 secs]			
O:I:give fact	21/a	David	(i)At least he's doing *well* – (ii)at least he's doing *well* in London.

P:elaborate	21/b		(iii) He's <u>cleaning them up</u>.
	22	Nick	( )
?R:re-challenge	23	David	(i) Well, he rang Roman – (ii) he rang Roman a week ago
R:track:confirm	24/a	Nick	(i) Did he?
R:c:disavow	24/b		(ii) I didn't know that.
R:track:clarify	24/c		(iii) What he rang Denning Road did he?
R:resolve	NV1	David	[nods]
R:track:check	26	Nick	(i) Yea?
R:track:probe	27	Fay	(i) Because Roman lives in Denning Road also?
R:resolve	28	David	(i) Yep.
R:register	29	Fay	(i) Oh.
R:D:extend	30/a	Nick	(i) Not for much longer.
P:enhance	30/b		(i) We're *too messy* for him.
R:D:elaborate	31	David	(i) That's what the cleaner – your cleaner lady cleaned my place thought
R:D:extend	32	Nick	(i) She won't come back to our place.
R:track:check	33	Fay	(i) Who == ?
R:track:probe	34	Stephen	== (i) So it's *that bad*?
R:resolve	35	David	(i) Yea.
R:track:check	36/a	Fay	(i) Who?
R:track:check	36/b		(ii) M?
R:track:clarify	36/c		(iii) What's her name?
R:resolve	37	Nick	(i)) It's Stephanie, I think.
R:register	38/a	Fay	(i) Stephanie!
R:track:clarify	38/b		(ii) Who's Stephanie?
R:resolve	39	Nick	(i) The cleaning lady.
R:resolve	40/a	David	== (i) That's our cleaning lady.
	40/b		(ii) She
R:s:register	41/a	Fay	== (i) Oh, the cleaning lady.
R:s:acknowledge	41/b		(ii) Well I'm sorry.
R:D:elaborate	42/a	David	[to Fay] (i) She used to be our mutual cleaning lady,
P:extend	42/b		(ii) except that she sacked these guys, except Roman.
O:I:demand:opinion	42/c		[to Nick] (iv) I mean you've got to admit (v) Roman is *absolutely* the *cleanest* guy in the flat.
R:c:contradict	43/a	Nick	(i) But he's *TOO clean*
P:enhance	43/b		(ii) Because you know like he gets *upset* about things.
R:D:extend	44	Fay	(i) He kept telling me (ii) I've got a <u>big</u> operation on with ( )
R:D:enhance	45/a	Nick	(i) The *trouble* with Roman though is that – (ii) you know he does still like cleaning up.

P:extend	45/b		(iii) But he but he y'know like, (iv) he has dinner parties *all the time,* (v) he – and he cooks *all the time,* (vi) he MAKES *all the mess all the time* as well, you know ( ) sort of.
C:monitor	45/c		(vii) You know?
R:c:contradict	46/a	David	(i) No.
R:challenge:counter	46/b		(ii) You don't understand Nick – (iii) you.
P:elaborate	46/c		(iv) Guys that do the cleaning up do all of the unseen things that you never thought of (v) like putting out the garbage and
R:refute	47	Nick	(i) I – (ii) no no – (iii) I always put out the garbage.
R:challenge:rebound	48	David	(i) When was the last time you put out the garbage?
R:refute	49	Nick	(i) Today.
R:rebound	50/a	David	[shocked amazement] (i) *ToDAY!*
R:track:clarify	50/b		(ii) What, before bridge?
R:challenge:detach	51	Fay	(i) So huh [non-verbal!]
R:challenge:detach	52	Nick	(i)) So <u>stick</u> that!
R:track:clarify	53	David	(i) Before bridge?
R:resolve	54	Nick	(i) Yes.
R:track:probe	55/a	Fay	(i) Does your garbage go on Sunday morning?
R:register	55/b		(ii) <u>Good grief!</u>
P:extend	55/c		(iii) Mine goes Monday morning.
R:resolve	56/a	Nick	(i) Ours goes Monday.
R:challenge:rebound	56/b		[to David] – (ii) *See!*
P:elaborate	56/c		(iii) I *even* know (iv) when garbage day is.
	57	David	( )
R:D:enhance	58/a	Fay	(i) Just making sure (ii) you don't <u>miss the boat.</u>
P:extend	58/b		(iii) I put it out on Monday mornings. (iv) I hear them. (v) I hate the trucks. (vi) They go == *roaring* up
R:D:extend	59/a	Nick	== (i) Well we've got a whole lot of garbage tins (ii) that's *good.*
P:extend	59/b		(iii) But you got to fill them up (iv) before everyone else does.
		Stephen	[into microphone of tape-recorder]
O:I:give opinion	60		(i) I hope (ii) this is a new one for the recorder.
R:s:nv	61	Nick	[laughs]
A:elaborate	62	Stephen	(i) A *garbage* discussion!
R:nv	NV2	All	[laughter]

Compared with text 4.1: Mates, the workplace conversation presented in Chapter 4, this conversation may seem rather tame, and much more politically correct. Compared with text 3.1: Philosophy, the family conversation, text 5.1: Allenby appears a far more evenly shared conversation. But perhaps the most striking difference between text 5.1 and the other texts we have seen so far is that for much of Allenby interactants are talking about absent others. Whereas in text 3.1: Philosophy, Brad and his interests were the major topic of conversation, and then in text 4.1: Mates the group collaborated to get John as both speaker and topic much of the time, in text 5.1: Allenby we find that the talk first deals with Allenby himself, then his sister, then a friend of his, Roman, and even Stephanie, the cleaning lady. It is only in the final section of the chat that the focus shifts to the participants, Nick and Fay, who are present at the dinner party.

We suggest that it is not accidental that the participants in text 5.1 talk about absent other people. Allenby is a conversation in which different levels of familiarity are operating among the five participants. Through their talk about absent third persons, the participants are able to signal and explore the different ways in which each participant present is involved with each other participant.

The choice of a topic-person, e.g. Allenby who is not known to some of the participants, provides a device for signalling one's status as a core insider while simultaneously excluding some interactants from full participation. For example, Liz, who does not know Allenby or his sister or friends, remains silent. However, the topic offers the others present useful openings for encouraging the development of closer affective involvement. For example, Fay and Nick both try to fill Liz in, in turns 4 and 5, and 9 to 14. For all the participants, then, the topic provides a means of exploring relationships within the group. This exploration would be far more restricted if the topic of talk were a present person, since other present participants might feel inhibited about expressing true opinions and reactions.

This talk about third persons, however, is not 'gossipy' in the way the talk about Tamara is in text 1.2. No particular stories are developed around the people mentioned, and there is as much positive appraisal of Allenby as there is negative censure of him. Nonetheless, a great deal of appraisal work is being done through the talk, as can be seen from Table 5.1, which summarizes Appraisal choices in text 5.1: Allenby.

As Table 5.1 shows, of the five interactants present only three are responsible for most of the talking. Of those three, Nick speaks most, with Fay and David producing an almost equal number of clauses. However, if we were to conclude from this that Nick, David and Fay play more or less equivalent roles in the conversation we would be very much mistaken. The Appraisal results provide the first evidence that these participants are involved in the conversation in quite different ways.

The most striking result captured by Table 5.1 is that while Nick and David use about equivalent amounts of appraisal as a proportion of their speaking time, Fay uses very little Appraisal. Nick appraises most and the most frequent category he uses is amplifications (both enrich and augment), although he also makes judgements of social esteem and social sanction. For David, judgement is the major category. This suggests that David is the most oriented to social evaluations. He seems to be willing to make judgements about people, and is concerned to classify people according to their social behaviour. Nick, on the other hand, is less judgemental, and more emphatic. He is concerned to express his affective responses and appreciation of people and events as much as he judges other people.

Table 5.1 Summary of Appraisal in text 5.1: Allenby

·	Nick	David	Fay	Stephen	Liz
total Appraisal items	21	16	5	2	0
total clauses	41	31	32	4	1
Appreciation					
reaction	1	1		0	
composition	1	0		0	
valuation	0	0		1	
total	2	1		1	
Affect					
un/happiness	0	0			
in/security	0	0			
dis/satisf/n	2	1			
total	2	1			
Judgement					
social sanction	0	1	1		
social esteem	2	7	2		
total	2	8	3		
Amplification					
enrich	2	1	1	0	
augment	12	5	1	1	
mitigate	1	0	0	0	
total	15	6	2	1	

Intriguingly, Fay seems excluded from expressing her own affective responses or appreciations. She judges minimally, and only following David's initiating judgements, for example, in turn 16.

The Appraisal results suggest that although Nick, David and Fay contribute almost equally to the talk, Nick and David are more willing to express their personal opinions than is Fay. This suggestion of different levels of familiarity or openness is reinforced by the Involvement patterns in the excerpt.

Only two vocatives are used in text 5.1, both produced by David and both targeting Nick only. This suggests that David is concerned to indicate a special relationship with Nick, to the exclusion of the women. David's use of slang when talking to Nick reinforces this (e.g. *hard time* in turn 6, and *cleaning them up* in turn 21).

The use of humour also suggests differential participation. Unlike text 4.1: Mates, there is little explicit humour in text 5.1, but what is there is produced by David and Nick, often during exchanges directed to each other. Nick offers a hyperbolic description of Allenby in response to David in turns 3 and 5, when he describes Allenby as *bloody raving on* and as someone who *just yap yap yaps all the time*. In turn 42, David quips that the cleaning lady *sacked* Nick and his flatmate; and in the latter part of the talk David banters with Nick about his claim to have put out the garbage (turns 48–54).

Fay does not initiate any humorous remarks, or if she does they pass unnoticed by the other participants. However, she does laugh at David's description of Allenby (in turn 9), and at Stephen's remarks to the tape recorder (turn 63).

Both Appraisal and Involvement analyses suggest therefore that the apparently equal amounts of talk produced by David and Fay are misleading: the two participants are playing very different roles in the conversation, particularly in the way in which each relates to the principal talker, Nick. But in order to uncover the different kinds of relationships interactants are constructing with each other, we need to look at not just *what* or *who* they are talking about, but *how* they are talking to each other. We need to look, in other words, at how the participants *interact*.

Looking at interaction involves looking at what interactants are doing in relation to each other. For example, when David says *This conversation needs Allenby* (in move 1) he is not just producing a modulated declarative clause about a loquacious bridge player known to some members of his audience. His declarative clause is making a conversational **move**, in this case stating an opinion. His move has implications for his relationships with other interactants, and for what his audience can do next: in stating an opinion (rather than, for example, asking for someone else's) he asserts his role as an initiator, a giver of information. By stating an opinion, and one that implies a negative evaluation of the group's conversational skills (rather than stating some factual information or even a positive opinion), he implies that he is sufficiently intimate with his interactants to present an opinion for discussion. As a negative opinion about the group, David's move carries expectations that it will be followed by further talk, as indeed it is. In her reaction in turn 2 (*Oh he's in London so what can we do?*) Fay positions herself as both co-operatively "in the know" (she provides the audience with further relevant information), while at the same time obliquely confronting the aptness of David's opinion. When Nick directly contradicts David in move 3 with *We don't need Allenby*, he positions himself in direct conflict with David, but also as dependent upon him in that Nick picks up on the proposition David has asserted and simply negates it. Thus, in the first three moves we see David enacting a role of conversational provocateur, Fay a role of essentially co-operative but mildly challenging reactant, and Nick enacting his opposition but also his dependence upon David. At the same time a more independent, less familiar relationship is suggested between Fay and David.

To construct these relationships, interactants draw on topics which are shared or of mutual interest, and they draw on the grammatical and semantic resources of the language: the systems of mood, appraisal, involvement and humour that we explored in Chapters 3 and 4. These ʳ ʲices express degrees of authority, directness, closeness, and dependency. ʲus, David produces a full declarative clause to set up the proposition for ʲiscussion, making the nominalization *this conversation* Subject and using ʲhe modality *needs* to depersonalize his claim (he does not begin *You guys are lousy conversationalists*). Fay's use of a modulated interrogative clause in turn 2 (*so what can we do?*) softens her challenge by offering David a possible way of backing down. He could react to her by saying *Oh yea, you're right, he's in London*. The absence of any modality in Nick's response in turn 3 makes it a clear contradiction, and his rewording of the Subject as *we* brings the real focus of David's judgement out into the open, and his intensifications (*bloody raving on*) add force to his contradictory position.

To account for how people construct relationships with each other through talk, we need then to go beyond the topics they talk about or the grammatical and semantic resources they deploy. We need to be able to give functional labels to the activities they are achieving *as* they talk to each other: activities such as 'questioning', 'challenging', 'supporting', 'stating opinions', etc. If we can label what interactants are doing, and relate the move types to the grammatical and semantic resources they use to do them, then we have very sophisticated tools for exploring the negotiation of interpersonal relationships in talk.

5.3 ANALYSING INTERACTIVITY: FROM GRAMMAR AND SEMANTICS TO DISCOURSE

One important implication of our discussion so far is that the grammatical and semantic analyses presented in Chapters 3 and 4 need to be augmented by an analysis of move types, what we call below **speech functions**. You may wonder why we cannot simply take each of the clause moods we identified in Chapter 2 and give a new 'move' label to each one. The reason for this is that there is not a one-to-one match between particular mood structures and particular discourse functions. For example, if we look at excerpt 5.1: Allenby, we can note the following:

- that the same grammatical structures can perform different interactive functions
- that the clauses of different mood types can achieve equivalent interactive functions

For example, consider the following moves from text 5.1: Allenby:

C:monitor	9b	Fay	(ii) D'you remember?
R:track:check	18	Nick	(i) Straight into the what?
R:track:probe	27	Fay	(i) Because Roman lives in Denning Road also?

All three moves are expressed by interrogative clauses. However, the function of each move differs: while move 9b is used to elicit confirmation of points already made by the speaker, move 18 is used to check on a detail that has been misheard, and move 27 is used to probe information left implicit.

Similarly, the declarative mood structure is sometimes used to start the flow of talk, while at other times declaratives are used in reacting to prior talk. For example:

| O:I:give opinion | 15/a | David | (i) Jill's very bright actually. (ii) she's very good. |
| R:s:agree | 16 | Fay | (i) She's extremely == bright |

While David's declaratives initiate by stating his opinion, Fay's declarative in 16 offers a supporting response.

As well as noting that clauses of the same mood type can perform different conversational jobs in different contexts, so we can note that clauses of different mood types can be doing the same things. Thus it is possible to challenge a speaker using a variety of moods, as the following examples indicate:

(i)   challenging using a declarative clause:

| R:challenge:counter | 46/b | David | (ii) You don't understand Nick – (iii) you. |

(ii)   challenging using an interrogative clause:

| R:challenge:rebound | 48 | David | (i) When was the last time you put out the garbage? |

(iii) challenging with a minor clause and non-verbal action

| R:challenge:detach | 51 | Fay | (i) So huh [non-verbal!] |

These examples indicate that there is an important distinction to be made between the grammatical structure of clauses and the discourse function they perform in a particular conversational context.

At the same time discourse function and grammatical form are somehow related. There does seem to be some kind of tie between the grammatical form 'interrogative' and the discourse function 'question', and the grammatical form 'imperative' and the discourse function 'command'. We need to retain this relationship of typicality between grammatical form and discourse function, while recognizing that what is typical need not, and does not, always occur.

Thus, we need two ways of looking at dialogue: from the point of view of grammar (the constituent mood structures of conversational clauses) and from the point of view of discourse (the types of moves made in an interactive context). The first tells us primarily about the linguistic rights and privileges of social roles in the culture; the second tells us primarily how, while enacting those social roles, participants are constantly negotiating relationships of solidarity and intimacy. The two together contribute to our understanding of how participants enact their interpersonal differences in casual conversation, and therefore how power is ongoingly negotiated through talk.

As indicated in Chapter 2, there are various different approaches to dealing with discourse interactivity, with major contributions coming from CA, with its account of the mechanics of turn-taking, Speech Act theory, with its identification of the different illocutionary forces of utterances, Pragmatics, with the meanings of utterances interpreted contextually, and the Birmingham School, with its hierarchy of discourse units identified on structural criteria. All these accounts contribute to our understanding of discourse structure. However, in this chapter we concentrate on developing the systemic functional model of dialogue, as initially presented in Halliday's functional-semantic account of dialogue (1984, 1994). We focus on Halliday's account for four reasons:

i) Halliday's analysis of dialogue sets out to describe exhaustively all moves in casual talk. While the description allows for variation in the degree of delicacy with which move classes are identified, it assigns all moves to one or other initial class, thus enabling the comprehensive coding of continuous conversational excerpts. This exhaustiveness contrasts with CA and Speech Act accounts, which deal only with certain very visible types of adjacency pairs or illocutionary acts.

ii) The systemic analysis explicitly relates move types to grammatical classes (i.e clause types), positing an 'unmarked' relationship between particular move types and their expression in particular mood classes. This means that criteria can be developed for identifying move types, and avoids the sometimes ad hoc or purely lexical basis of analytical categories in CA or logico-philosophic accounts.

iii) Because the account of discourse structure in systemics is incorporated within a comprehensive contextual model of language, it provides a way of relating patterns in move choices to the interpersonal context of interaction. Through the register variable of tenor, patterns in discourse interactivity can be related to contextual variables such as status relations, affective involvement and frequency of contact. This semiotic perspective avoids the mechanistic explanations of CA and the cognitive-intentionalist explanations of logico-philosophic approaches, neither of which we find adequate to explain the relationship between micro-interactional patterns and macro-social structures.

iv) The functional-semantic account of dialogue proposed by Halliday (and extended by other scholars, as reviewed below) proposes an extremely rich description of the meanings of moves in talk. As such it renders largely unnecessary the application of rigid exchange formula of the type developed within the Birmingham School. While such constituent models of conversational sequences have been demonstrated to have relevance in the description of the interactive structure of pragmatic interactions, they do not transfer easily to casual conversational data. Our discussion will demonstrate that a great deal can be said about the conversational exchange without the imposition of a higher level structural unit.

5.4 A FUNCTIONAL-SEMANTIC INTERPRETATION OF INTERACTION

In the following sections we summarize Halliday's functional-semantic interpretation of dialogue, before considering its implications for the unit of discourse analysis. We then present our own extensions of the description for the analysis of casual conversational data.

5.4.1 Halliday's model of dialogue

Halliday (1984, 1994: 68–71) approaches interaction from a functional-semantic perspective, offering both a way of describing dialogic structure explicitly and quantifiably, and a way of interpreting dialogic structure as the expression of interpersonal relations.

He points out that whenever someone uses language to interact, one of the things they are doing is establishing a relationship: between the person speaking now and the person who will probably speak next. Halliday (1984: 11) suggests that dialogue is "a process of exchange" involving two variables:

1. a commodity to be exchanged: either information or goods and services
2. roles associated with exchange relations: either giving or demanding.

The simultaneous cross-classification of these two variables of exchange-commodity and exchange-role define the four basic **speech functions** of English, i.e. the four basic types of moves interactants can make to initiate a piece of dialogue. These basic speech functions are displayed in Table 5.2.

Table 5.2 Speech roles and commodities in interaction

Speech role	Commodity exchanged	
	Information	Goods-and-Services
Giving	statement	offer
Demanding	question	command

Source: based on Halliday 1994: 69

The built-in interactivity of dialogue arises from the implication that speech roles position both speaker and potential respondent:

> When the speaker takes on a role of giving or demanding, by the same token he assigns a complementary role to the person he is addressing. If I am giving, you are called on to accept; if I am demanding, you are called on to give. (Halliday 1984: 12)

We also need to see that there is a choice between initiating and responding moves. For example, in text 5.1: Allenby, when David states in move 1 *This conversation needs Allenby* he is making a statement (in this case of his own opinion), and his statement is largely independent of prior talk. Linguistically, this independence is marked by two main features of David's speech:

- he uses a full determiner + noun nominal group (*this conversation*) rather than a presuming reference item (e.g. *it*);
- he produces a complete non-elliptical clause, with a Subject, Finite/Predicator and Complement.

Fay's comment *Oh he's in London so what can we do?* is said in reaction to David's comment, and is therefore a responding move. A number of linguistic features mark Fay's comment as dependent on David's initiation:

- she begins her move with the continuity Adjunct *oh*, explicitly signalling that her contribution relates to prior talk and implying that her utterance is a qualification to that prior talk (the *oh* implies *oh BUT*)
- she replaces David's use of the name *Allenby* with the pronoun *he*, thus tying the interpretation of her move back to David's.

As Halliday's notion of speech roles implies, our choice of responding moves is constrained by the initiating move that has just been made. This is the functional-semantic reinterpretation of CA's notion of sequential implicativeness (discussed in Chapter 2). Every time speakers take on a role, they assign to the listener(s) a role as well. Every time a speaker initiates an interaction, the listener is put into a role of Responding if they want to interact. As Halliday explains:

> Even these elementary categories already involve complex notions: giving means 'inviting to receive', and demanding means 'inviting to give'. The speaker is not only doing something himself; he is also requiring something of the listener. Typically, therefore, an 'act' of speaking is something that might more appropriately be called an 'interact'; it is an exchange in which giving implies receiving and demanding implies giving in response. (1994:68)

Halliday captures this interactivity by pairing each of the four basic initiating speech functions with a desired or expected response, which may or may not be verbalized. These expected responses constitute the preferred second-pair part of the adjacency pair. Since there is always the possibility of an interactant producing a response other than the expected one, Halliday also recognizes 'discretionary alternatives', the dispreferred responses of CA.

These alternative responses can be broadly differentiated as either supporting or confronting. Supporting responses enact consensus and agreement. For example, acknowledging a statement or answering a question are both supporting moves. Confronting responses enact disagreement or non-compliance. For example, disclaiming knowledge rather than acknowledging, declining to answer a question or refusing an offer all enact (verbally) some degree of confrontation.

The labels supporting/confronting avoid the use of terms such as 'preferred/expected' and 'dispreferred/discretionary' which imply that these responses differ principally in terms of frequency. The issue is not whether preferred or predicted responses occur more frequently – in registers like casual conversation dispreferred responses are actually more common, for reasons we will come to later. The difference has to do with the implications for the exchange. While both types of responses engage with the proposition put forward in the initiation (i.e. they do not seek to challenge or undermine it), supporting responses tend to close off the exchange, as the proposition has been resolved. Confronting responses, on the other hand, are often followed by further negotiation, as respondents may either volunteer or be asked to provide justifications or explanations.

Incorporating this relabelling, we can now summarize Halliday's outline of the semantics of dialogue in Table 5.3.

Thus far, Halliday's account can be read as a reinterpretation in functional-semantic terms of the adjacency pair. However, Halliday extends on CA and also Speech Act theory interpretations of conversational structure by linking this discourse structure to both context (what is going on in the dialogic situation) and to grammar (the clause system of mood).

The link between speech function and context is that the social role that participants are occupying in an interaction will constrain the speech functions they have access to when interacting with specific others. Thus,

Table 5.3 Speech function pairs

Initiating speech function	Responding speech functions	
	supporting	confronting
offer	acceptance	rejection
command	compliance	refusal
statement	acknowledgement	contradiction
question	answer	disclaimer

Source: adapted from Halliday 1994: 69

for example, the social role of 'teacher' gives access to the full range of initiating speech functions when interacting with students, while the social role of 'student' places constraints on both the frequency and types of initiations that can be made to the teacher (and to other students).

This link between social context and linguistic choices recalls the analysis of text 3.1: Philosophy in Chapter 3, where analysis suggested that social roles constrain grammatical choices. Adding speech functions to our account now allows us to clarify this relationship between social context and language as each speech function is associated with a typical mood structure, as summarized in Table 5.4.

Table 5.4 Speech functions and typical mood in clause

Speech function	Typical mood in clause
statement	declarative
question	interrogative
command	imperative
offer	modulated interrogative
answer	elliptical declarative
acknowledgement	minor (or non-verbal)
accept	minor (or non-verbal)
compliance	minor (or non-verbal)

While suggesting this pattern is the **congruent** one (involving an unmarked association between discourse function and grammatical form), Halliday points out that very frequently we encounter **incongruent** realizations of speech functions. This occurs when a speech function is *not* realized by the predicted mood type. For example, consider David's clause selection in move 6 of text 5.1: Allenby:

O:I:question:opinion	6	David	(i)S'pose he gives you a hard time Nick?

Here David uses a declarative to ask Nick for his opinion (rather than the congruent interrogative *Does he give you a hard time Nick?*). Incongruence also occurs in move 42c:

O:I:demand:opinion	42/c	[to Nick] (iv)I mean you've got to admit (v)Roman is absolutely the cleanest guy in the flat.

In this move the declarative David uses is an incongruent way of demanding Nick's agreement. Congruently he might have used an imperative structure: *Admit Roman is the cleanest guy.*

Table 5.5 summarizes congruent and incongruent mood choices for the four basic speech functions:

Table 5.5 Congruent and incongruent realizations of speech functions

Speech function	Congruent clause mood	Incongruent clause mood
command	imperative	modulated interrogative, declarative
offer	modulated interrogative	imperative, declarative
statement	declarative	tagged declarative
question	interrogative	modulated declarative

5.4.2 Units of discourse analysis: turns and moves

As we have noted above, grammatical form and discourse function are not equivalent: we are dealing with two different types of patterns, closely related but distinct. One of the implications of this is that the discourse patterns of speech function are carried not by grammatical units, such as the clause, but by a discourse unit, a unit sensitive to interactive function. The most obvious discourse unit is the turn: all the talk produced by one speaker before another speaker gets in. However, although turns are very important units in casual talk, we cannot use them to analyse speech function because, as we can easily demonstrate, one turn can realize several speech functions. For example:

R:D:elaborate	42/a	David	[to Fay] (i)She used to be our mutual cleaning lady,
C:extend	42/b		(ii)except that she sacked these guys, except Roman.

O:I:demand:opinion	42/c		[to Nick] (iv)I mean you've got to admit (v)Roman is absolutely the cleanest guy in the flat.

Here we see that within a single turn at talk, David is in fact achieving at least two quite different discourse tasks. First, he is responding to Fay's query about Stephanie, and second he is provoking Nick into a discussion of the relative cleanliness of the people flat-sharing in Denning Road. This change of addressee clearly indicates that David is making a number of moves in a single turn. However, multi-purpose turns can still happen even when the addressee remains constant. For example, we have already pointed out that when Nick responds to David's first move, he is actually achieving two tasks in a single turn:

R:c:contradict	3/a	Nick	(i)We don't want – (ii)we don't need Allenby in the bloody conversation.
C:enhance	3/b		(iii)'Cause all you'd get is == him bloody raving on

He both declares his disagreement, and he offers a justification for doing so. The fact that two rather than just one task are being performed here can be seen by realizing that Nick could have stopped at the end of his first move, at which point we would only have known his position, but not his justifications, which David might then have tried to elicit.

Examples like these demonstrate that while the turn is indeed a significant unit in the analysis of conversation, it is *not* necessarily equivalent with discourse functions.

As explained above, Halliday's account of dialogue sets up speech function as a separate discourse level of analysis, expressed through grammatical patterns. These two types of patterns are carried by different linguistic units. As we saw in Chapter 2, the grammatical patterns of mood are expressed through **clauses**. Halliday suggests that the discourse patterns of speech function are expressed through **moves**.

Moves and clauses do not relate to each other in terms of size or constituency: moves are not 'made up of' clauses, and clauses are not 'parts of' moves. The relationship is one of expression, or, more technically, **realization**: moves, which are discourse units, are expressed in language through clauses, which are grammatical units.

While you may feel that this account makes life very complex for the conversational analyst by recognizing both clauses and moves, there are good reasons for needing two separate (though related) units. Just as we saw earlier in this chapter that one mood type could be achieving different speech functions in different contexts, so we find that a single speech function can sometimes be achieved through a single clause, as in move 1 in text 5.1: Allenby:

> O:l:give opinion   1   David   (i)This conversation needs Allenby.

At other times, however, a speech function is achieved through several linked clauses (i.e through a sentence), as with move 15a from text 5.1.

> O:l:give opinion   15/a   David   (i)Jill's very bright actually. (ii)she's very good.

In this example two clauses realize the single speech function of stating an opinion.

Although we need to recognize the distinction between moves and clauses, we also need to recognize their close association, which can again be described in terms of congruence. Just as there is a congruent relationship between speech functions and mood choices (e.g. a command is congruently realized as an imperative), so we find that congruently a move is realized as a clause. However, we also need to be able to analyse those instances of incongruence, where a move is realized by a grammatical unit other than a clause.

While Halliday identified the move as the unit which expressed speech functions, he did not discuss the identification of moves in any detail and so did not address the complex issues which face the analyst of authentic casual conversation. In the following section we detail the criteria we have developed for the identification of moves in casual talk.

5.4.3 Identifying 'moves' in casual conversation

As the above discussion implies, the move is closely related to the turn-taking organization of conversation. In fact, we regard the move as a functional-semantic reinterpretation of the turn-constructional unit (TCU) of CA (discussed in Chapter 2). The end of a move indicates a point of possible turn-transfer, and therefore carries with it the idea that the speaker "could stop here". A move is a unit after which speaker change could occur without turn transfer being seen as an interruption.

From a practical perspective, however, we need to know just how to recognize moves in a stretch of talk. As explained above, the move is a unit of discourse organization, not of grammar, and is therefore a separate unit from the clause. However, while the clause and the move are distinct units, so fundamental to language structure is the clause that most of the time a move is realized by a clause: that is, most clauses are moves, and most moves are clauses.

In determining whether in a particular instance a clause is a move, two criteria must be considered together:

i)   the grammatical dependence or independence of the clause (whether the clause has made independent mood selection);

ii)   prosodic factors (whether the end of a clause corresponds to the end of a rhythmic/intonational unit).

These two criteria capture the dual identity of the move as *both* a unit encoding mood choice *and* a unit sensitive to turn-taking. We will briefly review each of these criteria.

i) Grammatical criteria in move identification Martin's (1992:40) definition of a move as *a clause which selects independently for mood* is a useful point of departure, although not sufficient on its own. Thus, clauses which do not select independently for mood (i.e. which for various reasons are bound to take the mood of a clause to which they are linked) generally do not function as separate moves. The most common reason for a clause not selecting independently for mood is that it is grammatically dependent upon, or subordinated to, a main clause. This means that the following three combinations of clauses frequently constitute a single move:

a) Dependent clauses and the main clause on which they depend. Where the dependent clause occurs in first position, it carries strong structural implications that the speaker has not yet finished their move. Hence examples such as the following are easy to treat as single moves:

| 25 | Dave | (i) If you're doing an Arts degree (ii) you got a lot of other garbage to do. |
| 60 | Brad | (i) If you wanted to (ii) you could do ... (iii) you could do ALL your points in the one year. |

With subordinated structures where the main clause comes *first* and the dependent clause(s) *follow*, we are usually dealing with a single move but here prosodic criteria need to be considered (see discussion below). For example, in turn 59 Nick states:

| R:D:extend | 59/a | Nick | == (i) Well we've got a whole lot of garbage tins (ii) that's good. |
| C:extend | 59/b | | (iii) But you got to fill them up (iv) before everyone else does. |

Here the dependent (subordinate) clause *before everyone else does* is produced after the main clause on which it depends, and without any pausing or break between them. The two clauses therefore constitute a single move.

b) Embedded clauses. An embedded clause is a clause operating within another clause, e.g. as a post-modification or noun clause. For example, text 5.1. turn 9/a:

| O:I:give fact | 9/a | Fay | (i) You met his sister that night we were doing the cutting and pasting up. |

In this turn *we were doing the cutting and pasting up* is a clause embedded as a post-modifier of the noun *night*. An embedded clause cannot select its own mood but is implicated in the mood choice of the clause within which it is embedded. For this reason, embedded clauses generally do not constitute separate moves, unless they are produced as 'add-ons' (see below).

c) Quoting or reporting clauses, both direct and indirect. Where one clause involves a verb of thinking or saying and the next or previous clause includes what was said or thought, the two function together as a single move, as again such clauses are grammatically dependent. For example:

O:I:demand:opinion	42/c	[to Nick] (iv)I mean you've got to admit (v)Roman is absolutely the cleanest guy in the flat.

Although there is a clause boundary after *admit*, the second clause which completes what it is that Nick has to admit, is bound to choose declarative mood as selected in the main clause. The two clauses are therefore just one move. This is also the case with a mental clause projection such as the following:

	Stephen	[into microphone of tape-recorder]
O:I:give opinion	60	(i)I hope (ii)this is a new one for the recorder.

Stephen's move is not complete after *I hope*: we need to know just what he hopes, and the declarative choice of the main clause must be echoed in the mood of the dependent clause. Hence the second projected clause is part of the same move. These criteria apply also to direct quoting of speech. For example, in turn 6/d from text 1.2 : Tamara:

8/a	Jenny	She said, "Have you seen any
8/b		photos of me at the fancy dress?"

Although this example consists of two clauses it is treated as only one move.

ii) Prosodic criteria in move identification Not all grammatically dependent clauses form moves with their main clause, nor are all grammatically independent clauses separate moves. The identification of a move depends also on rhythm and intonation, as these systems interact with grammatical structure to signal points of possible turn transfer, i.e. move boundaries. There is significant pressure in casual talk to minimize turn-length, especially in multi-party talk, where competition is high. The clause is signalled as a "complete" unit, not only through its grammatical structure but also through prosodic patterns: clauses express a complete tone contour (one at least), and are frequently followed by brief or extended pauses. While grammatical boundaries of the clause generally signal points at which turn-transfer can occur, speakers can delay turn-transfer, or make it less likely, by not aligning grammatical and prosodic boundaries. Thus, rather than breaking between clauses, slowing down and finalizing tone contour, speakers can instead speed up, delay tone realization and rush on into the second or subsequent clause. This is the phenomenon of **run-on**.

Two clauses which are grammatically independent (and therefore may select independently for mood), may be produced with run-on: i.e. no rhythmic or intonational break at the clause boundary. Since run-on is a strategic manoeuvre which speakers use to try to avoid losing the turn, run-ons are treated as a single move. For example:

R:challenge:rebound	2/a	Fay	(i)Oh he's in London (ii)so what can we do?

Here Fay rushes straight on from her first clause to produce a second, co-ordinated clause. Although the second clause is grammatically independent and each clause selects a different mood, prosodically the two clauses are packaged as a single discourse unit, and are therefore treated as a single move.

Subordinated structures, where the main clause appears first and is then followed by its dependent(s), may also be produced with or without run-on. Where there is no run-on, each clause is functioning as a separate move since the speaker "could have stopped" after the first clause. For example:

R:c:contradict	43/a	Nick	(i)But he's TOO clean
C:enhance	43/b		(ii)Because you know like he gets upset about things.

Here Nick's second clause is added as an afterthought, and so is considered a second move.

What we are claiming here, then, is that move identity depends on the co-occurrence of grammatical and prosodic boundaries, as indeed was recognized (although not systematically stated) by Sacks *et al.* (1974). This claim points to the importance of transcription in conversational analysis, as also noted by CA. While it is not necessary to be highly skilled in the rhythmic and intonational analysis of the kind developed by Halliday (1994), it is important to listen repeatedly to the original taped data in order to determine move boundaries. However, if in doubt about move division, the safest criteria to fall back on are grammatical ones, as outlined above.

5.4.4 Applying the basic speech function classes

Once an excerpt of talk has been divided into moves, the speech function system outlined by Halliday can be used to code the talk exhaustively, which shows the distribution of initiating to responding, giving to demanding roles. Such information tells us about the relationships between the interactants in a situation, particularly in terms of the distribution of power amongst them. For example, we can use the twelve basic speech function labels to analyse text 1.4 (the pragmatic interaction in the post office presented in Chapter 1). This analysis is presented in Table 5.6.

Table 5.6 Speech functions in text 1.4: Post Office

Turn	Speaker	Talk	Speech function
1	Salesperson	yes please	OFFER
2	Customer	can I have these two like that	COMMAND
3	S	yes	COMPLIANCE
4	S	one's forty-five	Compliance (cont.)
5	S	one's twenty-five	Compliance (cont.)
6	C	and have you got ... the ... first day covers of ...	COMMAND
7	S	yes	COMPLIANCE
8	C	(Anzac)	Command (cont.)
9	S	how many would you like	OFFER
10	C	four please	ACCEPTANCE
11	S	two of each?	QUESTION
12	C	what have you got	QUESTION
13	S	uh there's two different designs on the -	ANSWER
14	C	I'll take two of each	ACCEPTANCE
15	S	uhum	–
16	S	right...that's a dollar seventy thank you	COMMAND
17	S	here we are	OFFER
18	C	thank you	ACCEPTANCE
19	S	thank you	–
20	S	dollar seventy that's two four and one's five	OFFER
21	C	thank you very much	ACCEPTANCE
22	S	thank you	–
23	S	they'll be right I'll fix those up in a moment	OFFER
24	C	okay	ACCEPTANCE

Source: data from Ventola 1987: 239–40

The findings from this analysis are summarized in Table 5.7.

Table 5.7 Summary of speech functions in text 1.4: Post Office

	Offer	Acceptance	Command	Compliance	Question	Answer
Salesperson	5	0	1	2	1	1
Customer	0	5	1	0	1	0

As Table 5.7 shows, in text 1.4 speech function use is not reciprocal: the interaction is driven by Offers produced exclusively by the Salesperson, and Acceptances in response from the Customer. Only the Salesperson takes on the roles of Complying and Answering, while both interactants Question and Command.

Already such an analysis gives important evidence of the non-reciprocal discourse demands of the social roles of client and postal clerk. However, in casual conversation the distinctions we need to capture are more subtle than that: it is in the *types* of initiations, and *types* of responses that we see differences created and maintained. While relationships may appear to be based on equality and sameness, a more delicate analysis reveals underlying patterns of inequality and difference. We turn now to our development of Halliday's initial classification to the analysis of speech functions in casual conversation.

5.5 SPEECH FUNCTION CLASSES IN CASUAL CONVERSATION

In order to capture the more subtle speech function patterns of casual conversation, the speech function description needs to be extended in 'delicacy' (i.e. sub-classification needs to be made more detailed). Over the next few pages we present a simplified set of speech functions for analysing casual conversation.[1]

The speech function classes presented are comprehensive, in that all moves should be assignable to one of the classes included. The speech function classes are shown in the form of a 'network', where categories at the lefthand side are the least delicate (most inclusive). Movement towards the right can be read as subclassification, indicating increasing delicacy in the description. Our network is data driven, having been based on the analysis of conversational data such as that presented in this book.

While our network offers a starting-point for the description of any excerpt of casual talk, more subtle subclassifications may need to be developed to reveal patterns of particular interest in specific types of conversational (or other interactive) data. Because of the tie Halliday suggests between speech functions and mood, speech function classes can be more delicately subclassified on a principled basis. The criteria for establishing speech function categories are linguistic, not intuitive: for each class of speech function, realization criteria can be specified drawing principally on the systems of interpersonal meaning. Thus, speech function classes can be defined not only functionally (what a move of each type does in conversation), but also grammatically, in terms of predictable selections of mood and modality, and semantically, in terms of predictable appraisal and involvement choices. Where no linguistic differences can be maintained between categories, the categories are not considered to be analytically justified. Thus, extending the network in delicacy involves specifying ever finer functional and linguistic distinctions between moves, based on a corpus of data.

Figure 5.1 presents an overview of the entire network, showing the major subcategories of speech function classes which will be presented.

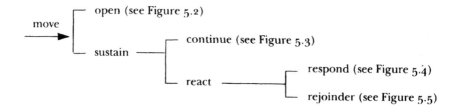

Figure 5.1 Overview of the speech function network

To simplify presentation, the network has been broken into four sections. The discussion which follows each section of the network deals with the following dimensions of each speech function class:

- the meanings of the different speech functions (their discourse purpose);
- their identification (congruent grammatical realizations);
- examples of each speech function class.

Once all the classes of speech functions have been presented, the analytical categories will then be applied to text 5.1: Allenby and text 3.1: Philosophy.

5.5.1 Opening speech functions

Figure 5.2 captures the main resources available to interactants to initiate a sequence of talk[2].

The network in Figure 5.2 captures the difference between conversational moves which begin sequences of talk, or open up new exchanges, and moves which sustain exchanges. Grammatically this difference is usually signalled by actual or potential ellipsis (including forms of replacement ellipsis known as substitution). That is, sustaining moves are related elliptically to prior opening or other sustaining moves, or could be made elliptically dependent upon them. For example, Nick's move 3b (*We don't need Allenby in the bloody conversation*) is not actually elliptical but potentially elliptical in relation to David's initiation (*This conversation needs Allenby*), since Nick could have responded simply *No we don't.* The non-elliptical response in this case may be due to the intervention of Fay.

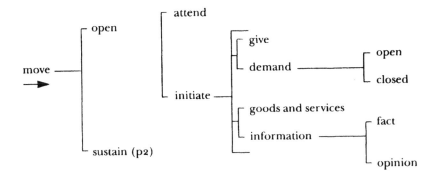

Figure 5.2 Opening speech functions in casual conversation

While opening moves are not elliptically dependent on prior moves, they are usually cohesive in other non-structural ways, such as through lexical or referential cohesion. For example, David's move *This conversation needs Allenby* is cohesive lexically with the earlier excerpt of this conversation presented as text 1.1. (*conversation* links back to *conversation, expressions, French*, etc.), and referentially (*this* refers to the same conversation as in turn 1, text 1.1). However, the move is not elliptically dependent, setting up its own Subject/Finite elements.

The distinction in the network in Figure 5.2 between attending and initiating moves captures the difference between moves which merely set the scene for an interaction, and those which actually get that interaction under way. Attending moves include salutations, greetings and calls, all of which function to prepare the ground for interaction by securing the attention of the intended interactant.[3]

The initiating move options are already familiar from Halliday's earlier work reviewed above, with the basic oppositions between giving and demanding, goods and services and information grammaticalized congruently as in Table 5.4. Only two extensions in delicacy which are outlined below are made in the network in Figure 5.2:

i) The differentiation between fact and opinion information for both statements and questions. For example, contrast *He plays the double-bass* (a statement of fact) with *This conversation needs Allenby* (a statement of opinion). The difference between facts and opinions is usually expressed lexically, with opinions containing either expressions of modality, or appraisal lexis. It is useful to keep track of the fact/opinion difference because degrees of affective involvement frequently impact on the extent to which interactants will freely discuss opinions. Fact and opinion initiations also tend to lead to different types of exchanges, and eventually genres, with opinion exchanges generating arguments, while fact exchanges often remain brief or develop into story-texts.

ii) The differentiation between two types of questions: open questions, which seek to elicit completion of a proposition from the addressee, and closed questions, which present a complete proposition for the support or confrontation of the addressee. Open questions are congruently realized by wh-interrogatives, while closed questions are realized by polar interrogatives. Again, degrees of power, affective involvement, contact and affiliation impact on these choices.

5.5.1.1 *The function of opening moves in casual conversation*

Opening moves, as the name indicates, function to initiate talk around a proposition. Because they involve a speaker in proposing terms for the interaction, they are generally assertive moves to make, indicating a claim to a degree of control over the interaction.

The speech function labels used in coding which derive from the opening move network are summarized in table 5.8.

Table 5.8 Speech function labels for OPENING moves

Speech function	Discourse purpose	Congruent mood	Example
attending	attention seeking	minor; formulaic	Hey David!
offer	give goods and services	modulated interrogative	Would you like some more wine?
command	demand goods and services	imperative	Look.
statement:fact	give factual information	full declarative; no modality; no appraisal	You met his sister
statement:opinion	give attitudinal /evaluative information	full declarative; modality and/or appraising lexis	This conversation needs Allenby.
question:open:fact	demand factual information	wh-interrogative; no modality; no appraisal	What's Allenby doing these days?
question:closed:fact	demand confirmation/ agreement with factual information	polar interrogative; no modality; no appraisal	Is Allenby living in London now?
question:open:opinion	demand opinion information	wh-interrogative; modality/appraisal	What do we need here?
question:closed:opinion	demand agreement with opinion information	polar interrogative; modality/appraisal	Do we need Allenby in this conversation?

5.5.2 Sustaining: continuing speech functions

While opening moves initiate negotiation of a particular configuration of Mood constituents, sustaining moves remain "with" the Mood structure set up in an initiation. In other words, sustaining moves keep negotiating the same proposition. Sustaining talk may be achieved either by the speaker who has just been talking (continuing speech functions), or by other speakers taking a turn (reacting speech functions). Figure 5.3 displays the speech function network for the first group of sustaining moves, the continuing moves.

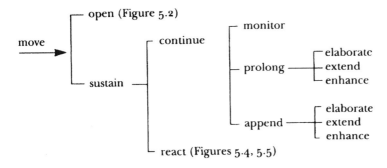

Figure 5.3 Sustaining: continuing speech functions in casual conversation

The part of the speech function network represented in Figure 5.3 captures the fact (noted by Sacks *et al.* 1974) that the turn-taking system of conversation allows for either the current speaker to keep talking (continue) or for another interactant to take over the speaker role (react). The continuing move subclasses then capture the options open to a speaker who retains the turn at the end of a move and who produces a move which is (meant to be) heard as related to an immediately prior move produced by the same speaker. The continuing status of a move will be realized by its potential or actual elliptical status in relation to the prior move. The prior move may be of any speech function class.

A continuing speaker has two main options: to monitor or to prolong. We will review each subclass in turn.

5.5.2.1 *Monitoring moves*

Monitoring involves deploying moves in which the speaker focuses on the state of the interactive situation, for example by checking that the audience is following, or by inviting another speaker to take the turn, in which case the invited response is set up as a supporting response. For example:

| O:I:give fact | 9/a | Fay | (i) You met his sister that night we were doing the cutting and pasting up. |
| C:monitor | 9/b | | (ii) D'you remember? |

In 9b Fay prompts Liz to acknowledge her statement, with a clause which is elliptically tied to 9/a (i.e. *D'you remember you met his sister?*). Here is a similar example:

R:D:enhance	45/a	Nick	(i) The trouble with Roman though is that – (ii) you know he does still like cleaning up.
P:extend	45/b		(iii) But he but he y'know like, (iv) he has dinner parties all the time, (v) he – and he cooks all the time, (vi) he MAKES all the mess all the time as well, you know ( ) sort of.
C:monitor	45/c		(vii) You know?

In move 45/c Nick offers the speaker role to David, implying that David will demonstrate agreement with his analysis of Roman's faults – even though he might know that the likelihood of David agreeing is very slight. Again, the monitoring move is elliptical, depending on all the prior clauses in his turn.

5.5.2.2 *The function of monitoring moves in casual conversation*

As monitoring moves imply a readiness to hand over the turn, they are moves which indicate an interest in deferring to or including other speakers, and in seeking support for one's own position.

5.5.2.3 *Prolonging moves*

Prolonging moves are those where a continuing speaker adds to their contribution by providing further information. These categories capture the fact that very often we do not say all that we want to say in one single move. To describe the prolonging options, we draw on Halliday's categories of logico-semantic relations (Halliday 1994: 225ff, 324–6), particularly the three types of expansion (elaboration, extension and enhancement, explained below). In Halliday (1994) elaboration, extension and enhancement are presented as grammatical categories referring to logico-semantic relations between clauses in clause complexes (sentences). In Halliday and Matthiessen (forthcoming), these logico-semantic categories are also used in a more abstract sense, to model relations between linguistic structures at various different levels. It is in this extended interpretation of expansion that we use its subcategories to describe the relationship between moves in sequence.

Thus, we interpret the relation between a speech function and its prolonging continuation as one of expansion: a prolonging move builds on or fills out the move it is logically connected with. More specifically, the relationship between a first move and its prolonging sequel(s) may be one of (i) elaboration, (ii) extension or (iii) enhancement.

i) Elaborations In elaborations, a move clarifies, restates or exemplifies an immediately prior move. An elaborating relationship could be made explicit by the insertion of conjunctions such as: *for example, like, I mean* between the two related moves. However, in rapid casual talk elaborating conjunctions are often left implicit, the relationship being implied by the juxtaposition of the moves. For example:

R:D:elaborate	4/a	Fay	[to Liz] == (i)He's a bridge player, a naughty bridge player.
P:elaborate	4/b		(ii)He gets banned from everywhere because of his antisocial or drunken behaviour ( )

In 4/b, Fay amplifies the information she has presented in 4/a. She could have introduced 4/b with an *I mean* or *for example*. Another example occurs in moves 20/a-20/b:

R:D:elaborate	20/a	David	(i)He was a good boy (ii)but just no tolerance for the alcohol.
P:elaborate	20/b		(iii)I've pulled him out of so many fights (iv)it's ridiculous.

Here David exemplifies his claim of Allenby's alcohol intolerance by continuing with an elaboration in 20/b.

ii) Extension In extension, a move adds to the information in an immediately prior move, or provides contrasting information. The prolonging extension could be, but need not be, explicitly linked with conjunctions such as: *and, but, instead, or, except.* For example:

R:D:elaborate	42/a	David [to Fay]	(i)She used to be our mutual cleaning lady,
P:extend	42/b		(ii)except that she sacked these guys, except Roman.

In move 41/b David adds information which contrasts with his claim in 41/a. Similarly:

R:D:enhance	45/a	Nick	(i)The trouble with Roman though is that – (ii)you know he does still like cleaning up.

| P:extend | 45/b | | (iii)But he but he y'know like, (iv)he has dinner parties all the time, (v)he – and he cooks all the time, (vi)he MAKES all the mess all the time as well, you know ( ) sort of. |
| C:monitor | 45/c | | (vii)You know? |

In move 45/b Nick continues to hold the floor after his first move by offering contrasting information about Roman. Later in the excerpt we find:

| R:D:enhance | 58/a | Fay | (i)Just making sure (ii)you don't miss the boat. |
| C:extend | 58/b | | (iii)I put it out on Monday mornings. (iv)I hear them. (v)I hate the trucks. (vi)They go == roaring up |

In move 58/b Fay continues as speaker by simply adding further information to her initiating statement.

iii) Enhancement In enhancement, a move qualifies or modifies the information in an immediately prior move by providing temporal, spatial, causal or conditional detail. The enhancing relationship could be, but need not be, made explicit through conjunctions such as: *then, so, because.* For example:

| R:c:contradict | 3/a | Nick | (i)We don't want – (ii)we don't need Allenby in the bloody conversation. |
| C:enhance | 3/b | | (iii)'Cause all you'd get is == him bloody raving on |

In move 3/b Nick continues as speaker by qualifying his contradictory response in move 3/a, offering a reason to justify his confronting position. Similarly:

| R:D:extend | 30/a | Nick | (i)Not for much longer. |
| P:enhance | 30/b | | (i)We're too messy for him. |

Here Nick's second move is related implicitly as an explanation (causally).

5.5.2.4 *The function of prolonging moves in casual conversation*

Prolonging moves enable speakers to flesh out their contributions, getting more than a single move in as speaker. Although it is assertive to keep the turn, prolonging moves often seem to pre-empt possible challenges or queries. Hence, prolonging can be used defensively as well as assertively in casual talk.

5.5.2.5 *Appending moves*

One final type of continuing move recognized in the network in Figure 5.2 is the Appending move. This move class is mid-way between a continuing:prolonging speech function (considered above) and a reacting:developing move (see discussion below). Appending moves occur when a speaker makes one move, loses the turn, but then as soon as they regain the turn they produce a move which represents a logical expansion of their immediately prior move. Thus, although turn transfer has occurred (another speaker has intervened), it is almost as though the initial speaker had never lost the turn. For example, in text 5.1: Allenby, Fay is explaining who Jill is to Liz:

R:D:elaborate	12	Fay	(i) That's David's sister.
R:s:acknowledge	13	Liz	(i) Oh right.
A:elaborate	14	Fay	(i) Jill.

Had Liz not intervened with her *Oh right*, Fay's next move (*Jill*) would have been either part of move 12 (so, only a single move), or a prolonging elaboration, depending on prosodic factors. However, although turn transfer has occurred, Fay's move 14 does not appear to be a reaction to Liz's move, but rather a continuation of her own contribution in turn 12. A similar sequence occurs in text 3.1: Philosophy:

R:refute	99	Fran	(i) They didn't have that either.
R:s:evaluate	100	Brad	(i) Yeah well exactly.
A:elaborate	101	Fran	(i) They were just clerks.

Fran's move 101 does not have the grammatical characteristics of a reacting move (being non-elliptical, for example), but can be interpreted as an elaboration of her previous contribution in move 99. The following example from text 3.1: Philosophy, shows that Appending is closely related to the pressure of turn-taking in casual talk.

R:refute	74/a	Brad	(i) Yeah but I don't LIKE people ... um ...
P:elaborate	74/b		(ii) I don't want to be INVOLVED with people.
P:elaborate			(iii) I'd rather be involved with == soil erosion
R:challenge:rebound	75/a	Fran	== (i) Everybody has to be though.
*	75/b		(ii) But I mean
A:extend	76	Brad	(i) or desalin == ation

Overlap indicates that Fran begins her turn in 75 before Brad has finished his. When Brad gets back in 76 he uses the opportunity not to react to her contribution, but to flesh out his own.

Enhancement is also possible in an Appending move, as in this sequence from text 3.1: Philosophy:

O:I:Command	1/a	Brad	(i)Look.
O:I:question	1/b		(ii)See that guy.
P:elaborate	1/c		(iii)He plays the double-bass
R:s:register	2	Fran	(i)Does he?
E:enhance	3/a	Brad	(i)In the orchestra.

In this exchange, Brad comes back in after Fran's intervention in turn 2 and produces a prepositional phrase which adds spatial detail to the information in his prior move, 1/c.

As these examples illustrate, while prolonging moves are typically non-elliptical clauses, appending moves are typically nominal or prepositional phrases only, indicating their dependence on the prior move produced by the same speaker. While appending moves illustrate the same subtypes as prolonging moves (elaboration, extension, enhancement), we recognize them as a separate category in order to keep track of the fact that, despite speaker transfer, the appending speaker takes a new turn to expand on their earlier contribution.

Table 5.9 summarizes the speech function labels for the continuing moves.

5.5.3 Reacting speech functions: responding

The remaining two segments of the speech function network capture the options available when turn transfer occurs, i.e. when one speaker reacts to a move produced by a different speaker. These networks therefore capture the essentially interactive options in conversation.

Our networks differentiate two types of reacting moves: responses and rejoinders.[4] Responses are reactions which move the exchange towards completion, while rejoinders are reactions which in some way prolong the exchange (rejoinders are discussed fully below).

Figure 5.4 displays the responding group of Reacting options in the speech function network. Responding reactions negotiate a proposition or proposal on the terms set up by the previous speaker: that is, the respondent accepts being positioned as a respondent, and accepts to negotiate the other's proposition. This is realized linguistically through ellipsis: many responding moves are potentially or actually elliptically dependent on prior moves by other speakers. They do not introduce new Subject^Finite nubs, although they may expand on what is on the table. They are congruently realized by elliptical declaratives or, if minor clauses, are produced with terminating (falling) intonation.

Table 5.9 Summary of continuing speech functions

Speech function	Discourse purpose	Congruent mood	Example
Continue:monitor	check that audience is still engaged	elliptical major clause or minor clause with interrogative intonation	You know? Right?
Prolong:elaborate	clarify, exemplify or restate	full declarative, linked (or linkable) by: for example, I mean, like	see moves: 4b, 10b, 17b, 17c, 20b, 21b, 46c, 56c in 5.1
Prolong:extend	offer additional or contrasting information	full declarative, linked (or linkable) by: and, but, except, on the other hand	see moves: 42b, 45b, 55c, 58b, 59b in 5.1
Prolong:enhance	qualify previous move by giving details of time, place, cause, condition etc.	full declarative, linked (or linkable) by: then, so, because.	see moves: 3b, 30b, 43b in 5.1
Append: elaborate	clarify, exemplify or restate previous move after intervention by another speaker	elaborating nominal group	see moves: 14, 20a and 62 in text 5.1
Append:extend	offer additional or contrasting information to previous move after intervention by another speaker	extending nominal group	see example from text 3.1 presented above
Append:enhance	qualify previous move after intervention by another speaker	enhancing prepositional/adverbial phrase	see example from text 3.1 presented above

However, while responding moves accept positioning towards exchange completion, they still enable resistance. Responses may be either supporting or confronting. Supporting moves are the preferred responses of CA or Halliday's predicted responses (discussed above), while confronting moves are dispreferred or discretionary alternatives (although note that we classify some dispreferred options as rejoinders – see below). But both support and confrontation are on the terms set up by the other speaker.

There are four main categories of supporting moves: (i) developing; (ii) engaging; (iii) registering; (iv) replying. These major subclasses of supporting speech functions differ in the degree and type of negotiation they enter into. We consider each type below.

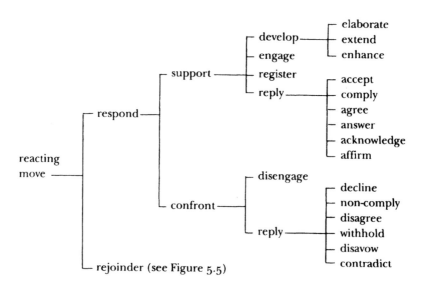

Figure 5.4 Sustaining: responding speech functions in casual conversation

5.5.3.1 Developing moves

Developing moves indicate a very high level of acceptance of the previous speaker's proposition, as they build on it, by expanding it experientially in the following ways, which are already familiar from the Continuing move network:

i) Elaborate A develop:elaborate move expands on a previous speaker's contribution by restating, clarifying or exemplifying what has been said. Develop:elaborate moves can be produced by a single speaker as two sentences linked by one of the elaborating conjunctions (*i.e. for example, I mean, like*). For example:

    R:D:elaborate   4/a   Fay   [to Liz] == (i) He's a bridge player, a naughty bridge player.

In move 4/a Fay produces a clarifying elaboration of David's earlier move (*This conversation needs Allenby*). David himself could have provided this elaboration – but significantly he did not. The following sequence offers a further example:

    R:D:extend   30/a   Nick   (i) Not for much longer.

P:enhance	30/b		(i)We're too messy for him.
R:D:elaborate	31	David	(i)That's what the cleaner – your cleaner lady cleaned my place thought

Here David's move expands on Nick's expansions, providing supporting exemplification.

Developing moves are very closely related to prolonging and appending moves, considered earlier. Sometimes it is difficult to tell whether a move is being produced in reaction to a prior move by a different speaker (in which case it is a developing move), or whether it represents a continuation by the speaker after an unplanned intervention by another speaker (in which case it is an appending move). The following sequence from text 5.1 provides an example:

O:I:give opinion	15/a	David	(i)Jill's very bright actually. (ii)she's very good.
R:s:agree	16	Fay	(i)She's extremely == bright
R:D:elaborate	17/a	David	== (i)Academ – academically she's probably brighter than David …
P:elaborate	17/b		(ii)David's always precocious with his …
P:elaborate	17/c		(iii)The only sixteen year old superstar ( ) arrives in Sydney (iv)to ( ) (v)and straight into the mandies

It is difficult to decide whether David's move 17/a is produced in reaction to Fay's move 16, or whether David was just too slow off the mark and Fay intervened before he had time to finish his contribution. We have called this one a developing elaboration (rather than an appending elaboration) because the move is realized by a non-elliptical clause.

ii) Extend A speaker may expand on a prior speaker's move by adding further supporting or contrasting details. A develop:extend move can be produced by a single speaker as two sentences linked by one of the extending conjunctions (*and, but, on the other hand*). For example, Nick contributes this statement in text 5.1:

R:D:extend	5	Nick	(i)And he just yap yap yaps all the time.

He produces a move here which could logically (but not interpersonally) have been produced by Fay, whose contribution he is extending.

iii) Enhance A speaker may enhance on a prior speaker's move by providing a temporal, causal or conditional qualification. A develop:

enhance move can be produced by a single speaker as two sentences linked by one of the enhancing conjunctions (*because, so, then*). For example:

R:D:enhance   58/a   Fay   (i)Just making sure (ii)you don't miss the boat.

In move 58/a, Fay builds on Nick's information about garbage day (move 56/a), by offering what seems to be an explanation for why he puts the garbage out so early. A filled out version of her move brings out its enhancing function: *So in putting the garbage out on Saturday when it doesn't go till Monday morning, you're just making sure you don't miss the boat.*

5.5.3.2 *The function of developing moves in casual talk*

The continuity between a Developing move and the move it expands on makes the Develop reaction a very co-operative conversational move. The speaker indicates interpersonal support for the initiator, while offering further ideational content for negotiation.

5.5.3.3 *Engaging moves*

Engaging moves are exchange-compliant reactions to attending moves. They are minimally negotiatory, as they simply agree to the negotiation going ahead. Engaging reactions include responses to the attention-getting attending moves. These are realized typically by minor clauses, often duplicating the lexical items and/or intonation of the opening salutation (e.g. hello – hello).

5.5.3.4 *Registering moves*

Registering reactions are reactions which provide supportive encouragement for the other speaker to take another turn. They do not introduce any new material for negotiation, and they carry the strong expectation that the immediately prior speaker will be the next speaker. It is into this category of registering reactions that we put feedback and backchannelling moves, as well as more evaluative reactions, such as *Oh* or *Really* said with an intonation expressing surprise (not doubt – then they could be taken as challenges, see below). They are generally realized by formulaic minor clauses of agreement, these verbal expressions frequently reinforcing accompanying non-verbal signals (e.g. head nods). For example:

R:s:register   41/a   Fay   == (i)Oh, the cleaning lady.

In 41/a Fay simply repeats the information provided by Nick, indicating that she has heard what he has said.

Some registering moves can be ritualistic expressions of sympathetic surprise, but these do not carry the implication of confrontation or the need for further resolution. For example:

R:track:probe	55/a	Fay	(i) Does your garbage go on Sunday morning?
R:register	55/b		(ii) Good grief!
P:extend	55/c		(iii) Mine goes Monday morning.

In 55/b Fay registers that she has heard and is surprised at Nick's information, but there is no implication that she is challenging or querying his response. Instead, she moves on to contrast his situation with her own.

We also treat as registering moves cases where a speaker follows up minimally on the response given by another speaker. For example:

R:track:probe	27	Fay	(i) Because Roman lives in Denning Road also?
R:resolve	28	David	(i) Yep.
R:register	29	Fay	(i) Oh.

Fay's *Oh* in move 29 effectively rounds off this short exchange, registering that she has heard (and, implicitly, accepts) David's information in move 28.

5.5.3.5 *Replying moves*

Replies are the most negotiatory of the responding reactions, although they negotiate the proposition given by a prior speaker. They are typically realized by elliptically dependent clauses, where the Subject^Finite comes from a prior speaker's move. As Figure 5.4 indicates, we subclassify replies as either supporting or confronting, as explained below.

5.5.3.6 *Supporting replies*

All initiations can be matched with supporting responses. Thus, for example, the supporting response to a statement of fact is to acknowledge it, as Nick, David and Liz do here in this sequence from text 5.1:

O:I:give fact	9a	Fay	(i) You met his sister that night we were doing the cutting and pasting up.
C:monitor	9b		(ii) D'you remember?
R:s:acknowledge	10/a	Nick	(i) Oh yea.
P:elaborate	10/b		== (ii) You met Jill.
R:s:acknowledge	11	David	== (i) Oh yea.
R:D:elaborate	12	Fay	(i) That's David's sister.
R:s:acknowledge	13	Liz	(i) Oh right.

Supporting responses to commands (compliance) and offers (acceptance) are often achieved non-verbally, as is also sometimes the case with affirmations and acknowledgements. For this reason it can be important to assign a non-verbal move number to such actions.

5.5.3.7 *The function of supporting replies in casual conversation*

Supporting replies indicate a willingness to accept the propositions or proposals of the other speakers. They are therefore non-assertive, even deferential. They create an alignment between initiator and supporter, but suggest that the relationship is one of dependence and subordination.

5.5.3.8 *Confronting replies*

Confronting responses range from either disengaging (refusing to participate in the exchange, for example, by responding with silence), or by offering a confronting reply. A range of confronting replies can be paired with typical initiations. For example, statements of facts or opinions can be confronted through contradictions:

R:c:contradict	3/a	Nick	(i) We don't want – (ii) we don't need Allenby in the bloody conversation.
P:enhance	3/b		(iii) 'Cause all you'd get is == him bloody raving on

In move 3/a Nick reacts to David's initiation with a contradiction, realized by simply negating the Finite element of David's move. Here is a further example which occurs a moment later in the same conversation:

O:I:question:opinion	6	David	(i) S'pose he gives you a hard time Nick?
R:c:contradict	7/a	Nick	(i) Oh I like David a lot.
P:extend	*7/b		(ii) Still but

Nick's move 7/a can be read as a contradiction of David's move 6, with Nick reading himself as the implied Subject of move 6, rather than Allenby. Thus his answer indicates that he is "hearing" move 6 as something like *So I s'pose you don't like David then (because he gives you a hard time)?*

A prior move can also be confronted through a disavowal, as in the following example from text 5.1:

?R:re-challenge	23	David	(i) Well, he rang Roman – (ii) he rang Roman a week ago
R:track:confirm	24/a	Nick	(i) Did he?
R:c:disavow	24/b		(ii) I didn't know that.
R:track:clarify	24/c		(iii) What he rang Denning Road did he?

In this sequence one of the three different reactions Nick produces to David's claim in move 23 is simply to disclaim knowledge of the relevant information.

Confronting responses to closed questions involve disagreeing with the polarity in the initiating question. For example, responding with negative polarity to a positive polarity question (*Is Allenby in London? – No he isn't.*) or with positive polarity to a negative polarity question (*Don't you like Allenby? – Yes I do.*). An open question can be confronted with a withholding response (*When do you put the garbage out? – don't know*).

Confronting responses to offers (decline) and commands (refusal) are often non-verbal, and should again be assigned non-verbal move numbers in the transcript so that the speech functions can be assigned.

5.5.3.9 The functions of confronting replies in casual conversation

Confronting replies indicate a dependency between the initiator and respondent, but do not imply the deference or alignment of supporting replies. They encode relatively weak forms of non-compliance with the positionings offered the respondent. Like supporting replies, they close the exchange off and avoid the overt negotiation of any differences.

The full range of responding speech functions is summarized in Table 5.10.

5.5.4 Reacting: rejoinder moves

It was pointed out above that the responding reacting moves comply with the expectation of exchange closure, achieved linguistically by negotiating only the proposition set up by the initiating speaker. Rejoinders, on the other hand, rather than completing the negotiation of a proposition or a proposal, tend to set underway sequences of talk that interrupt, postpone, abort or suspend the initial speech function sequence. Thus rather than just negotiate what is already on the table, rejoinders either query it (demanding further details) or reject it (offering alternative explanations). Figure 5.5 captures the subclasses of rejoinders.

As the segment of the network in Figure 5.5 indicates, there are two main subclasses of rejoinders: **tracking** moves and **challenging** moves. These two subclasses correspond to the supporting and confronting alternatives available in the responding move classes, with tracking moves supporting (although prolonging) negotiation, while challenging moves confront a prior move. We consider each rejoinder type and its subtypes below.

5.5.4.1 Tracking moves

Tracking moves are moves which check, confirm, clarify or probe the content of prior moves. They are supporting in the sense that they merely delay anticipated exchange completion, without indicating disagreement with it. Their dependency on prior moves is realized through

Table 5.10 Summary of sustaining responding speech functions

Speech function	Discourse purpose	Congruent mood	Example
engage	show willingness to interact by responding to salutation, etc.	minor: typically "yea" or matched response	Hi-*Hi*; Nick? – *Yea?*
register	display attention to the speaker	repetition of speaker's word(s); paralinguistic expressions such as Mmm, Uh huh; ritual exclamations; minor clauses	see moves: 29, 38a, 41/a, 55/b in text 5.1
comply	to carry out demand for goods and services	non-verbal; expressions of undertaking (e.g. "OK")	Can you pass the salt, please? – *Here/ [passes it]*
accept	to accept proffered goods and services	non-verbal; expressions of thanking	Have another? – *Thanks/ [takes one]*
agree	to indicate support of information given	Yes; positive polarity;	see move 16 in text 5.1
acknowledge	to indicate knowledge of information given	expressions of knowing	see moves 10/a, 11, 13, 41/b in text 5.1
answer	to provide information demanded	complete missing structural elements	Where's Allenby? – *In London*
affirm	to provide positive response to question	Yes; positive polarity	Have you heard from him lately? – *Yes, I have/only yesterday*
disagree	to provide negative response to question	negation of proposition	Is he in London now? – *No*
non-comply	to indicate inability to comply with prior command	non-verbal; no expressions of undertaking; negation of verbal command	Could you pass me the salt, please? – *sorry/can't reach/got my hands full*
withhold	to indicate inability to provide demanded information	negative elliptical declarative	When is he due back? – *I've no idea*
disavow	to deny acknowledgement of information	expressions of disclaiming knowledge	see move 24/b in text 5.1
contradict	to negate prior information	No; switched polarity	see moves: 3/a, 7/a, 43/a, 46/a in text 5.1

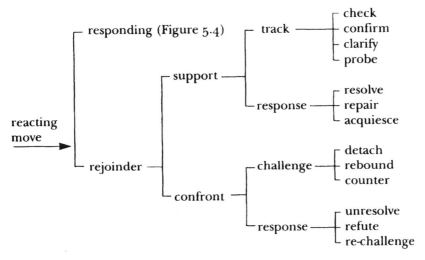

Figure 5.5 Rejoinder speech functions in casual conversation

their actual or potential ellipsis. Their recycling function is realized through their interrogative structure and/or rising intonation. There are four main types of tracking moves:

i) Checking moves. These moves check on content which has been missed or may have been misheard. For example, in move 18 Nick uses an elliptical interrogative to send the exchange "back", requesting a filling in of the information he has missed:

R:track:check   18   Nick   (i)Straight into the what?

Checking may involve specifically requesting clarification, as in Brad's move 14/a from text 3.1: Philosophy:

R:track:check   14/a   Brad   (i)Whaddya mean?

It may also involve querying a move which has more or less been missed altogether, as in this example from text 4.1: Mates, when Keith seems to have lost track of the flow:

R:track:check   54   Keith   Eh?

ii) Confirming moves These moves seek verification of what the speaker indicates they have heard. For example:

?R:re-challenge   23   David   (i)Well, he rang Roman – (ii)he rang Roman a week ago

R:track:confirm	24/a	Nick	(i) Did he?
R:c:disavow	24/b		(ii) I didn't know that.
R:track:clarify	24/c		(iii) What he rang Denning Road did he?

In move 24/a Nick indicates that he has heard David's claim and wants it confirmed.

iii) Clarifying moves   These moves seek additional information in order to understand a prior move. In the example presented above, Nick continues in move 24/c with a clarification, offering his own filling in of assumed information. Another example is:

R:rebound	50/a	David	[shocked amazement] (i) ToDAY!
R:track:clarify	50/b		(ii) What, before bridge?

In move 50/b David seeks clarification of what he assumes to be implied in Nick's move 48.

Also classified as clarifications are requests for elaboration. For example, in move 18 above, had Nick responded with *What are mandies?* the move would be clarifying information that has been heard, but is simply not intelligible to the listener. Clarification moves typically delay the presentation of the speaker's reaction, on the basis that inadequate information is available.

iv) Probing moves   These moves offer further details or propose implications for confirmation by the initial speaker. Probes thus introduce new propositional material, but it stands in a logico-semantic relation with the moves being tracked. That is, a probing move involves offering for confirmation an elaboration, extension or enhancement of a prior move. Probes are typically realized as tagged declaratives (building on information in another speaker's prior turn), or elliptically or logically dependent interrogatives. For example:

R:track:probe	27	Fay	(i) Because Roman lives in Denning Road also?

Here Fay suggests an enhancement of the argument so far, offering a causal explanation to make sense of both David's and Nick's comments. Like all the tracking moves, probes keep the interaction going, but they make a more substantial original contribution than other types of tracking moves.

Tracking moves call more or less directly for further talk from the prior speaker – they thus get responded to. The responses may be supporting, as when a tracking request is resolved or a challenge acquiesced with. For example, Fay immediately resolves Nick's query in move 18 of text 5.1:

R:track:check	18	Nick	(i) Straight into the what?

R:track:resolve	19	Fay	(i) Mandies. [laughs]

And later in the same text David resolves Fay's probe:

R:track:probe	27	Fay	(i) Because Roman lives in Denning Road also?
R:resolve	28	David	(i) Yep.

Tracking moves may also be responded to with repair moves, as in the following sequence from text 3.1: Philosophy:

O:I:state fact	105	Brad	== (i) That guy that that Bangladeshi that used to live with us he was a a a Limnologist or whatever it's called.==
R:track:check	106	Fran	== (i) A WHAT?==
R:track:check	107	Dave	== (i) Who?
R:repair	108	Brad	(i) Oh not == Limnologist.
R: repair	109	Fran	== (i) Ichthyologist.
R:repair	110/a	Brad	(i) He studied fish.
P:elaborate	110/b		(ii) He studied ... (iii) he was a ... (iv) he was a ...Dip ...
R:track:query	110/c		(v) Oh what is it called? ...
R:resolve	110/d		(vi) PhD in Science.

In this sequence, Brad's initiating statement of fact is tracked by both Fran and Dave. Brad reacts by offering a repair move, as Fran almost simultaneously offers an alternative repair. Lost in the technical terms, Brad repairs again, descriptively this time. However his continuing elaboration again brings him up against technicality, and he both tracks and then resolves his own query.

Confronting responses to tracking moves generally fall under the challenging category considered next.

5.5.4.2 *Challenging moves*

This second type of rejoinder move confronts prior talk by attacking it on one of several fronts: e.g. by actively rejecting negotiation or by querying the veracity of what has been said or the sayer's right to say it. We will differentiate three main types which are outlined below:

i) Detaching moves These moves seek to terminate the interaction, to avoid any further discussion. For example, in text 5.1 both Fay and Nick respond to David with this form of challenge:

R:challenge:detach	51	Fay	(i) So huh [non-verbal!]
R:challenge:detach	52	Nick	(i) So stick that!

ii) Rebounding moves   These moves send the interaction back to the first speaker, by questioning the relevance, legitimacy or veracity of another speaker's move. For example:

O:I:give opinion	1	David	(i)This conversation needs Allenby.
R:challenge:rebound	2/a	Fay	(i)Oh he's in London (ii)so what can we do?

While the modulation and choice of interrogative in Fay's response in 2/a soften her challenge, she is nonetheless confronting and rejecting David's opinion. Unlike a simple contradiction (e.g. such as is offered by Nick in the following move), Fay's rebound provisionally puts David back into the position of having to justify or modify his initiating opinion.

iii) Countering moves   These moves express confrontation by offering an alternative, counter-position or counter-interpretation of a situation raised by a previous speaker. For example:

R:c:contradict	46/a	David	(i)No.
R:challenge:counter	46/b		(ii)You don't understand Nick – (iii)you.
P:elaborate	46/c		(iv)Guys that do the cleaning up do all of the unseen things that you never thought of (v)like putting out the garbage and

In this sequence David rejects Nick's assertion (that Roman is too clean) not by merely contradicting him (*e.g. Roman is NOT too clean*) but by asserting a counter-proposition: that the problem lies with Nick and not with Roman. He then elaborates on this challenge by providing exemplification.

Like tracking moves, challenging moves more or less obligate the prior speaker to respond. However, very often the responses are themselves confronting: a query cannot be resolved, a counter is refuted, or a re-challenge launched. Reactions to rejoinder moves have themselves a certain rejoinder quality about them, and often lead in turn to further challenging or tracking. It is not uncommon in casual talk to find lengthy sequences of such moves, as in the sequence of moves 46 to 54 in text 5.1: Allenby.

5.5.4.3 *The function of rejoinders in casual talk*

The frequency of rejoinders in casual talk, and their relative absence from more formal spoken interactions, relates to their potential to sustain the interaction. While pragmatic interactions aim at closure and completion, casual conversations need to be sustained if their goals are to be met. The building and reaffirming of relationships and identity is never finally achieved, hence the need to use the linguistic resources to keep the channels open for as long as possible. Tracking moves contribute to sustaining the interaction by keeping an exchange open, without implying any interpersonal confrontation. They thus express a willingness to maintain contact, and imply alignment (or at least potential alignment) with the addressee's position. Challenging moves, on the other hand, directly confront the positioning implied in the addressee's move, and thus express a certain independence on the part of the speaker. Because they invariably lead to further talk, in which positions must be justified or modified, challenging moves contribute most assertively to the negotiation of interpersonal relationships.

Table 5.11 summarizes the rejoinder reacting moves reviewed above.

Table 5.11 Summary of sustaining rejoinder speech functions

Speech function	Discourse purpose	Congruent mood	Example
check	to elicit repetition of a misheard element or move	elliptical polar interrogative	see moves: 18, 33, 46b in text 5.1
confirm	to verify information heard	elliptical wh-interrogative; wh/element from prior move	see move 24a in text 5.1
clarify	to get additional information needed to understand prior move	elliptical interrogative; wh/new element (not in prior move)	see move 24c in text 5.1
probe	to volunteer further details/implications for confirmation	full clause, new subject, etc. but in logico-semantic relation with the moves it's tracking or tagged declarative	see move 27 in text 5.1
resolve	to provide clarification, acquiesce with information	elliptical declarative; mood adjunct of polarity or modality	see moves: 28, 35, 37, 39 in text 5.1
detach	to terminate interaction	silence; expression of termination	see move 52 in text 5.1
rebound	to question relevance, legitimacy, veracity of prior move	wh-interrogative, elliptical	see moves: 2a, 48 in text 5.1
counter	to dismiss addressee's right to his/her position	non-elliptical declarative; negation of understanding/rightness	see move 46b in text 5.1
refute	to contradict import of a challenge	elliptical declarative; negation	see move 47 in text 5.1
re-challenge	to offer alternative position	elliptical interrogative	see move 23 in text 5.1

5.6 SPEECH FUNCTION CODING

Having now introduced all the speech function classes that we will be using, we will work through the steps involved in a speech function analysis, demonstrating its usefulness as an explanatory and interpretive tool for analysing casual conversation.

5.6.1 Identifying moves

The first step in the analysis of interactive structure is to divide the transcript into moves, according to the criteria suggested under section 5.4.3 above. Moves can be numbered within turns using the a, b notation, as in the presentation of text 5.1: Allenby. This method ensures that turns are also numbered, which makes it straightforward to determine the number of turns produced by each participant and the amount of functional work achieved in each turn (i.e. how many speech functions per turn).

For purposes of coding, analysis must deal also with incomplete moves and non-verbal realizations of moves. Where a speaker restarts a clause, producing an identical but completed version second time around, we assign the same move number to both attempts. For example:

O:I:give fact   21/a   David   (i)At least he's doing well – (ii)at
                                           least he's doing well in London.

Just as we recognized incomplete clauses, so we recognize (and number) incomplete moves, i.e. where a move is abandoned before completion.

Finally, actions which are significant in the interaction (i.e. to which speech functions can be assigned) are given non-verbal move numbers. While speech function coding focuses on moves, it is important to still keep track of clauses, as eventually the speech function analysis will be related to mood analysis to reveal patterns of congruence or incongruence, and choices in modality. From this chapter on, all transcripts in which interactivity is being analysed will be numbered for moves.

5.6.2 Coding speech functions

Once the transcript is divided into moves, each move is assigned a speech function label, based on the most righthand categories in the networks presented above. A speech function coding sheet can be prepared, most directly by writing the speech function choices on the transcript, as has been done with text 5.1 at the beginning of this chapter.

There is a fundamental difference between coding for mood and coding for speech function. While in grammatical coding each clause can be coded in isolation from the clauses around it, speech function coding, like coding for appraisal, can only be done contextually: that is, the function of each move can only be decided by looking at its relationship to prior moves. This is what CA recognized as the sequential implicativeness of interaction: what each move means is in large part dependent on what has just been said. For example, we can only classify Nick's move 3 in text 5.1 as a contradiction by relating it back to David's initiation in move 1. Had David just said *Bloody Allenby would be a pain in the neck if he were here!* then Nick's move would be classified as a supporting answer, an entirely different speech function.

A second principle needs to be invoked to keep coding manageable. Although there is a strong sense in which all moves in talk relate to many (even all) previous moves, in initial coding it is advisable to interpret the function of each move in relation to only *one* other move, i.e. the nearest relevant prior move. That is, we prefer single rather than multiple coding. This is straightforward with dialogue, where typically what each person says relates to the immediately prior turn by the other person. However, it is more complicated with multilogue where the queue of people speaking means that one move may actually be relating back to something several moves earlier. For example, if we coded moves 2 and 3 in text 5.1 in a strictly linear sequence, we would have to show Nick's move 3 a as related to Fay's move 2. However, the mood structure of Nick's move 3 provides strong evidence for interpreting it as a reaction to David's initiation, giving us two reactions in sequence. At a later stage it is always possible to deepen the analysis by considering whether some moves need to be given multiple codings: e.g. Nick's move 3/a, which constitutes a confronting reaction to David, is in a sense a supporting extension of Fay's response in move 2. Double coding can thus capture the full effects of sequential implicativeness, but the complexities it introduces are best avoided first time through.

5.7 INTERPRETING SPEECH FUNCTION ANALYSIS

Once the speech function analysis has been carried out over the whole text, patterns can be explored from two perspectives: (i) synoptically, by quantifying overall choices per speaker; (ii) dynamically, by tracing through the speech function choices as the conversation unfolds. We will briefly discuss the results of each perspective for text 5.1: Allenby.

5.7.1 Synoptic interpretation of discourse structure

Table 5.12 is a quantification of the discourse structure choices in all moves by the three dominant speakers in text 5.1: David, Nick and Fay. Moves made by Liz and Stephen will be discussed separately. To simplify presentation, speech function classes which are not used by any of the speakers are not shown on the table.

Table 5.12 Summary of speech function choices in text 5.1: Allenby

Speech function	David	Nick	Fay
no. of turns	19	21	18
no. of moves	26 (2) (NV1)	30 (2) (NV1)	27
no. of clauses	35 (2)	40 (1)	35
Open			
question:opinion	1	–	–
state:fact	1	–	1
state:opinion	3	–	–
total	5	0	1
Continue			
monitor	–	1	1
prolong:elaborate	5	2	1
prolong:extend	1	2	2
prolong:enhance	–	3	–
append:elaborate	2	–	–
total	8	8	4
react: responding			
register	–	–	4
develop:elaborate	–	–	4
develop:extend	4	4	1
develop:enhance	–	1	1
replying:supporting	–	–	2
confronting	1	2	–
total	5	7	12
react: rejoinder			
tracking:clarify	2	1	2
tracking:confirm	–	1	–
tracking:check	–	2	3
tracking:probe	–	–	2
reacting:resolve	4	4	1
challenging:detach	–	1	1
challenging:rebound	1	1	1
challenging:counter	1	–	–
challenging:refute	–	1	–
challenging:re-challenge	1	–	–
total	9	11	10

Table 5.12 reveals the following patterns:

- Dominant and incidental participants. Bearing in mind that Liz produces only one turn and Stephen three, we can see from this table that there are two distinct sets of interactants participating in text 5.1: the dominant ones (Nick, David and Fay) and the incidental ones (Liz and Stephen).

This suggests that Liz and Stephen are both marginalized, Liz perhaps by her lack of shared background (she does not know Allenby and so is effectively excluded from a lengthy section of the talk), and Stephen perhaps because he is less available than usual due to his responsibilities as host. Certainly Liz plays a very passive role throughout, with her only move being a supporting acknowledgement, while Stephen produces one initiating statement of opinion, one elaborating continue and one supporting reaction (acknowledgement).

- Number of turns. As noted at the beginning of the chapter, there is a remarkably close similarity in the number of turns for each of the dominant players, with Nick just beating the others. This suggests that the three are competing for turns, or at least consider themselves to have the right to equal turns at talk, as would match our intuitive definitions of casual conversation as 'talk among equals'. Nick is revealed as the most assertive interactant.
- Number of moves. The number of moves produced by each interactant is also very similar, realizing again the equality of friends. However, proportions have changed slightly: Nick emerges as speech functionally dominant (he gets more moves into his turns), while Fay also gets more value out of her turns, producing more moves though fewer turns than David.
- Number of clauses. Nick produces more clauses for his number of turns/moves. This confirms that he gets more airspace than the others, more value from his role as speaker. It also reveals that there is substantial, but certainly not total, congruence between moves and clauses, as we would expect in a casual context.

If we now consider the categories of moves produced by the three speakers, Table 5.12 shows the following:

- David dominates openings, with Nick never opening and Fay only once. This shows that Nick is strikingly dependent on the other interactants: he talks most, but only in reaction to the contributions of others.
- As an opener, David favours statements of (his) opinion, suggesting that he enacts a role of 'stirrer'. It also indicates a certain egocentricity. Fay's single opening is a statement of fact, suggesting that she does not risk presenting her own opinions for debate. This ties in with the findings for appraisal choices reported at the beginning of this chapter.
- Nick continues more often, although there is proportionally little difference. However, when David continues, he elaborates: i.e. he says the same thing in a different way, suggesting that while he might kick things off, he does less to broaden subsequent discussion. Nick is more inclined to qualify/justify, thus using more argumentative strategies, while Fay prefers to add information, a neutral means of broadening the field.
- Both Nick and Fay monitor once, while David does not. Slight though these figures are, they suggest that David sees his role as provoking others

to interact, rather than checking to see that they are still with him.
- In responding reactions, we see that David produces fewest, and Fay the most, even though she does not talk as much as the men. In fact, nearly half of her responses are registers (very minimal supporting reactions) or elaborating develops, with two supporting replies. Thus, all her responses are supporting, and many are minimal in negotiatory terms. She appears to be using language to construct a role for herself as a facilitator and supporter.
- David's responses, on the other hand, are mostly developing elaborations, a continuation of the pattern he preferred in continuing moves. Thus, he tends to re-say what he or someone else has already said.
- It is striking to note that Nick is the only participant to use confronting responses. He also uses no elaborations but prefers extensions and enhancements, a continuation of his pattern in continuing moves. These results indicate that he plays a more confrontational role, in which he also adds more to extend the discussion, while the others tend to keep things on the same terms.
- The results for rejoinders are equally revealing. The number of rejoinders produced by each speaker are about equal, indicating that all speakers contribute to the maintenance and open-endedness of the talk. However, almost all of Fay's rejoinders are tracking moves (i.e. supporting), and the majority of those are checking moves. This shows not only her role as supporter, but also her partial exclusion (she is not often in the position to resolve someone else's tracking moves). While her dependence is supportive, she is also the only one to probe, indicating the work she does to promote continued talk.
- Both David and Nick get to resolve a lot, enacting their positions as insiders relative to Fay. David clarifies while Nick checks, a further indication of the contrast between provocateur and dependent-respondent. In the challenges, David is more willing to send a challenge back with an alternative, while Nick prefers either to detach or refute. These results show Nick's essentially dependent discourse behaviour.

Overall then, the speech function analysis shows us that, despite the apparent equality with which casual conversation is assumed to operate, interactants differ subtly but significantly in the roles they play. These role differences in text 5.1 can be summarized as follows:

- David takes on the role as a provocative initiator, but offers little new information after his initiations. He is willing to engage with Nick's confronting reactions, but offers little in support of others' contributions.
- Nick talks the most but gives the least, relying on others to open and elaborate. His role is to react, frequently confrontationally, taking time to justify and develop his position.
- Fay is dialogically active, but again largely through reacting to others' contributions. Her reactions are overwhelmingly supporting, and overall her linguistic behaviour indicates a concern to facilitate and uphold the talk.

Although based on the analysis of just one short excerpt, these findings tie in with other studies of mixed gender groups, where women have been found to talk less than men, and to perform various forms of conversational "shitwork" (Fishman 1980, Nordenstam 1992). There are also implications for male conversational roles, with David and Nick functionally complementing each other: David opens, Nick reacts. Their linguistic roles thus imply a mutual dependence, rather than competition: they need each other more than either needs Fay, perhaps enacting the close male bonding of Australian mateship. Choices of speech function, then, can be related to cultural expectations about the roles of different social groups.

If we now relate the speech function patterns to mood choices we gain further insight into the identities and differences being enacted in the talk. Table 5.13 summarizes mood choices for David, Nick and Fay in text 5.1: Allenby. Mood classes which are not selected by any speaker are not shown.

This table for mood choices both confirms and extends on the picture which emerged from the speech function analysis. In summary, table 5.10 shows the following patterns in text 5.1:

Declaratives Approximately half of Nick's and Fay's contributions are full declaratives, but for David the figure is much higher. This is consistent with his contributions being more initiating than responsive. One surprise is that Nick uses so many full declarative clauses although we have seen from the speech function analysis that he never actually initiates. This is accounted for in his production of many qualifications and explanations of his reactions: his develop and continue moves are non-elliptical structures. This is further evidence that he does indeed get more value for his turns than other speakers, making full comments rather than elliptical reactions.

Interrogatives If we aggregate all the interrogatives (David: 3; John: 3; but Fay: 5) the results are consistent with suggestions that women in mixed company ask more questions than do men. The supportive/facilitative nature of Fay's questions is implied in her preference for wh-interrogatives (which give the respondent more room to respond) than the more limiting polar questions, which the men prefer.

Negation Negation is not used at all by David while Nick produces three negated clauses. This shows that although David makes confronting moves, he does not employ the negative and contrary realizations that Nick prefers.

Subject choice Analysis shows that Nick is by far the most egotistical of the speakers: his involvement in the conversation is highly personal, as he frequently talks about himself. In contrast, David never makes himself Subject. His preference for getting absent people, Nick, and generalizations as Subject is further evidence of his lack of personal engagement: he is getting the talk going, but it does not closely touch him. Meanwhile Fay also

Table 5.13 Summary of mood choices in text 5.1: Allenby

Mood (clause type)	David	Nick	Fay
number of clauses	35 (2)	40 (1)	35
declarative full elliptical	20 2	22 5	16 5
polar interrogative elliptical	2	2	
tagged declarative full		1	
wh-interrogative full elliptical	1 –	– 1	3 2
imperative		2	
minor	4	4	3
most frequent Subject choice	3rd p. pronouns: Allenby, Jill, Roman nominalization: this conversation; complex NP: guys that do the cleaning up you (Nick)	I; we; he (Roman)	3rd p. pronouns: Allenby, Jill Roman you (Liz, Nick)
negation		3	1
adjuncts:total circumstantial interpersonal textual	16 6 3 7	23 9 3 11	16 9 1 6
modalization (i) probability (ii) usuality	2 (s'pose; probably) 1 (always)	1 (I think) 1 (always)	
modulation (i) obligation (ii) capability	2 (got to; needs) –	1 (got to) –	– 1 (can)
total no. of modalities	5	3	1
incongruence mood/speech function	2		1

prefers third person subjects, but does also make Liz the Subject (the only time Liz gets included) and she also makes Nick the Subject, again indicating her supportive orientation.

Adjuncts While we find much the same proportion of circumstantial Adjuncts for all speakers (i.e. half the number of clauses), the results show that Fay produces a higher proportion of circumstantials, while the others produce more textuals than circumstantials. This seems to suggest that Fay's moves are concerned more with adding extra details, and less with establishing coherence and continuity. In fact, it is sometimes difficult to appreciate the relevance of Fay's moves (e.g. moves 44 and 58a).

Modalities Figures for total modalities show that David uses most, followed by Nick, then Fay. In fact, Fay uses no modalization, and just one modulation (a *can* of capability). So while the others do debate their judgements of certainty and obligation, Fay exposes less of her own judgements. This ties in with the results of the appraisal analysis, discussed at the beginning of the chapter.

Congruence/incongruence of speech functions/mood Relating mood choice to speech functions, we can see that David is the most incongruent, with Nick relentlessly congruent throughout. These few examples of incongruence are accounted for as follows:

- In move 6, David uses a modalized declarative to elicit an opinion. (Congruent: *Does he give you a hard time?* or *Don't you like Allenby then?*). Here the incongruence allows David to avoid negation and/or the closed question, thereby producing a potentially more open and provocative initiation.
- In move 42c, David again uses a modulated declarative *I mean you've got to admit.* This could have been expressed congruently as an imperative (*Admit Roman is the cleanest guy*). The modulation allows him to represent his opinion as if it were an undeniable fact.
- In move 27 Fay probes using a declarative structure overlaid with an interrogative intonation: *Because Roman lives in Denning Road also?*. The declarative structure here contrasts with the congruent realization of this probe through an interrogative: *Does Roman live in Denning Road also?* The effect of her choice of the declarative enables her to offer a suggestion, rather than merely request confirmation.

5.7.2 Summary of analysis

Synthesizing the results of mood, appraisal, involvement and now speech function analysis we can see that in text 5.1: *Allenby* the three major participants are playing very different roles, enacting very different relations between themselves and others. For all her talk, Fay is working to support the males in their relationship of co-dependency. The Nick – David relationship is the closest one, with Fay weakly aligned with Nick against David's provocative, impersonal stance. Nick may dominate in talk-time and evaluative contribution, but is totally dependent on David for the opportunity to express himself.

Thus detailed analysis of interactive patterns, combined with the analysis of grammatical and semantic patterns, can capture some of the ways in which, as each participant talks, they enact aspects of their subjective identity. The analysis also suggests that the identities they enact are not personal but social: in creating relations of provocation, dependence or support, interactants display patterns of relations which operate between men and men, and men and women, in the broader cultural context of white Australian society.

5.7.3 The dynamics of conversational structure: tracing the conversational exchange

The analysis presented so far helps us to uncover overall patterns of choices in a "slice" or phase of conversation. Such analysis can capture the lack of reciprocity in discourse behaviours, and provides evidence of the different levels of familiarity or attachment being enacted between participants. Although the synoptic quantification of the analysis captures important information about the identities the interactants adopt, it does not display the unfolding of the interaction across time. This means that it does not show clearly, for example, the relationship of contradiction/confrontation that operates between David and Nick, nor does it show exactly to whom Fay enacts her supportive role (to both the others, or just to one of them). We therefore suggest one further step in speech function analysis: the discussion of the sequential unfolding of the exchanges in the excerpt. This not only permits us to follow the shifting relationships, but also sheds light on a theoretical issue which has concerned structural-functional approaches to conversation since the work of Sinclair and Coulthard (1975): the nature of the conversational exchange.

The speech function analysis can lead us to identify units larger than moves in the flow of talk: i.e. **exchanges**. An exchange can be defined as a sequence of moves concerned with negotiating a proposition stated or implied in an initiating move. An exchange can be identified as beginning with an opening move, and continuing until another opening move occurs. The general structure of the conversational exchange is therefore one opening move followed by all related continuing and sustaining moves. We have shown the exchange boundaries in text 5.1: Allenby by using shaded lines.

Applying this definition of the exchange, we can see that excerpt 5.1 consists of seven exchanges, ranging in length from one move to thirty moves, with a build-up to two dominant exchanges, before a trailing off. We will now review briefly the dynamic unfolding of the particular exchanges in context and the implications for the interpersonal relationships being constructed.

Exchange 1: moves 1–5 (total: 7 moves) In exchange 1 we see David taking up his role of provocateur, and the generally confrontational tone of the interaction is set with the two reactions his opening elicits. But while the relationship between David and the others is initially defined as one of confrontation (of different degrees), we see Nick supporting Fay in the final moves of the exchange, where they collaborate to offer supporting information for the outsider, Liz.

Exchange 2: moves 6–8 (total: 4 moves) In exchange 2, Nick again responds to David by confronting him, and then (in a parallel to exchange 1) we see Fay co-operating to elaborate on Nick's information – or at least the information so far on the table. Again, the collaboration is intended for Liz. We thus see that Liz's presence provides a mechanism for aligning Fay and Nick.

Exchange 3: moves 9a–14 (total: 8 moves) Fay is the pivotal player in this exchange, which is completely supporting: Nick and David support Fay in her efforts to include Liz. Again, all participants are united in their efforts towards Liz, who makes her only verbal contribution in this exchange. The sequence of supporting responses leads to a trailing off as this exchange has nowhere to go.

Exchange 4: moves 15a–20b (total: 9 moves) This is an exchange dominated by the Fay–David relationship, and is another all-supporting exchange, again involving collaboration to include the excluded Liz. However, this exchange develops through expansion, with frequent logical relations (elaboration and extension) and a resolved tracking sequence. Thus this is an exchange of collaboration and support. Here we see then an attempt to prolong the interaction, but in the absence of confrontation the exchange peters out.

Exchange 5: moves 21a–42b (total: 30 moves) Exchange 5 is far more dynamic than any of the earlier ones, and exchange structure is denser. This is still a largely supporting exchange, in which we see the increase in dynamic rejoinder moves, with tracking the dominating structural relation. The obvious effect of these tracking moves is to prolong the exchange. In the first part of the exchange, David is set up as 'controller', but eventually both Nick and David come jointly to resolve Fay's and Stephen's queries, creating a new alignment in which Fay is an outsider to a Nick–David collaboration.

Exchange 6: moves 42c–59b (total: 29 moves) Dominated by David and Nick, this complex exchange sees confronting moves exceed supporting moves for the first time, and rejoinders far outweigh responses. This is therefore the most open-ended of the exchanges, and displays most clearly the dependency between Nick and David, with the other interactants largely relegated to providing an audience for this display of male bantering.

Exchange 7: moves 60–62 (total: 3 moves)   In this final exchange we see Stephen providing some release/relief from the level of confrontation of the previous exchange. The brevity of this exchange suggests it will be a transitional exchange, and indeed the interactants take the option and let the argument drop. The conversation resumes after a short pause, with Fay providing a monologic recount of garbage collection in her street.

5.7.4   Summary of analyses of discourse structure

The combination of a synoptic and a dynamic perspective on the speech function analysis allows us to capture both who takes on which roles in the interaction, and the dynamic negotiation of relationships of inclusion and exclusion, support and confrontation, alignment and distance. The discussion of exchange structure in text 5.1: Allenby, shows that the talk provides opportunities for different relationships to be worked on at different points in the unfolding interaction. Comparative degrees of involvement can be inferred from the frequency and types of moves each interactant makes towards the others.

The dynamic perspective also reveals the fundamental importance of rejoinder moves, and particularly confronting move options, in casual talk. When responding options only are chosen, negotiation leads to the termination of the exchange, particularly if responses are supporting. The selection of rejoinder moves provides a major resource for sustaining any individual exchange, and thereby prolonging the conversation. Confronting reactions are the reactions most likely to engender further talk. Casual conversation thrives on confrontation, and wilts in the face of support. These findings lend support to claims such as Kress's (1985) that text is born in the exploration of difference.

5.7.5   Discourse structure in text 3.1: Philosophy

While space does not allow a detailed review of other texts, a brief summary of interactive structure in text 3.1: Philosophy will be offered. Speech function analysis of this text shows the following patterns:

- Brad made 11 opening moves, compared with 5 openings by Dave and only 1 by Fran. This confirms the impression gained from mood analysis, that Brad not only dominates the number of turns, but also controls the direction of the negotiation.
- Dave's openings were predominantly questions, indicating his dependence on Brad and his preference for interacting only with his son

(to the exclusion of his wife).

- Brad's openings involved an equal number of statements of opinions and statements of facts, indicating that he considered initiations about his own opinions and activities to be of interest to the group.
- Brad was the only speaker who produced continuing moves (a total of 36 in the excerpt), of which one-third were elaborations. This provides clear evidence of his domination of the speaker role. A significant proportion of these continuations were Appending moves, showing that he frequently ignored intervening contributions by other speakers.
- Brad also dominated the responding moves (28 to Fran's 15 and Dave's 7). This was the largest category of Fran's talk, allowing us to confirm that she used minor and elliptical clauses to respond.
- 11 of Fran's 15 responses were registering moves, i.e. minimally supporting reactions (feedback, backchannelling), whereas a majority of Brad's responses were developing moves. So while Fran contributed little in her responder role, Brad used his responses to get more information (about himself) into the discussion.
- However, Fran's linguistic behaviour comes closest to Brad's in the rejoinder category, where Brad produced 25, Fran 15 and Dave only 7. This suggests that Fran makes discourse choices which are likely to sustain the interaction.
- Of her rejoinders, the majority were tracking moves (9), most being clarifications. Brad's tracking moves were mostly resolving moves (he did not ask, he gave), further evidence of how Brad is set up as the centre of attention in the interaction.
- Fran made 6 challenging moves, 4 rebounds and 2 counter challenges. Brad made 10 (7 rebounds and 3 counters), and Dave only 1. These findings indicate that Fran was willing to argue with Brad, thereby sustaining the interaction in the process of standing up to him, while Dave made little contribution to the maintenance of the interaction and preferred to elicit answers rather than to debate positions.

These results supplement the account of status relations which emerged from the mood and semantic analyses presented in Chapters 3 and 4. The speech function choices made by the three interactants further confirm the 'work' the parents do to provide discursive space for the son, his willingness to take it, the unequal supportive role taken on by the mother, and the lack of linguistic connection between father and son.

5.8 CONCLUSION

In Chapters 2, 3 and 4 we have introduced the first steps in a comprehensive analysis of casual conversation. Choices in mood, appraisal, involvement, the use of humour, and now patterns in conversational structure have allowed us to analyse and reflect on the roles and relationships being enacted in excerpts of casual conversation from a variety of different contexts. We have shown how detailed grammatical, semantic and discourse analysis can begin to lay bare the linguistic behaviours which are associated with certain social roles and the interactive behaviours which enable participants, consciously and unconsciously, to position themselves and their fellow interactants as sociocultural subjects.

NOTES

1. The speech function network presented in this chapter is an adaption of the networks found in Eggins (1990) and Martin (1992).
2. The network in Figure 5.2 simplifies Halliday's (1984) speech function oppositions by listing only final category labels (e.g. command, offer, etc.) rather than displaying underlying oppositions (giving vs. demanding, goods-and-services vs. information). This caters for readers who may not be familiar with systemic formalisms.
3. See Martin (1992: ch. 2) for further subclassification of attending moves.
4. The term rejoinder is our label for the category of dynamic moves identified in Martin (1992: ch. 2).

6 Genre in casual conversation: telling stories

6.1 INTRODUCTION

In the previous chapters we have explored the lexico-grammatical and discourse-semantic resources used in casual conversation. Excerpts presented in these chapters were examples of highly interactive sequences of spoken language, characterized by a rapid transfer of turns from one speaker to another. In this chapter we turn to examples of casual conversation where interactants get to hold the floor for extended turns at talk. These extended turns or 'chunks' of talk display patterns of internal structuring which are not found in the 'chat' sections of casual conversation.

We will use the concept of 'genre' in developing a description of the internal structuring of these longer turns at talk. As outlined in Chapter 1, the concept of genre originated in literary studies but, more recently, this concept has been broadened, within the fields of functional linguistics and critical theory, to describe both literary and non-literary texts. In this chapter we will consider:

- what we mean by 'chunks' or text-types in conversation;
- principles of generic description of extended turns;
- generic analyses of a range of storytelling texts which interactants commonly produce in casual conversation;
- the different kinds of genres which occurred in casual conversation data collected in three workplaces during coffee breaks.

6.2 CHUNK AND CHAT SEGMENTS IN CASUAL TALK

The spoken language data presented in previous chapters has involved the frequent exchange of turns, involving almost competitive interaction. However, not all casual talk involves such frequent turn-taking as we saw in text 1.3: Dr Flannel, where one speaker (Bill) dominated for a sustained period of time.

As you read the following text, consider in what respects it is different from the previous texts we have presented. You might also like to suggest who you think the interactants are (for example, are there any clues as to the gender of the participants?).

Text 6.1 Cockroaches

Turn	Speaker	
1	S1	I hate cockroaches more than rats
2	S2	I don't like cockroaches either
3	S3	But cockroaches are just the thing – you just get them anywhere
4	S1	Yeah but when you tread on them they crunch [laughter]. A rat just squelches
5	S3	Actually over at Manly along the promenade, if you walk along there at night, they're that big [gesture] – they're huge but they're, they're a different ... um brand
6	S2	Big roaches, are they?
7	S3	Yeah, they're big ones, real big ones
8	S1	I remember we were sitting for our analytical chemistry exam and it was the final exams and they have sort of like bench desks where there's three to a bench normally and they had the middle seat empty and two sat either side and I was sitting there and I thought 'Geez I can feel something on my foot.'
9	S2	uuhh
10	S1	And I thought 'No, no, don't worry about it,' you know 'what on earth is this chemical equation?' and I am trying to think 'but there's something on my foot!' and I looked down and there was this cockroach like this [gesture] – and I just screamed and jumped up on the chair and as I did that I knocked the bench and it went up and all Geoff's exam stuff went into the bin next to him, and I was standing on this chair screaming and the exam supervisor came running over, 'what's going on there?' [laughs] And I said 'there's a cockroach down there' [laughs] 'cause you're not allowed to speak, sneeze, cough, anything in those final exams, and um, there's me screaming on the chair.
NV1	All	[laughter]
11	S3	Ran into Anna this morning, boy she gets around.
12	S1	Yeah, did you find out what she does?
13	S3	Yeah, she's part of a team.
14	S1	Yes ... whose team? Doctor John's?
15	S3	Yeah, she does terminal patients.

(Slade's data)

As with the texts in the previous chapters, in this text there are several interactants who are all contributing at some stage and the conversation is obviously informal and spontaneous. But, unlike the majority of the texts presented so far, at one point in this interaction (turns 8–10) the participant S1 takes the floor and is allowed to dominate the conversation for an extended period.

We can recognize that what S1 is doing in turns 8 to 10 is telling a story, which is enabled by the chat leading up to it in which all participants co-operate in 'setting the scene'. It is this highly interactive, multiparty talk which makes it possible for S1 to then hold the floor until her story is finished. We can also see that the 'story' goes through some predictable stages: almost as soon as we hear *I remember we were sitting ...*, we have expectations that S1 is going to hold the floor (or at least is making a bid to do so) and will most likely recount some events in her life. Compare this to text 3.1: Philosophy for example, where there was little predictability beyond each exchange. So, while 'chat' could be very thoroughly described by looking at micro-structural patterns (mood and speech function), texts like 6.1 invite a more macro-structure analysis.

Storytelling is very common in casual conversation. It provides conversationalists with a resource for assessing and confirming affiliations with others. For example, the story in text 6.1 entertains and amuses, but more significantly it gives the participants the opportunity to share experiences and to display agreement and shared perceptions. Stories involve both representations of the world (e.g. narrating a sequence of events located in time and place), and reactions to those events (e.g. sharing an attitudinal response). In stories we tell not just what happened, but also how we feel about it. Thus, in stories values, attitudes and ways of seeing the world are created and represented.

Stories emerge from social experience, and are shared in social contexts. The way interactants tell their stories expresses dimensions of their social identity, such as gender, class, and ethnicity. For example text 6.1 involves the telling of an embarrassing incident, which is at the expense of the speaker. The disclosure this represents indicates a particular level of contact between the interactants, and a willingness to look the fool. This also suggests the gender of the interactants, or at least that of S1 (a woman). Recent research on gender differences in storytelling (Coates 1995, Johnstone 1993) suggests that stories in which speakers show themselves in fearful, embarrassing or humiliating situations are far more likely to be told by women than by men. Later in this chapter we will see that male speakers seem to prefer to feature as heroes in stories which are about danger, violence, heroic deeds, etc. In our culture men do not usually tell stories about their own foibles.

The story in text 6.1 is embedded within an interactive context, and the right to tell a story must be negotiated with the other participants. Conversationalists display awareness of when to take turns and when to relinquish turns. For example, in text 6.1 above S1 signals that the story is about to finish when she says:

| 10 | S1 | 'cause you're not allowed to speak, sneeze, cough, anything in those final exams, and um, there's me screaming on the chair. |

This is a comment on the inappropriateness of her own behaviour and it sums up why the narrative was amusing and worth telling. The laughter which greets this summing up is followed by S3, whose contribution marks a shift in the interaction:

11   S3   Ran into Anna this morning, boy she gets around.

The shift of topic in this turn suggests that S3 would like the floor and that she is likely to proceed with a gossip text. However, before S3 is able to hold the floor for an extended turn, there is another chat segment which is highly interactive, in which the participants indicate a willingness and agreement for S3 to gossip about Anna. The conversation then continues with S3 becoming the primary speaker.

To summarize, text 6.1 develops as a sequence of 'chat' followed by a 'chunk' (a story) followed by more 'chat'. After this the conversation moves into another 'chunk' which is an example of a gossip text. It appears, therefore that conversation consists of different kinds of talk: what we have called the 'chunks' and the 'chat'. One problem in analysing conversation is that we need ways of describing both the chunks and the chat segments of conversation. The 'chat' segments are those where structure is managed 'locally' that is, turn by turn. The 'chunks' are those aspects of conversation which have a global or macro-structure, where the structure beyond the exchange is more predictable. The 'chat' segments are amenable to analysis of the type outlined in the previous chapters, i.e. analysis that models conversation in terms of the micro-interaction, describing the move by move unfolding of talk. On the other hand, the chunk segments need an analysis which can capture the predictable macro or global structure. These different analyses can be combined to build a more complete description of casual conversation. With the analysis of the 'chunks' we need ways of describing:

- the kinds of 'chunks' that can happen in spontaneous casual conversation. We need to ask, for example, what kinds of chunks other than stories can occur;
- the way these chunks are typically structured;
- the different subtypes of particular genres that we find in casual conversation in English. Can we identify different kinds of storytelling texts? If so, what do they have in common and how do they differ?

Before we look in detail at a range of storytelling genres we will review the steps involved in a generic analysis.

6.3   PRINCIPLES OF GENERIC ANALYSIS

In Chapter 1 we introduced the concept of genre and reviewed its different theoretical orientations. Following Fairclough, genre is defined as 'a socially ratified way of using language in connection with a particular type of social activity' (Fairclough 1995a: 14). It is an institutionalized language activity which has evolved over time to have a particular text structure. Genre theory is therefore 'a theory of the unfolding structure texts work through to achieve their social purposes' (Eggins and Martin in press). Six steps involved in generic structure analysis are outlined below.

i) **Recognizing a chunk** Certain factors indicate that a segment of conversation is a chunk which is amenable to a generic description. These are:

- when one participant takes the floor and is allowed to dominate the conversation for an extended period. Even in highly interactive genres, there is usually one speaker who dominates the floor for that period (although sometimes it may be two or even more speakers who are doing the co-telling). In other conversations where the interactivity disrupts the flow of the genre the adequacy of a generic description may be affected.[1]
- when the chunk appears to move through predictable stages.

In text 6.2: One Night, presented below, the participants allow John to dominate the floor when he signals that he is about to tell a story by saying:

1	1a	John	I went home with a couple of Vietnamese one night,
	1b		and I thought it was ridiculous.

The story then moves through specific stages which lead to its completion. These stages are labelled in the transcript of text 6.2 below.

In text 6.2 John is telling his story during a coffee break at work to his workmate, Keith, who is around 50 years old, and Mary. Mary is a university academic in her mid-thirties who is visiting the workplace and who joins the conversation for a short period. All the transcripts from now on are presented in turns and moves, numbered down the lefthand side.[2]

Text 6.2 One Night

Turn	Move		
Abstract			
1	1a	John	I went home with a couple of Vietnamese one night,
	1b		and I thought it was ridiculous.
Orientation			
	1c		I was sitting in the back of the car,
2	2	Mary	== mm
3	3a	John	== reading the paper ...

Complication

	3b		and … two Australian fellows in the car in front ended up just blocking the roadway,
	3c		wouldn't let them go past.

Evaluation

4	4	Mary	== Really?
5	5a	John	== Wouldn't let us go past,
	5b		they were going about ten kilometres an hour, at least.
	5c		I felt, you know, really angry.
6	6	Mary	Just because they were == Vietnamese in the car?
7	7	John	== Yeah
8	8	Mary	Isn't it == terrible!

Resolution

9	9a	John	And then we == got to the railway station
	9b		and … just near the hump,
	9c		you know that hump we go over near Fairfield, Johnny?
	9d		Um, just there,
	9e		and they stopped in the middle of the railway line
	9f		so I just jumped out of the car,
	9g		walked over towards them
	9h		and when they seen an Australian jump out,
	9i		they == took off.

Coda 1

10	10	Mary	Isn't that == terrible!
11	11	John	== It's ridiculous
12	12	Keith	Some of the people == do that
13	13a	John	To me == it wouldn't worry me,
	13b		I was just sitting there reading me paper,
	13c		but just to me,
	13d		it just bugged me
	13e		because … they're people that are different.
14	14	Mary	mm
15	15	John	That's all … people who're different.

Coda 2

16	16a	Mary	And you just,
	16b		you start realizing what they == must
17	17	John	== Oh yeah
18	18a	Mary	What they must get all the time.
	18b		What they must have to put up with, because …
19	19a	John	That's right,
	19b		yeah they must get that all …
	19c		because I asked them, I asked them,
	19d		I said "Do you get that often?"
	19e		They said, "Yeah … everywhere they go."

(Slade's data)

ii) Defining the social purpose of the chunk and labelling the genre The second step in generic analysis is to clarify the overall function or social purpose of the genre. For example, whether the primary function of the genre is to tell an amusing or entertaining story, or whether it is to gossip about someone or to exchange opinions etc. More specifically, we need to identify the way the text type constructs social reality: what social practices are referred to and how attitudes and values are formed by and reflected in the text (these points are taken up in more detail in the discussion of gossip in Chapter 7).

Once the social purpose of the text has been defined, a functional label needs to be provided. As there are different kinds of storytelling texts, these labels need to be more specific than, for example, "telling a story". We will see in the next section that there are four different kinds of stories which people commonly tell in casual conversation in English: narratives, anecdotes, exemplums and recounts. Text 6.2 is a canonical narrative of personal experience of the kind described by Labov and Waletzky (1967)[3] where the focus centres around a disturbance or crisis in the usual flow of events which must, somehow, be resolved. However, text 6.1: Cockroaches, is an example of the anecdote genre.

iii) Identifying and differentiating stages within a genre A genre is made up of constituent stages. The third step of generic analysis is, therefore, to identify the constituent stages and to explain how they relate to each other in constituting the whole. This can be achieved by using functional labels in the generic description.

Functional labelling involves asking what functional role each stage is playing, and how each stage contributes towards achieving the overall social purpose of the genre. We divide the text into functional constituents by recognizing as a stage only those turns or groups of turns which fulfil a function relative to the whole. This means that we only call something a stage if we can assign to it a functional label.[1] The aim is to describe what the stage is doing, relative to the whole, in terms as specific to the genre as can be found.

Labels such as 'beginning', 'middle', 'end', 'introduction', 'body' and 'conclusion' should be avoided as they are not genre specific. These are textual labels and therefore do not distinguish the different purposes being achieved by the different stages of a genre.

In text 6.2 we can recognize narrative stages of the type identified by Labov and Waletzky (1967: 39).

Abstract:	The purpose of the abstract is to provide a summary of the story in such a way that it encapsulates the point of the story.
Orientation:	The purpose of the orientation is 'to orient the listener in respect to place, time and behavioural situation. (Labov and Waletzky 1967: 32)
Complication:	The purpose of the complication is to present temporally sequenced events which culminate in a crisis or problem. It is the main section of a narrative.

Evaluation:	The purpose of the evaluation is to reveal 'the attitude of the narrator towards the narrative'. (Labov and Waletzky 1967: 37)
Resolution:	The purpose of the resolution is to show how the protagonist's actions resolve the crisis.
Coda:	The purpose of this concluding stage is to make a point about the text as a whole. It can be 'a functional device for returning the verbal perspective to the present moment'.

These stages are exemplified in section 6.4.1 below.

As pointed out in Chapter 2, in casual conversation there are often deviations from or disruptions to the generic flow. However, the reason that we can recognize these deviations or disruptions as such is that there is an underlying abstract structure to each generic type. To recognize deviations from a pattern is a verification of the facts of the underlying pattern. Because there is this generic expectation, participants are able to negotiate in any instance the actual unfolding of talk. For example, in text 6.4: Skiing Holiday, presented below, the listener does not contribute to the successful generic unfolding of the story. After the speaker makes his bid to tell a story, the listener digresses and does not co-orient to the story but the speaker persists and by extending the Orientation is able to proceed with telling the story.

Such deviations or disruptions demonstrate that there is an underlying abstract structure which speakers recognize and which is potentially open to negotiation at any point. The structure can be derailed, diverted or aborted altogether but more usually it will proceed through the expected stages.

iv) Specifying obligatory and optional stages   As we saw in Hasan's analysis of the service encounter genre reviewed in Chapter 2, there are obligatory and optional elements of generic structure, and the stages are ordered with respect to each other.

The obligatory elements of generic structure are defining of the genre and they are the key elements in recognizing a genre. For example, in a narrative the Orientation, Complication, Evaluation and Resolution stages are all obligatory.

On the other hand, the optional elements are not a defining feature of a particular genre and can occur across genres. For example, in a narrative the Abstract and the Coda are optional stages: they are not essential to the production of a well-formed narrative, and these stages can occur in other storytelling genres such as exemplums and anecdotes.

As explained in Chapter 2, these obligatory and optional elements can be recursive: an element or set of elements can occur more than once (Hasan 1979, Halliday and Hasan 1985).

v) Devising a structural formula   The next step in generic analysis is to devise a structural formula to describe the genre. The stages are written in a linear sequence and the symbol ^ is placed between them to indicate how they are ordered with respect to one another. The stages within the brackets

( ) are optional, occurring only in some instances of the genre. Recursions are marked by " and the domain of recursion is indicated by square brackets [ ]. For example, the structural formula for narratives such as text 6.2 above is:

(Abstract) ^ Orientation ^ Complication ^ Evaluation ^ Resolution ^ (Coda)

vi) Analysing the semantic and lexico-grammatical features for each stage of a genre Although identifying the schematic structure of a genre is a major part of generic analysis, it cannot be performed accurately without an analysis of the semantic and lexico-grammatical realizations of each stage of schematic structure. For a systematic generic analysis, semantic and grammatical justification for differentiation of text stages needs to be provided.

There are two features to note about genres in terms of semantics and lexico-grammar:

- Texts of different genres reveal different lexico-grammatical choices. Thus realization patterns will differ across genres. This will be illustrated in the next section when we outline the differences between the four storytelling genres in casual conversation.
- Each genre is made up of functionally related stages and this means that the different stages will reveal different lexico-grammatical patterns. Thus realization patterns will differ across generic stages. However, it is not that different stages will use totally different lexico-grammatical structures. Rather, it is that different stages use different configurations of lexis and grammar, different clusterings of patterns.

The semantic and lexico-grammatical analysis reveals how text types realize particular social purposes; how the participants and participant relations are constructed; how the text systematically relates to the contextual factors and how particular ideological (gender, class, ethnicity) positions are constructed and represented. This detailed language analysis is an essential aspect of genre analysis; it is not useful to conceive of genres simply in terms of their generic structure.

In the next section we will apply generic analyses to a range of authentic storytelling texts which occurred in our casual conversational data. We will describe in more detail the stages of a narrative as exemplified in text 6.2, and will define these stages by their semantic and lexico-grammatical realizations. We will also review text 6.1. We will then examine the different kinds of genres which occur in casual conversation in English and the relationship between the chunk and the chat segments of casual talk.

6.4 STORYTELLING GENRES

Following Plum (1988) we have categorized the storytelling texts into four genres: anecdote, exemplum, recount and narrative. Plum's research (1988) into texts which were produced in socio-linguistic interviews found that speakers produced a range of narrative-type genres in response to the same question. Martin and Rothery's (1986) research into children's narratives produced in the school context similarly indicated that there were a range of narrative-type genres produced by children (see Martin 1984a)[5]. These storytelling genres are all based on a time line of events, or as Martin says:

> they are built up around a set of narrative clauses ...; in addition they share basic structural elements at their beginning and ends – for example Abstract, Orientation and Coda. (1992: 564)

The differences between these storytelling genres are evident in their different generic structures, in particular in the distinctive middle stages of each genre. Plum's (1988) staging structure for these genres is outlined in Table 6.1.

Table 6.1 Generic structure of storytelling genres

	Beginning	Middle	End
Narrative	(Abstract) ^ Orientation	^ Complication ^ Evaluation ^ Resolution ^	(Coda)
Anecdote	(Abstract) ^ Orientation	^ Remarkable Event ^ Reaction	(Coda)
Exemplum	(Abstract) ^ Orientation	^ Incident ^ Interpretation ^	(Coda)
Recount	(Abstract) ^ Orientation	^ Record of Events ^ Reorientation	(Coda)

These storytelling genres are outlined in detail below with particular reference to casual conversation.

Narratives Plum (1988) uses the term 'narrative' for those texts which have the middle phase structure of Complication followed by Resolution (Complication ^ Resolution). These texts increase in tension or excitement, culminating in a crisis followed by a resolution of that crisis. These stories project a world in which the protagonists face experiences which are regarded as problematic in some way and which they must resolve. The events of narratives are given their significance through the evaluative meanings. Successful narratives have a telos. They give listeners a sense that they are moving towards some end point, towards a resolution of some conflict which has occurred in the experience of an individual or individuals. Protagonists within narratives may be represented as powerful or powerless, as acting alone or with others.

Text 6.2 above is a prototypical narrative with the crisis building up and culminating when the protagonist resolves the complication by jumping out of the car and frightening off the Anglo-Australian drivers. A detailed analysis of this text is given below.

Anecdotes   An anecdote is closely related to a narrative in that the focus is similarly on a crisis. However, in an anecdote there is no explicit resolution. Rather than being explicitly resolved, the crisis is reacted to in some way: by an expression of amazement, frustration, embarrassment, humiliation, etc.

For example, text 6.1: Cockroaches, presented at the beginning of this chapter, is an anecdote where the purpose, like that of narratives, is to tell a story to entertain or amuse. But, unlike text 6.2: One Night, in text 6.1 there is not a crisis that somehow gets resolved, but rather the disturbance of normality builds up and ends with the narrator highlighting the bizarre or unusual nature of the events by expressing her reaction (*and I was standing on this chair screaming*), which then results in an outburst of laughter. Thus the events in the anecdote are not explicitly resolved but rather the crisis is simply reacted to with laughter.

Exemplums   In exemplums there is an explicit message on how the world should or should not be.

For example, text 6.4: Working for Charity, presented below, is more concerned with making the point that *one day you can be on the inside and the next day you're right out* than with telling the story of a particular incident. The incident is described in order to illustrate the point being made. As Plum argues:

> What matters in exemplums is not the representation of events as problematic, something typical of both narrative and anecdote and reflected in their respective generic structures, but instead it is the cultural significance of the macro-event, that is the significance of the events in the context of culture in which the text is told. (Plum 1988: 225)

Recounts   Recounts, on the other hand, simply involve the retelling of events with a prosody of evaluation running throughout to make the story worth telling, but the evaluation is not realized discretely. Recounts retell events, sequenced in time, but they do not necessarily deal with a problem. The point of a recount is to retell the events and to share the speaker's appraisal of those events.

In each of these storytelling genres it is the evaluation running through the text which sustains the story and establishes its contextual significance. The evaluation may appear at any stage of the text but in some genres it increases in volume as the text proceeds until a culminating focal point is reached. We will demonstrate this increasing intensity of evaluative meanings in the analysis of text 6.1, re-presented below.

The four genres outlined above are different functional varieties of storytelling texts, each with different goals and different purposes. These variations cannot be accounted for satisfactorily in terms of the differences between individual narrators as Labov and Waletzky suggest (1967: 40). Instead we need to recognize that culturally shared practices result in functional varieties of stories, with text types differing according to the different social purposes they are fulfilling.

Although such generic variation has tended to be ignored in many functional paradigms, a subcategorization is essential to account for the different kinds of stories that are told in casual talk in English. An analysis of such stories is not only of theoretical importance for a description of casual conversation in English but, as stories are a reflection of peoples' identities, such an investigation can also shed light on the construction of social identities and sociocultural worlds.

It is important to stress that these generic forms should not be interpreted as fixed or rigid schema. The generic structure description is an abstraction which describes the underlying abstract structure that participants, within particular cultural contexts, orient to. As we said earlier, speakers frequently deviate from this ideal type but such deviations will be interpreted in relation to an understood generic convention. As Fairclough suggests:

> when people produce or interpret texts, they orientate towards conventions as ideal types ... In saying that conventions have the status of ideal types I am not suggesting they are purely imaginary; there are texts which closely match ideal types (as well as others which do not), so that people learn from concrete textual experience. (1995a: 13)

Some texts which speakers produce will be examples of socially recognized and ratified activity types and will adhere tightly to a generic structure. These texts represent 'ideal types'. However, some texts will be a complex mix of genres, while others will contain deviations from the expected generic flow. These more complex texts can be interpreted in relation to the potential, or, using Fairclough's term, to the 'ideal type'.

For analytical purposes, the concept of genre is a useful tool for describing the ideal type, for describing the generic structures which have evolved over time to achieve particular social purposes. However, this concept needs to be seen as a useful heuristic device for describing the globally structured moments in casual conversation and not as a rigid formula.

In the next section we will examine storytelling texts in more detail. We will begin with an analysis of narratives exemplified by text 6.2: One Night. This analysis will focus on the lexical and semantic realizations of each of the generic stages of the text. We will then present an analysis of anecdotes focusing on text 6.1: Cockroaches, followed by an analysis of exemplums with text 6.4: Working for Charity. Finally, the structure and realizations of recounts will be exemplified with the text 6.5: And Then We Became Friends.

6.4.1 Narratives[6]

Narratives are stories which are concerned with protagonists who face and resolve problematic experiences. The social purpose of the narrative is realized through a number of stages which are examined in detail below.

Each stage of the narrative has a particular function in relation to the narrative as a whole. The Abstract in narratives functions as a generic indicator which signals that a story is about to be told and establishes the point of the text. In text 6.2: One Night, John signals in turn 1 that a story is about to be told when he says:

1	1a	John	I went home with a couple of Vietnamese one night,
	1b		and I thought it was ridiculous.

This turn functions as the Abstract stage of the genre. The first move sets up expectations as to what the text is going to be about by naming the activity sequence that is going to be problematized (i.e. *going home*). The point of the story is established in John's second move, where the activity sequence is appraised as out of the ordinary, as problematic. This is realized grammatically by the attributive (descriptive) clause, where the Attribute is realized by the attitudinal epithet *ridiculous*.

The Orientation stage of a narrative orients the listeners to what is to follow. It is concerned with detailing people, actions, time and place. There are three semantic properties of the Orientation:

1. a locative setting in time and/or place;
2. an account of a behavioural situation which may be customary or unique;
3. the introduction of the principal character or characters who participate in the events (Rothery 1990: 182).

In text 6.2 the Orientation is expressed in John's third and fourth moves:

	1c		I was sitting in the back of the car,
2	2	Mary	== mm
3	3a	John	== reading the paper ...

In moves 1c and then 3a, John specifies the location and signals that it is a first-person narrative. As the speaker is discussing ongoing or repetitive behaviour, the present-in-past tense is used.

The Complication stage foregrounds experiential meanings and involves a problem culminating in a crisis. Semantically, the Complication involves a disruption to the usual sequence of events and in this way the actions that follow become problematic and unpredictable. The unexpected change in the usual sequence of events is indicated by John saying: *and . . . two*

Australian fellows in the car in front ended up just blocking the roadway, which then culminates in the crisis, *wouldn't let them go past.*

As the Complication stage involves retelling past events, it is typically realized grammatically by material processes in the simple past tense. Material processes are typically processes of 'doing' or 'action', for example, in text 6.2 we have the material processes of 'blocking' and 'passing' in the Complication stage.

As explained above, the Resolution stage of a narrative explains how the protagonist manages to resolve the crisis. In text 6.2, the Resolution occurs after the Evaluation, in turn 9:

9	9a	John	And then we == got to the railway station
	9b		and ... just near the hump,
	9c		you know that hump we go over near Fairfield, Johnny?
	9d		Um, just there,
	9e		and they stopped in the middle of the railway line
	9f		so I just jumped out of the car,
	9g		walked over towards them
	9h		and when they seen an Australian jump out,
	9i		they == took off.

This stage of the text is where usuality is restored, here in the final move of the turn (*they took off*). The Resolution marks a return to temporally sequenced clauses involving sequences of action processes in the past tense, for example, 'got', 'stopped', 'jumped'. In the Resolution the relationship between the processes tends to be one of temporal succession. These relationships can be realized explicitly in the text through conjunction or they can be left implicit. This is demonstrated below for the clauses from the Resolution of text 6.2. The processes are underlined, the explicit conjunctive relationships are shown in bold and the implicit conjunctive relationships are shown in parentheses:

1	And **then** we got to the railway station
2	and just near the hump, ...
3	they stopped in the middle of the railway line (then)
4	**so** I just jumped out of the car and
5	and **then** walked over towards them
6	and when they seen an Australian jumped out, (then)
7	they took off

The Evaluation stage, Labov argues, is what gives the text significance; it establishes the point of telling the story. As it occurs between the Complication and the Resolution, it creates a feeling of suspense and marks a break between these two action stages. Labov argues that this stage is obligatory as without it a narrative is incomplete:

Evaluation devices say to us: this was terrifying, dangerous, weird, wild, crazy; or amusing, hilarious, wonderful; more generally, that it was strange, uncommon, or unusual – that is, worth reporting. It was not ordinary, plain, humdrum, everyday, or run of the mill. (Labov 1972a: 371)

The Evaluation in text 6.2 occurs in turns 4 to 8:

4	4	Mary	== Really?
5	5a	John	== Wouldn't let us go past,
	5b		they were going about ten kilometres an hour, at least.
	5c		I felt, you know, really angry.
6	6	Mary	Just because they were == Vietnamese in the car?
7	7	John	== Yeah
8	8	Mary	Isn't it == terrible!

In these moves both Mary and John express incredulity and their reactions confirm the events as remarkable or unusual. John also expresses his personal reaction to the events (*I felt, you know, really angry*). With the change of focus from ideational to evaluative meanings, the Evaluation stage disrupts the activity sequence and suspends the action of the Complication. With his repetition of *wouldn't let us go past*, John draws attention to the crucial part of the narrative and thereby gives significance to the following Resolution. Rothery lists the semantic properties of the Evaluation stage as:

1 the expression of attitudes or opinions denoting the events as remarkable or unusual;
2 the expression of incredulity, disbelief, apprehension about the events on the part of the narrator or a character of the narrative, including highlighting the predicament of characters;
3 comparisons between usual and unusual sequences of events in which participants in the narrative are involved;
4 predictions about possible course of action to handle a crisis or about the outcome of the events. (Rothery 1990: 203)

Evaluative comments, however, do not only occur as a discrete stage but are usually spread throughout the text. For example, in text 6.2 there are evaluative comments in the Abstract when John says *and I thought it was ridiculous* (move 1a), as well as in Coda 1 when both Mary and John offer appraisals:

10	10	Mary	Isn't that == terrible!
11	11	John	== It's ridiculous

Labov distinguishes between those evaluations that appear inside from those that appear outside the fixed position clauses of narratives. The former he refers to as embedded evaluations, and he points out that such embedded evaluations do not disrupt the dramatic continuity (Labov 1972a: 372). The latter he refers to as external evaluations. Labov outlines five types of evaluations which range from wholly external to embedded, as summarized below:

i) Wholly external evaluations where the narrator stops the narrative to address the listener directly and to express an evaluation of the event (see Toolan 1988). For example:

Wouldn't let us go past, they were going about ten kilometres an hour, at least. I felt, you know, really angry (from text 6.2)

ii) Evaluations where the narrator attributes the evaluative remark to him/herself at the moment that the story happened. So it is what the narrator thought to him/herself at the time of the events. This is an external evaluation that does not overtly break the flow of the story and it is thus an intermediate step between external and embedded evaluations. For example:

*And I thought, 'isn't this terrible, just because they were Vietnamese'.
(* = hypothetical example)

iii) Evaluations where the narrator embeds a comment made to another participant at the time of the action. For example:

*So I said to Mary, 'This makes me really angry'.

iv) Evaluations which come from another participant in the action. For example:

*And after it all happened, Mary said 'It's really frightening, it happens to us all the time'.

v) Evaluative action when the narrator tells what people did rather than what they said. For example:

*I just prayed that they would drive on.

To these five categories we can add another:

vi) Evaluative Conclusion: this occurs where an evaluative comment is embedded in the Coda. For example:

To me it wouldn't worry me, I was just sitting there reading me paper, but just to me, it just bugged me because ... they're people that are different (from text 6.2)

The Coda in text 6.2 contains other evaluative comments. Mary, the female participant, in move 10, says *Isn't that terrible* which evaluates the events in terms of 'ethics' (see Chapter 5) or morality (the expression of incredulity) whereas John, the male narrator, evaluates the incident as unusual or out of the ordinary with his comment *its ridiculous* (move 11). John evaluates it, therefore, as remarkable rather than unethical.

The Coda often refers back to the theme of the Abstract, and makes an overall statement about the text. This is done in text 6.2 in the first Coda with the speaker repeating *it's ridiculous*. One of the functions of the Coda is to return the text to the present and by doing so to evaluate the whole event.

The use of appraisal lexis such as *terrible* and *ridiculous* provides summary evaluations and the clause *some of the people do that* relates the Coda to the here and now by commenting on its significance. The narrator's comment:

13	13a	John	To me == it wouldn't worry me,
	13b		I was just sitting there reading me paper,
	13c		but just to me,
	13d		it just bugged me
	13e		because ... they're people that are different.

resembles a concluding comment that provides a thematic summary of the whole story and so it signifies the end of Coda 1 and it is where the story could have finished. Following this, Mary makes a comment which links the preceding text to a wider context (moves 16a–19g) and so initiates another Coda which is produced interactively and where the relevance of the narrative to the broader social context is commented on.

Table 6.2 outlines some of the language features typical of the different stages of a narrative. It is important to emphasize that what distinguishes the different stages of a genre is that they fulfil functionally distinct roles and therefore lexico-grammatical realizations vary from one stage to another. The functional motivation of the genre is seen in its distinctive generic structure and lexico-grammatical features: the linguistic forms are as they are because of the functions they serve.

6.4.2 Anecdotes

The second story genre we will review is the anecdote. The primary function of an anecdote is to enable interactants to share a reaction to a remarkable event. Anecdotes create a crisis but do not resolve it explicitly. The generic structure of an anecdote is:

(Abstract) ^ Orientation ^ Remarkable Event ^ Reaction ^ (Coda)

The Remarkable Event consists of temporally ordered actions, outlining a remarkable event, which the narrator wants to share his/her reaction to. The Reaction stage, as with the Evaluation in narratives, highlights the

Table 6.2 Semantic and lexico-grammatical realizations of the stages of text 6.2: One Night

Genre: Narrative
Purpose: To deal with unusual or problematic events and their outcome.
Stages: (Abstract) ^ Orientation ^ Complication ^ Evaluation ^ Resolution ^ (Coda)

Stages	Moves	Language features
Abstract Establishes the point of the text and signals that a story is about to be told	1a–1b	Thematic prediction of what the text is going to be about Names the activity sequence (i.e. going home) that is going to be problematized Attitudinal lexis, e.g. *ridiculous*
Orientation Orients listeners to what is to follow in terms of people, actions, time and place	1c–3a	A locative setting in place Past action material processes
Complication Temporally orders actions leading to a crisis	3b–3c	Protagonists as theme Temporally sequenced Material processes, e.g. *blocking, go*
Evaluation Evaluates or presents appraisal of crisis	4–8	Suspends the action of the complication by the use of repetition – *he wouldn't let us go past/* the use of intensifier – *really/* a confirmation check/the use of an exclamative – *isn't that terrible* Tension is produced by the disruption to the activity sequence
Resolution Actions resolve crisis	9a–9i	Protagonist resolves complication Temporally sequenced clauses Sequence of action processes in past tense, e.g. *got, stopped, jumped, took off* Usuality restored – *they took off*
Coda 1 Makes point about text as whole Returns text to present	10–15	The use of attitudinal lexis, such as 'terrible', 'ridiculous' Move 12 returns text to present Moves 13a–15 provide thematic summation of narrative
Coda 2	16a–19e	Evaluation of the whole event Return to present Use of quoted speech for dramatic effect

significance or tellability of the events, often by drawing on assumed cultural knowledge. The Reaction is an interpersonally loaded representation of the speaker's reaction to their own story, where the event is evaluated and the significance of the story established.

We will look at two anecdotes. Text 6.1: Cockroaches, introduced earlier in the chapter, is an anecdote told by a woman to her colleagues (one woman, one man). Text 6.3: Skiing Holiday, presented below, is told by a man to an all-male group. Both the conversations took place during coffee time at work.

6.4.2.1 The analysis of text 6.1: Cockroaches

Text 6.1 is re-presented below, this time with the generic stages indicated on the left. There are three participants: Pat, Pauline and Gary. They are clerical staff who have worked together for over two years. They regularly have lunch and coffee breaks together and they are all in their mid to late twenties. They are all Anglo-Australians.

Text 6.1 Cockroaches

Turn	Move	Speaker	
1	1a	Pat	I hate cockroaches more than rats
2	2a	Pauline	I don't like cockroaches either
3	3a	Gary	But cockroaches are just the thing –
	3b		you just get them anywhere
4	4a	Pat	Yeah but when you tread on them they crunch [laughter].
	4b		A rat just squelches
5	5a	Gary	Actually over at Manly along the promenade,
	5b		if you walk along there at night
	5c		they're that big [gesture]
	5d		they're huge
	5e		but they're, they're a different … um brand
6	6	Pauline	Big roaches, are they?
7	7	Gary	Yeah, they're big ones, real big ones

Orientation

8	8a	Pat	I remember we were sitting for our analytical chemistry exam
	8b		and it was the final exams
	8c		and they have sort of like bench desks
	8d		where there's three to a bench normally
	8e		and they had the middle seat empty
	8f		and two sat either side

Remarkable Event

	8g		and I was sitting there
	8h		and I thought 'geez I can feel something on my foot'
9	9	Gary	uuhh
10	10a	Pat	And I thought 'no no don't worry about it'
	10b		you know
	10c		'what on earth is this chemical equation'
	10d		And I am trying to think
	10e		but there's something on my foot
	10f		and I looked down
	10g		and there was this cockroach like this [gesture]
	10h		and I just screamed
	10i		jumped up on the chair
	10j		and as I did that I knocked the bench
	10k		and it went up
	10l		and all Geoff's exam stuff went into the bin next to him,

Reaction

	10m		and I was standing on this chair screaming
	10n		and the exam supervisor came running over 'what's going on there!' [laughs]
	10o		And I said 'there's a cockroach down there!' [laughs]

Coda

	10p		'Cause you're not allowed to speak, sneeze, cough, anything in those final exams,
	10q		and um there's me screaming on the chair.
11	11	All	[laughter]

(Slade's data)

Pat may well have been intending to tell a story when she said *I hate cockroaches more than rats*. However, as we do not know this from the co-text, this move cannot be interpreted as the beginning of the story. It may equally well be the case that Pat's story was prompted by Gary's previous two turns

(turns 5 and 7). This highlights the importance of taking into account the co-text in interpreting the generic flow. This conversation demonstrates the embedding of a generically structured text, a chunk, in the dynamic flow of talk.

Pat's anecdote actually starts in turn 8, with an Orientation that first sets the general context (the exam) and then in moves 8b to 8f provides more specific, contextual information. It is a prototypical anecdote in that the Remarkable Event takes the listeners up to the climax of the crisis and then the story suddenly stops. It does not resolve the crisis but finishes the story amid chaos with the Reaction stage which follows explaining why the behaviour was inappropriate but amusing.

By contrast, if it were a narrative, it would have had an explicit Resolution such as:

> The supervisor killed the cockroach, I picked up Geoff's exam stuff and went back to my exam paper.

However, in an anecdote it is not the resolution of the crisis which is important. In fact, by not providing an explicit Resolution, it is understood within this cultural context that normality was restored. It is the Reaction which follows the Remarkable Event and the evaluative comments throughout the anecdote which establish the significance of the story. Reactions can include an outburst of laughter, a gasp indicating horror or fear or an expression of amazement.

The embedded evaluative comments which occur throughout this anecdote start with Pat's comment in move 10a: *And I thought, no, no, don't worry about it.* Throughout the Remarkable Event the interpersonal contribution increases in amplification until move 10o and the tension is increased by three factors:

- the disruption of the activity sequence with the intrusion of the quoted thought in move 10a (*And I thought, no, no , don't worry about it*);
- the shift from the simple past (*I thought*) to the present in present (*I am trying to think*);
- the increased interpersonal intensity with *I just screamed and jumped up on the chair* in moves 10h and 10i.

The evaluation running throughout the story reaches a peak in moves 10m to 10o when Pat says:

10m	and I was standing on this chair screaming
10n	and the exam supervisor came running over 'what's going on there!' [laughs]
10o	And I said 'there's a cockroach down there!' [laughs]

The Reaction is the focal point of the evaluative comments and the shift from the Remarkable Event stage to the Reaction stage is realized grammatically by:

- a shift in tense from simple past (*looked down, screamed, jumped up*) to the use of present in past (*was standing*);
- the occurrence of two instances of quoted speech, in move 1on (*what's going on there!*) and in move 1oo (*And I said 'there's a cockroach down there!'*);
- the use of an amplified behavioural process realizing affect in move 1om – '... *screaming'* and the amplification in move 1on – '... *came running over'*.

The Reaction then increases in intensity with Pat's interpersonal comments continuing in the Coda and culminating in move 1oq (*and um there's me screaming on the chair*). This reiteration of '*screaming on the chair'* has the effect of emphasising the unusual or inappropriate nature of the events.

As the story Pat tells does not have a Resolution, the events outlined in the story end at the Reaction stage with the outburst of laughter indicating that the story has worked and it needs no resolution.

Text 6.1 contains a story told by a woman and it is in the Remarkable Event, from move 1oe onwards, that the story starts sounding like a story told by a woman. The story is a self-deprecating one, about an embarrassing incident, where the protagonist represents herself as behaving in an inappropriate and humiliating way. The inappropriateness of the behaviour is what makes it amusing. In the Reaction stage Pat reminds her listeners of the location of the events – 'the exam room' – and by doing so, explicitly reinforces the inappropriateness of her actions. In the Coda she comments yet again on the inappropriate behaviour and thereby sums up why the anecdote was amusing and worth telling. Table 6.3 identifies some of the language features typical of the different stages of an anecdote with reference to text 6.1: Cockroaches.

6.4.2.2 Analysis of text 6.3: Skiing Holiday

We will now look at an anecdote told by a man in an all male group in a similar setting, at a coffee break at work. Text 6.3: Skiing Holiday involves three men, two Anglo-Australians, Willie and John, and Keith who is a first generation Italian–Australian. They are supervisors in a car factory, all in their mid-forties to mid-fifties.

The generic stages of text 6.3 are indicated and the moves are numbered down the left hand side of the transcript below.

Table 6.3 Semantic and lexico-grammatical realizations of the stages of
text 6.1: Cockroaches

Stages	Moves	Language features
Orientation Orients the listeners to what is to follow, in terms of people, actions, time and place	8a–8f	Setting in time and place Moves 8a and 8b set the general context Moves 8c–8f provide more specific contextual information
Remarkable Event Temporally orders actions outlining a remarkable event which the narrator wants to share her reaction to	8g–10j 8g–8h 10a–10e	Narrator as theme – *I was sitting, I can feel, I thought* Suspends the action by the quoted thought, and a shift from the simple past to the present in present. Tension is produced by the disruption of the activity sequence in move 10a Present in present tense in move 10c Temporally sequenced clauses
Reaction The evaluation of the events establishes the significance of the story	10m–10o	Use of quoted speech for dramatic effect Shift in tense from simple past to present in past – *was standing* Intensity of interpersonal contribution increasing, e.g. *screamed, jumped up* Outburst of laughter
Coda Makes point about text as a whole Returns text to present	10p–11	Evaluation of the whole event Return to the present

Text 6.3 Skiing Holiday

Turn	Move	Speaker	

Orientation

1	1a	Willie	Me son got back from a skiing holiday,
	1b		== ah last Friday.
2	2	John	== mmhm
3	3	Willie	Some of the funny stories he == he
NV1			== [Laughter]
4	4a	John	He can have that for me.
	4b		Was too bloody cold for me yesterday afternoon.

5	5a	Willie	Ah well the wife's been skiing,
	5b		the rest of the family
	5c		but I haven't been down there.
6	6	John	I was only down there one time.
7	7a	Willie	He said he said once you start down a slope its there's no way you can stop.
NV2			== [Laughter]
8	8	John	== Yeah.
9	9	Willie	He said [Laughs] whether you're starting down on your backside == or on your skis.
10	10a	John	== Eh, I went down there once.
	10b		I froze all the time.
	10c		I said == never again.

Remarkable Event

11	11a	Willie	== He eh he came down
	11b		and he he was coming down this track in fact,
	11c		I think it was was it Perisher?
	11d		No it wasn't,
	11e		uh I forget where it was.
12	12	John	Smiggins.
13	13a	Willie	No no no no further Guthega.
	13b		He went up to Guthega.
	13c		He was coming down this this track
	13d		and he's been a few times
	13e		so he's got some idea of it um
	13f		so he said that he he saw this slight rise,
	13g		so he said he headed up the rise
	13h		== and he found out it was a ski jump.
NV3		ALL	== [Laughter]
14	14a	Willie	He he'd lost one ski at the top
	14b		and eh apparently he was flying through the air with one leg up in the air with a ski on it
	14c		and he he landed head first in the snow
	14d		but he caught his head.
	14e		His mate with him
	14f		he hit a tree on the way down.
	14g		Came back all bruised and scraped down one side of his face.

Reaction

| 15 | 15 | John: | And they say Rugby League's rough. |
| NV4 | | All | [Laughter] |

Coda

| 16 | 16a | Willie | He he said to me when he got out of the snow bank |

16b	he he saw a fella flat on his back.
16c	And he'd collapsed there laughing.
16d	First time going over this jump.

(Slade's data)

Text 6.3 demonstrates interesting gender differences in the telling of stories. The text deals with a funny incident related by a man about his son. Although the story is about a skiing accident, it is told from the point of view of the son surviving and laughing and, in contrast to text 6.1, it is told in a way that does not make the son look foolish or incompetent. Although Willie's son falls over in the snow, this event is presented not as his fault or because of incompetence, but because of the ski jump. The story foregrounds the amusement, not the embarrassment. This is partly achieved by the fact that this is told through the boy's eyes and not the eyes of the onlookers.

Although they represent different story genres, there is an interesting similarity between text 6.3 and the narrative we analysed above, text 6.2: One Night. In these two stories, both narrated by men, the events are satisfactorily resolved by the intervention of the protagonist as 'hero' who deliberately undertakes a course of action to set things right.

Recent research on gender and language has indicated that stories told by women are significantly different from stories told by men. Research on the talk of women friends (Coates 1995, 1996) has argued that the female protagonist in stories of personal experience finds herself in impossible, fearful, humiliating or embarrassing situations. Women, Coates argues, present a mundane world where problems can be shared, and usually where something is being 'done' to the protagonist rather than the protagonist being the doer. This is in contrast to men who tend to tell personal stories about danger, violence, heroic deeds, etc. Barbara Johnstone's (1993) research involving the analysis of 58 personal experience narratives demonstrates that:

> women's stories tend to be about community, while the men's tend to be about contest. The men tell about human contests – physical contests such as fights as well as social contests in which they use verbal and/or intellectual skill to defend their honour. They tell about contests with nature: hunting and fishing... The women's stories, on the other hand, revolve around the norms of the community and joint action by groups of people. The women tell incidents in which they violate social mores and are scared or embarrassed as a result. (1993: 69)

By examining the different kinds of narratives produced by men and women we can be more specific about the function of this kind of talk. The overall purpose of storytelling in the culture is to entertain or amuse through the exploration of experience. However, more specifically, the purpose of narratives in women's talk is to bind women together in sustaining and creating new worlds and in experimenting with possible selves (Coates, 1995,1996). Coates also argues that such stories can be a means of implicitly questioning and criticising dominant values. Although women present themselves as powerless and as reactive rather than proactive, they also often hint at other ways of behaving and other ways of seeing the world. This is particularly evident in the gossip texts discussed in Chapter 7.

With generically structured segments of talk there will be one or more participants in a primary listener role. An examination of this primary listener role reveals other interesting gender differences in the type of contributions participants make to the interaction. Gardner (1994) outlines seven different types of listener contributions that are common in casual talk in English. These are:

i)   continuers which function to immediately hand the floor back to the last speaker, e.g. 'mmhm', 'uh', 'huh';
ii) acknowledgments which claim agreement or understanding of the previous turn, e.g. 'mm', 'yeah';
iii) assessments which are appreciative in some way of what has just been said, e.g. 'how awful', 'shit', 'wonderful';
iv) newsmarkers which mark the speakers turn as news e.g. 'really', 'is it!';
v)   questions that indicate interest by asking for further details or questions which are asked in order to repair some misunderstanding;
vi) collaborative completions, when one participant finishes another's utterance;
vii) non-verbal vocalizations, e.g. laughter, sighs, etc.

These are the unmarked contributions which can be made by participants in a primary listener role. However, sometimes listeners will produce more substantial turns which can be disruptive of the generic flow.

In text 6.3: Skiing Holiday, John's first *'mmhm'* in move 2 is a continuer which does not really indicate involvement. It is neutral feedback rather than an encouragement to continue telling the story. In moves 4a and 4b, John is less than encouraging: he does not give a go-ahead to tell the story, rather he treats Willie's previous three moves (1, 2 and 4a) as an announcement to which he indicates a negative evaluation. Willie persists in trying to proceed with the anecdote but once again, in moves 10a-10c, John does not give a go-ahead and continues to digress from Willie's story. In both these cases John's contributions are disruptions: they are not questions that encourage Willie's story to be continued but rather are comments about himself that interrupt the flow of the story. In the case of the second interruption in moves 10a–10c, the comments are ignored and Willie continues with the story.

We can contrast this with the feedback which Mary gives in text 6.2: One Night. Mary's comments in move 4 (*really?*) and in move 8 (*isn't it terrible*) are supportive assessments which encourage the narrator to continue. Generally, women are more likely, in these cultural contexts, continually to insert supportive minimal responses or questions to elicit further details (see Fishman 1983 on the differences between male and female feedback strategies in English informal conversation).

John's contributions in text 6.3 which disrupt the generic flow also demonstrate that, although participants are oriented to the generic structure, the stages still need to be negotiated at every move. If the participants do not immediately co-orient to the story, the Orientation may need to be extended before the speaker can move into the next stage, or the participants may be successful in blocking the story altogether.

One other interesting gender difference highlighted by the stories in this conversational data is the degree of evaluative comments provided by the speakers throughout their story. In text 6.3: Skiing Holiday, the evaluative comments are restricted to move 3: *Some of the funny stories he == he* and move 15: *And they say Rugby League's rough*, where the focal point of evaluation is provided by another participant (John). By contrast, in text 6.1: Cockroaches, the woman narrator evaluates the events explicitly all the way through the story. The evaluative comments start in move 10a and increase in intensity until move 100: *And I said 'there's a cockroach down there!' [laughs]*

In Table 6.4, the generalized features of anecdotes are exemplified through the significant language features of each stage of text 6.3: Skiing Holiday.

As the analysis in Table 6.4 indicates, text 6.3: Skiing Holiday is told without an Abstract. The setting and tone of the story is clearly established, in the Orientation, before the actual events are described. This is done by:

- thematizing the son in move 1 in the Orientation and thus introducing him as the protagonist;
- foreshadowing a funny incident in move 3 – *Some of the funny stories he he;*
- foreshadowing that it is going to be a skiing story in move 7a – *He said he said once you start down a slope its there's no way you can stop* and in move 9 – *He said whether you're starting down on your backside or on your skis.* Move 7a also immediately establishes the point of the story.

The Remarkable Event is temporally sequenced and Willie uses reported speech as well as a shift from the simple past to present in past tense to heighten dramatic effect, e.g. *he was coming down the track.* Moves 13d and 13e break the storyline and, by doing so, create an expectation that a crisis is about to happen.

We will now briefly apply this generic structure analysis to the story segment of Text 1.3: Dr Flannel, presented in Chapter 1, demonstrating the generalizability of this formula.

Table 6.4 Semantic and lexico-grammatical realizations of the stages of text 6.3: Skiing Holiday

Stages	Moves	Language features
Orientation	1–3; 7a–10c Moves 4a–6 are an interruption by another speaker	Introduction of characters and setting them in time and place (move 1) Foreshadows events/action (moves 3, 7a and 9) Point of story established (e.g. in move 7a by the use of an existential clause with generic participants) and the reason is given why the story is worth telling
Remarkable Event Temporally orders actions outlining a remarkable event which the narrator wants to share his reaction to	11a–14g	Events sequenced in time Temporal links are implicit, the text follows events in time Use of reported speech which is a feature of retelling anecdote featuring a third party Present in present tense in move 11b to heighten dramatic effect – in contrast with the simple past tense typical of this stage. Moves 13d–13e provide a break in the storyline and by doing so create an expectation that some crisis is about to happen
Reaction The evaluation of the events establishes significance of story	15 and NV4	Jointly constructed Outburst of laughter (in amusing anecdotes) often occurs after remarkable event.
Coda Makes point about text as a whole Returns text to present	16a–16d	An elliptical relational clause is used 'First time going over this jump' to emphasise signficance of story.

Text 1.3 Dr Flannel (re-presented from Chapter 1)

Turn Abstract	Speaker	
1	Bill	I had to laugh. I walked into David Jones's and they're always nice ... people in there, you know
2	Mavis	Mmm ==
3	Alex	== Yeah

Orientation

| 4 | Bill | And there was two girls behind a counter |

Remarkable Event

		and I didn't know which ... where to go, to go to ahh ... And she said, I said ah "Good Morning ladies" and one of the girls == said "Thank you. You're a thorough gentleman."
NV1	Mavis and Alex	== [laughter]
5	Bill	And I said [laughing slightly] "Could you direct me in the direction where the men's singlets are? I'm after ... a Dr Flannel. She said "DR FLANNEL!" She said "What's that?" I said "WAIT A MINUTE!" [Makes motion of tearing shirt open].
NV2	Mavis and Alex	[laughter]
6	Alex	And showed her [laughs]
7	Bill	I said "THAT!" [pointing at singlet]
NV3	Mavis and Alex	[laughter]
8	Alex	And she screamed and == called security. [laughs]
9	Bill	== And I said "Do ya wanta have a look at the hairs on me chest?" I said "Have a look!"
NV4	ALL	[laughter]
10	Mavis	You haven't got any have you?
11	Bill	NO! Haa! [loud laughter] And they started laughin' And another woman came over and said "What's goin' on here?"
NV5	Mavis and Alex	[laughter]
12	Bill	She said "Oh this gentleman here wants to know where the ... the Dr Flannel are. He's just showed us his chest ... == and the hairs on his chest". [laughs]
NV6	Mavis and Alex	== [laughter]
13	Bill	and they said "HE HASN'T GOT ANY!"
NV7	ALL	[laughter]
14	Mavis	What store do you have to go to? Is there a men's store and a women's store?
15	Bill	Yeah. The men's store.
16	Mavis	Yeah. The men's store. Yeah, I was gonna say...
17	Bill	Ha ha [laughing] And
18	Mavis	They usually
19	Bill	she ha ha she said. "You've got a decent old scar there"... I said "Oh yeah. [laughing slightly] I said "I'm not gonna == show you where it ends!"
20	Mavis	== Mmm
NV8	ALL	[laughter]
21	Bill	[still laughing] And she said "Why?" I said "It goes a fair way down!" [laughs]

22	Mavis	Did you tell her what you've had?
23	Bill	Yeah ha [laughing]. She said "What you've had an operation?" I said "Yeah, I had a bypass operation". She said "That's what they do?" I said "Yeah". I said "They
24	Mavis	Cut you right open
25	Bill	"Get a saw" I said. And she said "They DON'T!" I said "They DO!"
26	Mavis	They DO! Yeah! They'd have to.
27	Bill	I said "They get like a ah … fret saw and it's got little, a revolving blade on it. And I said "They go zoom, straight down your chest".
28	Mavis	They cut open your breastbone to … == pull it back
29	Bill	== Yeah
30	Mavis	Don't they? To be able to do it … == Open … Yeah.
31	Bill	== Yeah pull it open like that.
32	Bill	And I said "I've got wire in there". I said "There's three lots of wire down there, figure-eighted". She said "No!"
NV9	Mavis and Alex	[begin laughing]
33	Bill	…. I said "Well", I said "You're not – gonna feel it, I can". [laughing]
NV10	ALL	[laughter]

Reaction

34	Bill	She said. You know the two of them, they said "You've made our day
NV11	Mavis and Alex	[begin laughing]
35	Bill	… It's always SOO dull" [laughs]
NV12	Alex	[laughs]
36	Mavis	Yeah it probably would be ( ) As I say …
37	Bill	Yeah. [still laughing slightly] She said "We'll remember you for a while."
NV13	Mavis	[laughs]

Coda

38	Bill	And when I was goin' out … They never had any … They directed me where to go.
39	Mavis	Mmm
40	Bill	[laughing] And when I was goin' out they're laughin' their heads off and wavin' to me [laughs]
NV14	Alex	[laughter]
NV15	Bill	[still laughing – the last to stop]
41	Mavis	Yea that, that's what they call them don't they? They call them flannels, don't they?
42	Bill	Yeah. Dr Flannel.

We see in text 1.3 that the Abstract establishes immediately that Bill is going to tell an amusing story and the Orientation provides the necessary contextual information. The Remarkable Event outlines the bizarre nature of events, culminating in Bill's punchline in turn 33. This causes an outburst of laughter from Mavis and Alex (there is no need for a Resolution) and then Bill repeats the shop assistant's reaction with: *You've made our day ... It's always SOO dull.* The anecdote ends, in a dialogically constructed Coda, with Bill highlighting how amusing the Events were and Mavis returning the text to the present with *They call them flannels, don't they?* (see Chapter 3 for a discussion of mood choice in this text, and Chapter 4 for a detailed discussion of humour in the text).

We will now look at an analysis of Exemplums which occur in casual conversation in English.

6.4.3 Exemplums

Plum (1988: 233) defines an exemplum as 'a moralising tale or parable; an anecdote designed to point a moral'. The moral point is made by reference to the broader cultural context, similar to the gossip texts we will be considering in Chapter 7. Both exemplums and gossip fulfil the function of prescribing behaviour, by making it clear what is considered to be appropriate behaviour.

Text 6.4: Working for Charity, presented below, is a conversation involving two women. The conversation took place during a coffee break at work. Judy is a clerical officer in her mid-twenties and Mary is a university academic in her mid-thirties who is a visitor to the workplace. They are both Anglo-Australians.

Text 6.4 Working for Charity

Turn	Move	Speaker	
Abstract			
1	1a	Judy	Yeah its m- quite amazing really,
	1b		one day you can be on the inside
	1c		and the next day you're you're right – out –
Orientation			
	1d		I I used to work for this charity
	1e		really this is a classic I reckon
	1f		a Christian charity right?
2	2	Mary	Yeah
3	3a	Judy	And em and depending on – depending on where
	3b		you know I was saying before I was the catering manager == there.
4	4	Mary	== Yeah right.
5	5a	Judy	And I was treated with the utmost respect really you know
	5b		and I I had a fabulous job
	5c		and I just loved every minute of it you know
	5d		and I was on the ad-administration staff you know
	5e		and everything was really wonderful

Incident

	5f		and then when they moved me and John to the you know the accommodation hhh
	5g		my God!
	5h		the attitude changed completely == you know.
6	6	Mary	== Why?
7	7a	Judy	From the man ... from the management which a which was the Chaplain you know
	7b		the the chaplain the head of it all.
8	8	Mary	Oh == yeah,
9	9a	Judy	== I was just a nobody
	9b		and from going from a position where I was included in absolutely everything
	9c		overnight I was put in a position where I was no longer ... I mean even just little things
	9d		like I was no longer invited to staff farewells.
	9e		Or they would they'd run up 5 minutes
	9f		because I lived on the premises
	9g		they'd run up 5 minutes before the person was due to go
	9h		and say 'oh Judy you know we forgot to tell you that there was an afternoon tea for so and so'
	9i		things like that you know

Interpretation

	9j		and == you used to get really hurt over that.
10	10a	Mary	== Why do you reckon...
	10b		why was that do you think?
11	11	Judy	hh cause it's not really a Christian organization
NV1		ALL	[Laughter]

(Slade's data)

The Abstract Judy offers in this text is in the form of an interpretation and establishes her reason for telling the story. She uses the generic 'you' to state the general relevance of the story. As with narratives and anecdotes, the Orientation orients the listeners to what is to follow in terms of characters, actions, time, place, etc. The more general field of 'charities' is first introduced by Judy in moves 1d to 1e- *I I used to work for this charity, really this is a classic I reckon* and then the more specific field is established in move 1f – *a Christian charity*, in move 3b – *you know I was saying before I was the catering manager there* and in move 5d – *and I was on the ad-administration staff you know.*

The difference in text structure between exemplums and the other storytelling texts is evidenced by the middle stages of Incident and Interpretation. The Incident represents a series of temporally sequenced events where the focus is on the significance of the events, on their interpretation and what they illustrate, rather than on their problematic nature.

Judy's interpretive comments run throughout the text (in particular occurring in this text in both the Abstract as well as in the Incident) but there is also a localized focal point that occurs after the Incident stage. The function of this stage is quite different from the Evaluation stage in narratives, or the Reaction stage in anecdotes. The evaluative comments in exemplums relate to the broader cultural context beyond the immediate context of the text, and make a moral point of some sort. For example, consider move 11:

| 11 | 11 | Judy | hh cause it's not really a Christian organization |

In this move Judy does not provide an appraisal of the crisis. Instead she offers her interpretation in terms of an ethical judgement on how organizations should treat people.

Past tense action processes are typically used in the Incident stage, just as they are in the Complication stage of narratives and the Remarkable Event of anecdotes. The function of the Incident is to provide evidence for the Interpretation which follows. In text 6.4 the pivotal point of the Incident is realized in move 9a where Judy characterizes her role with the following descriptive/attributive clause:

| 9 | 9a | Judy | == I was just a nobody |

Table 6.5 lists some of the main semantic and lexico-grammatical realizations of each of the stages of an Exemplum with particular reference to text 6.4.

6.4.4 Recounts

Recounts are about a temporal sequence of events in which the narrator is involved. The narrator's attitude towards the events is outlined, but this evaluation is not realized discretely. Recounts do not necessarily deal with a problem, although often they tell about slight disruptions that have to be overcome. The purpose of Recounts is to tell how one event leads to another. Unlike narratives and anecdotes, they are concerned with an expected activity sequence rather than with highlighting a remarkable event. The point of the Recount is simply the succession of events. The generic structure of a Recount, as reformulated by Martin (1992) is:

(Abstract) ^ (Orientation) ^ Record of Events ^ (Coda)

The Record of Events stage comprises a series of events about a given field or fields. It usually involves a step-by-step progression which is given significance by the interpersonal contributions that occur throughout the text. In text 6.5: And Then We Became Friends, presented below, interpretation and evaluation run throughout but they are not amplified at the point of disruption as would be the case in a narrative or an anecdote. Recounts involve ongoing evaluation which is in contrast to anecdotes where evaluation comes to an amplified climax at the point of the disruption to the activity sequence.

As with the other storytelling texts, Recounts have a telos giving the listeners a sense that they are moving towards an end point, that the activity sequence will be completed.

Table 6.5 Semantic and lexico-grammatical realizations of the stages of text 6.4: Working for Charity

Stages	Moves	Language features
Abstract Establishes the point of the text Signals that a story is about to be told	1a–1c	Use of generalized *you* to state general relevance of story Attitudinal lexis *quite amazing* An attributive clause in move 1 is elaborated in moves 1b–1c
Orientation Orients the listener to what is to follow in terms of people, actions, time and place	1d–1f	Introduces wider field (charity) and then more specific fields (Christian charity, catering manager) Use of circumstances of location Use of generic statements (e.g. move 1d) Point of story established in moves 5a–5e where appraisal of whole experience is given *Every minute* and *everything* are markers that this is a general comment, thereby establishing the significance of the story
Incident Outlines temporally sequenced events in order to elucidate interpretative comments or moral judgement	5f–9i	Past tense action processes Time sequence
Interpretation A moral interpretation or judgement of incident is relayed	9j–1l	Use of anaphoric extended text reference *that* in move 9j Refers back to whole incident Use of descriptive/attributive clauses which may be interpersonally modalized and/or the attributes interpersonally loaded

The next text we will consider, text 6.5: And Then We Became Friends, is a coffee break conversation involving a group of women at work. The three women (Jessie, Di and Judy) are supervisors in a hospital kitchen and they are in their mid to late twenties. Di is telling the story of how she first met her boyfriend in London: she had been writing to him for the two years before they met.

Text 6.5 And Then We Became Friends

Turn	Move	Speaker	
Abstract			
1	1a	Jessie	Right.
	1b		Right and so when did you == actually meet him?
2	2	Di	== So we didn't actually meet until that night.
3	3	Jessie	Until that night.
4	4	Judy	Oh hysterical [laughing]!
Orientation			
5	5a	Di	Well, I met him that night.
	5b		We were all, we all went out to dinner
Record of Events			
	5c		So I had champagne and strawberries at the airport
6	6a	Jessie	And what was it like the when you first saw him?
	6b		Were you really == nervous?
7	7a	Di	== Well I was hanging out of a window watching him in his car,
	7b		and I thought 'oh God what about this!'
NV1		Jessie/Judy	[Laughter]
8	8a	Di	And he'd combed his hair
	8b		and shaved his eyebrows == and
9	9	Jessie	== Had you seen a photo of him?
10	10a	Di	Oh yeah,
	10b		I had photos of him, photos ...
	10c		and I'd spoken to him on the phone.
11	11	Jessie	Did you get on well straight away?
12	12a	Di	Uh, well we sort of.
	12b		I'm a sort of nervy person when I first meet people,
	12c		so it was sort of ... you know.
	12d		== just nice to him.
NV2		Jessie	== [laughter]
13	13a	Judy	"Come on lets go downstairs with all the other people ..."
	13b		shhh ...
	13c		dragging him away.
14	14a	Di	Um and then I got sick.
	14b		I had this Filipino flu,
	14c		or Hong Kong flu
	14d		or whatever they like to call it,
	14e		and then um then we fought like cats and dogs for == about a week.
15	15	Jessie	== Oh really == [laughing]!
16	16a	Di	== He was going to send me back.

	16b		And um and then we called a truce and started again.
	16d		And then we sort of became friends.
Coda			
19	19	Judy	Became friends [laughing]
20	20a	Jessie	Great.
	20b		Very close friends in fact [laughing]
	20c		Great.

(Slade's data)

As with the other storytelling texts, the Abstract stage in text 6.5 refers to the whole text, thereby providing a thematic prediction of what is to come. The activity sequence of 'meeting the boyfriend' is immediately introduced and then the rest of the text expands on this. Jessie's question in move 1b – *Right and so when did you actually meet him?*, is typical of the type of question which will elicit a Recount.

As with the middle stages of the other storytelling genres, the Record of Events stage is concerned with the retelling of a temporal sequence of events and it is typically realized by material processes, for example, *hanging out, dragging him, fought*. There is no significant disruption to the activity sequence and there is no focal point of evaluative comment which suspends the action, as would happen in a narrative. Although there is a slight problem in move 14a – *um, and then I got sick*, the time line is not broken but continues until the end of the Record of Events stage.

In the Coda, Judy returns the text to the present by providing a gloss on the story. It tells the listener that, despite a few minor problems, the couple ended up together.

Table 6.6 lists some of the main semantic and lexico-grammatical realizations of each of the stages of a Recount with particular reference to text 6.5.

6.4.5 Summary of story genres

In this section we have detailed the similarities and differences between different storytelling texts.

The storytelling genres are all centred around temporally sequenced events and all make some kind of evaluative comment which marks the significance of the events described. However, as our analysis has demonstrated, the genres differ from one another in important respects. These differences are summarized in Table 6.7.

The four different story types identified in this chapter represent a resource for conversationalists to share their experiences and their evaluations of those experiences. Plum (1988: 223) suggests that the different generic types can be associated with different "entertainment values":

Table 6.6 Semantic and lexico-grammatical realizations of text 6.6: And Then We Became Friends

Stages	Moves	Language features
Abstract Establishes the point of the text Signals that a story is about to be told	1–4	Thematic prediction of what the text is going to be about by naming the activity sequence (i.e. meeting the husband) Attitudinal lexis (e.g. *oh hysterical*) establishes the point of telling the story
Orientation Orients the listeners to what is to follow, in terms of people, actions, time and place	5a–5b	A locative setting in place (*dinner*) Past action material processes (e.g. *went out*)
Record of Events Provides a sequence of events with ongoing appraisal	5c–16d	Past tense action processes Events sequenced in time Temporal links are implicit, the text is following event time, except for move 14a – *and then I got sick* Use of reported speech for dramatic effect (e.g. move 13a – *Come on let's go downstairs ...*) Present in present tense (e.g. move 13c – *dragging him away.*)
Coda Makes a point about the text as a whole Returns text to present	19–20c	Evaluation of the whole event Return to the present

Table 6.7 Summary of differences between the story genres

Narratives	• the Evaluation stage provides a break between the Complication and the Resolution stages • the culmination is in the explicit Resolution
Anecdotes	• the focus is on the reaction to the crisis rather than on the crisis itself • the culmination is in a highly affectual Reaction
Exemplums	• the focus is on the interpretation or the moral point being made about the Incident rather than on the crisis which is resolved • culmination is in the judgement or the moral point being made
Recounts	• the focus is on the way events relate to one another • involve ongoing appraisal but the evaluative comment is not realized discretely

> Both anecdote and narrative may be said to be primarily concerned with 'entertaining' a hearer with a textual artefact which, in order to be successful needs to have a status independent of the experience it represents. On the other hand, ... exemplum (is) much more concerned with 'making a point' rather than with entertainment, something which is achieved by creating a link between the text as representation of experience and something outside it.

Stories are a reflection of people's identities and these representations then, in turn, shape the way the world is. As Johnstone (1993: 68) puts it:

> talk and worlds are connected in a variety of ways. Talk is certainly often about the world and reflects what the world is like. At the same time, though, worlds are created in talk. This is in fact most obviously true of narrative talk, since stories, by means of introductory abstracts, summary codas, and other linguistic devices, explicitly take teller and audience out of the "storyworld" in which their conversation takes place into a "talerealm" in which the narrative takes place.

It is through the exchange of stories that social life, in all its aspects, is represented and shaped. Stories are not just a reflection of a pre-existing state but they also shape reality.

When we talk we do more than just talk for talk's sake: we build up and establish shared attitudes and identities, shared ways of seeing the world. Our social worlds are created through talk; this has resulted over time in there being recognizable language activities with distinct purposes: we tell stories, we gossip, we exchange opinions, we joke, etc. As speakers of a language, we know how to structure these language activities in ways that are appropriate to their cultural contexts, for example, how to make the stories interesting, entertaining or worth telling. A genre analysis is concerned with the description of these linguistic activities. It provides semantic and grammatical explanations for classifying and grouping texts with similar social purposes into text types, but it also gives us analytical tools for the explanation and description of why and how texts are structured in different ways according to the different social goals they are achieving. It provides us with the basis for critical evaluations of the meanings we make in conversation, and their role in constructing systems of values, social reality and the social identities.

So far in this chapter we have used the concept of genre to distinguish between different kinds of storytelling texts which occur in casual conversation in English and to describe their text structure. The concept of genre is also useful for identifying the other kinds of text types which can occur in casual conversation. In the next section we will use the concept of genre to characterize and quantify a large body of casual conversational data, allowing a comparison of preferred conversational genres among different gender groups.

6.5   CASUAL TALK AT WORK: A GENERIC CHARACTERIZATION

In this section we will use a generic categorization to describe three hours of casual conversation data collected during coffee breaks in three different workplaces. The conversations involved three different groups of participants.[8]

i)   all-male group;
ii) all-female group;
iii) mixed group with men and women.

Although the conversations involved people from many different first language backgrounds, all the interactants were fluent speakers of English. The participants were work colleagues and acquaintances but not close friends. The frequency and distribution of all the text types according to gender are listed elsewhere (see Slade 1995).

6.5.1   Genres in casual conversation

The different types of talk which occurred across the three groups were identified and these are listed below:

- Narratives
- Anecdotes
- Recounts
- Exemplums
- Observation/Comment
- Opinion
- Gossip
- Joke-telling
- Sending Up (friendly ridicule)
- Chat

Table 6.8 outlines the relative frequency of the genres that occurred in the coffee break conversations across the three groups.

Table 6.8 Frequency of genres in coffee break conversations at work (across the three different groups)

Text type	Percentages
Storytelling	43.4
Observation/Comment	19.75
Opinion	16.8
Gossip	13.8
Joke-telling	6.3

Table 6.8 indicates the weighting of the genres in relation to each other: i.e. what percentage of the generically structured sections of talk each genre represents.

The storytelling texts (i.e. narratives, anecdotes, exemplums and recounts) occurred most frequently across the three groups[9] with Observation/Comment texts and Opinion texts also occurring frequently.[10]

Segments of talk labelled 'sending up' (teasing) and 'chat' are not included in Table 6.8 as these do not display a generic structure. These segments of casual talk which cannot be captured by a generic analysis are discussed below.

Of the storytelling texts, the anecdotes were by far the most frequent across all the three groups. These were followed by recounts and exemplums with the least frequent being narratives. Narratives occurred more in the mixed group of men and women, infrequently in the all-male group and not at all in the group of all women. The men told more stories where there was an explicit resolution, of the kind of a hero overcoming adversity. The women told more anecdotes which involved embarrassing, humiliating or worrying situations, where the story culminated in a reaction, such as an outburst of laughter.

The results of this study suggest that the frequency of any particular storytelling genre may depend on the degree of familiarity and contact between the participants. If the participants are in regular contact or quite familiar with each other, then anecdotes and recounts are likely to be more frequent. Sharing an emotional reaction to an event, particularly if the event is embarrassing or makes the storyteller look foolish, is more likely to occur in contexts where the participants are more familiar with one another. Similarly, merely recounting events can be quite mundane and therefore this is likely to occur when participants know each other well or are in regular contact. On the other hand, narratives and exemplums are more likely to occur than recounts in situations where participants are less familiar or have less contact with one another. This can be represented on a cline such as the one below:

High contact			Low contact
Recount	Anecdote	Exemplum	Narrative
mundane – nothing out of the ordinary	affect	judgement	unusuality

Sharing an anecdote is likely to be more personal than sharing a moral judgement. In situations where participants are less familiar, narratives, which deal with overcoming the unusual, are more likely to be told.[11]

Opinion texts occurred across all the three groups. These texts propose, elaborate, defend and exchange opinions about people, things or events. They are expressions of attitude not of fact. They express an individual or a societal judgement as to the rightness or wrongness, the goodness or badness, the desirability or otherwise of a state of affairs in the real world. The generic structure of opinion texts, as identified by Horvath and Eggins (1995) is:

Opinion ^ Reaction ^ (Evidence) ^ (Resolution)

Once the opinion is given the interactant is required to react. Where disagreement occurs, the speaker will almost certainly provide evidence for his/her opinion and after an exchange of opinions the interactants need to reach a resolution of some sort before the text is closed.[12] Opinion texts occurred most commonly in the all-female group and the mixed gender group and because these were acquaintances and not close friends, they rarely involved disagreement.

Observation/Comment texts are a type identified by Martin and Rothery (1986). They deal with events or things and factuality is what matters. An observation is made on a fact and then a comment follows. Hence the obligatory elements of structure are:

Observation ^ Comment

These texts involve no time line of events and so are not classified as storytelling texts.

Gossip occurred frequently in the all-women group, not at all in the all-male group and only minimally in the mixed group. The gossip texts are discussed in detail in Chapter 7.

Table 6.9 lists the generic structure of the different types of talk that occurred in the workplace coffee-break conversation data with relevant references.

6.5.2   Variation across the groups

There were a number of variations in the text types which occurred across the three groups and some of these are outlined below:

i) All-male group Apart from the chat segments of talk, the most frequently occurring stretch of talk in the all-male group was teasing or sending up (friendly ridicule). An example of sending up from these conversations was examined in Chapter 4 (text 4.1: Mates). Gossip did not occur at all in this group and there were few storytelling texts with only three anecdotes, two narratives, two exemplums and three recounts. This compares with twenty-two stories in the mixed group and sixteen in the all-women group. The men very rarely discussed personal details and their chat tended to be about work, rugby, soccer, etc.

ii) All-female group There was no sending up at all in this group. The two

Table 6.9 Generic structures of text types

Genre	Generic structure
Narrative	(Abstract) ^ (Orientation) ^ Complication ^ Evaluation ^ Resolution ^ (Coda) [Labov and Waletzky 1967]
Anecdote	(Abstract) ^ (Orientation) ^ Remarkable Event ^ Reaction ^ (Coda) [Plum 1988, Rothery 1990]
Exemplum	(Abstract) ^ (Orientation) ^ Incident ^ Interpretation ^ (Coda) [Plum 1988, Martin 1995]
Recount	(Abstract) ^ Orientation ^ Record of Events ^ (Coda) [Plum 1988, Rothery 1990, Martin 1992]
Observation/ Comment	(Orientation) ^ Observation ^ Comment ^ (Coda) ^ (Completion) [Martin and Rothery 1986]
Opinion	Opinion ^ Reaction ^ (Evidence) ^ (Resolution) [Horvarth and Eggins 1995]
Gossip	Third Person Focus ^ Substantiating Behaviour ^ (Probe)/ Pejorative Evaluation ^ (Defence) ^ (Response to Defence) ^ (Concession) ^ (Wrap-up) [Slade 1995]
Joke-telling	Generic structure not yet explored
Sending Up	Cannot be characterized in generic terms
Chat	Cannot be characterized in generic terms

most frequent text types were gossip and the storytelling genres. In the chat segments women discussed quite personal details including boyfriends, weddings, marriages, children and relatives. They also discussed their future plans and past activities in detail, e.g. weekends, holidays, etc. Opinion texts occurred more frequently than with the men and there were more storytelling texts.

iii) Mixed group with men and women   In the mixed group amusing or surprising stories dominated the conversation and so there were many more storytelling texts including anecdotes, narratives, recounts and exemplums. Joke telling was more frequent than in the all-female group. There was some sending up but not nearly as much as in the all-male group.

6.5.3   Exploring difference and similarity

One interesting finding of the study was that sending up was the most dominant text type in the all-male group and gossip was the most frequent text type in the all-female group. Gossip did not occur at all in the all-male group and sending up did not occur at all in the all-women group. The interpretation of these findings draws on tenor differences of contact and affective involvement (see Chapter 2). While we would not want to claim from the findings of these data that men do not gossip or that women do not send each other up, we consider that it is more likely that in these particular subcultures, men will send each other up when they are getting to know each other and gossip only when they are close friends. Conversely, for women in these contexts, we believe that gossip is a way of showing mateship and a willingness to get to know each other. Women, in these cultural contexts, are only likely to send each other up when they are close friends.[13]

Both sending up with the male acquaintances and gossiping with the female acquaintances are fulfilling a similar function: they are a way of building up and establishing shared attitudes and values, ways of exploring similarities and likenesses. In the gossip texts, by criticizing an absent third person, the women are explicitly or implicitly saying what the appropriate way to behave is. Similarly, by ridiculing each other for deviant physical or behavioural manifestations, the men are establishing normative boundaries and implicitly asserting group values.

It is the **exploration of similarity**, therefore, that is the motivation behind such talk for people who are getting to know each other. We can then distinguish this from conversations between close friends which are motivated by the **exploration of difference**. The functional motivation of gossip, as well as the differences in structure between the gossip of workplace acquaintances and that of close friends, is explored in detail in the next chapter.

6.6 THE LIMITATIONS OF A GENERIC ANALYSIS: THE CHAT SEGMENTS

When analysing the casual conversation data collected from these workplace contexts, it became clear that a generic analysis could account for a significant proportion of the casual conversation data. However, there were other segments of the data which could not be analysed generically. These chat segments constituted about half the talk and it is interesting to note that the percentages are very similar across the three workplace groups.[14]

Table 6.10 shows the percentage of chat as a proportion of the total conversations.

Table 6.10 Chat segments as a proportion of total conversations

All women	Chat	58%
	Text types	42%
Men and women	Chat	47%
	Text types	53%
All men	Chat	52%
	Text types	48%

Although we have distinguished above between generically structured talk (chunks) and non-generically structured segments (chat), in fact our data suggested that casual talk can be represented on a line, such as the one below:

| storytelling texts | opinion | gossip | chat |

This cline positions segments of conversation as either more or less amenable to generic analysis. At the left pole of the cline we place the narratives which display a clear generic structure, while at the righthand pole we place chat, (for example, as in text 4.1: Mates).

There are two factors that influence the adequacy of a generic description: the degree of interactivity of the genre and the degree to which interpersonal or experiential meanings are foregrounded. With the chat segments, a generic analysis does not succeed at all and an analysis is needed that focuses on the micro-interaction, as we detailed in Chapters 3 to 5.

The text types in the middle of the cline (opinion and gossip texts) tend to be more highly interactive than narratives, for example, with interpersonal meanings highly foregrounded.[15] Although these text types can be described as having a schematic structure, and can be assigned a generic structure formulation, they also need an analysis that can capture the more open-ended nature of this kind of talk, an analysis that can capture the dynamic unfolding of text. The generic and micro analyses of these highly interactive genres are detailed in the next chapter when we explore the nature and description of gossip in English.

6.7 CONCLUSION

Because casual conversations involve both moments of rapid, highly interactive turn-taking as well as moments of relative stability of speaker role, we have argued that we need to develop an analytical model which can describe both the 'chat' and the 'chunks'. In this chapter we have focused on the description of the 'chunks'. These 'chunks' are the parts of casual conversation that need not only a micro or localistic analysis of their turn-by-turn organization, but also an analysis that can focus on their global or macro text structure. The principles of generic analysis presented in this chapter build on the analyses outlined in the previous chapters, providing an additional perspective on the structure of casual conversation in English.

The strength of a generic approach is that it stresses the relationship between language and its social context, between the linguistic realization of a text and its social and cultural function. In order to understand why a text is structured as it is, we must understand the cultural and social purpose it fulfils. The social purpose of the text, then, is not only reflected in its generic structure but also in the particular language choices made within each stage. Analysing the language of a text together with analysing its social function is a dialectical task: it needs to be seen as a two-way relationship between text and the broader social and cultural context.

In the next chapter we demonstrate the application of the cumulative analyses developed so far (grammatical, semantic, discourse and generic) to the description and interpretation of a type of talk which plays a significant role in everyday social life: gossip.

NOTES

1. See, for example, the analysis of the 'probe' stages in the gossip genre, detailed in Chapter 7.
2. The move is the basic semantic unit of interaction – See Chapter 5 for a detailed definition.
3. Labov and Waletzky's (1967) description of narratives of personal experience is detailed in Chapter 2.
4. The issue of what to do with the sections of talk embedded in a genre that cannot effectively be assigned a generic label will be looked at in the next chapter.
5. Also Martin's work with the team of researchers at the Disadvantaged Schools Program from 1993 to 1995 was responsible for extensive research into the different kinds of genres produced at school and in the workplace. (See, for example, Martin 1995, and Rothery and Stenglin 1994 and Iedema, Feez, and White 1993 and Iedema, 1995.)
6. This section should be read in conjunction with Chapter 2 where we detail Labov and Waletzky's description of narratives as well as Martin and Rothery's work on genre within the Systemic Functional Linguistic school (see, for example, Martin 1992, 1995).
7. Many years ago this text was discussed in detail with Guenter Plum; many thanks for his contribution.
8. For further discussion of these data see Slade (1995, 1997).
9. As it is spontaneous casual conversation data, unlike the narratives elicited by Labov and Waletzky from sociolinguistic interviews, these texts were dialogic and so involved interruptions, continual feedback, etc. All of the stories (except text 1.3: Dr Flannel) discussed in the previous section of this chapter are from this data set.
10. This has important implications both for the description and teaching of casual conversation in English. Although there has been quite extensive research on narratives across disciplines, only recently has attention been paid to such genres as gossip (Coates 1988, Bergmann 1993), opinion texts (Horvath and Eggins 1995) and joke-telling (Sacks 1992a). In the applied linguistic context there has been very little emphasis on the application of such descriptions. For example most of the genres listed above are not represented in language teaching materials at all. Yet all these genres play a significant role in the way peoples' identities are established and in the way social worlds are created.
11. We are grateful to Jim Martin for discussions on these storytelling texts.
12. Gossip can be seen to be agnate to exemplums, as they both involve judgement. Exemplums tell stories which lead into or justify the judgements whereas gossip texts have a judgement and then they exemplify

       the judgement (sometimes only minimally).

13.   This speculation is supported by Eggins's data of close friends at a dinner party where, although involving mixed gender groups, there is frequent sending up and gossiping between all parties.

14.   The percentages for Table 6.10 were worked out in the following way. Those portions of the text that did not appear to have a generic structure were described as 'chat'. The complete transcripts were numbered into moves (as defined in Chapter 5). Calculations were then based on the number of moves in the 'chat' sections and the number of moves in the generically structured sections. The generically structured text consisted of those genres outlined in this chapter.

15.   This is not to say that some narratives are not dialogically constructed but even with the more interactive narratives, the unfolding of the narrative works through the stages towards completion. Whereas with gossip, as will be shown in the next chapter, there is a much greater capacity for recursion where the interactive segments probe for more gossip thereby expanding the text.

7 Gossip: establishing and maintaining group membership

7.1 INTRODUCTION

In the previous chapter we applied techniques of genre analysis to describe those segments of casual conversation that display a global structural organization. We reviewed the different story genres interactants produce in talk, and we also demonstrated that a generic analysis provides a way of characterizing a large corpus of casual conversational data.

In this chapter we will look at gossip, one of the most commonly occurring and socially significant genres in English casual conversation. We will show that gossip is a highly interactive genre, which, although it has some chunking elements, also includes parts which are more like the 'chatty' texts looked at in Chapters 3, 4 and 5. We will analyse gossip using the steps of generic analysis which we presented in Chapter 6. These steps are:

- establishing that there is a distinctive genre of gossip;
- defining and labelling the genre of gossip;
- establishing the social function of the gossip;
- identifying and differentiating the text stages;
- specifying obligatory and optional stages and devising a structural formula;
- specifying the semantic and lexico-grammatical realizations for each stage.

The analysis of the language of gossip presented in this chapter reveals a great deal about the social role and function of gossip in our society as a form of talk through which interactants can construct solidarity as they explore shared normative judgements about culturally significant behavioural domains. We demonstrate that gossip is a culturally determined process with a distinctive staging structure that can be described. However, we also argue that in order to describe gossip (and in particular the 'chat' like elements that are dispersed throughout) the generic perspective needs to be complemented by a dynamic analysis that focuses on the unfolding of the talk, move by move. In the final sections of the chapter we bring together the techniques developed in this book to provide a comprehensive analysis of the gossip text presented in Chapter 1, text 1.2: Tamara. We will demonstrate that it is through these cumulative perspectives that a systematic approach to the analysis and interpretation of casual conversation can be achieved.

7.2 ESTABLISHING THAT THERE IS A DISTINCTIVE GENRE OF GOSSIP

The fact that we can designate something as gossip in our everyday experience, and that we can recognize certain sorts of conversation as gossip, suggests that it does have a distinctive and characteristic linguistic structure and that, like narratives and other storytelling texts, it is a genre in its own right. Listeners can, from an initial trigger utterance such as '*This reminds me of Tamara*' (text 1.2), recognize that a gossip text is about to occur.

To establish whether gossip is a distinctive genre, differences from other agnate genres need to be identified. Text 7.1: A Classic Affair, is from a coffee-break conversation at work and involves a group of women who are discussing a work colleague, Anna. There are three women in the group who are all in their mid to late twenties. When the conversation was recorded, Jo and Donna had been working in the hospital for about four months and Sue had only recently started. They regularly have coffee breaks together but they do not see each other outside the workplace (i.e. they are not close friends).

When you are reading text 7.1, you might like to consider how it is similar to and how it is different from the story texts we analysed in Chapter 5.

Text 7.1 A Classic Affair

Turn	Speaker	
1	Jo	We had ... there was an affair, a classic, a classic was here. There was an affair going between a a kitchen a er the cook == and ... this other girl you know I mean she'd come over any excuse she'd be over
2	Sue	==Oh yeah
3	Jo	I mean it was the laughing stock of the whole hospital and we got we got to the stage where we'd really play on it because if we needed anything from the other side we'd sort of ring up and say 'oh Anna if you're not doing anything', I mean she'd run you know whatever you == wanted
4	Sue	== Did she know that you knew?
5	Donna	I don't == think so
6	Jo	== No I don't think she was that cluey.
7	Donna	No == I don't think she was aware of the fact that so many people == knew
8	Jo	== Yeah [Laughs]
9	Donna	== She'd come in and ... and [laughs] I reckon she got pissed around left right and centre just to keep her out of the kitchen because everytime you turned around and she'd wear she'd ...
10	Sue	Yeah
11	Jo	I know, then all of a sudden she started wearing make-up,

		it was a real classic [Laughs]
12	Donna	A girl that never really wore make-up
13	Sue	And what happened in the end. Are they == still together?
14	Donna	Oh == she left her husband and she's um ...
15	Sue	They're still together?
16	Donna	Yeah
17	Sue	She left her husband?
18	Jo	Yeah
19	Sue	== Gosh!
20	Donna	== Oh its pretty ... it's sad but it happened while I've been away
21	Jo	She'd be ringing up on the weekend as if you know ... and we could hear her voice on the phone, all through the week, and then on the weekend she'd pretend (she didn't you know) she was someone different (laughs)
22	Sue	Oh really. What'd she do?
23	Jo	She'd sort of makes [ ] she works in the assembly room
24	Sue	Right
25	Jo	They used to work over here; that's how how they met [Laughs]
26	Sue	And is he still here?
27	Donna	Yeah
28	Jo	he's on holidays at the moment.
29	Sue	== mmm
30	Donna	== Is she on holidays, I haven't seen her since I've been back?
31	Jo	No no she's not [Laughs]
32	Donna	Actually it's really ridiculous. I mean I think she's made an absolute fool of herself because there is a girl who rings him every afternoon from Canberra. He originally comes from Canberra this guy and I quite often used to pick up the phone. Now it's not her
33	Sue	So you don't know what's going on?
34	Donna	I think she's atrocious.
36	Jo	Oh they haven't had those phone calls for ages though.
37	Donna	Been careful, have they?
38	Jo	Yeah but she left her husband ... she left her husband for him.
39	Donna	Yeah, six years to get (a leg in) this girl had nothing to lose.

(Slade's data)

There are parts of this text which seem similar to a storytelling text in that there is an unfolding of events in a temporal sequence. As with storytelling texts, we can identify evaluative comments, such as *I mean, it was the laughing stock of the whole hospital* and *Actually, it's really ridiculous* which similarly have an important functional role in establishing the significance and point of the text.[1] And yet, if we try to apply a narrative generic structure analysis to this text, we find that not all the stages are there. The difference between this text and a narrative text is that there is no problem which culminates in a crisis, there is no Complication stage and there is no Resolution.

There is, however, some temporal unfolding of events as illustrated in turn 3 below:

> 3 Jo I mean it was the laughing stock of the whole hospital and we got we got
> to the stage where we'd really play on it because if we needed anything
> from the other side we'd sort of ring up and say 'oh Anna if you're not
> doing anything', I mean she'd run you know whatever you == wanted

However the focus here is not on the events but rather on justifying the speaker's negative opinion of Anna and the affair she was having. Where narratives have a basic ideational orientation (what happened when, and what went wrong), text 7.1 has a more intense interpersonal orientation: it is the evaluations of the people being gossiped about which appear to be what motivates the conversation.

The major motivation for narratives and anecdotes is to share experiences which somehow go wrong and in these texts people classify the experiential world in terms of what is likely and what is not. In gossip texts, on the other hand, people classify the world in terms of what people should or should not be doing. In gossip the events are not experientially unusual but interpersonally unacceptable: this different functional motivation of gossip is why it cannot be classified as a storytelling genre.

Essentially, telling stories and gossiping are both about affirming and reconfirming friendships and in this they reflect the primary goal of casual talk which is to establish and maintain relationships. However, they do this in quite different ways. Stories are about sharing unusual experiences, thereby confirming what is considered usual, affirming ways of understanding the world, as well as new worlds being collaboratively constructed and negotiated. Gossiping, on the other hand, involves sharing opinions and judgements about a person's behaviour or physical attributes, and by doing so implicitly asserting appropriate behaviour or defining a physical norm. In this way gossip reinforces and maintains the values of the social group.

Gossip is a highly interactive genre: participants frequently co-construct the gossip, recipients provide continual feedback to indicate interest (and complicitness with the gossip) or ask questions to elicit more details.[2] There are usually highly interactive segments in a gossip text which are similar in structure to the chat segments of talk (see Chapter 3). For example, there are segments of text 7.1 above which seem to be quite different in nature from other parts of the text and which do not seem to fit into the overall generic structure. Two examples of these segments are presented below:

Example 1

4	Sue	== Did she know that you knew?
5	Donna	I don't == think so
6	Jo	== No I don't think she was that cluey.
7	Donna	No == I don't think she was aware of the fact that so many people knew
8	Jo	== Yeah [Laughs]

Example 2

13	Sue	And what happened in the end. Are they == still together?
14	Donna	Oh == she left her husband and she's um ...
15	Sue	They're still together?
16	Donna	== Yeah
17	Sue	== She left her husband?
18	Jo	Yeah
19	Sue	== Gosh!

In these sections the other participants appear to be doing more work in moving the text forward. These are examples of chat segments which occur throughout the text. Although there was some degree of interaction in the storytelling texts presented in Chapter 5, text 7.1 is more highly interactive and is therefore different in two important ways:

i) The feedback from Sue is necessary for the text to move forward as it indicates her implicit approval of the gossip, such approval being essential for a gossip text to continue. Gossip realizes or construes an ongoing, negotiated solidarity.

ii) The gossip is dialogically told. There are two primary speakers with Jo and Donna both relating incidents which provide evidence and fuel the gossip.

This structural difference between the storytelling genres and gossip indicates that gossip is in fact achieving a different purpose: the sharing of an opinion about an absent third person (often a friend) is potentially face-threatening and therefore there needs to be explicit or tacit approval given for the gossip to proceed.[3] This approval is indicated by all participants sharing in the gossip, at the very least by asking questions or using assessments or newsmarkers (see Chapter 6, section 6.4.2) to indicate interest and involvement.

This is not to suggest that there is no interaction or feedback from listeners in other genres of casual conversation; of course there is: all casual conversations are interactive. It is that gossip appears to have a greater potential to keep going than, for example, the storytelling texts: by asking questions or by providing more details, participants can stimulate a fresh round of incriminating evidence and allegations. It is possible, for example, for the participants in the conversation all to contribute to the gossip, each building up layer upon layer of evidence to reinforce the negative judgement. Gossip is inherently dialogic: speakers work together collaboratively to construct the discourse.

7.3 · DEFINING AND LABELLING THE GENRE

In popular currency the term gossip is used in many different ways. In the most general sense it can refer to any 'idle' chat about daily life; it can, on the other hand, be used to characterize women's talk in general (and therefore sometimes used as a sexist put-down of such talk), or it can be used more specifically to refer to conversations between two or more people about another person behind his/her back. In this book, gossip is broadly defined as talk which involves pejorative judgement of an absent other. More specifically the focus is on talk which is meant to be confidential (or at least not reported back to the third party), and is about an absent person who is known to at least one of the participants. This kind of talk frequently occurs both in the conversational data of workplace colleagues (acquaintances), as well as in dinner party conversations between close friends (see Slade, 1997 for a more detailed discussion of this definition).[4]

The pejorative comment, which helps to identify the text as gossip, is about the attribute or action of the absent person. The pejorative comment element distinguishes it from 'spreading news' about someone: this definition does not include, therefore, conversations which merely involve reporting a fact about a friend, for example, 'John just moved in next door' where opinions and judgements are not elaborated.

Gossip is defined here in a more specific sense to that used by other linguists such as Jones (1980: 243) who defines gossip as "a way of talking between women in their roles as women" and Coates who uses this definition as the basis of her study (1988: 95). Their use of gossip encompasses talk by women in all-women interactions and as such is much broader than the generic sense in which we are using it. Similarly, Tannen's definition in *You Just Don't Understand* (1990), although more specific than Jones's, is also broader than our use. Tannen says:

> Telling details about others' lives is partly the result of women's telling their friends details of their own lives. These details become gossip when the friend to whom they are told repeats them to someone else – presumably another friend. (97)

Tannen equates telling gossip as a "grown-up version of telling secrets" (97). Bergmann similarly defines gossip as "news about the personal affairs of others" (1993: 45). Tannen and Bergmann's definitions encompass the passing on of any details about a friend's life. Only if such conversations were extended, and pejorative opinions of the friend were exchanged and elaborated, would they fit our definition of gossip.

The definitions offered by Jones or Tannen are too general to classify gossip as a particular text type or genre with a definable and generalizable generic structure. We are concerned with a particular type of gossip that is specific enough in functional motivation to be defined as a distinctive genre. This specific functional motivation is to establish solidarity through shared values and agreed ways of seeing the world. In the next section we will explore the role gossip plays in the construction and maintenance of our social identities and social relationships.

7.4 THE SOCIAL FUNCTION OF GOSSIP

Every day a considerable amount of time for millions of people is consumed by gossip and as such it is a powerful socializing force: one that is at the same time reflective and constitutive of the sociocultural world from which it arises. More than thirty years ago, the anthropologist Max Gluckman said:

> It has taken the development of anthropological interest in the growth and break-up of small groups to put gossip and scandal into their proper perspective, as among the most important societal and cultural phenomena we have been called upon to analyse. (1963: 307)

More recently, Robin Dunbar (1992),[5] in an article entitled 'Why gossip is good for you' in the *New Scientist*, argued even more strongly that gossip was in fact at the heart of the evolution of language. He claimed that, from the beginning of human civilization, gossip has been one of the most important ways of integrating a large number of social relationships, thus enabling big groups to cohere and to control the behaviour of group members. He wrote that:

> By talking to one person, we can find out a great deal about how other individuals are likely to behave, how we should react to them when we actually meet them and what kinds of relationships they have with the third parties. All these things allow us to coordinate our social relationships within a group more effectively. And this is likely to be especially important in the dispersed groups that are characteristic of humans. This would explain our fascination for social gossip in the newspapers, and why gossip about relationships accounts for an overwhelming proportion of human conversations. Even conversations in such august places as university coffee rooms tend to swing back and forth between academic issues and gossip about individuals ... What we have here is ... a new theory of evolution of language that ... explains why gossip about people is so fascinating. (31)

Whether such a strong claim – that gossip is at the heart of the evolution of language – can be upheld is open to debate. But what is far less controversial, and now the focus of a great deal of attention in social anthropology is the argument that gossip is an essential aspect of group cohesion (see, for example, Harding 1975, Haviland 1977, Brenneis 1988).

We will now consider the social function of gossip by looking at text 7.2 below. This is an excerpt from another coffee-break conversation involving the same group of women as in text 7.1. In this conversation Donna, Sue and Jo are discussing another work colleague, Richard, and criticizing his attitudes towards work and his behaviour in the workplace.

As you read the text, consider what Sue is doing when she initiates the gossip about Richard and what is achieved by the end of the interaction.

Text 7.2 Richard

Turn	Speaker	
1	Sue	Mmm, what's happened about Richard?
2	Jo	Ah about Richard. Ah nothing [laughs]. He's been spoken to. It'll be a sort of a watch and wait == something ==
3	Sue	== Yeah, what do you reckon is going to happen?
4	Jo	Not a thing
5	Donna	Um, no, I don't know
6	Donna	It depends on the == attitude
7	Jo	== The trouble is here if you've got a member of staff against you, you can't just sack them, you know; and this is the whole problem you've got to resort to reneg ...
8	Sue	and that's where they do all these nasty things.
9	Jo	Yeah, because they just didn't work out. Yeah because you just can't == that's it
10	Sue	== You reckon something's going to happen to him? What could they do to him?
11	Donna	Richard's not a very nice person anyway. He just doesn't fit into the system in general. It's not nice what's happening to him but the thing is he is em creating the situation just as much as what they ... BECAUSE HE'S BEEN CAUGHT DRINKING ON THE JOB [whisper] which is no good you know and he hasn't been really doing his job properly == anyway
12	Sue	== Do the girls like him?
13	Donna	No, because he's got this attitude 'I am superior' you know. He talks down to people which automatically puts people's backs up.
14	Sue	right
15	Donna	and the trouble is that's why right from the word go people didn't like him because he talked down to people he should be talking up to sort of in a == fashion
16	Sue	== yeah
17	Donna	But he has his airs and graces and I'm superior sort of thing. And basically really here there aren't that even though say I'm the supervisor and he's the catering aide and there's the workers sort of thing. There really isn't all that much difference you know, you're not God and they're in the middle rung and the people are on the

bottom rung thing. Basically catering aides are just fellow workers the same as those people out there and when they get out there saying 'you've got to do this' and 'I told you', you know, talking down to them and making them feel small. It just doesn't work. They won't do anything for you.

18	Sue	What do you think they'll do to set him up?
19	Donna	I think they've given up on that idea. I think they'll just [everyone laughs] mmm they'll just mm bide their time because he's going to hang himself they don't have to do anything they've realized that now
20	Sue	What's he going to do? What do you mean == hang himself?
21	Donna	== Well when he's over in the other ... when he was working in Gloucester House he used to lock himself in the office, pull down the blinds, put his feet on the desk, turn on his radio, listen to the races, and drink and smoke
22	Sue	shit
23	Donna	Made himself unavailable when he's supposed to be working.
24	Sue	really
25	Donna	and uh do his TAB's[6] in the afternoon.
26	Sue	and expect to get away with it.
27	Donna	== uh huh
28	Sue	== Can't he ... did he just just think he wasn't ever going to get caught?
29	Jo	yeah
30	Sue	mmmm
31	Donna	Yeah, no one's going to put me in. I'm the boss sort of thing, you know because in the afternoons the catering aide was the only person you know sort of like supervising like in that area, and basically most of the supervisors uh don't go over to that area. It's a private section of the hospital it's supposed to be self-contained and run itself.
32	Sue	right, yeah
33	Donna	because they produce their own food and everything – but they found a problem with him because by accident somebody had to go over there one day and see the dietetics department which is another offshoot of the research department. They share that office and they could never get in and that's where the complaints started coming through probably and they saw him drinking
34	Sue	uh huh
35	Donna	You cannot drink on the job
36	Sue	Right yes and if they did set him up what would they do? I mean how could you get him sacked –?
37	Jo	Well they just would –
38	Donna	Really in a way they don't really have to get anybody I mean to say if you are not doing the right thing and you feel there's this pressure on and they watch you like a hawk ... in the end you're really going to crack

(Slade's data)

Text 7.2: Richard starts with Sue initiating the gossip. Initially Donna and Jo are reluctant to start gossiping but Donna does respond to Sue's second request for gossip about Richard with her explicit judgement, *Richard's not a very nice person anyway.* Sue's encouragement of the gossip is interpreted as tacit agreement and this encourages Donna and Jo to continue gossiping. Analysis of the conversational data of workplace colleagues or acquaintances revealed that the speaker must receive some confirmation of consensus after introducing the third person. If this confirmation does not occur, then the speaker is likely to back away from the gossip. The data also revealed that, if the participants in these contexts do not agree with the gossip, they are more likely to be non-committal to enable the gossip to continue.

In turn 11, Donna immediately establishes that Richard is outside the group when she says, *he just doesn't fit into the system.* She then provides evidence for her negative evaluation of Richard in turn 11 – *he's been caught drinking on the job,* in turn 13 – *he talks down to people* and again in turn 15 – *he talked down to people he should be talking up to.* By expressing these judgements, Donna states what she regards as unacceptable work behaviour, and by implication makes it clear what she considers to be appropriate behaviour. These negative judgements are then used as a hook on which to hang the evaluation: *but he has his airs and graces and I'm superior sort of thing* (turn 17).

The first part of the gossip is jointly produced with Sue probing for the gossip from Donna and Jo. After Donna takes over and holds the floor, providing evidence as to why she judges Richard's behaviour as unacceptable, Sue and Jo continually offer supportive minimal responses (*right, yeah*), indicating not only their active attention but also their tacit approval of the gossip. Other minimal responses, such as *shit* (turn 22) and *really* (turn 24) indicate more explicit support for the negative opinion of Richard. Sue, after her initial question which triggered the gossip, asks seven more questions and collaboratively completes one of Donna's utterances with *expect to get away with it* (turn 26). She is therefore very active in co-constructing the gossip and by doing so, showing that she agrees with the values being expressed.

The negative evaluations of both Richard (*not a very nice person anyway*) and of his behaviour (*drinks on the job, talks down to people, smokes and drinks in his office*) run throughout the text. By the end of the conversation all the participants have indicated that they support the judgement that being lazy at work, drinking on the job and talking down to people are unacceptable forms of behaviour. Thus in this respect, the gossip has helped to establish their similarity, their shared attitudes to work and made clear what they believe are appropriate work standards.[7] A certain level of 'trust' and group membership has been extended to Sue.

This text demonstrates two critical social functions of gossip which are outlined below:

i) Gossip functions to establish and reinforce group membership Gossip is a way of asserting social unity. It unifies a group but it can also provide a means of entry into a group. It provides a means of exploring similarity and shared values; this exploration of similarity being the mechanism by which people develop social bonds.

Gluckman (1963) argues that the right to gossip about certain people:

> is a privilege which is only extended to a person when he or she is accepted as a member of the group or set. It is the hallmark of membership. Hence, rights to gossip serve to mark off a particular group from other groups. (313)

For example, a way to make a non-member feel ill at ease is to begin to gossip about someone the person does not know. Gossip draws boundaries between a 'we' and a 'they'; it forges ties that bind a group together.

Not only are in-group members entitled to comment on and evaluate the behaviour of other group members, but there is an obligation to do so. If any member does not join in the gossip, their reticence can be seen as not wanting to share confidentialities. If they continue to do so over time, they can marginalize themselves. Gossip, therefore, becomes a 'duty of membership of the group' (Gluckman 1963: 313). This is reflected particularly in the gossip texts of close friends at a dinner party, as we will see later in this chapter. In the conversation between close friends, which is motivated by the exploration of difference, the social function of gossip as a hallmark and duty of in-group membership particularly applies.

ii) Gossip functions as a form of social control Text 7.2 above also demonstrates the second major functional motivation of gossip: to exert social control. This text is motivated by significant interpersonal goals to define normative boundaries. Donna and Jo quite clearly establish their values and the work standards they hold as important. In this sense, their gossip reaffirms their sociocultural values: it is one of the forms of discourse through which people make sense of their world. It maintains, modifies and reconstructs reality by labelling and judging various elements of experience in terms of the actions or behaviour of an absent third person. For this reason anthropologists such as Gluckman (1963), Haviland (1977) and Cox (1967) have argued that gossip is a vehicle for maintaining 'the unity, morals and values of social groups' (Gluckman 1963: 308). It is a way of asserting collective values and increasing group cohesion and it also enables the group to control the behaviour of its members. Group values are asserted in gossip and this is done by the third person, often an in-group member, being judged for failing in some way to live up to the group values. Gossip labels the actions or the behaviour of the third person as deviant and unacceptable and in this way makes clear what is considered appropriate behaviour. Gossip is, therefore, concerned with departures from normality, people finding such departures more interesting to talk about. Hence gossip can be seen to reflect and maintain social structures and social values and 'to keep people in line'.

Gossip is a form of talk usually associated with women, and the term 'gossip' is often used by men to denigrate women's talk. However, despite some people's denials (especially men's), gossip is a form of talk that most of us, perhaps all of us, engage in to differing degrees and in differing contexts. It plays a significant role in the construction and maintenance of our social identities and friendships: it is not something to be denigrated, but rather is one of the most important social phenomena to analyse.

In this section we have looked at the social functions of gossip. In the next we will identify the generic structure of gossip and the optional and obligatory elements of this structure. In section 7.6 the lexico-grammatical realization of each of the stages will be outlined. The generic structure and the linguistic features will be seen to be realizations of the functional motivation of gossip. That is, the linguistic forms are as they are because of the functions they serve.

In the final section of this chapter, we will complement a generic analysis with a move by move analysis of text 1.2: Tamara (from Chapter 1), enabling us to capture both the dynamic unfolding of the text as well as its generic structure. A gossip text of close friends at a dinner party (text 7.3 below) will also be examined for comparative purposes. From these analyses the generic structure formulation will be seen as defining the gossip texts in our data set; such a description being a generalizable formula for describing instances of texts of that genre as they typically occur within particular cultural contexts.

7.5 IDENTIFYING AND DIFFERENTIATING THE TEXT STAGES: THE GENERIC STRUCTURE OF GOSSIP

In this section the stages of the generic structure of gossip will be identified by examining text 7.1: A Classic Affair, and text 7.2: Richard, as two examples of gossip between workplace colleagues.

As we pointed out in Chapter 6, a generic structure description is an account of the expected unfolding of the genre, as it occurs within specific cultural contexts. There is an underlying structure to a generic type and within given and shared cultural contexts there is an expectancy of a particular generic sequence. Frequently, however, this sequence is deviated from. A generic structure description is therefore an account of the ideal type. It is not to be interpreted as a fixed or rigid schema: it is a description of the underlying abstract structure which participants orient to.

There was a specific and consistent organization across the gossip texts in our data and they all displayed specific core stages which will be outlined in the following subsection.

7.5.1 Obligatory and optional elements of the generic structure of gossip

We will now look at the consistent organization of gossip by describing the obligatory elements in the structure. These occur in a specified sequence and are defining of this genre. The elements are:

Third Person Focus ^ Substantiating Behaviour ^ Pejorative Evaluation

Third Person Focus functions to introduce the third person and in most cases to frame the deviant behaviour. It is this stage which establishes the 'we' versus 'they', the 'us' versus 'them'.

Substantiating Behaviour is also an obligatory element where the speaker or speakers provide evidence or information which enables the participants to make a negative evaluation. The speaker describes an event which highlights some departure from normality and this is then used as a hook on which to hang the evaluation. It is this building up of evidence that allows the participants to establish shared attitudes and values and therefore in the case of the workplace acquaintances, it is a way of establishing similarity; it is a way of getting to know each other better. Similarly, with close friends this stage functions to justify the speaker's negative evaluation of the third party and by doing so to elaborate on what is thought to be the appropriate way to behave. With close friends, therefore, this stage functions to consolidate and reconfirm shared attitudes and values.

The text is given meaning by the negative evaluation which runs throughout. This negative evaluation is also realized discretely where the events outlined in the Substantiating Behaviour are evaluated and commented on: this stage has been labelled **Pejorative Evaluation**. It is these Pejorative Evaluations which motivate the gossip and drive the text forward. The function of the Substantiating Behaviour stage is to provide evidence or a justification for the subsequent negative evaluation. The Substantiating Behaviour stage is at the service of the interpersonal; it ideationalizes the interpersonal meanings that are foregrounded in the Third Person Focus and the Pejorative Evaluation stages.

The obligatory elements of the generic structure are demonstrated below, through an analysis of the first section of text 7.1: A Classic Affair, presented above:[8]

Text 7.1: A Classic Affair: a generic analysis – displaying obligatory elements of structure

Turn	Move	Speaker	
Third Person Focus			
1	1/a	Jo	We had … there was an affair
	1/b		A classic
	1/c		A classic was here.
	1/d		There was an affair going on between the cook == and this other girl, you know.

Substantiating Behaviour (1)

	1/e		I mean she'd come over
	1/f		any excuse,
	1/g		she'd be over
2	2	Sue	== Oh yeah

Pejorative Evaluation (1)

3	3/a	Jo	I mean, it was the laughing stock of the whole hospital

The three elements displayed here are the obligatory elements of structure. We will now outline the optional elements of structure. When the optional elements are analysed, the differences in structure between gossip in coffee-break conversations between work colleagues (acquaintances) and that of close friends at a dinner party become apparent. We will first describe the optional elements of structure that are applicable to both these contexts.

In each of the gossip texts analysed, a recursive cycle is set up in which speakers provide evidence for ways in which the behaviour of the third person is inappropriate/unacceptable (Substantiating Behaviour), they then follow this by giving the Pejorative Evaluation, after which someone (often another speaker) provides further evidence. This cycle of Substantiating Behaviour followed by Pejorative Evaluation is often prompted by another speaker requesting more details. This element of structure in which the request is made has been labelled **Probe**. Probes are stages in the talk where participants probe for more details, for more gossip (see, for example, moves 13–19, and 22/b–31 below). We will argue later that these Probes are different in kind to the other elements of generic structure.

The final stage of the structure has been labelled **Wrap-up**. This optional element provides a thematic summation of the event or behaviour outlined in the text. It often picks up on the deviant behaviour mentioned in the Third Person Focus.

The stages of Substantiating Behaviour and Pejorative Evaluation may be repeated a number of times and so may the sequence from Substantiating Behaviour through to Wrap-Up. For example in text 7.1 (analysed below) each of the Probes prompts another round of further evidence or further Substantiating Behaviours which are used to fuel more negative judgements about Anna. In this text there are five different Substantiating Behaviours and the whole sequence of Substantiating Behaviour through to Wrap-Up is repeated twice.

Recursion is much more likely to occur in gossip texts than in narratives: in gossip, events known to the participants can be repeated and retold, because the focus is not on what happened, but rather on the way in which the events illustrate the negative attributes of the person being gossiped about. By contrast, in storytelling, adults do not usually immediately repeat an incident which they know other participants have already heard.

The complete text 7.1: A Classic Affair has been analysed below for generic stages.[9] In this analysis we can see that moves 1 to 12 show the first cycle of the obligatory and optional elements of structure. The remainder of the text demonstrates the recursivity of Substantiating Behaviour, Pejorative Evaluation and Wrap-Up.

Text 7.1: A Classic Affair: a generic analysis

Turn	Move	Speaker	
Third Person Focus			
1	1/a	Jo	We had … there was an affair
	1/b		A classic
	1/c		A classic was here.
	1/d		There was an affair going on between the cook == and this other girl, you know.
Substantiating Behaviour (1)			
	1/e		I mean she'd come over
	1/f		any excuse,
	1/g		she'd be over
2	2	Sue	== Oh yeah
Pejorative Evaluation (1)			
3	3/a	Jo	I mean, it was the laughing stock of the whole hospital
Substantiating Behaviour (2)			
	3/b		and we got to the stage where we'd really play on it
	3/c		because if we needed anything from the other side
	3/d		we'd sort of ring up and say
	3/e		"Oh Anna, if you're not doing anything."
	3/f		and she'd run, you know
	3/g		Whatever you == wanted
Probe (1)			
4	4	Sue	== Did she know that you knew?
5	5	Donna	I don't == think so.
6	6/a	Jo	== No
	6/b		I don't think she was that cluey.
7	7/a	Donna	No
	7/b		== I don't think she was aware of the fact that so many people == knew.
8	8	Jo	== Yeah
Substantiating Behaviour (3)			
9˙	9/a	Donna	== She'd come in and … [laughs]
	9/b		I reckon she got pissed around left right and centre
	9/c		just to keep her out of the kitchen
	9/d		because everytime you turned around

	9/e		and she'd wear, she'd ...
10	10	Sue	Yeah
11	11/a	Jo	I know.
	11/b		Then all of a sudden she started wearing make-up.

Wrap-Up (1)

	11/c		It was a real classic [laughs]
12	12	Donna	A girl that never really wore make-up.

Probe (2)

13	13/a	Sue	And what happened in the end?
	13/b		Are they == still together?
14	14/a	Donna	Oh, == she left her husband
	14/b		and she's um...
15	15	Sue	They're still together?
16	16	Donna	Yeah
17	17	Sue	She left her husband?
18	18	Donna	Yeah
9	19	Sue	== Gosh!

Substantiating Behaviour (4)

20	20/a	Donna	== Oh, it's pretty ... sad
	20/b		but it happened while I've been away
21	21/a	Jo	She'd be ringing up on the weekend as if, you know,
	21/b		and we could hear her voice on the phone all through the week
	21/c		and then on the weekend she'd pretend (she didn't, you know,) she was someone different
22	22/a	Sue	Oh really?

Probe (3)

	22/b		What'd she do?
23	23	Jo	She'd sort of make { } she works in the assembly room.
24	24	Sue	Right
25	25/a	Jo	They used to work over here
	25/b		That's how they met [laughs]
26	26	Sue	And is he still here?
27	27	Donna	Yeah
28	28	Jo	he's on holidays at the moment
29	29	Sue	== Mmm.
30	30/a	Donna	== Is she on holidays?
	30/b		I haven't seen her since I've been back
31	31	Jo	No, no, she's not.

Pejorative Evaluation (2)

32	32/a	Donna	Actually, it's really ridiculous
	32/b		I mean, I think she's made an absolute fool of herself

Substantiating Behaviour (5)

32/c			because there is a girl who rings every afternoon from Canberra.
32/d			He originally comes from Canberra this guy
32/e			and I quite often used to pick up the phone
32/f			now it's not her

Probe (4)

33	33	Sue	So you don't know what's going on?

Pejorative Evaluation (3)

34	34	Donna	I think she's atrocious.

Probe (4-Cont.)

35	35	Jo	Oh, they haven't had those phone calls for ages, though.
36	36	Donna	Been careful, have they?
37	37/a	Jo	Yeah
	37/b		But she left her husband...
	37/c		She left her husband for him
38	38/a	Donna	Yeah

Wrap-up (2)

38/b		Six years to get a {leg in}
38/c		this girl had nothing to lose.

(Slade's data)

The analysis captures the fact that the Third Person Focus in text 7.1 introduces the offending situation – *there was an affair* and then introduces the two people who are going to be gossiped about: *the cook and this other girl.*

The evaluative, interpersonal contribution in this text starts in the Third Person Focus in move 1/b, *A classic,* where 'a classic' is not overtly judgemental, but appreciation (see appraisal analysis Chapter 4, section 4.3) where 'the affair' is treated as an object, a cultural artefact ('a classic' is usually a description of a film, or a work of art, not of human behaviour). It is amplified, by repetition, which has the effect of intensifying the comment. 'A classic' is therefore a term that is borrowed from another field: a rhetorical ploy where Appreciation (rather than the more explicit Judgement) is used with the desired effect that it is immediately evident that gossip is about to take place. The word 'affair' usually has negative connotations in our culture, and hence the listeners are immediately positioned to expect that negative evaluations of the people having the affair are likely to follow.

The Third Person Focus stage is followed by the first Substantiating Behaviour which provides evidence to justify Anna's behaviour being considered excessive. This fuels the subsequent Pejorative Evaluation stage when in move 3/a Jo says, *It was the laughing stock of the whole hospital.* This is the first explicit judgement with the grammatical metaphor *laughing stock* used to indicate the ridiculousness of the situation and the word *whole* used as an amplification. This explicit judgement legitimizes the appraisal. It is this Pejorative Evaluation stage that drives the rest of the text as most of the following stages (Substantiating Behaviour (2) through to Substantiating Behaviour (5)) provide evidence for this judgement.

In Substantiating Behaviour (2), when Jo says *and she would run, you know. Whatever you wanted*, she again demonstrates that Anna's behaviour was foolish. This is experiential evidence of what Jo explicitly expressed in the previous Pejorative Evaluation, i.e. that both the affair and Anna were the laughing stock of the whole hospital. It is interesting to note here the gender values that are being perpetuated, in that it is Anna who is being criticized as making a fool of herself and not the man involved in the affair.

The intensity of Jo's contribution decreases after Substantiating Behaviour (2). In move 6/b, *I don't think she was that cluey*, her judgement is softened through the modalized *I don't think*. At this stage Donna takes over the interpersonal work. In Substantiating Behaviour (3) Donna provides evidence to justify why Anna's behaviour is considered unusual and, although there is no explicit judgemental lexis, the judgement in Move 11/b (*then all of a sudden she started wearing make-up*) is evident.

In the first Probe (moves 4–8) Sue indicates that she is a compliant listener (reflecting functional motivation of establishing similarity and building up solidarity) and Donna similarly indicates agreement with Jo's evaluation that the woman being gossiped about is foolish or silly, when she says in move 7/b: *I don't think she was aware that so many people knew.* Donna interprets Jo's interpersonal commitment, and Sue's probing for more information as a springboard for her explicit judgement. After Jo stops, therefore, Donna picks up the gossip and her interpersonal judgement increases in intensity as the text continues. For example, Wrap-Up (1), move 12, *a girl that never really wore make-up* is an implicit judgement but by moves 32/a to 34 Donna's judgement has intensified.

We can see this increased intensity, in move 32/a (Pejorative Evaluation (2)) *Actually, its really ridiculous* in which three Appraisals are expressed. The judgement is explicit and *really* amplifies the judgemental lexis creating the effect of a stronger judgement. There is, though, in this move also a mitigating amplification, *actually* which is used to soften the otherwise very strong judgement. Detailed analysis thus clarifies the foregrounding of interpersonal meanings in this utterance (see Chapter 4).

Move 32/a cohesively links back to the Third Person Focus, while move 32/b *I mean, I think she's made an absolute fool of herself*, is a springboard for the following Substantiating Behaviour. Move 32/b is an explicit modalized judgement, in which the judgement is intensified with the amplification *absolute*, emphasizing the totality of the judgement. As the judgement is so strong, Donna uses interpersonal metaphors of modality *I think* to soften the negative judgement; as well as an elaborating conjunction, *I mean* which functions in a similar way to soften the judgement. There are many examples of '*I mean*' in these gossip texts; these function to mitigate or downplay the judgement. As would be expected, there are also other mitigating strategies (see Chapter 4) used in this text, such as *just, sort of,* which are used when speakers want to soften the negative judgements they are making.

Move 32/b is a prospective judgement that projects the following Substantiating Behaviour. In most cases, the Substantiating Behaviours fuel the Pejorative Evaluations which follow. However, in this case, the Pejorative Evaluation both refers back to Substantiating Behaviour (4) and projects forward to Substantiating Behaviour (5).

These are explicit judgements, increasing in intensity, culminating in Donna saying, in Pejorative Evaluation (3), move 34: *I think she's atrocious.*'" In Donna's contribution there is an increase in the use of explicitly judgemental lexis whereas Jo is trying to constrain it. The evaluation increases in intensity and reaches a peak of prominence in each of the discrete Pejorative Evaluation stages.

The analysis of text 7.1 suggests that the primary function of the talk is to draw Sue in, but it also involves negotiation between Donna and Jo about how critical to be. Donna is quite explicit until move 35 when Jo says: *Oh, they haven't had those phone calls for ages, though.* In this statement Jo tries to modify the criticism and to counter Donna's claim. The judgement of atrocious is explicitly rejected indicated by Jo's implicit *but* in move 35. Donna concedes to Jo in move 36 when she says, *Been careful, have they?.* Jo then comes in with another implicit judgement in moves 37/a to 37/c, *Yeah, but she left her husband. She left her husband for him,* thereby reaching a consensus with Donna which paves the way for the text to close.

The text may well have finished after Wrap-Up (1) but Sue, probing for more information, signals not only her tacit approval for the gossip, but eagerness to hear more. The Wrap-ups often refer back to the Third Person Focus as Wrap-Up (1) does.

Up until Substantiating Behaviour (4) the evaluative meanings in each stage of the gossip are linked back to Pejorative Evaluation (1):

| 3 | 3/a | Jo | I mean, it was the laughing stock of the whole hospital |

This is the first explicit judgement. The subsequent Substantiating Behaviours link to the second Pejorative Evaluation *I mean, I think she's made an absolute fool of herself* providing evidence for these increased judgements.

The elements of structure labelled Probe have the function of indicating agreement or at least compliance for the gossip: by asking questions, or by reacting, or by simply exclaiming (such as *gosh* in move 19), the other participants indicate that they share these attitudes, or at least are encouraging the gossip to continue.

We can see from this analysis how judgement is smeared throughout the text and how it increases in intensity as the text proceeds. The analysis has shown how the Pejorative Evaluation (1), move 3/a: *It was the laughing stock of the whole hospital* drives most of the rest of the text. The Substantiating Behaviours mostly contain implicit judgements: these lead up to the peak of intensity in Pejorative Evaluation (3) which paves the way for the text to close. By tracking these evaluative meanings (see Chapter 3) we can see the interpersonal texture that contributes to the semantic coherence of this text.

One pattern which is consistent across all the gossip texts is that the Third Person Focus lays the foundation for the negative evaluations. The Substantiating Behaviours all provide evidence for the negative judgement, they are experiential cloaks on which to hang the explicit judgement. These then build up to the Pejorative Evaluations that are explicit judgements. The Pejorative Evaluations increase in intensity as the text proceeds, culminating in the Wrap-Ups, which contain implicit judgements.

7.5.2 Devising structural formulae for gossip

We can now capture the generic structure for the gossip of acquaintances in a linear sequence. This sequence, which is set out below, includes the obligatory and optional elements of structure as well as the elements which can be recursive.

Third Person Focus ^[[Substantiating Behaviour •
{(Probe)/Pej.Evaluation}]"^(Wrap-up)]"

Key:
.^   = is followed by
•   = occur in either sequence
( ) = optional
[ ] = domain of recursion or sequencing
{   = either/or
"   = recursion

Essential to the success of gossip in the data of workplace colleagues is the audience's implicit and explicit agreement. Without this agreement the gossip text will not proceed. Disagreement rarely occurs in any parts of these conversations, whether participants are telling a story, recounting or gossiping, but it is particularly the case with the gossip texts. A speaker is likely to back down after introducing the third person, if they do not receive some sort of confirmation from the listeners. There is a 'willing suspension of doubt',[11] that is, even if a participant does not agree with every detail, they need to be seen to accept the speaker's version of events. The listeners need to indicate agreement and the etiquette of gossip dictates how far the person initiating the gossip can go. If the speaker is judged to gossip too excessively or too pejoratively, then the gossip can turn against the speaker. An example of this is presented below. It is from a conversation involving the same group of women as texts 7.1 and 7.2 above. Example:

Sue: And when you said for example that Jenny didn't speak to you any more did you, have you ever approached her about that? Have you ever actually said

to her look em.
Donna: No I don't think it matters.
Sue: Okay, now getting back to biz.

In this example, Sue requests gossip but she interprets Donna's response as a lack of willingness to pursue it and so to save face immediately withdraws.

In contrast, the gossip between close friends does not display this preference for agreement. This can be illustrated by text 7.3: Clara and Stephen, presented below. This is a conversation which took place at a dinner party involving close friends. There were six people at the dinner party, Mark, Sally, Chris, Graham, Sue and Jim. They were all Anglo-Australians, aged in their mid-twenties to mid-thirties. They had all met many years before through their shared interest in bridge. The particular people participating in the conversation are Mark, Sally and Chris (and Graham gets referred to). They are discussing an affair which two of their friends, Clara and Stephen, are having. Clara is married to Andrew Harrison who is referred to throughout this conversation as 'Andy', 'Andrew' or 'Harrison'. The gossip starts with Mark telling the others how Stephen recently told Clara's husband about the affair.

As you read text 7.3 you will notice the additional elements of generic structure which are not present in the workplace conversation analysed above.

Text 7.3: Clara and Stephen

Turn	Move	Speaker	

Third Person Focus

| 1 | 1/a | Mark | See Stephen did something that I find particularly weird. |

Substantiating Behaviour (1)

	1/b		He told me, when I first got back, that the whole business was clandestine
	1/c		but == that ...
2	2	Sally	== Everybody knew about it.
3	3/a	Mark	Yeah
	3/c		Well, generally though the husband's the last to know
	3/d		and you see it was sort of an open secret.
	3/e		and Stephen thought that was terrible,
	3/f		right,
	3/g		cause it smacked of dishonesty
	3/h		so he fronted Andy, quote unquote,
	3/i		right

Pejorative Evaluation (1)

| | 3/j | | Which like what a thing to do! |
| | 3/k | | == Really! |

Defence (1)

4	4	Chris	== Well, you almost did that.
5	5	Mark	How?
6	6	Chris	You were very intent on sort == of
7	7	Sally	== Getting out in the open
8	8	Chris	Very veiled sort of message to Mark.
9	9	Mark	I'm Mark.
10	10/a	Chris	Oh, to Graham. (laughter)
	10/b		about losing things and people and things like that,
	10/c		You remember all those …
	10/d		You kept on giving him all these cryptic lines
	10/e		and even he worked out what they == meant

Response To Defence (1)

11	11/a	Mark	== Yeah…
	11/b		that was very good.
	11/c		but still that's really weird of Stephen

Pejorative Evaluation (2)

	11/d		because the whole situation right
	11/e		basically what he and Clara do is …
	11/f		I mean both of them do nothing == but sort of …
12	12	Sally	== They feed off Harrison I think
13	13	Mark	Well, other people in general, Stephen
14	14	Sally	Stephen off everybody
15	15	Mark	Stephen and Clara both
16	16	Sally	Yeah

Substantiating Behaviour (2)

17	17/a	Mark	Umm, they just sort of
	17/b		you know they ring up someone who they know is rich
	17/c		and they say
	17/d		what are we doing for lunch?
18	18	Sally	Yeah
19	19/a	Mark	You know its amazing
	19/b		and they …
	19/c		I don't understand
	19/d		I don't think either of them enjoy drinking
	19/e		but they get drunk every == day
20	20	Sally	== Mmm
21	21/a	Mark	== I've never seen either of them drunk
	21/b		and um but it's pretty bizarre thing to do to Clara's security
	21/c		cause she's == you know …

Defence (2)

22	22/a	Chris	== Yeah

| | 22/b | | I sort of understand it |

Response To Defence (2)

| 23 | 23/a | Mark | Well, you don't understand the English though. |

Substantiating Behaviour (3)

	23/b		You see Andrew prefers it all technically a secret.
24	24	Sally	Yeah, that ...
25	25/a	Mark	Clara's allowed to occasionally make a veiled comment
	25/b		which means that he really knows,
	25/c		right,
	25/c		and he enjoys that.
	25/c		But when you go up and ...
	25/d		anyway one way or another Stephen fronted Harrison,
	25/e		his own words,
	25/f		and now the deal is that they're allowed to do
	25/g		what they like
	25/h		as far as I can understand it.
	25/i		But Stephen's not allowed to be there
	25/j		when Andrew is.
	25/k		I don't know.
	25/l		Maybe Clara has some function in Andrew's business you know
	25/m		make him appear straight
	25/n		I think ...
	25/o		Wasn't that the whole motivation for the marriage or whatever?
	25/p		That was the impression I got.
	25/q		That he needed a wife to appear sort of respectable == and the rest of it
26	26	Sally	== yeah

Defence (3)

| 27 | 27 | Chris | == They're quite useful things to have ... |

Response to Defence (3)

28	28	Sally	Yeah
29	29/a	Mark	Yeah,
	29/b		its possible
	29/c		but I think well Clara was good for him in many ways
	29/d		because Clara's like ...
	29/e		her social set in Perth was all very rich people.
30	30	Sally	Yeah
31	31	Mark	And so Andrew got to ...

Pejorative Evaluation (3)

32	32	Sally	He sounds like the most crooked ...

Defence (Aborted)

33	33/a	Mark	Oh, he isn't really
	33/b		but he you know sort of ...

Pejorative Evaluation (4)

34	34/a	Chris	I think he's really nice just to talk to
	34/b		but I'd hate to have to depend on him

Defence (4)

35	35/a	Mark	Andrew's all right
	35/b		Andrew does business same way everyone does
	35/c		but it's just like he's a fraction more open about it all, you know
	35/d		he gets people drunk
	35/e		gets them to sign things
36	36/a	Chris	Yeah
	36/b		but that's not really true
	36/c		A lot == of ...

Response To Defence (4)

37	37/a	Sally	== But it seems such a peculiar ...
	37/b		cause Stephen and Clara spend most of their time bitching about ...
38	38	Mark	== Andrew
39	39/a	Sally	== Andrew
	39/b		and yet they == both
40	40	Mark	== Well, that's their ...
41	41/a	Sally	you know, are so dependent on him
	41/b		and she wouldn't leave him in a pink fit
	41/c		because he's got money.
	41/c		and Stephen's got no money
	41/c		and has no intention of, you know
	41/d		he's not interested in being ...

Concession (1)

42	42/a	Mark	Yeah,
	42/b		kind of ...
	42/c		but Andrew sort of enjoys all the abuse he gets to some extent
43	43	Sally	Mmm
44	44/a	Mark	Seems like terribly poor form
	44/b		You know this girl Kim.

(Eggins's data)

As you can see in this text there is not an obligation to agree; on the contrary, the participants disagree with each other and exchange quite different opinions about the person being gossiped about. With each of the gossip texts between close friends, participants frequently disagreed with the speaker's interpretation of events, often defending the person being criticized. The gossip is more likely to be about another close member of the group where participants feel they have the right, as established members of the group, to discuss another group member. In each case of gossip in the workplace, the person being gossiped about was not a close friend of any of the participants, which made the gossip 'safer' and less potentially face threatening.

It has been argued that co-operativeness is typical of all women's talk and competitiveness is more likely to characterize men's talk (see Coates 1988: 99). However, co-operativeness depends on the functional motivation of the conversation and how well the participants know each other. In conversations between close friends, which are motivated by difference, the participants are more likely to vie for turns, to disagree and to contradict each other. In the conversations of work colleagues, the participants work together to share likenesses and to establish shared ways of seeing the world. Co-operativeness characterizes the workplace coffee-break conversations (at least with the mixed gender and the all-women groups). Given the nature of the workplace context, conversations there tend to be between people who are in frequent contact but with low affective involvement (to use two of the variables for tenor, see Chapter 1). Conversely the data of mixed gender groups of close friends are characterized more by competitiveness.

This functional motivation of conversations among close friends to explore difference is manifested in three additional elements of structure. These are Defence, Response to Defence and Concession. Defence is where a listener disagrees with the speaker by defending some aspect of the person being gossiped about. This is followed by the speaker responding to the defence. Following these two elements a compromise position is usually reached when one or other of the parties concedes. This demonstrates that, even with close friends where some degree of solidarity and shared understanding is assumed, there is a need to reach consensus before a conversation can switch topic.

It appears from the conversational data of close friends that the only time concession is not obligatory is when the Defence is only very mild and so does not pressure the other speaker to concede. An example of this occurs in moves 22/a and 22/b in text 7.3 where Chris comes in with a mild Defence when Mark is criticizing Clara and Stephen:

Defence (2)

22	22/a	Chris	== Yeah
	22/b		I sort of understand it

Mark does not concede to this Defence when he remarks in move 23/a, *Well, you don't understand the English though* and so he proceeds (with another Substantiating Behaviour) to provide more evidence for his negative evaluation. Defence and Response to Defence appear to be obligatory stages in the data of close friends. Although the stage of Concession occurs in most cases, it is optional.[12] Once consensus is reached it paves the way for completion of the text.

Defence, Response to Defence and Concession are unlikely to occur in the conversations of acquaintances because, in these conversations, there needs to be explicit or implicit agreement for gossip to proceed.

In text 7.3. Mark indicates in the concession that agreement has been reached and therefore he implicitly signals that the topic can be changed. In this case the concession functions to close the gossip text and so there is no Wrap-up.

We can now develop an overall structural formula which applies for both the close friends and acquaintances data:

Third Person Focus ^[[Substantiating Behaviour •
{(Probe)/Pej.Evaluation} ^(Defence)^(Response to
Defence)]"^(Concession)^(Wrap-up)]"

What distinguishes the stages of gossip texts from each other is that they fulfil a functionally distinct role. Each stage displays semantic differences as well as some significant lexico-grammatical differences (see section 2.6.2.6, Chapter 2). A defining feature of a generic stage is the particular semantic strategies employed and these in turn are realized by particular grammatical features. In the next section we will outline the semantic and grammatical realization of each of the obligatory stages.

7.6 SPECIFYING SEMANTIC AND LEXICO-GRAMMATICAL REALIZATIONS FOR EACH STAGE OF A GOSSIP TEXT

In this section we will briefly discuss the three obligatory stages of a gossip text. We will also examine the optional stage of Probe because it is structurally different to the other elements of structure. The Pejorative Evaluation stage will be presented in detail in order to show what a more elaborate analysis can reveal. The different semantic strategies employed by participants in the Pejorative Evaluation will be presented in a semantic network and this will be followed by a discussion of some of the lexico-grammatical features.

We will draw mainly on examples from text 7.1: A Classic Affair, but will use some examples from text 7. 2: Richard, and 7.3: Clara and Stephen.[13]

7.6.1 Obligatory stages

7.6.1.1 Third Person Focus

The Third Person Focus, which is the initial obligatory stage of gossip, introduces the person or people being gossiped about. In some texts the personal attribute or behaviour which is disapproved of is also mentioned. This is where the functional motivation of establishing and maintaining in-group membership is immediately reflected in the text by setting up the 'us' versus 'them'. The third person is immediately established as outside the group by being the object of the group's judgement. For example, in text 7.1 when Jo says, *We had an affair* the use of the word *'we'* establishes a symbolic relationship between being in the dialogue and being outside it. The dialogue is a type of metaphor for being in the group in the first place. The Third Person Focus also serves to give a thematic prediction that a gossip text is about to begin and this makes the listener 'tune in' to what is to follow.

The Third Person Focus can be in the form of a request for a gossip text, as in text 7.2: Richard, turn 1: *What happened about Richard?*. It can also take the form of someone initiating a gossip text which is the case with text 7.3, *see Stephen did something that I find particularly weird*. Whether you are giving or demanding gossip the simultaneous semantic options available to initiate the text are to focus either on the offending situation or on the offender. For example move 1/a in text 7.1, focuses on the offending situation when Jo says, *There was an affair*. On the other hand, move 1/a in Text 7.3 focuses on the offender when Mark says, *see Stephen did something that I find particularly weird*. If the focus is on the situation then in most cases the offender is also introduced. For example, in text 7.1 the situation is introduced first in move 1/a, *There was an affair* but this is followed by mention of the offender in move 1/d, *There was an affair going on between the cook and this other girl, you know*.

7.6.1.2 Substantiating Behaviour

While the Third Person Focus sets up the interpersonal focus, the Substantiating Behaviours legitimize the judgements by providing evidence for the negative evaluations. Therefore, the main function of the Substantiating Behaviour stage is to provide evidence of how the third person acts uncharacteristically, excessively, inappropriately or unacceptably. This function of the Substantiating Behaviour stage is illustrated in Table 7.1 with reference to texts 7.1 and 7.3:

Table 7.1: The function of the Substantiating Behaviour

Type of 'deviant' behaviour	Text	Stage and moves	Evidence of behaviour
unusual, uncharacteristic or atypical behaviour	text 7.1: A Classic Affair	Substantiating Behaviour 3 ● moves 9/a–11/b	uncharacteristic: wearing of make-up
excessive behaviour	text 7.1: A Classic Affair	Substantiating Behaviour 1 ● moves 1/e–2	offender accused of going over to other section of hospital too frequently
unacceptable or inappropriate behaviour	text 7.3: Clara and Stephen	Substantiating Behaviour 3 ● moves 9/a–11/b	Andrew accused of marrying Clara to appear '*straight*' and '*respectable*'

Each of these semantic strategies separate the person being gossiped about from the group who gossip. They frame what is considered to be deviant behaviour and by doing so clearly establish the groups values.

This semantic nucleus of Substantiating Behaviour is then realized in various ways in the lexicogrammar. A straight projection of group membership is realized throughout all Substantiating Behaviours by grammatical oppositions which are set up. For example, in texts 7.1 and 7.3 there are two major referential chains of 'I' and 'we' on the one hand and 'he' and 'she' on the other. In text 7.1: A Classic Affair, the first 'she' chain is introduced in the first Substantiating Behaviour and this is followed through in all the other Substantiating Behaviours.

Many of these Substantiating Behaviour stages deal with a sequence of behaviours which lead to a concluding behaviour which marks the behaviour as unusual. This occurs, for example, in text 7.1: A Classic Affair in:

- Substantiating Behaviour (3) in move 11/b – *then all of a sudden she started wearing make-up*
- Substantiating Behaviour (5) in move 66 – *Now, it's not her*

This point of culmination acts like a coda to the Substantiating Behaviour stage and is often realized by a thematic, temporal adjunct. For example, in text 7.1 in move 11/b – *then all of a sudden* and in move 32/f – *now*.

7.6.2 Pejorative Evaluation

Evaluative meanings occur throughout gossip texts but at each Pejorative Evaluation stage there is a peak of evaluative prominence. It is in these stages that the judgements, which have been fuelled by the Substantiating Behaviours, are made explicit. The two aspects of the functional motivation of gossip, i.e. as a form of social control and as an indicator of in-group membership, are reflected in the semantic and linguistic strategies of the Pejorative Evaluation.

The semantic network details the semantic options available, demonstrates how these social meanings are expressed in language and shows the range of options in meaning which can be adopted in the Pejorative Evaluation stage.

The semantic network provides a bridge between the social meanings and the linguistic forms, an interface between context and lexicogrammar. It is a way into the linguistic system from the context. As Halliday (1973) suggests, this kind of analysis is saying 'these are the meanings; now this is how they are expressed' rather than 'these are the forms, now this is what they mean'. The semantic strategies are quite specific but these can be realized in different parts of the grammar.[11] As Halliday says:

> Whereas the social meanings, or behaviour patterns, are specific to their contexts and settings, their linguistic reflexes are very general categories such as those of transitivity, of mood and modality, of time and place, of information structure

and the like. The input to the semantic networks is sociological and specific; their output is linguistic and general. (Halliday 1973: 80)

The semantic network in Figure 7.1 outlines the semantic strategies available for Pejorative Evaluation. This semantic network indicates that there are two broad semantic categories which realize Pejorative Evaluation. These are outlined below:

i) **The offence-oriented strategies** focus on the offender, i.e. the person being gossiped about. Here the Pejorative Evaluation ascribes a negative attribute either to the offender ('evaluation of offender') or to their behaviour ('evaluation of behaviour'). If the feature 'evaluation of behaviour' is selected, then the negative attitude can be realized in two ways:

- It can be realized in a relational attributive clause ('as attribute'). For example, in text 7.1: A Classic Affair – move 32/a: *it's really ridiculous* assigns a negative attribute to Anna's behaviour.
- Alternatively, it can be realized in a relational: identifying clause, e.g. in text 7.1: A Classic Affair – move 3/a: *it was the laughing stock of the whole hospital* where the situation ('it') is identified as having a particular function or status ('the value').

  If the feature 'evaluation of offender' is selected then, similarly, the negative attitude can be realized either:

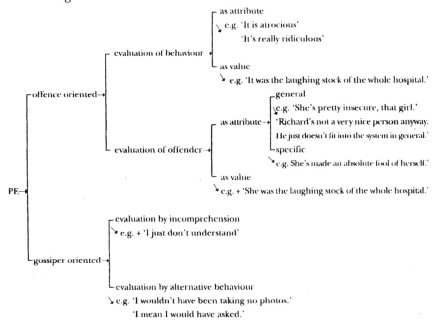

Figure 7.1 Semantic network for Pejorative Evaluation

- by a relational: attributive clause; where the negative attribute is expressed in general terms. For example, in text 7.1: A Classic Affair: move 34: *I think she's atrocious* and in text 7.2: Richard: turn 10: *Richard's not a very nice person anyway. He just doesn't fit in to the system* or where the negative attribute is tied to a specific situation, as in text 7.1: move 32/b *I mean, I think she has made an absolute fool of herself.* Each of these cases assign a negative attribute to the 'offender'.
- or by a relational: identifying clause where the value identifies the 'offender' as having a particular negative status. For example: *She was the laughing stock of the whole hospital.*

ii) With the '**gossiper-oriented**' strategies there are two choices:

- 'Evaluation by alternative behaviour' is where the Pejorative Evaluation is in the form of the speaker saying what they would have done instead. It is projected into hypothetical reality as in text 1. 2 : Tamara in Chapter 1:

| Donna | == I wouldn't be taking any photos. == I mean, I would have asked. |
| Jenny | == I mean, if anyone had taken any photos of me at the fancy dress I'd want them to == burn them. |

- 'Evaluation by incomprehension' is where the speaker expresses incomprehension of the offender's behaviour, e.g. *I just don't understand, it's beyond me.*

These two broad categories represent the semantic meaning selections that might be expected to occur in the Pejorative stage of a gossip text. The offence-oriented strategies clearly state that the behaviour or actions of the offender are inappropriate or unacceptable. The gossiper-oriented strategies indicate what is considered to be appropriate behaviour in certain contexts or make explicit the gossiper's disapproval of the offender's behaviour. Each of these strategies assert and reconfirm the values of the group as well as indicate in-group membership. The Pejorative Evaluation is important in establishing agreement with the primary gossiper and in paving the way for the gossip text to continue. It then continues with more evidence (a Substantiating Behaviour) to support the negative judgements.

Each of these semantic strategies of Pejorative Evaluation clearly marks the behaviour as outside that which is regarded as acceptable by the group.

Modalized metaphors are frequently used in the Pejorative Evaluation stage, for example:

- 'I think', 'I reckon' and 'I mean' function as interpersonal adjuncts.
- 'I mean' and 'I mean to say' are incongruent elaborating conjunctions but they can be seen to fulfil the same function.

Each of these forms serve explicitly to modalize the proposition and by doing so soften the negative judgement. For example:

- Text 7.1: A Classic Affair: Move 3/a – *I mean, it was the laughing stock of the whole hospital*
- Text 7.1: A Classic Affair: Move 34 – *I think she's atrocious.*
- Text 7.1: A Classic Affair: Move 32/b – *I mean, I think she's made an absolute fool of herself.*

Coates claims that these incongruent forms are frequently used by women to 'hedge assertions in order to protect both their own and addressee's face' (Coates 1989: 114). As gossip poses a potential risk to 'face', it is not surprising that these forms are prevalent in these conversations.

7.6.3 Probe

We will now look at those sections of gossip which have been labelled 'Probe'. We will examine text 7.1: A Classic Affair and consider whether the Probe stage functions in the same way as the other elements of generic structure.

The first two probes of text 7.1: A Classic Affair are presented below:

Probe (1)

4	4	Sue	Did she know that you knew?
5	5	Donna	I don't think so.
6	6/a	Jo	No
	6/b		I don't think she was that cluey.
7	7/a	Donna	No
	7/b		I don't think she was aware of the fact that so many people knew.
8	8	Jo	Yeah

Probe (2)

13	13/a	Sue	And what happened in the end?
	13/b		Are they still together?
14	14/a	Donna	Oh, she left her husband
	14/b		and she's still with ...
15	15	Sue	They're still together?
16	16	Donna	Yeah
17	17	Sue	She left her husband?
18	18	Donna	Yeah
19	19	Sue	Gosh!

Both these sections of the gossip text start with Sue asking a question. Sue is the person who does not have previous knowledge of the affair and so she has not been involved in supplying evidence, i.e. she does not provide any Substantiating Behaviour. The Probe sections basically consist of Question ^ Answer, with an optional follow-up.

These sections are labelled 'Probe' as they are probing for more information. They are different in kind to the other elements of structure and do not function in the generic structure in the same way as the Substantiating Behaviour or Pejorative Evaluation stages.

The Third Person Focus, Substantiating Behaviour, Pejorative Evaluation and Wrap-up stages can be represented as elements in a multivariate structure in that they are functionally distinct stages. In other words, Substantiating Behaviour is functionally distinct with reference to Pejorative Evaluation and Wrap-up. This means that each element or stage has a point to it, and this point is significant for the achievement of that particular discourse type or genre. In addition, some of the elements are constrained to occur in a particular order. It is these obligatory elements and their sequence that define the genre and have a role in bringing the genre to an end. They are elements or stages that lead to the completion of the text.

By contrast, probes are not functionally specific to the completion of the text but they enable the text to continue. For example, after the first Wrap-Up in text 7.1, the text could have finished, but Sue's probe in move 13/a, '*And what happened in the end?*' enabled the text to continue. By asking questions and by showing interest and implicit agreement with the gossip, Sue encourages Jo to supply more information.

Probe can occur in other genres of casual conversation and hence it is not defining of any particular genre: this is because it serves more general interactional goals.

Probe stages are different from other elements of structure for three reasons:

- They are not functionally specific to the genre.
- They do not lead to the completion of the text.
- They are distinctively dependent on the previous elements in a way that the other elements of generic structure are not.

Having Probe in the generic structure formulation disguises the fact that its relationship to other elements of structure is different from the relationship of other elements to each other. Probes can function within the rapid turn taking segments of chat and can function to sustain both chat and chunk segments of talk.

In gossip texts we see Probes functioning to sustain and extend the genre in the same way as Probing moves extend exchanges by probing the content of prior moves. Probing moves have a similar function to Probes in gossip texts. Both these types of probing strategies are supportive of talk in the sense that they delay anticipated exchange or genre completion, without disrupting the flow of talk. They also both display dependency on the previous moves or stages of a text.

In the Probes, we see the chat segments of casual conversation embedded in the chunks. Therefore, in such highly interactive genres as gossip, a generic perspective needs to be complemented by an approach which can describe the dynamic unfolding of chat.

A generic account of texts provides part of the picture in that it specifies the generic agenda which interactants have to address. This macro perspective is important as it can account for what constitutes a complete text. However, we need to complement this perspective with one which can describe the interpersonal dimension of talk and which can allow us to describe how conversation is locally open ended, i.e. how the conversation can, in principle, expand indefinitely move by move.

In the next section we will return to the gossip text presented in Chapter 1, text 1.2: Tamara, and bring together the analyses outlined in chapters 4 (analysis of interpersonal meanings) and 5 (move and speech function) and combine these with the generic account outlined in this chapter. A comprehensive picture of casual conversation thus requires different analyses being brought to bear on any particular text. The particular analyses to foreground will depend on the particular excerpt; in this gossip text the generic structure and interpersonal analyses will be foregrounded.

7.7 THE GENERIC AND MICRO STRUCTURE OF THE GOSSIP TEXT 1.2: TAMARA

The generic structure of the first section of text 1.2: Tamara is outlined below. On the left hand side, the analysis of the conversational structure of the text is outlined, and the Appraisal analysis of interpersonal meanings is indicated by italics. The analysis will be followed by a discussion of the interpersonal dimension of the text in relation to the generic stages and then the speech function analysis will be discussed briefly to illustrate the micro-interaction of the gossip text.

Conversational structure	Turn/ move	Speaker	Text
Third Person Focus			
O:I:give opinion	1/a	Donna	But this reminds me of Tamara.
Substantiating Behaviour (1)			
P: elaborate	1/b	Donna	She comes back from two months away
P: extend	1/c		organizes an extra month the following year
P: extend	1/d		and how she accumulates so many holidays is beyond me.
R:D:elaborate	2/a	Jo	She hasn't *even* come up for ten years' service
P: enhance	2/b		so it can't *even* be == classed as long service leave
R:s:acknowledge	3	Jenny	== Oh, I don't know.
R:D:extend	4	Donna	I'm coming up for that, love

Probe (1)

R:track:probe	5	Jo	Did she see the photos in her coz?[15]

Substantiating Behaviour (2)

R: resolve	6/a	Jenny	She walks in …
C:enhance	6/b		She *stopped me*
C:enhance	6/c		She *stopped me*
C:enhance	6/d		and she said, umm "Oh, by the way, have you seen any photos of == me?"
C:enhance	6/e		I thought, you know, you're *a bit sort of*, you know …
R:D:extend	7	Jo	== No-one told her there were photos.
C:enhance	8/a	Jenny	She said, "Have you seen any photos of me at the fancy dress?"
C:enhance	8/b		And I said,
C:enhance	8/c		I said, "Well, as a matter of fact, I've seen one or two, um, of you *Tamara*, but you know, nothing …"
C:enhance	8/d		And, um, she said "Do you know of anyone else who's taken == any photos of me at the fancy dress?"

Pejorative Evaluation (1)

R:D:elaborate	9/a	Donna	== I wouldn't be taking any photos.
C:elaborate	9/b		==I mean, I would have asked.
R:D:elaborate	10	Jenny	== I mean, if anyone had taken any photos of me at the fancy dress I'd want them to == burn them.
R:D:enhance (Rhetorical question)	11	Jo	== Why does she always want to get her picture ( )

Substantiating Behaviour (3)

R:D:elaborate	12	Jenny	She said, "I just wanted to see how well the costume turned out."

Pejorative Evaluation (2)

R:D:elaborate	13	Jo	*She's pretty insecure, that girl.*

Substantiating Behaviour (4)

(False start)	14/a	Donna	I told her …
O:I:give opinion	14/b		You know what she said?

P:enhance	14/c		== I can't believe it.
R:D:extend	15/a	Jenny	== *You know what she wore?*
P:extend	15/b		She wore this suit with a no top, a pair of Lurex tights without feet in them, you know and then,
P:extend	15/c		and ... she had this old green olive green jumper that her mother must of had ...
R:D:enhance	16/a	Donna	Yeah, its her mother's.
P:enhance	16/b		She told me that
P:enhance	17/a	Jenny	And then she had her face painted green ...
P:extend	17/b		had her hair in a tight plait or something == down her back
R:s:acknowledge	18	Jo	== Yeah, yeah.
P:extend	19/a	Jenny	*And she had her face painted green* with turquoise upside her long nose and *around and up and down,*
P:enhance	19/b		and it had *all* glitter *around here.*

Pejorative Evaluation (3)

R:resolve	20/a	Jo	Yes.
P:enhance	20/b		*she's a tart.*

Substantiating Behaviour (5)

R:D:enhance	21/a	Jenny	And then she had. . .
	21/b		I can't think what else,
P:extend	21/c		I know, ... eye shadow and the whole bit
P:enhance	21/d		and then she had this old stick with a star on it.
P:extend	21/e		Um, and she had this stick thing ... this stick thing that had a star on it,
P:enhance	21/f		and then she had a cape around her shoulders or something,
P:enhance	21/g		and went [poof] or something to people
P:enhance	21/h		and then started laughing.

Wrap-Up

R:D:elaborate	22/a	Donna	== Yeah, here's something.
P:elaborate	22/b		You'd just go and break off a tree
P:extend	22/c		and stick a star on it.

(Slade's data)

In this text, the Third Person Focus is initiated by Donna when she says, *But this reminds me of Tamara.* This is a prototypical gossip opener which utilizes the semantic strategy of focusing on the offender (see section 7.6.1.1). Jo and Jenny, as established in-group members, would immediately know whether the gossip is going to be negative or positive. What they would not know at this stage is what kind of judgement is going to be made (that is, whether Tamara's integrity is going to be questioned or her ethics or morality or whether she is going to be accused of being incompetent or foolish or of being deceitful or cowardly).

The particular kind of judgement is made obvious through the first Substantiating Behaviour which, although implicit, makes it clear that the speaker thinks Tamara is deceitful (by taking more holidays than she deserves). So early on in the text, even before any explicit judgement, the other participants are being positioned to think that Tamara is playing the system to her own gain.

The Tamara text differs from the other gossip texts presented in this chapter as there is very little explicit judgement made by the participants. However, there is still a smearing of judgement throughout the text which increases in intensity and culminates in move 20/b when Jo says, *she's a tart*.

To establish how the attitudinal meanings are spread throughout this text we need to see how the judgement is implicitly coded: that is how it is coded not through interpersonal lexis but rather through the building up of experiential meanings that implicitly code these judgements.

In Substantiating Behaviour (2), moves 6/a to 8/d, Jenny clearly establishes her judgement of Tamara as vain through repetition (amplification: *She stopped me, She stopped me*) and quoting Tamara, for example: *by the way have you seen any photos of me?*. Jenny's judgement then fuels Donna who comes in with a negative evaluation in Pejorative Evaluation (1). However, Donna still does not use explicit judgemental lexis but implies a judgement by stating what she would have done instead, in moves 9/a and 9/b, *I wouldn't be taking no photos, I mean I would have asked*. This is an example of a semantic strategy of 'evaluation by alternative behaviour'. This strategy enables the speaker to make a negative evaluation by discussing alternative behaviour rather than focusing on the offender such as in move 13 when Jo says, *she's pretty insecure, that girl.*

In this stage, both Jenny and Donna use the incongruent elaborating conjunction, *I mean* and this serves explicitly to modalize the proposition and by doing so softening the negative judgement.

Judgement is not made explicit until move 13 in Pejorative Evaluation (2), when Jo says: *she's pretty insecure that girl.* This is a judgement of social esteem (see Chapter 4, section 4.3.3). Here Jo is softening a little in her judgement. However, in Substantiating Behaviour (4), Jenny comes in with heavy artillery, the increased intensity of judgement being achieved by amplification through repetition in move 14/b: *You know what she said?,* move 15/a: *You know what she wore?,* and again in move 17/a: *she then had her face painted green.* Increased intensity of judgement is also achieved by multiple judgements. Tamara is constructed as unethical, then as looking ridiculous and foolish. These judgements start with judgements concerning Tamara's unethical behaviour in moves 15/a and 15/b which pave the way

for the explicit statement of the same judgement in move 20/b: *she's a tart'*
It is only because the foundation of judgement is laid in the preceding
section of the gossip (through the Substantiating Behaviours) that this is
said with no modality or hedging.

The multiple judgements continue in Substantiating Behaviour (5)
where Tamara is constructed as daggy and incompetent. This amplification
of judgement culminates in a proliferation of meaning leading up to this
penultimate Pejorative Evaluation (3).

There is a crescendo of evaluation in the Wrap-up at the end of this text
where Donna is saying that Tamara, on top of everything else, is also stupid and
incompetent (by saying that she is uncreative with her wardrobe). This really
amounts to the final insult leaving nowhere left to go. It is at this stage that the
topic changes with Jo saying *Reminds me of my Mum with a Christmas tree.*

Unlike the participants in text 7.1: A Classic Affair, all the interactants in
the Tamara text have been in the workplace for some time. They are all
familiar with Tamara and each of the participants collaborate in the gossip.
This explains why there is only one Probe, which occurs when Jo asks a
question in move 5, *'did she see the photos in her coz?'.* She knows that this
single question will elicit further evidence for their judgements of Tamara.

These analyses also shed light on the pattern of contribution from the
different participants. Donna orchestrates the gossip by beginning and
ending it. Jenny makes her opinions obvious by building up evidence
through Substantiating Behaviours, whereas Jo makes the interpersonal
undercurrent explicit (11, 13, 20/a, 20/b). Jo also uses many negatives
(2/a, 2/b, 7) and questions (5, 11). Jo provides explicit judgements while
Jenny provides more of the evidence on which Jo hangs her evaluations.

This text demonstrates the social function of gossip as a vehicle for
maintaining the unity, morals and values of social groups. Taking too many
holidays, wanting photos to be taken of yourself, dressing inappropriately or
daggily, are clearly established as inappropriate ways to behave. These
behaviours represent what this group asserts as the undesirable qualities of
deceit, vanity and foolishness. This conversation, although on the surface
about Tamara, is more about the maintenance of a social order, and the
perpetuation and assertion of normative boundaries.

7.7.1 Speech function analysis

A conversational structure analysis of the Tamara text shows us that
the gossip is collaboratively constructed with Donna and Jenny initiating
most of the statements and Jo showing both her compliance and agreement
with the judgements by responding and also probing to move the text
forward. Her question in move 5, *did she see the photos in her coz?*, was the only
non-rhetorical question and this opened up the possibility for further gossip
about Tamara. This also shifted the judgement from Tamara's deceit to her
vanity. Jenny responds to this with a detailed Substantiating Behaviour
where she provides evidence that paints Tamara as vain and conceited.

By move 6/e each participant has indicated judgement and inside knowledge of Tamara and by doing so they have marked their membership in the group. At the same time each participant has clearly stated what type of behaviour they endorse and what type they condemn. As they have all established membership, there is no functional role for more Probes. The only other questions in the remainder of the text are rhetorical questions, e.g. move 11, *Why does she always want to get her picture...?* and move 14/b, *You know what she wore?*. Both these rhetorical questions are devices to encode judgement.

A speech function analysis also shows the relationship between the Pejorative Evaluations and the Substantiating Behaviours. In each case the Pejorative Evaluations have a Reaction: Developing structure with the responses being fuelled by the evidence provided in the previous Substantiating Behaviour. Similarly, the Wrap-Up has a Reaction: Developing structure which shows that this final step responds to the entire preceding text by providing a thematic conclusion – in this case, by saying that Tamara, on top of everything else, is also stupid and incompetent (by saying that she is uncreative with her wardrobe).

By tracking these discourse and semantic features as well as the global or macro structure of gossip, we can see how values and ideological positions are built up through the text, how agreement and compliance pave the way for the gossip to continue, and how, by sharing attitudes and values (by agreeing with views on how not to behave) solidarity is achieved.

7.8 CONCLUSION

This chapter has built on the descriptive techniques outlined in the previous chapters by developing analytical tools for describing the more interactively oriented genres. The analysis of the language of gossip presented in this chapter reveals a great deal about the social role and function of gossip in our society as a form of talk through which interactants can construct solidarity as they explore shared normative judgements about culturally significant behavioural domains. The analysis has demonstrated that gossip is a culturally determined process with a distinctive staging structure that can be described. It has also demonstrated the dialectical relationship between the linguistic form and the social purpose of gossip. However, in order to describe gossip (and in particular the 'chat' elements that are dispersed throughout) the generic perspective needs to be complemented by a dynamic analysis that focuses on the unfolding of the talk, move-by-move. A comprehensive picture of casual conversation thus requires that different analyses be brought to bear on each particular text.

NOTES

1. In the gossip texts, however, the evaluation is different in nature. In the gossip texts the evaluations are about the behaviour or action of a third

person, whereas in narratives the evaluations are concerned with the release of tension with respect to the Complication ^ Resolution structure.

2. We listed in Chapter 6 (see section 6.4.2) the different types of contributions made by participants when they are in a primary listener role. It seems that gossip utilizes more probing types of questions and makes more negative assessments than storytelling texts.

3. In all the gossip texts, whether it be between close friends at a dinner party or between workplace colleagues, interest and involvement in the gossip needs to be indicated for the gossip to proceed. The difference is, as discussed later in the chapter, that close friends may often disagree and argue about the judgements being made of the person being gossiped about whereas with the workplace colleagues, who are not close friends, tacit agreement is necessary for the gossip conversation to continue.

4. None of our data of the conversations of close friends and acquaintances included conversations about prominent figures, such as Princess Diana, who were not known to any of the participants. Hence, data of this kind have not been analysed, although such texts are likely to fit the generic structure description outlined for gossip in this chapter.

5. Dunbar is referring to the broader sense of gossip as the passing on of news.

6. TAB refers to official agency for placing bets on horse races.

7. This text demonstrates the hegemonic nature of gossip: the judgements made of Richard socially sanction this kind of behaviour; gossip in workplaces performs a similar function, although not addressed directly to the person in question, of an institutionalized reprimand.

8. All the analysed texts in Chapters 6 and 7 are numbered into turns and moves (see Chapter 5 for a definition of the move).

9. This structure is also applied to three other texts in this chapter. See Slade (1997) for an analysis of further gossip texts, demonstrating the generalizability of this generic structure.

10. This is not a felicitous response to the question in Probe (4): *So you don't know what's going on?*, which is why it is coded, not as part of Probe, but as a separate stage.

11. This is following Sacks, (1992a), who used the term 'willing suspension of disbelief'.

12. Using a courtroom analogy, terms such as defence and concession as well as 'offender' and 'offending situation' are used. With the gossip between close friends the offender is on trial and the verdict is negotiated whereas in the data of workplace acquaintances there is consensus or agreement on the verdict.

13. For a detailed linguistic analysis of each of the stages of gossip see Slade (1997).

14. These semantic strategies are the strategies that someone learning English as a Second Language may need to be familiar with to be able to recognize or participate in a gossip text in these or similar cultural contexts. This analysis can show the strategies that someone will need to be familiar with to understand gossip in the particular cultural contexts. It is an analysis that can show how the complementary roles in gossiping are achieved and what linguistic resources ESL learners will need to have to take up one of these roles.

15. "Coz" is common Australian slang for "costume".

8 Conclusion

8.1 INTRODUCTION

In this final chapter we summarize the major issues presented in the book, suggest the relevance of analyses presented in the previous chapters, and reiterate our arguments for the analysis of casual conversation.

8.2 SUMMARY

As we indicated in Chapter 1, our book has had two main aims: to develop a comprehensive set of analytical techniques for describing language patterns in casual conversation; and to offer a critical explanation of the role casual conversation plays in our development as socialized beings.

In Chapter 2 we reviewed the approaches to discourse analysis that we have found most relevant to the analysis of casual conversation. The range of approaches considered in that chapter underlined our conviction that casual conversation is sufficiently complex to require exploration from many different theoretical and descriptive perspectives.

We began by drawing on the CA characterization of conversation as an 'interactional achievement', i.e. as a collaborative, functional and social behaviour, and acknowledged insights from ethnography, sociolinguistics, variation theory, speech act theory, pragmatics, and the Birmingham School. We have drawn on the functional-semantic theory of systemic linguistics, which has provided a range of detailed, systematic analyses of linguistic patterns at different levels, as well as an explicit model of the relationship between the contextual dimension of 'social roles and relations' and its expression through the interpersonal meanings of talk.

We have also drawn on critical discourse analysis. CDA has provided us with a theoretical orientation which seeks to connect the private with the public, the interpersonal with the macro-institutional. We have taken from CDA a theory of talk as motivated and sustained by the negotiation of differences whose relevance exceeds the private contexts of our casual interactions. Our work also represents an exploration of CDA's methodological suggestions, that it is not enough to describe what goes on in talk, but that a useful analysis of casual conversation involves explaining both how casual talk connects us to the public, institutional structures of our cultural context, and how it is that most of the time we are unaware that such a connection is operating.

We believe that the analytical techniques presented in Chapters 3 to 7 satisfy our aim to enable comprehensive rather than fragmentary analysis of casual conversation. In Chapters 3, 4 and 5 we presented techniques for the analysis of grammatical, semantic and discourse patterns in casual conversation. Our interpretations of the results of these analyses allowed us to consider the negotiation of status relations, degrees of familiarity, and differential affiliations in conversations involving family groups, workplace colleagues and close friends. The inclusion of a discussion of humour in casual talk allowed us to explain in part why casual conversation is frequently both enjoyable to participate in as well as crucial in the affirming and enacting of social identities and relationships. Our analyses of humour in the conversations from different contexts suggested that humour is a strategic conversational resource that enables interactants to distance themselves from the contradictions and differences they are negotiating, while making it look and feel as though they are not actually doing anything serious at all.

In Chapter 6 we added to these techniques the further descriptive apparatus of genre analysis, which we have found useful in describing the macro-structure and social motivation of more monologic excerpts in casual talk. The application of an explicit typology of storytelling genres illustrated the range of different social purposes for which interactants tell their stories in casual talk. The application of genre analysis to account for a corpus of workplace conversations revealed the different text types or genres that commonly occurred in these conversations, as well as some interesting comparisons between the conversations in single-sex and mixed-sex groups.

Finally, in Chapter 7 we brought the micro-structural analysis and the genre perspective together in exploring the interactive conversational achievement of gossip. Through our analysis of the grammatical, semantic, discourse and generic characteristics of gossip talk, we developed an interpretation of the social effects of gossip to enable the enactment and confirmation of sociocultural values among groups of workplace colleagues and close friends.

Throughout the book we have demonstrated how the techniques presented permit both the quantitative analysis of synoptic characteristics of casual talk, and the more dynamic analysis of patterns in the unfolding of the talk move by move.

In presenting this extensive repertoire of analyses, we do not mean to imply that it would be necessary to apply all kinds of analysis to understand any excerpt of talk. Instead, we consider that the particular questions one is asking of the text would lead to the foregrounding of particular analyses over others. However, we have demonstrated that, for a comprehensive account of any casual conversational excerpt, a systematic working through of analyses from the grammatical to the generic is extremely useful.

Although in this book we have focused on analysing casual conversation, most of the techniques presented here could be applied to the analysis of spoken interactions from other more public contexts (e.g. pragmatic and pedagogic interactions). As such, our work goes beyond the analysis of conversation and represents a contribution to discourse analysis.

In order to meet our second aim, that of pursuing a critical interpretation of casual talk, the framework we have used has consistently linked the analysis of the language with the 'social work' the talk is doing in its cultural context. Our data provide support for Sharrock and Anderson's claim that:

> The character of the social situation and the nature of the social relationships between the participants are audible in the talk. Give someone a transcript and they can, very often, get quite a definite sense of who the parties to the talk are, in what capacities they are relating to one another, what kind of personal relationships they have and a great deal more beside ... One can do this by examining the way in which social relations are 'audibly present' in verbal exchanges, seeking to determine just what it is about a sequence of talk which makes it quite audibly (say) a conversation between old friends, a student ringing a teacher at home, a member of the public calling an organization in search of help or service? (1987: 317–18)

Our analyses of mood, appraisal, involvement, humour, speech function and genre have displayed systematically some of the ways in which interactants' social relations become 'audibly present' in talk. Drawing on critical theories of the 'reconstituting' relationship between private, everyday interactions and public social structures, we have connected these social relations to questions of difference and power. Our data have also lent support to Kress's claim that:

> Dialogue is ... the linguistic mode which is fundamental to an understanding of language and its uses. In dialogue the constitution of texts in and around difference is most readily apparent. Here it can be most readily discovered, analysed and described, and the processes of resolution of differences traced to their more or less satisfactory conclusions. (1985a:15)

We have thus explored how interactants draw on the grammatical, semantic and discourse resources of the language to enact and construct their social identities out of the problematics of sociocultural difference, so that what is 'audibly present' in casual talk is not just the interpersonal relations between particular participants at particular moments, but in fact the values, beliefs and interests of the culture within which any casual conversation takes place.

8.3 RELEVANCE OF THE BOOK

We believe that the analysis of casual conversation of the type presented in this book has immediate relevance in a number of contexts, of which we single out just two for brief comment: (i) in the teaching of English as a second or foreign language (and in applied linguistics generally); and (ii) in linguistics.

8.3.1 Relevance of analysing casual conversation in ESL/EFL teaching

We noted in our first chapter that the teaching of English as a second or foreign language is one area in which understandings about casual conversation would seem to be extremely useful. Without the ability to participate in casual conversations, people from non-English speaking backgrounds are destined to remain excluded from social intimacy with English speakers, and will therefore be denied both the benefits (as well as the risks) of full participation in the cultural life of English-speaking countries.

However, language teaching has tended to regard casual conversation as unstructured and therefore unteachable in any explicit sense. As a consequence there has been a general assumption that all one can do is get students "up talking". Such an attitude dooms students to a hit-or-miss approach, and limits their ability to make (and learn from) generalizations about casual conversational behaviour in English-speaking cultures.

The analyses we have presented in this book have demonstrated that casual conversation does have a consistent and describable structure, at a number of distinct levels. Systematic descriptions of the kind offered in this book could form the basis of a syllabus design for language teachers. Our analyses suggest that explicit features of casual conversation can be taught at two levels: (i) the generic; and (ii) the micro level of the clause, move and speech function.

At the generic level, the commonly occurring genres outlined in Chapters 6 and 7 can be presented and discussed. Cross-cultural comparisons can be highlighted, e.g. by exploring how gossiping, telling stories, or exchanging opinions are achieved differently in different cultures. Quite explicit language work can be dealt with at this generic level.

At the micro level of clause and move, the different speech functions outlined in Chapter 5 can be identified. The degree of delicacy presented in this chapter would obviously need to be simplified, but interactionally significant distinctions between, for example, opening and sustaining moves, types of continuing moves, responses and rejoinders, tracking and challenging could be presented and systematically related to linguistic realizations.

Syllabus design then can be complemented by a communicative methodology whereby the students are actively involved in practising and doing the task of casual talk in English. We hope that our analyses have also demystified the use of authentic texts in the language classroom, demonstrating that authentic excerpts of casual talk constitute fascinating documents on the culture.

Beyond the specifically ESL/EFL domain, our work also has relevance in applied linguistics and language in education areas, particularly for classroom-based research. We hope that the techniques presented in this book will encourage teachers and teacher trainers to collect and analyse their own samples of conversational data or spoken language of the classroom.

8.3.2 Relevance to linguistics

In addition to its relevance in applied linguistic contexts, we believe that analysis of the kind presented in this book has relevance to 'pure' linguistics, as the analysis of casual conversation reveals important facts about how language is structured to enable us to interact. While linguistic grammars have traditionally been based on written language corpora, Halliday has long stressed the importance of developing a grammar that can take account of both the written and the spoken language:

> It is in spontaneous, operational speech that the grammatical system of a language is most fully exploited, such that its semantic frontiers expand and its potential for meaning is enhanced. This is why we have to look to spoken discourse for at least some of the evidence on which to base our theory of the language. (1994: xxiv)

We believe that for a description of English to be described as 'systematic', it must offer an account of the register that most fundamentally shapes our social identities: that of casual conversation. Casual talk cannot be treated as some kind of "deviation" from the system of formal, written English, but must be analysed for an account of the systematic resources it has been shaped to offer its users in achieving social life.

8.4 CONCLUSION

Finally, we count as the major contribution of this book that, in developing a comprehensive approach to the analysis of casual conversation, we have been able to explore what it means to claim that casual conversation is critical in the social construction of reality. As Berger and Luckman (1966) pointed out, the reality maintenance and construction achieved through casual conversation is largely implicit, not explicit: the fascinating paradox of casual conversation is that the social functions of casual talk remain largely invisible to its participants.

It has been our aim to make these functions at least partly visible: to show how social structures are negotiated, how attitudes and values shaped by differences of concern to the institutionalized social context are reflected in and modified by casual talk. In exploring the subtle and complex meanings interactants make as they chat, we have come to share with Michael Halliday a fascination for the systematic resources which lie behind the 'magic' of everyday interaction:

> The magical power of talk derives from the fact that it is, in every instance, the manifestation of a systematic resource, a resource which has been built up through acts of conversation in the first place, and which goes on being modified in each one of us as we talk our way through life. (1984: 32)

References

Adelsward, V. (1989) Laughter and dialogue: The social significance of laughter in institutional discourse. *Nordic Journal of Linguistics* 12: 107–36.

Atkinson, J. and Heritage, J. (eds) (1984) *Structures of Social Action: Studies in Conversation Analysis*. Cambridge University Press, Cambridge.

Austin, J. (1962) *How to do Things with Words*. Clarendon Press, Oxford.

Bakhtin, M. M. (1986) *Speech Genres and Other Late Essays*. Translated by V. W. McGee. University of Texas Press, Austin.

Bateman, J. and Paris, C. (1991) Constraining the deployment of lexicogrammatical resources during text generation: towards a computational instantiation of register theory, in E. Ventola (ed.) *Functional and Systemic Linguistics: Approaches and Uses*. Mouton de Gruyter, Berlin (Trends in Linguistics Studies and Monographs 55), 81–106.

Bateson, G. (1973) *Steps to an Ecology of Mind*. Granada/Paladin, London.

Berger, P. and Luckmann T. (1966) *The Social Construction of Reality: A Treatise in the Sociology of Knowledge*. Doubleday, New York.

Bergmann, J. R (1993) *Discreet Indiscretions: The Social Organization of Gossip*. Aldine de Gruyter, New York.

Bergson, H. (1950) *Le Rire: essai sur la signification du comique*. Paris, Presses Universitaires de France.

Berry, M. (1981a) Systemic linguistics and discourse analysis: a multi-layered approach to exchange structure. Mimeo. Abridged version in M. Coulthard and M. Montgomery (eds) *Studies in Discourse Analysis*, Routledge and Kegan Paul, London, 120–45.

Berry, M. (1981b) Polarity, ellipticity, elicitation and propositional development, their relevance to the well-formedness of an exchange. *Nottingham Linguistics Circular* 10(1): 36–63.

Bhatia, V. K. (1993) *Analysing Genre: Language Use in Professional Settings*. Longman, London and New York.

Biber, D. and Finegan, E. (1989) Styles of stance in English: lexical and grammatical marking of evidentiality and affect. *Text* 9(1): (special issue on the pragmatics of affect): 93–124.

Boden, D. and Zimmerman, D. (eds) (1991) *Talk and Social Structure*. Polity Press, Cambridge.

Brenneis, D. (1984) Grog and gossip in Bhatgaon: style and sunstance in Fiji Indian conversation. *American Ethnologist* 11: 487–516

Brenneis, D. (1988) Language and disputing. *Ann. Rev. Anthropol.* 17: 221–37.

Brown, P. and Levinson, S. (1978) Universals in language usage: politeness phenomena, in E. Goody (ed.) *Questions and Politeness*. Cambridge University Press, Cambridge.

Burton, D. (1978) Towards an analysis of casual conversation. *Nottingham Linguistics Circular* 17(2): 131–59.

Burton, D. (1980) *Dialogue and Discourse*. Routledge and Kegan Paul, London.

Burton, D. (1981) Analysing spoken discourse, in M. Coulthard and M. Montgomery (eds) *Studies in Discourse Analysis.* Routledge and Kegan Paul, London, 61–81.

Butt, D., Fahey, R., Spinks, S. and Yallop, C. (1995) *Using Functional Grammar: An Explorer's Guide.* National Centre for English Language Teaching and Research (Macquarie University), Sydney.

Button, G. and Casey, N. (1984) Generating topic, in J. Atkinson and J. Heritage (eds) *Structures of Social Action: Studies in Conversation Analysis.* Cambridge University Press, Cambridge, 167–90.

Button, G. and Lee, J. (eds) (1987) *Talk and Social Organization.* Inter-communication 1 (series eds Howard Giles and Cheris Kramarae). Multilingual Matters, Clevedon.

Cameron D. (1992) Not gender difference but the difference gender makes: explanation in research on sex and language. *International Journal of the Sociology of Language* 94: 13–26.

Channell, J. (1994) *Vague Language.* Oxford University Press, Oxford.

Christie, F. (1989) Curriculum genres in early childhood education: a case study in written development. PhD thesis, Department of Linguistics, University of Sydney.

Christie, F. (1991a) First and second order registers in education, in E. Ventola (ed.) *Functional and Systemic Linguistics: Approaches and Uses.* Mouton de Gruyter, Berlin. (Trends in Linguistics Studies and Monographs 55), 235–56.

Christie F. (1991b) Pedagogical and content registers in a writing lesson. *Linguistics and Education* 3: 203–24.

Coates, J. (1988) Gossip revisited: language in all-female groups, in J. Coates and D. Cameron (eds) *Women in Their Speech Communities, New Perspectives on Language and Sex.* Longman, London and New York.

Coates, J. (1995a) Hedges and hedging in women's talk. Paper presented at the University of Technology, Sydney.

Coates, J. (1995b) The role of narrative in the talk of women friends. Paper presented at the University of Technology, Sydney.

Coates, J. (1996) *Women's Talk.* Blackwell, London.

Cope, B. and Kalantzis, M. (1993) *The Powers of Literacy: A Genre Approach to Teaching Writing.* Falmer, London.

Coulthard, M. and Brazil, D. (1979) *Exchange Structure.* Discourse Analysis Monograph No. 5. English Language Research, University of Birmingham, Birmingham.

Cox, B. A. (1967) What is Hopi gossip about? Information management and Hopi factions. *Man* 2: 278–85.

Cranny-Francis, A. (1993) Gender and genre: feminist subversion of genre fiction and its implications for critical literacy, in B. Cope and M. Kalantzis (eds) *The Powers of Literacy.* Falmer Press, London.

Douglas, M. (1975) *Implicit Meanings.* Routledge and Kegan Paul, London.

Drew, P. (1987) Po-faced receipts of teases. *Linguistics* 25: 219–53.

Drew, P. and Heritage, J. (eds) (1992) *Talk at Work: Interaction in Institutional Settings.* (Studies in Interactional Sociolinguistics 8), Cambridge University Press, Cambridge.

Dunbar, R. (1992) Why gossip is good for you? *New Scientist* 21 November: 28–31.

Eggins, S. (1990a) Conversational structure: a systemic-functional analysis of interpersonal and logical meaning in multiparty sustained talk. PhD thesis, Department of Linguistics, University of Sydney.

Eggins, S. (1990b) Keeping the conversation going: a systemic-functional analysis of conversational structure in casual sustained talk. Unpublished PhD thesis, Department of Linguistics, University of Sydney.

Eggins, S. (1994) *An Introduction to Systemic Functional Linguistics.* Pinter, London.

Eggins, S. (1996) Some functions of humour in spoken interactions. Plenary paper presented to the 23rd International Systemic Functional Congress, University of Technology, Sydney, 15–19 July.

Eggins, S. and Martin, J. R. (in press) Genres and registers of discourse, in T. van Dijk (ed.) *Discourse: A Multidisciplinary Introduction.* Sage, London.

Fairclough, N. (1989) *Language and Power.* Longman, London.

Fairclough, N. (1992) *Discourse and Social Change.* Polity Press, Cambridge.

Fairclough, N. (1995a) *Critical Discourse Analysis.* Longman, London.

Fairclough, N. (1995b) *Media Discourse.* Edward Arnold, London.

Firth, J.R. (1957) *Papers in Linguistics 1934–51.* Oxford University Press, Oxford.

Fishman, P. (1980) Conversational insecurity, in H. Giles *et al.* (eds) *Language: Social Psychological Perspectives.* Pergamon Press, Oxford, 127–31.

Freud. S (1905) *Jokes and their Relation to the Unconscious.* Routledge and Kegan Paul, London.

Fries, P. and Gregory, M. (eds) (1995) *Discourse in Society: Systemic Functional Perspectives, Meaning and Choice in Language: Studies for Michael Halliday.* Vol. 50 in the series Advances in Discourse Processes. Ablex, Norwood, NJ.

Gardner, R. (ed.) (1994) Spoken Interaction Studies in Australia Special Volume of Australian Review of Applied Linguistics Series S, Number 11

Garfinkel, H. (1967) *Studies in Ethnomethodology.* Prentice Hall, Englewood Cliffs, New Jersey.

Gerot, L. and Wignell, P. (1994) *Making Sense of Functional Grammar.* Antipodean Educational Enterprises, Sydney.

Gluckman, M. (1963) Gossip and scandal. *Curr. Anthropology* 4: 307–16.

Goffman, E. (1959) *The Presentation of Self in Everyday Life.* Anchor Books, New York.

Goffman, E. (1967) *Interaction Ritual.* Anchor Books, New York.

Goffman, E. (1974) *Frame Analysis.* Harper and Row, New York.

Goffman, E. (1981) *Forms of Talk.* University of Pennsylvania Press, Philadelphia.

Grice, H. (1975) *Logic and conversation.* William James Lectures, Harvard University. Reprinted in P. Cole and J. Morgan (eds) *Syntax and Semantics Vol. 3: Speech Acts.* Academic Press, New York, 43–58.

Gumperz J. (1982a) *Discourse Strategies.* Cambridge University Press, Cambridge.

Gumperz, J. (1982b) *Language and Social Identity.* Cambridge University Press, Cambridge.

Gumperz J. and Hymes, D. (eds) (1964) The ethnography of communication. *American Anthropologist* 66 (6): 103–14.

Gumperz, J. and Hymes, D. (eds) (1972) *Directions in Sociolinguistics.* Holt, Rinehart & Winston, New York.

Halliday, M. A. K. (1961) Categories of the theory of grammar. *Word* 17(3): 241–92.

Halliday, M. A. K. (1973) *Explorations in the Functions of Language.* Edward Arnold, London.

Halliday, M. A. K. (1975) *Learning How to Mean: Explorations in the Development of Language.* Edward Arnold, London.

Halliday, M. A. K. (1978) *Language as Social Semiotic.* Edward Arnold, London.

Halliday, M. A. K. (1984) Language as code and language as behaviour: a systemic-functional interpretation of the nature and ontogenesis of dialogue, in R. Fawcett, M. A. K. Halliday, S. M. Lamb and A. Makkai (eds) *The Semiotics of Language and Culture Vol 1: Language as Social Semiotic.* Pinter, London, 3–35.

Halliday, M. A. K. (1985) *Spoken and Written Language.* Deakin University Press, Geelong.

Halliday, M. A. K. (1991) The notion of 'context' in language education, in T. Le and M. McCausland (eds) *Language Education: Interaction and Development.* Proceedings of the International Conference held in Ho Chi Minh City, Vietnam, 30 March–1 April. University of Tasmania, Launceston.

Halliday, M. A. K. (1994) *An Introduction to Functional Grammar,* 2nd edn., Edward Arnold, London.

Halliday, M. A. K. and Hasan, R. (1976) *Cohesion in English.* Longman, London.

Halliday, M. A. K. and Hasan, R. (1985) *Language, Context, and Text: Aspects of Language in a Social-semiotic Perspective.* Deakin University Press, Geelong.

Halliday, M. A. K. and Kress, G. (eds) (1976) *Halliday: System and Function in Language.* Oxford University Press, Oxford.

Halliday, M. A. K. and McIntosh, A. (1966) *Patterns of Language: Papers in General, Descriptive and Applied Linguistics.* Longman, London.

Halliday, M. A. K. and Plum, G. (1983) On casual conversation, in R. Hasan (ed.) *Discourse on Discourse.* Occasional Papers no. 7, Macquarie University, Sydney.

Halliday, M. A. K. and Mathiessen, C. M. I. M. (forthcoming) *Construing Experience : A Language-based Approach to Cognition.* De Gruyter, Berlin and New York.

Hammond, J. (1995) The grammatical construction of literacy: an analysis of two primary school literacy programs. PhD thesis, Department of Linguistics, University of Sydney.

Harding, S. (1975) Women and words in a Spanish village, in R. R. Reiter (ed.) *Towards an Anthropology of Women.* Monthly Review Press, New York.

Hasan, R. (1979) On the notion of text, in J. S. Petofi (ed.) *Text vs. Sentencezz: Basic Questions of Textlinguistics.* Helmet Buske, Hamburg.

Hasan, R. (1984) The nursery tale as a genre. *Nottingham Linguistic Circular* 13 (special issue on Systemic Linguistics): 71–102.

Hasan, R. (1985) *Linguistics, Language and Verbal Art.* Deakin University Press, Geelong.

Haviland, J. B. (1977) *Gossip, Reputation and Knowledge in Zinacantan.* University of Chicago Press, Chicago.

Hodge, R. and Kress, G. (1988) *Social Semiotics.* Polity Press, Cambridge.

Hodge, R. and Kress, G. (1993) *Language as Ideology,* 2nd edn., Routledge and Kegan Paul, London.

Holmes, J. (1984) Hedging your bets and sitting on the fence: some evidence for hedges as support structures. *Te Reo* 27: 47–62.

Horvath, B. and Eggins, S. (1995) Opinion texts in conversation, in P. Fries and M. Gregory (eds) *Discourse in Society: Systemic Functional Perspectives.* (Volume L in the series Advances in Discourse Processes). Ablex, Norwood, NJ, 29–46.

Hymes, D. (1972a) Towards ethnographies of communication: the analysis of communicative events, in P. Giglioli (ed.) *Language and Social Context.* Penguin Books, Harmondsworth, 21–33.

Hymes, D. (1972b) Models of the interaction of language and social life, in J. Gumperz and D. Hymes (eds) *Directions in Sociolinguistics: the Ethnography of Communication*. Holt, Rinehart & Winston, New York, 35–71.

Hymes, D. (1974) The ethnography of speaking, in B. Blount (ed.) *Language, Culture and Society*. Winthrop, Cambridge, Mass, 189–223.

Iedema, R. S. (1995) *Administration Literacy (Write it Right Literacy in Industry Research Project – Stage 3)*. Metropolitan East Disadvantaged Schools Program, Sydney.

Iedema, R., Feez, S. and White, P. (1993) *Media Literacy: Phase 1 of the Write it Right Industry Research Project*. Metropolitan East Disadvantaged Schools Program, Sydney.

Jefferson, G. (1972) Side sequences, in D. Sudnow (ed.), 294–338.

Jefferson, G. (1979) A technique for inviting laughter and its subsequent acceptance/declination, in G. Psathas (ed.) *Everyday Language: Studies in Ethnomethodology*. Irvington Publishers, New York, 74–96.

Jefferson, G. (1984) On stepwise transition from talk about a trouble to inappropriately next-positioned matters, in J. Atkinson and J. Heritage (eds), 191–222.

Jefferson, G. (1985) An exercise in the transcription and analysis of laughter, in T. van Dijk (ed.) *Handbook of Discourse Analysis*. Academic Press, London, vol. 3, 25–34.

Jefferson, G., Jefferson, J. and Lee, J (1992) The rejection of advice: managing the problematic convergence of a 'troubles-telling' and a 'service encounter', in P. Drew and J. Heritage (eds), 470–521.

Jefferson, G., Sacks, H. and Schelgoff, E. (1987) Notes on laughter in the pursuit of intimacy, in G. Button & J. Lee (eds) *Talk and Social Organization*. Multilingual Matters, London, 152–205.

Johnstone, Barbara (1993) Community and contest: Midwestern men and women creating their worlds in conversational storytelling, in D. Tannen (ed.) *Gender and Conversational Interaction*. Oxford University Press, New York, 62–80.

Jones, D. (1980) Gossip: notes on women's oral culture, in C. Kramarae (ed.) *The Voices and Words of Women and Men*. Pergamon Press, Oxford, 193–8.

Koestler, A. (1964) *The Act of Creation*. Hutchinson, London.

Kress, G. (1985a) *Linguistic Processes in Socio-cultural Practice*. Deakin University Press, Geelong.

Kress, G. (1985b) Ideological structures in discourse, in T. van Dijk (ed.) *Handbook of Discourse Analysis*. Academic Press, New York.

Kress, G. (1987) *Communication and Culture: An Introduction*. UNSW Press, Sydney.

Kress, G. (1987b) Genre in a social theory of language: a reply to John Dixon, in I. Reid (ed.) *The Place of Genre in Learning: Current Debates*. Deakin University Press, Geelong, 35–45.

Kress, G. and Hodge, B. (1979) *Language and Ideology*. Routledge and Kegan Paul, London.

Kress, G. and Van Leeuwen, T (1996) *Reading Images: The Grammar of Visual Design*. Routledge and Kegan Paul, London.

Kress, G. and Van Leeuwen, T. (1990) *Reading Images*. Deakin University Press, Geelong.

Labov, W. (1970) The study of language in its social context. *Studium Generale* 23: 30–87.

Labov, W. (1972a) *Sociolinguistic Patterns*. University of Pennsylvania Press, Philadelphia.

Labov, W. (1972b) Rules for ritual insults, in D. Sudnow (ed.) 120–69.

Labov, W. (1972c) *Language in the Inner City: Studies in the Black English Vernacular.* University of Pennsylvania Press, Philadelphia.

Labov, W. and Fanshel, D. (1977) *Therapeutic Discourse: Psychotherapy as Conversation.* Academic Press, New York.

Labov, W. and Waletzky, J. (1967) Narrative analysis: oral versions of personal experiences, in J. Helm (ed.) *Essays on the Verbal and Visual Arts.* American Ethnological Society, proceedings of Spring Meeting 1966. University of Washington Press, Washington, DC, 12–14.

Lakoff, R. (1975) *Language and Woman's Place.* Harper & Row, New York.

Leech, G. (1983) *Principles of Pragmatics.* Longman, London.

Lehrer, A. (1974) *Semantic Fields and Lexical Structure.* Elsevier, Amsterdam and London.

Levinson, S. (1983) *Pragmatics.* Cambridge University Press, Cambridge.

Lyons, J. (1977) *Semantics, Volume 2.* Cambridge University Press, Cambridge.

McTear, M. (1984) *Children's Conversation.* Basil Blackwell, London.

Martin, J. R. (1984a) Types of writing in infants and primary school, in L. Unsworth (ed.) *Reading, Writing, Spelling.* (Proceedings of the Fifth Macarthur Reading/Language Symposium), Macarthur Institute of Higher Education, Sydney, 34–55.

Martin, J. R. (1984b) Language, register and genre, in F. Christie (ed.) *Children Writing: Reader.* Deakin University Press, Geelong, 21–30.

Martin, J. R. (1992) *English Text: System and Structure.* Benjamins, Amsterdam.

Martin J. R. (1993) Genre and literacy – modelling context in educational linguistics. *Annual Review of Applied Linguistics* 13: 141–72.

Martin, J. R. (1994) Course notes for the subject 'Writing'. MA in Applied Linguistics Program, Linguistics Department, University of Sydney.

Martin, J. R. (1996) Evaluating disruption, in R. Hasan and G. Williams (eds) *Literacy in Society.* Addison-Wesley, London.

Martin, J. R. (in press) Beyond exchange: appraisal systems in English, in S. Hunstan and G. Thompson (eds) *Evaluation in Text.* Oxford University Press, Oxford.

Martin, J. R. and Rothery, J. (1986) *Writing Project Report No. 4.* (Working Papers in Linguistics), Linguistics Department, University of Sydney.

Matthiessen, C. M. I. M. (1993a) Instantial systems and logogenesis. Paper presented at 3rd National Chinese Systemic Symposium, Hangzhou University, Hangzhou, July.

Matthiessen, C. M. I. M. (1993b) Register in the round, in M. Ghadessy (ed.) *Register analysis. Practice into Theory.* Pinter, London.

Matthiessen, C. M. I. M. and Bateman J. (1991) *Text Generation and Systemic Linguistics: Experiences from English and Japanese.* Pinter, London.

Maynard, D. (1980) Placement of topic changes in conversation. *Semiotica* 30(4):263–90.

Mitchell, T. F. (1957) The language of buying and selling in Cyrenaica: a situational statement. *Hesperis* 26: 31–71.

Mulkay, M. (1988) *On Humour.* Polity Press, London.

Nordenstam, K. (1992) Male and female conversational style. *International Journal of the Sociology of Language* 94: 75–98.

Norrick, N. (1993) *Conversational Joking: Humor in Everyday Talk.* Indiana University Press, Bloomington.

O'Toole, M. (1994) *The Language of Displayed Art.* Pinter, London.

Palmer, F. (ed.) (1968) *Selected Papers of J. R. Firth 1952–1959.* Longman, London.

Plum, G. A. (1988) Text and contextual conditioning in spoken English: a genre-based approach. PhD thesis, University of Sydney.

Plum, G. A. (1993) Types of spoken narrative. Paper given at the 1993 LERN Conference: Working With Genre, University of Technology, Sydney.

Poynton, C. (1984) Forms and functions: names as vocative. *Nottingham Linguistic Circular* 13: 35–70.

Poynton, C. (1985) *Language & Gender: Making the Difference.* Deakin University Press, Geelong.

Poynton, C. (1990) Address and the semiotics of social relations: a systemic-functional account of address forms and practices in Australian English. PhD thesis, Department of Linguistics, University of Sydney.

Psathas, G. (ed.) (1979) *Everyday Language: Studies in Ethnomethodology.* Irvington Publishers, New York.

Roger, D. and Bull, P. (eds) (1989) *Conversation: An Interdisciplinary Perspective.* Multilingual Matters, Clevedon.

Rothery, J. (1990) Story writing in primary school: assessing narrative type genres. PhD thesis. Department of Linguistics, University of Sydney.

Rothery, J. (1994) *Exploring Literacy in School English.* (Write it Right Resources for Literacy and Learning), Metropolitan East Disadvantaged Schools Program, Sydney.

Rothery, J. and Stenglin, M. (1994a) *Exploring Narrative in Video: A Unit of Work for Junior Secondary English.* (Write it Right Resources for Literacy and Learning), Metropolitan East Disadvantaged Schools Program, Sydney.

Rothery, J. and Stenglin, M. (1994b) *Spine-chilling Stories: A Unit of Work for Junior Secondary English.* (Write it Right Resources for Literacy and Learning), Metropolitan East Disadvantaged Schools Program, Sydney.

Sacks, H. (1972a) An initial investigation of the usability of conversational data for doing sociology, in D. Sudnow (ed.), 31–74.

Sacks, H. (1972b) On the analyzability of stories by children, in J. J. Gumperz and D. Hymes (eds), 325–45.

Sacks, H. (1974) An analysis of the course of a joke's telling in conversation, in R. Bauman and J. Sherzer (eds) *Explorations in the Ethnography of Speaking.* Cambridge University Press, Cambridge, 337–53.

Sacks, H. (1975) Everyone has to lie, in B. Blount and M. Sanches (eds) *Sociocultural Dimensions of Language Use.* Academic Press, New York, 57–80.

Sacks, H. (1978) Some technical considerations of a dirty joke, in J. Schenkein (ed.), 249–70.

Sacks, H. (1984) Notes on methodology, in J. Atkinson and J. Heritage (eds), 21–7.

Sacks, H. (1992a) *Lectures on Conversation*, vol. I. Blackwell, Cambridge, Mass.

Sacks, H. (1992b) *Lectures on Conversation*, vol. II. Blackwell, Cambridge, Mass.

Sacks, H., Schegloff, E. and Jefferson, G. (1974) A simplest systematics for the organization of turn-taking for conversation. *Language* 50(4): 696–735.

Schegloff, E. (1972) Notes on a conversational practice: formulating place, in D. Sudnow (ed.), 75–117.

Schegloff, E. (1980) Preliminaries to preliminaries: 'Can I ask you a question?', in *Sociological Inquiry* 50, 104–152.

Schegloff, E. (1981) Discourse as an interactional achievement: some uses of 'Uh huh' and other things that come between sentences, in D. Tannen (ed.), 71–93.

Schegloff, E. and Sacks, H. (1974) Opening up closings, in R. Turner (ed.)

Ethnomethodology. Penguin, Harmondsworth, 233–264.

Schegloff, E., Sacks, H. and Jefferson, G. (1977) The preference for self-correction in the organization of repair in conversation. *Language* 53: 361–382.

Schenkein J. (1978) *Studies in the Organization of Conversational Interaction.* Academic Press, New York.

Schiffrin, D. (1985a) Conversational coherence: the role of well. *Language* 61: 640–67.

Schiffrin, D. (1985b) Everyday argument: the organization of diversity in talk, in T. van Dijk (ed.) *Handbook of Discourse Analysis Vol 3: Discourse & Dialogue.* Academic Press, New York, 35–46.

Schiffrin, D. (1987) *Discourse Markers.* Cambridge University Press, Cambridge.

Schiffrin, D. (1990) The management of a cooperative self in argument: the role of opinions and stories, in A. Grimshaw (ed.) *Conflict Talk.* Cambridge University Press, Cambridge.

Schiffrin, D. (1994) *Approaches to Discourse.* Basil Blackwell, Cambridge, Mass.

Searle, J. (1969) *Speech Acts: An Essay in the Philosophy of Language.* Cambridge University Press, Cambridge.

Searle, J. (1976) A classification of illocutionary acts. *Language in Society* 5: 1–23.

Sharrock W. and Anderson, R. (1987) Epilogue: the definition of alternatives: some sources of confusion in interdisciplinary discussion, in G. Button and J. Lee (eds), 290–321.

Sinclair, J. and Coulthard, R. (1975) *Towards an Analysis of Discourse.* Oxford University Press, Oxford.

Slade, D. M. (1986) Teaching casual conversation to adult ESL learners. *Prospect* 2 (1): 68–87.

Slade, D. M. (1995) Gossip: two complementary perspectives on the analysis of casual conversation in English. *ARAL,* (special edition on Spoken Discourse Studies): 47–83.

Slade, D. M. (in preparation) The texture of casual conversation: a multidimensional interpretation. PhD thesis, Linguistics Department, University of Sydney, Sydney.

Slade, D. M. and Norris, L. (1986) *Teaching Casual Conversation, Topics, Strategies and Interactional Skills.* National Curriculum Resource Centre, NSW.

Stubbs, M. (1983) *Discourse Analysis: The Sociolinguistic Analysis of Natural Language.* Basil Blackwell, London.

Sudnow, D. (ed.) (1972) *Studies in Social Interaction.* Free Press, New York.

Swales, J. (1990) *Genre Analysis: English in Academic and Research Settings.* Cambridge University Press, Cambridge.

Tannen, D. (1984) *Conversational Style: Analyzing Talk Among Friends.* Ablex, Norwood, NJ.

Tannen, D. (1989) *Talking Voices: Repetition, Dialogue, and Imagery in Conversational Discourse.* Cambridge University Press, Cambridge.

Tannen, D. (1990) *You Just Don't Understand: Men and Women in Conversation.* Ballantine Books, New York.

Taylor, T. and Cameron, D. (1987) *Analysing Conversation: Rules and Units in the Structure of Talk.* Pergamon Press, Oxford.

Toolan, M. J. (1988) *Narrative: A Critical Linguistic Introduction.* Routledge and Kegan Paul, London.

Ventola, E. (1983) Contrasting schematic structures in service encounters. *Applied Linguistics* 4(3): 242–58.

Ventola, E. (1987) *The Structure of Social Interaction.* Pinter, London.

Ventola, E. (1995) Generic and register qualities of texts and their realization, in P. Fries and M. Gregory (eds), 3–28.

Wells, C., Montgomery, M. and MacLure, M. (1979) Adult–child discourse: outline of a model of analysis. *Journal of Pragmatics* 3: 337–80.

Index

Page numbers in *italics* indicate a table or figure.

Printed in the United States
206617BV00003B/394-405/A

9 781845 530464